Mental Processes

Explorations in Cognitive Science
Margaret Boden, general editor

Mental Processes

Studies in Cognitive
Science

H. Christopher Longuet-Higgins

A Bradford Book
Published in cooperation with
The British Psychological Society

The MIT Press
Cambridge, Massachusetts
London, England

This book was set in Palatino by Asco Trade Typesetting Ltd., Hong Kong, and printed and bound by Halliday Lithograph in the United States of America.

Library of Congress Cataloging-in-Publication Data

Longuet-Higgins, H. C.
  Mental processes.

  (Explorations in cognitive science; 1)
  "Published in cooperation with the British Psychological Society."
  "A Bradford book."
  Includes index.
  1. Cognition.   2. Intellect.   3. Human information processing.   4. Artificial intelligence.   I. Title.   II. Series.
  BF311.L665   1987   153   86-20996
  ISBN 0-262-12119-0

Contents

II   Music

Introduction   57

III Language

V Memory

Preface

This is the log book of an expedition into the mostly uncharted territory of the mind. When in 1967 Richard Gregory and I packed our bags for Edinburgh, it was in the shared conviction that the workings of the mind could not possibly be as tedious as the psychologists made them out to be, or as peripheral as the physical scientists tended to assume. We were welcomed to our new university by Donald Michie, the British pioneer of "machine intelligence", C. H. Waddington, not so much a biologist as a Renaissance Man, and James Thorne, an eloquent expositor of the linguistic theories of Noam Chomsky. Sparks flew, as anyone might have predicted, between those of us who regarded human intelligence as a source of inspiration and those who planned to supersede it in the next five (or possibly ten) years.

My own students and colleagues during those turbulent times included David Willshaw, Peter Buneman, Mark Steedman, Stephen Isard, Richard Power, Anthony Davey, and Geoffrey Hinton, and I feel immensely proud of our collective achievements—and of their friendship. We knew, I think, that we were the children of a revolution in the science of the mind, though not, perhaps, in psychology, if that was merely "the science of behaviour", as my colleague David Vowles used to insist. The revolution was to see psychology as part of a much wider complex of disciplines—the "cognitive sciences"—concerned with the mechanisms and potentialities of information-processing systems in general. The idea of the brain as an information-processing system was not new; engineers and mathematicians from Babbage and Boole to Turing and von Neumann had long aspired to emulate mental processes in computing machines. What was new, perhaps, was the suggestion that it was time to begin couching psychological theories in computational terms—a proposal that has seemed by no means so bizarre since the publication of Terry Winograd's SHRDLU program and David Marr's posthumous book *Vision*, with its awe-inspiring subtitle

A Computational Investigation into the Human Representation and Processing of Visual Information.

The Edinburgh years (1967–1974) were, I suppose, the most formative as far as I was concerned. They encompassed the preparation and publication of the joint Gifford Lectures on the Nature of Mind, by A. J. P. Kenny, J. R. Lucas, C. H. Waddington, and myself, and the organization, by Waddington, of a marvellous series of meetings on theoretical biology—a subject that was and still is waiting to be born. By the time I moved to Sussex to join Stuart Sutherland in his Centre for Research in Perception and Cognition, the mental nihilism of behaviourist psychology had been effectively discredited, though pockets of resistance could still be found in the older universities. Sussex is where I have enjoyed the collaboration of Richard Power on language and Christopher Lee on music. And it is in Sussex that I have been finally cornered by Margaret Boden, the doyenne of British philosophers of artificial intelligence, and made to gather these thoughts together.

So much for the background of this book; now for its structure. The only sensible way of organizing the chapters was by subject matter; thus there are four special sections, concerned with music, language, vision, and memory, and an opening section, whose title (Generalities) tacitly admits that general reflections and speculations—to which the artificial-intelligentsia are particularly prone—tend to be less indigestible, if more ephemeral, than proposed detailed solutions to technical problems. The first of the special sections comprises the papers on music (the earliest of which were written before I left Cambridge and theoretical chemistry) and is addressed as much to the musician as to the cognitive scientist. The next two sections, on language and on vision, are more difficult; the vision papers will appeal only, I imagine, to readers who enjoy straightforward mathematical problems. The last section, on memory, must be treated indulgently as the first attempt of a physical scientist to climb out of the mindless world of atoms and molecules into the real world of subjective experience. (It is remarkable how many scientists have arrived at similar ideas independently.) The sections are separately introduced, and there are occasional asides on points of obscurity or wider interest.

My thanks are due to many people, especially my collaborators, though to thank them might seem as impertinent as it is sincere. To Richard Gregory, who also staked his career on the new psychology, and to Michael Swann, then Principal of Edinburgh University, who covered our bets. To Donald Michie and James Thorne, who introduced me to computing and to theoretical linguistics respectively, and to "Wad", the eternal pioneer, for some much-needed encouragement and wisdom. To Stuart Sutherland, not only for enabling me to join the University of Sussex but also for his untiring efforts to cure my psychological illiteracy. To Chris Darwin, Aaron Sloman, Arnold Smith, and all my other colleagues, in both Experimental Psychology and Cognitive Studies, to whose efforts are owed the excellent environment that the cognitive sciences enjoy at Sussex University.

Particularly I must thank Anne Mill and Mary Walton, for many years my long-suffering secretaries, for their part in preparing so many of these papers for publication and making cups of tea at critical moments. Finally, in addition to those publishers who have granted permission for the republication of some of the essays, I would specially like to thank my editor at The MIT Press for his sensitivity to the misgivings of a potential author and for all the trouble he and the Press have taken to make a silk purse out of a sow's ear. For various periods my work has been supported by the Nuffield Foundation and by the Science and Engineering Research Council and its predecessors the S.R.C. and the D.S.I.R., but it is the Royal Society of London to which I have owed my livelihood as a Research Professor for virtually the whole of my time as a cognitive scientist.

I

Generalities

The volume begins with a piece that tries to recreate the atmosphere of one of the meetings organized by Waddington at the Villa Serbelloni, Bellagio, on the shores of Lake Como. The proceedings of those meetings appeared in a series of volumes entitled *Towards a Theoretical Biology*, with the subtitles *Prolegomena*, *Sketches* and *Drafts*, published over the years 1968–1970 by the Edinburgh University Press. There being no recognized discipline of theoretical biology, each of us could interpret the phrase in his or her own way. I had recently said goodbye to theoretical chemistry, but my former colleagues supposed that I was merely planning to apply chemical and physical concepts to the workings of the brain. In fact my chemical expertise was to be of no further use to me, except as a paradigm of the scientific outlook; quite new concepts were going to be needed for getting to grips with the logic of the mind, as opposed to the chemistry of the brain, and of this I was already aware. In his introduction to the volume that included "The Seat of the Soul", Waddington shrewdly recognized it as a dialogue between me and my former self.

Chapter 2, "The Failure of Reductionism", is taken from *The Nature of Mind*, the published account of the joint Gifford Lectures given in 1971 and 1972 by A. J. P. Kenny, J. R. Lucas, C. H. Waddington, and myself. The idea of such a collaborative effort was due to Michael Swann, then Principal of Edinburgh University; we were all on the platform together, and the main speaker's remarks were prepared; but the succeeding discussion was spontaneous and is published more or less verbatim. At the time the lecture was delivered, the philosophical implications of the computational concept of mind were largely unexplored; at the time of this writing, the concept of artificial intelligence has already provoked several books by philosophers of mind, though not all of them are sympathetic to the more extreme claims of its proponents. (See Hubert L. Dreyfus, *What Computers Cannot Do—The Limits of Artificial Intelligence* [New York: Harper & Row, 1979; first edition 1972], and J. R. Searle, *Men, Machines and Minds* [London: BBC Publications, 1984].)

Chapter 3, "Artificial Intelligence", was commissioned by the British Medical Bulletin as a contribution to a special issue on cognitive psychology—a fact which dates the "coming out" of that subject to the turn of the 1970s. There are two main strands in the essay: a warning to the psychologists not to underestimate the explanatory power of computational accounts of the mind and a warning to the artificial-intelligence community to moderate its claims about the ability of machines to perform tasks, such as the education of small children, that call for real human understanding.

Chapter 4, "Artificial Intelligence—A New Theoretical Psychology?", was commissioned by the psychology journal *Cognition* for a special issue on artificial intelligence. It is tempting to regard its date (1981) as marking the final acceptance of AI into polite psychological society. The occasion offered an opportunity to reflect on the proper relationship between the two, and I took the liberty of suggesting that it was none other than the relation between the theoretical and the experimental aspects of any branch of science—between, for example, theoretical and experimental physics. It may be of some sociological interest that a year or so later the *New Universities Quarterly* invited Margaret Boden and me, among others, to contribute articles on AI to a special issue on that subject. I offered this essay for republication. When the issue eventually appeared, the editor had excised the subtitle and had sandwiched our contributions between a pair of pieces obviously designed to "rubbish" them. It appeared that at least one academic newssheet still felt a need to protect its virginity from the perils of the new paradigm.

Chapter 5, "Comments on the Lighthill Report", is an excerpt from *Artificial Intelligence—a Paper Symposium"*, published by the Science Research Council of the U.K. The Science Research Council had commissioned Sir James Lighthill, Lucasian Professor of Applied Mathematics in the University of Cambridge, to review the subject of artificial intelligence, and Sir James's report had expressed some scepticism about certain aspects of the subject. The symposium was intended to correct the balance by publishing the report along with some alternative views. The political background to the symposium has long since passed into history, but perhaps the document is still of interest for its first use of the phrase "the cognitive sciences". It may help the reader to understand why such a motley collection of subjects as vision, memory, language, and music should be brought together in a volume of this kind.

Chapter 6, "In Our Image?", was written in 1968 for *The Humanist Outlook*, a collection of essays by members of the humanist movement in Britain. There is no particular set of beliefs that humanists hold; what unites them is a common determination to understand and improve the human condition. Believing that much harm is caused by silly ideas about the theological uniqueness of *Homo sapiens*, I decided to trail my coat with a deliberately animistic account of the computer-assisted typewriter (which might be regarded as a primitive word-processing device). But the argument then leads on to a serious suggestion about how we might best set about understanding the human mind—a proposal that has since been so widely adopted that it is hard to recollect the disdain with which it was received at the time. (The editor obviously never read to the end of the essay; in his introduction he said "Professor Longuet-Higgins writes about computers and their power to economize labour". As he was good enough to apologize afterwards, he shall retain his anonymity.)

1   The Seat of the Soul

H. C. Longuet-Higgins

[Scene: The garden of a timeless Italian villa. A biologist and a physicist are strolling on the terrace.]

Physicist: I must say, B, you and your friends have done some most impressive work lately on the molecular mechanism of biological replication. I've been looking out for a new set of problems to give my graduate students, and it seems as if your field is one to which we physicists might well address ourselves. Have you any suggestions about research topics in biology which might be ripe for a rigorous physical approach?

Biologist: It's nice to feel you're interested, P, but before I make any detailed suggestions I shall have to ask you whether you want to go on doing physics or to move into biology.

P: I'm not quite sure I understand your question. But suppose I said that we wanted to go into biophysics, would that help?

B: Yes, it would help a bit; I presume you mean that you'd want to work on physical problems relevant to biology. If so, there are plenty.

P: What sort of problems are you thinking of?

B: Well, we'd like to know more about the transport of ions across membranes, for example. Then there are problems in fluid dynamics, such as the flow of blood through elastic capillaries; problems in quantum mechanics, such as the way in which energy quanta move through aggregates of chlorophyll molecules; there are thermodynamic problems such as the effect of pressure on the partial specific volume of water in cartilage. . . .

P (interrupting): Yes, yes, of course, I do appreciate what you say. Obviously there are a lot of important problems of that sort. But, actually, my students are—if I may say so—an unusually bright lot. I think they might be just a little—how shall I say?—under-motivated to tackle problems in hydrodynamics or classical chemistry. Their really strong suit is quantum mechanics, and we give them an intensive course on many-body theory and Green function techniques before they are allowed to start research.

Two of them are at a summer school in Uppsala at the moment, hearing about some fascinating work on proton tunnelling—how it affects mutations, cancer, and all that. And another is spending a few months in Paris, where I'm told there's a most lively school of quantum biology. I'd like them to have the chance of being around when the big breakthrough comes.

B: Sorry, I'm afraid I've lost you. What do you mean, "the big breakthrough"?

P: Well, I take it we're agreed that within the next three or four years biology is going to be put on some really firm scientific foundations?

B: Er—well; the firmer the better, of course, but I'm not quite clear what you mean by "foundations".

P: Well, take chemistry. Forty years ago it was just a kind of advanced cookery. Then, hey presto, along comes Pauling—no, I mean Mulliken—and now it all makes good sense, on the basis of quantum mechanics.

B: I think I see what you're driving at. But don't forget that a tremendous amount of first-rate chemistry—and I include theoretical chemistry—was done long before 1927, and even now that we have the Schrödinger equation there are still an awful lot of chemical facts that are not understood. Take the chemistry of natural products, for instance. People still do it in much the same way as they did fifty years ago. I have a chemist friend who recently synthesized ATP, and he doesn't understand a word of quantum mechanics.

P: All right, so science doesn't always develop logically. But surely you must admit that if we were really prepared to spend a bit of money on an all-out effort, we should soon manage to pin down the quantum-mechanical basis of biology?

B: I'm not quite sure what you're proposing. I happen to think that we have—or rather you physical scientists have—already pinned down the quantum-mechanical basis of biology, as you put it. But as we might have expected, biology is no less mysterious for all that. You might think molecular biology was an exception, but there the real insights have come not from quantum mechanics but from a combination of bacterial genetics, crystallography, and chemistry, and now that we know the structures of a number of proteins we discover that we're not really as interested in them as we thought we should be. It's the way in which they're organized that really seems to count.

P: How do you mean? Surely if we knew all the structures of all the molecules in a cell, we could in principle work out everything about the cell from quantum-statistical-mechanics?

B: Well, for a start, you know as well as I do that when someone says something is possible "in principle" he really means that it is impossible in practice. But even if it were possible in practice, such a ghastly calculation would dissatisfy both of us. A quantum-mechanical calculation on one particular bacterial cell would be incorrect for every other cell, even of the same species, a point which was made by Elsasser when he stressed the heterogeneity of the material with which the biologist has to deal. We biologists, no less than you physicists, want to be able to make valid *general* statements about our material—statements which hold for all the individuals in a species, and even more widely if possible.

P: If I understand you correctly, you are saying that descriptive biology is not enough; that what biology needs is a more quantitative approach. Could we physicists not help you here with, for example, statistical techniques? Statistics has been highly fruitful in physics, and I am told that it is now regarded as one of the biologists' most useful tools.

B: No, I wasn't really thinking along those lines. Of course I wouldn't deny the importance of statistics in experimental biology, but the recent revolution in molecular biology hasn't owed much to statistics. On the contrary, the "central dogma" of the molecular biologist—about the dominant role of DNA and the subservient role of proteins—is framed in descriptive, not quantitative, terms.

P: But surely you can't deny that biology depends upon physics, and that quantitative prediction is the essence of physical law?

B: No, of course not. But you've just used the word "depends". Certainly biology depends on physics, but I happen to think that it's not the same subject. We biologists are trying to find the right language in which to talk about living things. The language of a science must be tailored to its subject matter. To a physicist one caterpillar may look very much like another, and both will seem completely different from a butterfly. But to a biologist the butterfly is the same organism as one of the caterpillars, but a totally different organism from the other caterpillar. One of the jobs of the biologist is to find a rationale for grouping together certain individuals or processes and distinguishing them from others, and such a rationale is not going to be founded on ordinary physical notions such as mass, charge, and so on.

P: You said a few moments ago, talking of proteins and such things, that it's the way they are organized which really counts. How does this assertion tie in with what you have just said about the need to find the right language for talking about living things?

B: Well, I should say that the word "organization" is a very good example of the kind of word that ought to belong in a biologist's vocabulary. The essential thing, though, is to make sure that when challenged we can explain exactly what such a word means. You might say that this is a philosophical problem, if you regard philosophy as the attempt to clarify concepts.

P: All right, so we have to try and define "organization". But is it an exclusively biological idea? Don't we physicists use it when we are thinking about perfect crystals, for instance?

B: Do you really? When I hear physicists talking about such things, they usually seem to use the word "order", not "organization".

P: All right, but is there a real difference?

B: Yes, and a very important one in my opinion. There are two quite different meanings of "organization", an active and a passive one. You could I suppose say that when you tidy your desk you produce a greater degree of organization, or that a sonnet manifests a certain kind of organization. But what you would really mean is that you create order, or that a sonnet displays a certain kind of order. I want to talk about organization in the active sense, meaning the process of writing a sonnet or the manner in which you tidy your desk; I should want to say that order is sometimes (but not always) produced by organization.

P: Very well, let's use the word in that way. But you still haven't given me any idea how you would define it more exactly, or how it relates to biology.

B: I can see it's time for me to show my hand. Let's just have a look at the new biology. What has been the most important biological discovery of recent years? Surely the discovery that the processes of life are directed by programs, in the most professional sense of that word. In nature, as opposed to computing labs, the really distinctive thing about living processes is that they manifest programmed activity, while non-living processes do not. All other distinctions which people have tried to draw between life and non-life have come to grief when confronted with some physical system or other. For example, many physical processes produce complicated ordered patterns such as snowflakes or convection cells. Feeding, replication, excretion, homeostasis, all these properties are manifested by fire: it consumes fuel, it multiplies, it produces ashes and it's hard to blow out. But it is not programmed.

P: But surely it is programmed? Don't the laws of physics, in particular the Schrödinger equation, constitute the program for combustion, and for every other physical process, living or non-living?

B: No, I can't agree. If the idea of a program has any meaning at all, it must be possible to distinguish different programs from one another; to say that there is just one program for everything is to make nonsense of the word. That is one thing. Another distinctive feature of a program is its conditional character. All programs of any interest contain instructions of the type "if then … do such and such, otherwise do something else". The "something else" may be to enter a particular subroutine, or to move to a different point in the program, either an earlier point or a later one.

P: I think I see what you are getting at. But surely, in any developing physical situation, what happens will depend upon various conditions, won't it? How do you distinguish objectively between living processes and other physical processes which are liable to interference—for example, from outside the system under consideration?

B: You have exposed your flank there, P, I am afraid. That word "consideration" is a tacit admission that scientific description can never be as "objective" as our grandfathers supposed. Surely we ought to have learned that lesson by now from quantum mechanics if not from philosophy. But I must resist the temptation to score debating points, and try and answer your question in more detail. If we had had this conversation fifty years ago, and I had asserted that the cell was controlled by a program, it might have been very difficult for me to justify this view in a convincing way. But the extraordinary thing, proved by Watson and Crick, is that one can now point to an actual program tape in the heart of the cell, namely the DNA molecule. And more recently people have actually discovered how the characters on the tape are translated into the twenty-letter alphabet of the amino acids, the basic building blocks of the proteins.

Computing scientists agree that the idea which made their whole subject possible was that of the stored program. Well, it seems that nature made this discovery about 1,000 million years ago.

P: Are you suggesting, then, that life is just programmed activity, in the computer scientist's sense of "program"? Because if so you will find yourself driven into saying that a computer is alive, at least when it is executing a program, and that strikes me as mildly crazy. How about that for a debating point?

B: Fair enough. But I wouldn't put it past computing scientists to construct a machine which we would have to treat as if it were alive, whatever our metaphysical objections to doing so. I think I should want to point out, though, that the programmed activity which we find in nature is marked by at least one characteristic which hasn't yet been successfully copied by the engineers. In nature the controlling programs do not merely determine the way in which an organism reacts to its environment. They also control the actual construction of the organism, and its replication, including the replication of the programs themselves. This is very important, because the small alterations which sometimes occur during replication lead to phenotypic variations upon which natural selection can then operate. So life is not merely "programmed activity" but "self-programmed" activity.

P: "Self-organization", in other words?

B: Precisely, but I am trying to spell out the meaning of this term more fully than other people who have used it before.

P: I can see that it could be a very useful one for helping one to think about morphogenesis and possibly about evolution. But I am sure you would agree that biology holds other equally fascinating problems. What about the brain, for example? How could brain function be fitted into your scheme?

B: I think it fits rather well. Ask yourself, what kinds of thing do we really want to know about the brain? I suggest that what we would like is a detailed account, among other things, of the "software". I mean what a computer scientist would mean: the logic of the master program which sees to it that the user's program is properly translated into machine code, and implemented according to his instructions without lousing up the programs of other users. It seems quite reasonable to regard this as the ultimate objective of psychology. Psychology joins hands with physiology at the point where questions about software raise questions about the hardware by which the behavioural programs are implemented.

P: You know, that idea raises rather an interesting question. You pointed out that in molecular biology the actual program tape was discovered rather late in the day. Do you think that we might hope to find a physical embodiment of the master program which underlies our mental activity?

B: Heaven knows. But it's quite on the cards that there is a special program in charge of all our various subroutines, which must not conflict with each other if we are to behave in an integrated way. And possibly its instructions reside in quite a small part of the brain.

P: The seat of the soul, in fact?

[Enter two waiters with tea trays from the villa, and the conversation ends abruptly.]

2   The Failure of Reductionism

H. C. Longuet-Higgins

Editor's note: See the introduction to this part of the volume for the context of this chapter.

It has fallen to me to open the bowling for the sciences, at the risk of being hit for six by Kenny, who is to be opening batsman for the humanities. Unfortunately, I shall not be able to do what might be expected of me by Lucas, which is to assert that everything except matter is immaterial—if he will excuse the pun. But I suppose I shall have to expound that view, if only to improve upon it, which is what I want to do in this lecture. In brief, I propose to examine the doctrine of scientific reductionism, to give reasons why I regard it as untenable, and to drop some hints as to what will actually have to be done by scientists, and is already being done, if we are to create a worthy science of the mind, rather than being condemned to mechanistic platitudes on the one hand and philosophical exhortations on the other.

The reductionist position, as I see it, takes several forms, varying in sophistication. The confident young scientist described by Lucas had obviously been impressed by the beauty and order of modern physics, and by its apparent ability to give a coherent account of all the phenomena— or nearly all—manifested by matter in motion. Objects as different as the sun and the moon, substances as different as chalk and cheese, influences as obscure as magnetism and x rays, could all—or so it seemed—be brought within the compass of the physical sciences, and made comprehensible in terms of a small number of basic concepts and fundamental constants of nature. It was a heady experience, calculated to provoke a conversion to the view immortalized in Rutherford's famous dictum "There is physics, and there is stamp collecting". There were, of course, many matters of detail which had not been fully cleared up. One could state with great accuracy the laws describing the motion of a falling apple, but people hadn't yet explained exactly how a pip grew into a Cox's Pippin. Living organisms were certainly very different in their observable behaviour from crystals, atoms, and bar magnets. But as far as one could tell, the laws of conservation of mass and energy, and even the second law of thermodynamics, applied with equal force to living and non-living matter. The organic chemists had already synthesized many of the complex molecules which are formed in the tissues of plants and animals, and vitalism had been rudely expelled from polite scientific society. What better proof could there be of the overriding supremacy of the physical sciences and their ultimate ability to illuminate the whole universe of our experience?

So much for the Zeitgeist from which naive reductionism has sprung, at least in my own generation, though I suspect that the pendulum is now swinging rapidly in the opposite direction. But what is the intellectual content of this position, as opposed to its emotional symptoms?

The starting point of the reductionist argument is the supremacy of physics, the doctrine that any assertion which carries implications about the properties of matter must either conform with the laws of physics or be discarded. Let me illustrate this entirely reasonable view with one or two examples. First, suppose someone asserted that by taking thought he could determine his velocity of motion through space. Would we take him seriously? Of course not. Why? Because one thing which we know for certain now about space and time is that absolute motion is not only impossible to detect but impossible to define, if we take seriously, as we must, the experiments and the reasoning on which relativity is based. My second example is clairvoyance, the claim to be able to perceive future events. At the heart of physics is the causality restriction: If two events are in a relation of temporal precedence, then causal influences cannot be propagated from the later one to the earlier one. If anyone is genuinely clairvoyant, then modern physics is fundamentally in error. There are no two ways about it. Finally, to anticipate our discussions on free will and determinism, does Heisenberg's principle of uncertainty represent a gap in physics, through which we can escape from the tyranny of physical determinism? No, says the physicist. The principle of indeterminacy is a principle of impotence. Unless quantum mechanics is all wrong, no one can predict the way an excited electron will jump, or explain why it jumped the way it did, in terms of antecedent circumstances. So if an electron in my head jumps in a certain direction when I make a free choice, I cannot afterwards account for the way it jumped by referring to my choice, or in any other way either. It would, in any case, seem very odd to advance such an explanation for a physical event.

Now, perhaps, we are in a better position to state the doctrine of scientific reductionism, and to see what important questions, if any, it leaves unanswered about the nature of mind. It is, in a sense, a natural extension of scientific materialism, if that label is taken to signify a rejection of any concept which cannot be directly related to the world of things and stuff. Reductionism makes a less sweeping claim. The laws of physics, which carry the ultimate authority about the material world, are taken to be irreducible. The reductionist recognizes, however, that there are other sciences, such as chemistry, which have almost as high standards of generality and precision, and that these must find a place in the scientific scheme. But he notes with satisfaction that, after many centuries of illusory independence, chemistry has been fitted into the framework of physics, at least in principle. As Paul Dirac remarked in the first chapter of his book on quantum mechanics, the whole of chemistry and a large part of physics could in principle be explained by the new theoretical discoveries. So chemistry, the reductionist claims, is really physics, and, furthermore, biology is really chemistry. Witness the resounding success of molecular biology, which unlocked the secrets of reproduction and inheritance under the noses of the classical biologists. So perhaps neurophysiology is really molecular biology? Some scientists studying the brain certainly think so. It is seriously, though in my view implausibly, suggested that DNA, which embodies the lessions of our evolution, is also the answer to the problems of memory, which nobody could deny is central to mental activity. What about psychology? There are, of course, old-fashioned psychologists who concern themselves with how human beings learn to speak or to adjust themselves to other people, but psychology is really neurophysiology; the most up-to-date psychologists need electrodes to stick into nerves and brains, knives for cutting bits out, and complicated electronic recording equipment for processing their measurements—though what the process of "processing" is intended to achieve is not always made quite clear. And so on. Sociology is really psychology, economics is really sociology, history is really economics, and there the trail becomes indistinct.

I have been deliberately satirical in so describing the scientific reductionist, because his position becomes clear only when carried to its logical conclusion. But where is the fallacy? Because if we cannot find one, we must follow the argument where it seems to lead, into an intellectual wilderness populated by mad scientists trying to measure the positions and velocities of all the molecules within reach. Perhaps the best place to pick holes would be at a rather low level, with the assertion that chemistry is really physics, and see what this assertion amounts to. Roughly speaking, chemistry is concerned with the properties of matter under rather special conditions, such as those which prevail on earth. Under these conditions we can recognize distinct chemical substances, and the business of the chemist is to reveal the internal structure of these substances, and to account for their properties, including the ways in which they react with one another. The identity of a substance depends on the manner in which its constituent atoms are joined together. Usually, but not always, the atoms are bound together into identical clusters called molecules, so that the study of molecules is the major part of chemistry. But molecules come in all shapes and sizes, and must be brought to order before the chemist can state any significant generalizations about their behaviour. It is important to realize that no one except a chemist is competent to do this; certainly not a physicist, if only because physicists are so contemptuous of chemical distinctions—of "stamp-collecting" in Rutherford's words. Let me take an actual example. In recent years there has been much interest among chemists in what are now called electrocyclic reactions. I imagine that only a handful of people in this room will have the slightest idea what electrocyclic reactions are, and I have no intention of trespassing on the ignorance of those who do not. Along comes a physicist, expert in quantum mechanics, which, he maintains, explains all chemistry in principle, and we ask him for an explanation of electrocyclic reactions. Does he offer one? No. His first words are "What *are* electro-cyclic reactions?". In order to answer his question we shall have to introduce him to chemical concepts which are not part of his intellectual armoury, and even then he may not understand why we asked the question. Actually to answer it he has to become, for the moment at least, a chemist. Only by so doing can he see what principles of physics may be relevant to its answer. Insofar as physics is what physicists do when they are left to get on with their own work, chemistry is not part of physics in any important sense. It has its own concepts and its own problems, the concepts being those which are relevant to the problems. This, of course, is not to deny that physical principles can be brought to bear on chemical phenomena, but the questions must be asked at the higher level before they can be examined at the lower.

But this is not the whole story; if it were, my objections to the reductionist position might seem tiresomely pedantic to, let us say, a molecular biologist engaged in the crystallographic study of virus particles. There is an even more cogent objection to the view that all higher-level concepts must derive in the last resort from concepts in physics. Let me give a historical example. After Newton and Laplace it seemed that the secret of the universe was to be found in the laws of mechanics. These laws were thought to be deterministic in the sense that, given the states of motion of all material particles at one time, they would prescribe the states of motion of all the particles at any later time. But in the nineteenth century, before there had been any hint of indeterminacy in mechanics, a quite independent set of physical concepts emerged. Certain phenomena, such as the passage of heat from a hot body to a cold one, proved impossible to describe in purely mechanical terms. They called for the new concepts of temperature and entropy which, like the idea of disorder, make sense only when applied to physical systems in which the states of motion of the constituent particles are largely unknown. Statistical mechanics, as the new subject was called, could obviously not be founded on mechanical principles alone, because heat and temperature were not mechanical but statistical concepts. There was nothing in mechanics itself to stop hot bodies from getting hotter, or cold bodies from growing colder. This in spite of the unquestioned authority of mechanics, when applied to systems in which the initial state was specified in every detail. So if, even within physics, one set of concepts are not reducible to another, what grounds can there be for asserting that the concepts and laws of any other science must be reducible to those of physics?

It will, perhaps, be as well if I try and summarize this critique of scientific reductionism before launching into our main topic, the nature of mind. It's all very well to say that one science rests upon another, if all we mean is that the laws of the former do not actually conflict with those of the latter. But this demand does not entail that the concepts of the higher science can necessarily be explicated in terms of the concepts of the lower science. Nor does it even imply that the laws of the higher science follow from those of the lower; this is clear from the universally conceded fact that thermodynamics does not follow logically from dynamics. Dynamics is quite indifferent to the arrow of time, and thermodynamics emphatically is not. Most thoughtful biologists implicitly accept this thesis. In his recent admirable book, *Le hasard et la nécessité*, Jacques Monod is at pains to lay bare the distinguishing features of living systems, or perhaps one should say, of life, in relation to the non-living world. He reinterprets the Darwinian thesis in modern terms, and shows how at every level, from the molecular to the visible, the evolution of life can be seen as the selection of what he calls "teleonomic" variations, and their preservation by the fidelity of the hereditary process. This, if I may call it the First Law of Biology, is in style and conception totally unlike a law of physics, or even of chemistry, as I am sure Waddington would agree. But there are other scientists who remain unconvinced.

I recently attended a series of scientific meetings near Paris at which a number of distinguished physicists and biologists were discussing the implications of theoretical physics for biology. It was a strange, indeed an unnerving, experience. In the politest possible way, some of the theoretical physicists seemed to be suggesting that if only the biologists would open their minds to certain theoretical possibilities which had been revealed by quantum mechanics, many of the more puzzling properties of living cells, and even of the brain, might become clear to them. The biologists, almost to a man, reacted to this advice with less than gratitude, and it was easy to see why. Indeed, at one point in the proceedings I could not help recalling the story of an Edwardian lady who found herself seated next to a stranger at dinner, and asked him about his work. "Madam", he replied, "I am a student of physics". "Oh really", she said, "my husband always says that anyone with a classical education could get up physics in a fortnight". But I must not give the impression that the scientific battle of the mind is being waged in the field of theoretical physics. To suggest that it was would be to incur the justified indignation of those scientists who actually study animals and their brains and their overt behaviour. An architect might well take offence if a town planner exchanged ideas over his head with a bricklayer, even though towns are ultimately built of bricks. So let us leave physics to the physicists, and see what the psychologists and neurophysiologists might be able to tell us about the nature of mind.

Psychology is still a young subject, struggling to be recognized as a science. I am not competent to review its history, but I suspect that it might make a rewarding Ph. D. study in the sociology of science. The enormous success of the physical sciences in the nineteenth and early twentieth centuries called for some explanation, and generated a theory of science which laid great emphasis on quantitative measurement. Not surprisingly, this theory suited physics and chemistry very well, having been inspired by their example, but on the biological sciences its influence was perhaps a mixed blessing. It put pressure on the biologist to make his observations quantitative where possible, or at least to submit them to statistical analysis, but, as a consequence, it undervalued descriptive or taxonomic observations and concepts which could not be worked into a quantitative mathematical theory. Little wonder, then, that psychology should suffer a severe attack of cold feet and disown one of its great men, Sigmund Freud, in favour of white-coated experimenters on the learning abilities of rats and pigeons. Not that Freud was above criticism for his lack of statistical rigour; but how could anyone conduct an honest statistical analysis of material as complex and diverse as human dreams, for example? Nor would I suggest that nothing of value can be learned from carefully controlled experiments on animal and human behaviour; but what sort of information do such experiments yield, and can it possibly be used to illuminate our understanding of thought, as opposed to physical activity?

The behaviourist approach to psychology, as I interpret it, is founded on the determination to do away with human testimony as essentially unreliable and incapable of quantification. People's reaction times and pulse rates can be objectively measured, but their opinions and their interpretations of their experiences, though they may be noted by the experimenter, do not count as scientific evidence. In effect, the behaviourist treats the subject as a black box, which he subjects to measurable stimuli of various kinds, and which emits measurable responses. He attempts to establish a functional relationship between the two, in whatever terms suggest themselves to him. Needless to say, this is very difficult, and there is a quite irresistible temptation to cheat. One way of cheating is to ask the subject why he responded as he did, but this would really give the game away. To prevent this kind of cheating, it is therefore recommended that all behavioural experiments should be conducted on dumb animals, but this does not prevent the experimenter from trying to interpret their behaviour by analogy with his own. The other way of cheating is, of course, to prise open the box and look inside. There must be some causal connection, surely, between the input stimulus and the output response; let us see if we can't trace the nervous pathways which lead from one to the other. At this point, of course, the behaviourist has turned into a neurophysiologist, so let us see what the professional neurophysiologist has to tell us.

To the neurophysiologist, the word "mind" is even more suspect than to the experimental psychologist. His intellectual orientation is set by the word "neuron", and anything which isn't neuronal isn't neurophysiology. The mind, whatever it is, certainly isn't composed of neurons, but the brain is. So let us put behind us the outworn concept of mind and try to understand how the brain works. It may take many years, or even decades, but patience and experimental skill will eventually be rewarded. We already know quite a bit about axons, dendrites, synapses, and what have you; ultimately we may hope to have a more or less complete map of the central nervous system, and we shall be home. This little caricature of the neurophysiologist is, I admit, quite unfair to those devoted scientists who have told us what we know about the structure of the most complex system in the universe, and it does very much less than justice to those who feel that we have a long way to go before we shall be able to understand even the main principles on which the brain works. But, loyalty to one's colleagues apart, I suspect that neurophysiology alone can never lead to a full understanding of the brain. The real difficulty, as I see it, is in defining the problem. It is all very well to ask for a neurophysiological interpretation of the physical activity of an animal, but how can the neurophysiologist provide us with an interpretation of its mental activity unless we can find an independent way of describing mental activity? It's no good defining mental activity in neurophysiological terms, because this would preclude explaining it in those terms. In short, if we want the neurophysiologist to help us to understand how the brain works, we must tell him, in non-physiological terms, what we mean by the word "works". And at this point we find ourselves on the frontiers of thought.

Again it will be as well if I summarise before continuing. In the last few decades—though this trend is less evident now—psychologists have tended to play down the significance of subjective evidence and to concentrate on those things that can be measured with clocks, electrodes, and chemical tests. But the baby is in danger of being thrown away with the bath water. We might, it is true, be able to control rats, pigeons, and other pests by feeding them with brain hormones or otherwise manipulating their stimulus-response patterns; but when it comes to human beings surely the only ultimate justification for a scientific study of the mind is to enable us to understand ourselves better, and if possible to improve our mental capacities. How can we possibly do this if we turn our backs on thought itself and consider only its physical manifestations? Surely it is time that we admitted mental concepts into the scientific study of the mind; but what is a mental concept?

At this point I leave the conventional sciences for a while to consider what other attempts have been made to elucidate the nature of thought. As usual, we find that many of the best ideas have a very long history. One of the oldest intellectual disciplines is logic—as Kenny said yesterday—the study of the validity of inferences. If there are any concepts which must find a place in a theory of the mind, then inference is surely among them, and logic used to be regarded as embodying the laws of thought. The phrase "the laws of thought" sounds strange to the modern ear at a time when scientific laws are taken to be business-like statements about down-to-earth matters like magnetism, or crystals, or cell membranes; and logic has come a long way since Aristotle. In a modern textbook of logic one is rather unlikely to discover any reference to the way our minds work. Certainly none of the arguments will appeal in any way to facts about human intelligence. The only symptom of concern with human thought is an occasional appeal to the reader's intuition as to how the symbolism may be informally interpreted, and perhaps a few examples for him to work out. If the author offers any apology for his subject, this is much more likely to refer to the foundations of mathematics than to human reasoning per se. All this is entirely healthy, so long as the ultimate goal of the enterprise is not overlooked. If logic is to be justified solely as a critique of mathematical reasoning, then what is the justification for mathematics itself, or rather, what *is* mathematics? To ask this question is to invite the sarcastic reply that mathematics is what mathematicians do, either for their own benefit, if they are pure, or for the benefit of others, if they are applied. But even this riposte leaves open the question: How are we to decide whether a particular piece of mathematics is right or wrong? And here an appeal to some independent court is unavoidable. In the last resort, a piece of mathematics must stand or fall by whether it meets the demands of human reason; and we are back in the realm of the mind. In any but the most formalistic age, it would seem entirely natural to suggest that our mathematics is inspired by the attempt to capture the essence of our own processes of reasoning.

Another idea of great antiquity, referred to yesterday by Kenny, is that the secret of human thought is to be found in the study of human language. Language may not be the only medium in which thoughts can be expressed, but it is the faculty which most obviously distinguishes us from other animals, and permits the philosopher to discuss, the scientist to describe, not only the world but the nature of man. As most members of this audience are undoubtedly aware, the study of language has suddenly entered a new age. The leader of the new linguistics was of course, the American linguist Noam Chomsky. Chomsky's special contribution to linguistic thought was his comparison between the grammatical sentences of a natural language and the theorems of a logical system. Modern logic is conducted in symbols, as language is conducted in words, and there are strict rules in logic for determining whether a string of symbols represents a theorem; that is, whether it can be derived from a particular set of strings called the axioms. To say this might give the impression that Chomsky's primary concern was with form rather than with content, and this impression would not be entirely misleading. But to Chomsky and his school the concept of form gives place to that of structure, and the structure of a sentence in a natural language is identified with the manner in which that sentence is derived from the vocabulary of the language by the application of grammatical rules. I shall not go into detail; I merely want to emphasize that language is an exceedingly rich mine of information about our mental processes, that its description is a highly non-trivial undertaking which has already led to some general insights which are far from obvious, and that the study of language is no less scientific an enterprise than the study of aggressive behaviour or of courtship patterns, as its primary data are equally open to observation and to theoretical interpretation. As in other branches of science, a particular observation, or its interpretation, must always be open to revision, but the categories within which ideas about language must be framed seem to be much more nearly in keeping with a science of the mind than those which must be used for interpreting, let us say, the blink reflex or the effects of narcotics upon attention.

So logic and linguistics seem to be directly concerned with the nature of mental processes in a way in which neurophysiology is not and physics could not possibly ever be. But how are they to be integrated into psychology, or at least into that part of psychology which has survived the ravages of behaviourism? Because the picture is not as black as I painted it; there are many psychologists who pay their subjects the compliment of attending to their reports and are prepared to incorporate into their theories concepts, such as recognition, or interpretation, or decision, which do not lend themselves readily to statistical analysis. I want to suggest that the problem of describing the mind becomes very much clearer if we recognise that in speaking of "the mind" we are not speaking of a static or passive entity but of an enormously complex pattern of processes, far too rapid for us to reflect upon as we carry them out. One of the most interesting psychological case-studies on record is that of the late Professor A. C. Aitken. Aitken was probably the most prodigious mental calculator in all history, as well as being a first-class mathematician. He was able to recount, in moderate detail, what happened in his mind when he was asked, for example, to work out the cube root of a nine-figure number; and his reports, which it would be perverse to disregard, reveal an ability to run through an incredibly complex set of mental processes in far less time than it took him to report them. He lived long enough to witness the marvels of modern computing, and it is said that he regarded the computer as an unfair competitor. And this brings me to my last point.

The computer is, without doubt, the most interesting of modern inventions. Many people see it as a threat, of course, but the threat arises from its ability to do what no machine has ever done before: to carry out logical operations. It is interesting to think what a neurophysiologist or a physicist might make of a computer if they had never set eyes on one before. The physicist would discover inside it a large number of magnetic memory elements, and there his interest would probably stop. The neurophysiologist would trace the wires leading in and out of the memory and make an anatomical map, including the various pieces of peripheral equipment; he might also note that sharp pulses travelled hither and thither and activated the peripherals in an irregular way. But neither of them would really understand what was happening unless someone came along and explained about programs, and about computing languages, in which programs are written. The analogy with human thinking begins to fail at this point, because human beings can of course think very well without being programmed; perhaps I shouldn't say without ever having been programmed, but without being programmed at the time they do the thinking. But it does bring out one point of substance for our discussions, namely that the whole enterprise of understanding our minds is doomed to failure unless someone—and it had better be the psychologist—is prepared to undertake the description of mental processes in terms at least as abstract as those which are needed for describing computing "software", as it is called. It is a commonplace to say that computing is the implementation of logical algorithms, that is, precisely ordered sets of logical instructions. Isn't it about time that psychology embraced the idea of an algorithm and began to formulate a theory of thought in algorithmic terms? The only risk I can see in adopting this strategy is that it might fail to throw any light on the nature of thought—which I very much doubt—or that it might fail to illuminate all our problems—which seems very likely but can hardly count as an argument against making the attempt.

In this talk I have probably done very much less than was expected of me. I have not attempted to analyse the essential nature of mind, or to list all those mental faculties which we hold most precious. Others are better qualified than I to do that. All I have tried to do is to show that neither neurophysiology nor behaviourist psychology will suffice for the construction of a science of the mind, because their concepts are not mental but physical. The initiative must come from a more abstract level of description, such as logic or linguistics, and a psychological theory worthy of the name must accommodate the concepts of these subjects. It goes without saying that the psychology of the future must harmonize with the findings of neurophysiology, just as chemistry must harmonize with physics; but neither physics nor physiology can possibly dictate the laws which describe how our minds work.

Discussion

Kenny

I've been asked to start the discussion, but perhaps I'm not a very good person to start, because I am in sympathy with ninety-five percent of what Longuet-Higgins said. In the first part of his paper he argued in a general way against the programme of reductionism in science, and with that I'm in entire agreement. In the second part of his paper, he argued more in particular that he thought that the science or the mind, which is as yet something rather in the future, could not be reduced to either of the existing sciences of behavioural psychology [and] neurophysiology. And here there were two points with which I disagree. Professor Longuet-Higgins admitted that his account of the neurophysiologist was something of a caricature. Though he didn't say so, I think that perhaps his account of the behaviourist was also something of a caricature, and, having myself last night been critical of behaviourism, I'd like to defend the behaviourist in one respect.

I think that behaviourism was characterized by Longuet-Higgins as an approach determined to do away with human testimony in investigating its subject matter. I think that he is wrong and that behaviourists are right in saying that one shouldn't pay much attention to people's testimony about their thoughts, if by testimony we mean the kind of thing which Longuet-Higgins seems to mean—the remarks made, say, by the late Professor Aitken, about what went on in his mind when he did his prodigious calculation, or for that matter the kind of thing which Waddington quoted last night from Einstein. What makes the thoughts of Einstein great—indeed, what makes them thoughts at all—is not what imagery or what visceral thrills he said occurred while he was thinking out the answer to his problems; it's rather that the answers, when he comes to express them in symbols, whether in mathematical symbols or in language, can be understood by others, can be criticized by others, can be used by others to guide and inform their own researches and their own experiments. If we are to study human intelligent thought, we mustn't take the expression of those thoughts as being mere causal results of the true hidden thought of which these are just the visible effects. The verbal expression of the thought is itself an instance, and indeed the paradigm instance, of the phenomenon which is to be studied. It's the preeminent instance of that phenomenon, and it's the first thing that we have to study. To this extent the behaviourist, it seems to me, is perfectly right, though I'm not sure how far Longuet-Higgins would in the long run disagree, since later in his paper he said that language is a primary datum which is open to observation, and that I certainly agree with.

In the second place I want to take up a remark which is perhaps unfair to take up because it was meant at least partly as a joke. Longuet-Higgins said that the late Professor Aitken regarded the computer as an unfair competitor of the mathematician. Now, though this was a joke, I think that Longuet-Higgins does really believe that computers can do arithmetic. In one sense, of course, it is obviously true that computers can do arithmetic, and can do it better than we can. But computers can do arithmetic better than we can in precisely the same sense as clocks can tell the time better than we can—in the sense that, if you want to know what the time is, you do better to look at a clock than to introspect or to ask a neighbour who hasn't got a watch. But of course, in another sense, clocks can't tell the time at all; it is we who tell the time, using clocks as our instruments. Clocks can't tell the time, because clocks can't know the time, and if clocks could tell the time they wouldn't know what to do with it when they told it.

Longuet-Higgins
Well, I should be ashamed to spoil that last point; let me take Kenny's earlier point. I think that Einstein's thoughts and Aitken's thoughts are interesting, and I think they are instructive and they tell us something about the way people think, or the way some people can think—and after all it's what the mind *can* do which is of more interest than what it always does. The highest manifestations obviously are exceedingly interesting; but if we didn't believe that it was of significance to tell other people what went through our minds when we solved problems, then what the hell is a university for? At a university we try to teach people how to think, and we do this by introspecting as best we can. There isn't very much theory about this yet, but we do describe to other people our own thought processes, hoping that the descriptions which we give them may appeal to them and may help them to direct their minds in a similar way. No, I just cannot allow that it's ultimately of no concern as to how Einstein solves his problems. If we could teach ourselves to think in the way that Einstein does, no doubt we'd think a great deal better.

Well now, the second point, arising out of that: I wasn't suggesting for a moment that one should disregard overt behaviour. I was merely suggesting that there are people who put blinkers on their scientific research. I wasn't criticizing behaviour*al* psychology, let me say; I was talking about a certain philosophical school in psychology, called the behaviour*ists*. I don't suppose there are any behaviour*ists* in this room, although doubtless there are many behavioural psychologists. But a behaviourist psychologist is a person who holds a certain dogma about psychology, and I couldn't find any other way in which to represent this dogma clearly, but to say that it excludes from serious consideration human testimony, so that we are only allowed to pay serious attention to the way that this thing responds when we do this and that to it. Of course, there are dangers in believing what people say, because people can be terribly misled about their own mental processes; but one doesn't want to disregard any clues which one might be able to use.

Lucas

I am in an awkward position, because I agree with Longuet-Higgins's conclusions, which are admirable and true and worthy to be believed, but my logical conscience doesn't allow me to accept the arguments by which he reaches them. That is to say, it seems to me quite evident, if one looks at the whole field of human knowledge, that reductionism doesn't work and is untrue. What is difficult, though, is to see how the reductionist arguments may be met, and I don't think as yet that their case has been properly answered. Some points have been made, for instance the stamp-collecting argument is a very important one, and I go entirely along with that. Aristotle was the first to put this forward—he called them "formal causes"—what sort of thing it is. And it's clearly of the greatest importance in chemistry, also in biology. Biologists have realised that it is so important that they have a special name for it (taxonomy), and if this isn't enough we can consider the case of doctors, where much the rarest skill and much the most important skill is that of diagnosis—"What is it that is wrong with you?" Now this far I go, with Longuet-Higgins, in seeing that there is more than one question that we have to face, and it's because there is more than one question that not all the sciences are the same science. Biology asks different questions, and therefore can't be reduced to chemistry or physics. But the difficulty is to be sure that the different questions don't get in the way of each other. And now I'm just going to raise two difficulties, and try and give one answer which may not do.

One point which I think is worth making, and that we are rightly worried about, is this: When the biologist is asking a question, we feel that what the chemist or the physicist has to say is going to be of very great importance; but then how come that it doesn't completely answer the question? For instance, one can't manage without air. It seems that if you know all about the oxygen supply surely you must know all about respiration. And in answer to this I want to put forward a slightly sophisticated logician's move, which is to talk about bound variables. The crucial point is that, whereas the Laplacean physicist thought that he would be able to know where every molecule of oxygen was, and every other molecule, and work out from an initial state description the whole of the subsequent course of the universe, the biologist doesn't need this information, and would find it entirely irrelevant, because from his point of view one molecule of oxygen is as good as another. And this indefinite replaceability is one of the ways by which we can distinguish what is true, in the reductionist's case, from what is false.

A second point, which I'm not so sure about, is to take the difficulty, which seems to arise as we think about the reductionist case, that if I know all about something very simple then I must be able to answer more complicated questions, because they must be definable in terms of necessary and sufficient conditions of the very simple. This is an old, old thesis, a thesis of logical atomism, and how this is to be answered I think can be partly seen by an analogy in the human disciplines, where we often have some rather general, vague concept—motive was suggested earlier— which clearly is connected with behaviour. I can't be really and truly generous if I don't ever give anybody anything; yet it's not to be defined in terms of behaviour, because I can be generous in this way, or that, or the other; my behaviour is evidence for my generosity or not, but it's always only *prima facie* evidence, which can be rebutted by further evidence of my failure to be generous on some other occasion. And what I want just simply to air for the moment is the possibility that we shall find part of the answer to the reductionist's case in moving from the logic of necessary and sufficient conditions to the logic which we are much more familiar with, in history, in the law court, in philosophy, of stating a case, facing objections to it, rebutting those objections, and then having those rebuttals again turned against ourselves.

Waddington
Could I make a remark about reductionism, because I think I'm somewhat more sympathetic to it than Longuet-Higgins. I've always in the past really considered myself rather strongly anti-reductionist. It's only after listening to him that I am beginning to have some doubts as to whether I'm as anti as I once thought.

The real snag of reductionism, it seems to me, arises if you suppose that we really know all there is to be known about the physical entities and laws. Now I've lived long enough to have been taught chemistry at a time when what I was taught is now totally changed. I was taught that molecules were made up of groups of atoms which stick together with valency bonds, like little hooks sticking out of them in certain directions, with which they could join together. This left absolutely no possibility of the very-large-scale protein molecules with their tertiary structure and allosteric behaviour and such things, which are now explained as depending on incomplete saturation of the bonds between the atoms that are primarily joined together in the basic molecule. That concept didn't occur forty years ago, at any rate in the chemistry I was taught; it's been added on since. You must, I think, always realise that we don't know all about the basic physical entities, we don't know all about the electron, we don't know all about the quantum. If we discover new phenomena, which can't be squeezed into what we already knew, we just add a bit to what we thought we knew about the original, elementary structures. At least, we can try to do that, but I don't think we always can do it. I am quite in agreement with Longuet-Higgins that mental phenomena have to be described in terms of mental systems, and the questions to ask about intentions and mental operations cannot be phrased into physical terms—or at least, they can't *as yet* be phrased into physical terms, in such a way that you could get an answer by any modification of basic physical concepts. Maybe we never will be able to. But I'm sympathetic enough to the reductionist position to say we should at least try to; that if we have complex mental phenomena, and have to describe them in a non-physical way, we will want to ask non-physical questions about them, but we can try to invent new physical explanations.

In biology, for instance, it might be said that to all the questions we want to ask about evolution we give an answer in terms of phenomena such as natural selection which you can hardly translate into physical terms, or if you did it would be so fantastically clumsy as to be unusable. You may have to apply different types of explanation to answer the questions you want to ask. But unless you try to get your answers in terms congruent with the other sciences as you know them already, you are liable to go off and invent specific explanations which you will never be able to incorporate into the rest of science. In the specific case of neurophysiology, have the physical factors told us anything relevant to mental events? The sort of questions one wants to ask about linguistics, or about logic, are questions that have to be framed in terms of things like algorithmic programmes, or in some sort of mentalistic terms, and cannot be framed easily in terms of the passage of currents among neurons. On the other hand, the fact that we know that when events are going on in the brain they take the form of electric currents passing through many cells in many different regions of the brain does give us some indication of the kind of animal we are dealing with; the kind of thing we are talking about. For instance, there are plenty of cells in the brain, many more single cells than are needed to provide one cell per word in the dictionary. I'm not certain whether there are enough to provide one cell for each sentence anybody says in his lifetime, but I shouldn't be terribly surprised. So you could have imagined that mental events involve single specific individual cells, or a smallish number of individual cells for each mental event. This would have meant that a mental event had quite a different basic character from that which it has when it involves a few millions of cells, reverberating and interacting, with currents passing between them. It does seem to me that, although the neurophysiological understanding is not yet refined enough to shed any bright light on mental concepts, it nevertheless does give us an indication of the kind of thing we are talking about when we speak about a logical algorithm.

Longuet-Higgins
I don't think I can really deal with John Lucas's point in a moment, but I think I might be able to say something in reply to Waddington. I think there is quite a difference between the reductionist position as it might have been before 1927 and the position as it is now, because—though it sounds terribly dogmatic to say so—we really do know that chemical phenomena are determined by the Schrödinger equation. The equation has survived a fantastic amount of testing, and it really seems to be right. So it's no good trying to fiddle with the foundations. As for the other point which you made: If you want to understand the tertiary structure of proteins, well, if you've got a relevant chemical concept *that* might need revision, indeed it might; which just goes to show how chemical concepts are not the same thing as physical concepts.

Just to make a remark about the brain, and all those neurons and so forth, I think the computer is particularly helpful here, helping one to think clearly about the relation between different kinds of problem. If I have a computing language, and a program, and a computer, I can ask different kinds of question about a computation. We can ask what's the logic of the computation, or we can ask how does the computer interpret the language. Finally we can ask how does the computer actually work—has it got solid-state circuits and so forth. If I advance a theory about the way this computation is implemented which simply doesn't fit with the actual physical structure of the computer, of course I'm talking rubbish. And it's in that sense that we can say that the higher-level (more abstract) concepts or assertions have got to square with the assertions at the lower level. It's very difficult to make a general statement making it clear quite how the higher-level generalisations relate to the lower-level restrictions, but I think this is a case in which we can see very clearly in what manner that relation is to be considered.

3   Artificial Intelligence

H. C. Longuet-Higgins

It is a sign of the times that a paper on artificial intelligence should make its appearance among a collection of papers on cognitive psychology. Twenty years ago the phrase "artificial intelligence" carried the same aura of incredibility as "anti-gravity" or "interstellar travel"; but quite recently things have been happening which would make even the most hardened sceptic sit up and take notice. Here, to whet the appetite, is a short extract from a conversation on the teletype between a human being and a computer which has been programmed to converse, in English, about an imaginary toy world which can be displayed on a screen and rearranged to order (Winograd 1970).

Man: Had you touched any pyramid before you put the green one on the little cube?
Comp.: YES, THE GREEN ONE.
Man: When did you pick it up?
Comp.: WHILE I WAS STACKING UP THE RED CUBE, A LARGE RED BLOCK AND A LARGE RED CUBE.
Man: Why?
Comp.: TO GET RID OF IT.
Man: Why did you do that?
Comp.: TO CLEAN OFF THE RED CUBE.
Man: Why did you clear off that cube?
Comp.: TO PUT IT ON A LARGE GREEN CUBE.
Man: Why did you do that?
Comp.: TO STACK UP THE RED CUBE, A LARGE RED BLOCK AND A LARGE GREEN CUBE.
Man: Why did you do that?
Comp.: BECAUSE YOU ASKED ME TO.
Man: How did you do it?
Comp.: BY PUTTING A LARGE RED BLOCK ON THE TABLE; THEN

LETTING GO OF IT; THEN PUTTING A LARGE GREEN CUBE ON IT; THEN LETTING GO OF THAT CUBE; THEN PUTTING THE RED CUBE ON THAT CUBE; THEN LETTING GO OF THAT CUBE.

Note, among other marvels, the program's extraordinary virtuosity in its use of the pronouns "one", "it", and "that". But what has all this got to do with human cognition?

Machines and Minds

The idea of constructing intelligent machines, with manlike faculties of thought and perception, tends to arouse passions and prejudices which endanger rational discussion. One school of thought claims that a human being is just a powerful computer wired up to a number of specialized peripheral devices—eyes, hands, and so forth—and that it is merely an exercise in "cognitive engineering" to make a heat-proof, shock-resistant model. Against this it is asserted that the construction of an artificial person raises philosophical problems with which the best minds have been grappling for centuries, and that the engineer had better beware of making a genie instead. To enter this arena is to risk being torn apart by one combatant or the other, so I shall keep a discreet distance and merely refer the prophet-seeker to a recent paper by Michie (1970). I shall argue in this essay that artificial intelligence and cognitive psychology are not two separate subjects but two different aspects of the same enterprise—to understand the nature of mental processes.

Misconceptions

Two misconceptions must be eradicated at the outset. One is that artificial intelligence is exclusively concerned with machines, and the other is that psychology is exclusively concerned with human beings. Let us take psychology first, because we can look at its historical development and see where it is leading. One of the major effects of Darwin's theory of evolution was that the study of man ceased to be an isolated curiosity and became part of a much wider range of problems, about the behaviour of living things in general and of animals in particular. This change of perspective has become apparent in the attention which modern psychologists pay to animal behaviour studies. The trend has gone so far, indeed, that we find Skinner and his disciples (see Skinner 1957) seriously maintaining that all kinds of human behaviour, even natural language, can be understood in terms as crude as those that describe the operant conditioning of pigeons.

One may feel that it is a poor psychological theory which rejects such concepts as motive, interpretation, and decision; but one does not have to accept Skinner's theory to appreciate the importance of comparisons and contrasts between human beings and other animals in their ability to cope with the problems presented by the environment.

The view that psychology is, or at least ought to be, a more general subject than human psychology, or even ethology, gains extra weight when we think about the possibility of intelligent life on other planets. We could hardly claim to have a comprehensive theory of mental processes unless we had one rich enough to enable us to formulate precisely the difference between the Martian mind and our own. We could certainly not do this if cognitive psychology were simply a set of observations about human beings; any science worthy of the name must go beyond the actual world and select from a multiplicity of possible worlds. In short, cognitive psychology may seem to be a private human affair; but in so far as it is really a science, and not merely a set of anecdotes, it must call upon concepts and principles which would be relevant to anything that could properly be described as mental activity.

Now for the second misconception—that artificial intelligence is exclusively concerned with machines. This is more tricky to deal with, not least because it seems to follow from the name of the subject, especially in the variant form "machine intelligence". There are, however, obvious historical reasons for the name "artificial intelligence" (often ambiguously abbreviated to "A.I.")—reasons which undermine the natural assumption that the subject is merely a branch of engineering. The pioneers of high-speed computing were among the first to realize that they were creating systems which could be compared in interesting ways with the human mind. In the early days—that is, twenty years ago—other people tended to interpret the comparison at the wrong level—between the computer and the brain. This understandably irritated many neurophysiologists, because computers and brains differ profoundly as pieces of "hardware", so that it is virtually impossible to compare them in any quantitative manner—though such comparisons are still sometimes made. But at the level of description where the word "mind" belongs, the operation of programs and computing "software" can certainly be discussed in psychological terms—and is, all the time, by computing scientists. It is then a natural step to start describing mental processes in the language of computer programs, and this is the direction in which cognitive psychology seems to be moving at the present time. The word "artificial" in the phrase "artificial intelligence" may then be seen as no more than an indication that one is engaged in constructive rather than purely anthropological work. Perhaps, indeed, the phrase will soon look a little dated, at least when we have agreed on a word to describe the study of cognitive processes as such. (Did the alchemists of some parallel universe ever think of describing their experiments as "artificial chemistry (A.C.)"?) But general arguments are never as convincing as actual case studies, so let us look at a few.

"Ideal" and "Real" Problems

Broadly speaking there are two kinds of problem in artificial intelligence— "ideal" and "real"—and the "real" problems are the really difficult ones. Typical "ideal" problems are the writing of game-playing programs, the discovery of "heuristic" procedures for solving mathematical problems of various kinds, and the construction of routines for searching logical networks. They have the common feature that the universe to which they relate can be fully described by the programmer, who can also specify the manner in which the problem is to be represented inside the computer. They are like the problems which are invented and solved by the pure mathematician, who need pay no attention to the world of physics, where no lines are straight and no measurements exact. An outstanding example of an "ideal" problem, and its successful solution, is the now classic "checkers program" of Samuel (1959), which is liable to damage the self-esteem of even the most expert player of the game. But Samuel's program can only indicate moves, not actually make them on a real board; and this is where the "real" problems begin.

By "real" problems I mean those which confront one in the noisy, squashy, untidy, fragile, unpredictable world outside the computer room. This is the world in which human beings operate with remarkable success—their success being even more remarkable when one tries to think exactly how they achieve it. Let us consider some of our cognitive faculties in detail.

Cognitive Faculties

Seeing

We share with most animals the ability to see. What is the use of sight? Obviously not just to delight the eye. Sight enables us to take our bearings in the world and to form expectations about it. The retinal image, as

Gregory (1966) has stressed, is useful in so far as it conjures up an internal model of the world, upon which we can then act for our purposes. A brief glimpse is often enough to enable us to adopt a working hypothesis, as when we duck to avoid a snowball. The central problem about vision is to discover how we establish internal models of the world on the basis of the retinal image—models which are adequate for the tasks that we must carry out in order to achieve our goals. This may all seem very obvious when baldly stated, but its implications are profound, both for conventional psychology and for artificial intelligence. It means that vision, whether in man or in robots, cannot be treated simply as a problem in pattern recognition, except in the very simplest applications such as optical character recognition; it must be treated as a problem of pattern *interpretation*. A line drawing of a cube is seen by a person not as a two-dimensional network of lines but as a three-dimensional structure composed of surfaces which meet in edges which in turn meet in vertices. Clowes (1971) has convincingly shown how the process of picture interpretation may be viewed as a process very similar in logical form to the assignment of meaning to an intelligible sentence. Furthermore, retinal images are constantly changing, and it is a safe prediction that the perceptual psychologists and the robot-builders will have much to learn from one another when it comes to making models of perception during movement. In this, as in so many other areas of cognitive psychology, it is difficult to imagine a more useful medium of expression for psychological ideas than the medium of artificial intelligence.

Hearing

Another "real" problem of the greatest interest is our ability to interpret what we hear, and in particular what other people say. Engineers have, of course, constructed matched filters which will "recognize" sounds of standard waveform, and the peripheral ear can be regarded in this way. But of more interest is the question of how we make sense of noises, including those which are not intended for our benefit. As I sit typing, with my back to the window, I can hear various sounds from the street. The noise of cars passing is quite unmistakable, but I can also tell that the road must be wet, from the high-frequency "sh" sound which each car makes as it passes. A moment ago I heard someone running past the window (not walking, note), and then someone thundered down (not up, I am sure) the stairs. What elaborate conclusions we reach with our ears as well as with our eyes! It is fascinating to consider how we integrate our auditory experiences into our world model; as far as I am aware, this problem has not yet been tackled by anyone in artificial intelligence. But the problem of speech recognition certainly has, with just enough success to show how extraordinarily difficult and profound a problem it is. One might have hoped that a battery of matched filters could be developed which would distinguish the forty-odd phonemes of English speech and transcribe them into a phonetic script from which a correctly spelled text could be generated with the aid of phonological rules and a dictionary. Such a view is no longer seriously entertained (Pierce 1969), although with great labour and ingenuity one can make a series of logic circuits which will distinguish, with about 95% fidelity, between a few dozen carefully chosen words spoken in isolation. The information carried by the speech-wave, in fact, resembles handwriting—very illegible handwriting—much more closely than it resembles a stream of digits. The relevant characteristic of the speech-wave seems to be its power spectrum, which varies continuously with time and can be exhibited as a series of marks on a long strip of paper. If one looks at the sound spectrum of an ordinary utterance, one immediately discovers that many of the expected phoneme patterns are completely missing, that others are heavily dependent on their neighbours, and that most of the silences occur not between words but within them. One rediscovers, in fact, what the phoneticians and linguists have known for some time, namely that we could never hope to understand what is said to us unless we were able to use contextual, intonational, syntactic, and semantic clues for decoding the actual sounds themselves. Here is a problem, if ever there was one, for the combined resources of cognitive psychology and artificial intelligence.

Speech, Language, and Classification

Similar problems arise, of course, when one thinks of making a robot actually talk. If one transcribes a potential utterance into a string of phonemes and feeds them one by one into a loudspeaker, one obtains a noise which is at best barely intelligible and could not possibly be mistaken for human speech. To produce anything remotely acceptable one must pay detailed attention, as Holmes, Mattingly, and Shearme (1964) have, to the rules that determine the precise timing of the successive acoustic events, and to the rules (as yet largely unformulated) that determine the underlying stress and intonation pattern of an utterance, given its syntactic structure, the mental attitude of the speaker, and the emphasis which he intends to convey. Again, there can be no doubt that our understanding of speech would be much increased if we were able to formulate, in the precise terms of artificial intelligence, the programs and processes that enable us to transform what we want to say into an acoustic signal.

Turning from speech to language in general, we find a whole range of problems in which artificial intelligence could be of immense help to linguistics, and vice versa. My excerpt from Winograd's conversation with his computer shows what remarkable results can be achieved by someone who not only has mastered the technicalities of advanced computing but is also prepared to contend with the problems of syntax and semantics as they arise in natural language, as opposed to the "ideal" languages which are used for programming computers. It would be impossible to use anything but an "ideal" language for writing computer programs themselves, because otherwise we could not be sure exactly how their instructions would be interpreted. Nevertheless, if we want to understand the nature of thought, we can hardly afford to ignore the way in which human beings actually think—even if we could—and there is no better window into the human mind than the words which we use for expressing our thoughts.

Another "real" problem which has been much canvassed by technological enthusiasts and desperate librarians is that of document "processing". (I put the word "processing" in inverted commas because its usual effect is to annihilate thought about what the process of "processing" is intended to achieve.) The fact is that human beings collectively generate vast amounts of printed matter, most of it worthless; but from time to time a human being needs—or thinks he needs—to lay his hands on a strictly limited set of documents relevant to his interests. Would it not be a great boon if all documents could be fed as soon as they are written into a computing system which would classify them in such a way as to make this possible? Of course it would, and efforts are being made to do this kind of thing. But such enterprises raise some of the most "real" problems in artificial intelligence. They also highlight our human ability to organize what we learn into a coherent system of knowledge, from which we can usually retrieve without trouble what we happen to need at any moment. It is arguable that the ability to classify is central to any system which could properly be described as intelligent, because it underlies the further ability to make inductive generalizations and hence to predict what is likely to happen in novel circumstances. It is therefore encouraging to note that the theory of classification is at present making rapid strides, in the hands of Jardine and Sibson (1971) among others; and, furthermore, that the cerebral cortex is now being viewed, by Marr (1970) in particular, as an adaptive information store which, among other things, classifies and reclassifies the input signals from the various sensory organs. In a related area, the theoretical work of Willshaw, Buneman, and Longuet-Higgins (1969) on associative memory—couched in purely logical terms—seems to fit in very well with the ideas of Marr (1969) and Brindley (1969) on the function of the cerebellum. From automatic document retrieval to human memory may not be so long a distance as one might imagine.

Artificial Intelligence and Aesthetics

I now digress briefly to say something about aesthetics, though the relation of aesthetics to artificial intelligence may seem rather remote. I will not say anything about computer-generated "poetry", or computer-generated visual displays, quaint or striking as they may be, because quaintness or visual impact are all that one can coherently attribute to them. I focus instead upon the seemingly mundane problem of interpreting the outward form of a piece of music. Music is particularly well suited to formal analysis because the composer presents it to the performer in a remarkably concise logical notation, which partly reveals the internal structure—for example, the metre, as indicated by the bar lines, and the key, as given by the key signature. But, when the performer plays the music, these structural elements are not made explicit, any more than the word boundaries or punctuation marks in a piece of text read aloud. They are, none the less, inferred with high reliability by the musically educated listener, so the question naturally arises: how does he do it? The problem would be trivial, perhaps, if the performer thumped at the beginning of each bar, or played the keynote particularly loudly; but even from an expressionless performance the metrical and harmonic structure of a classical composition is quite easy to discern. Steedman and I (1971) have been examining this problem— which properly belongs to cognitive psychology—in relation to the music of Bach. We have achieved only fair success so far, but perhaps this fact is less interesting than the means that we employ. Our approach is to develop programs which express our ideas about the cognitive processes of the listener, and which can then be supplied with the notes of a Bach fugue subject as they might be played on an organ. The output is a statement of the harmonic relations between the notes, including the key, and the metrical structure. The considerable agreement between this output and Bach's own indications suggests that at least some of the elements of musical appreciation may be described in programmatic form—provided, of course, that the composer writes in a consistent style. It also lends indirect support to the view that music is a language, rather than (as Charles Lamb would have it) "the noise which they make on purpose".

Artificial Intelligence and Education

My most controversial example of the aspirations of workers concerned with artificial intelligence relates to education, and especially to the education of small children. About this, Michie (1970) has written:

It is generally agreed that an important application for advanced computer systems will be in educational technology.... Anyone who has watched 6 year olds wrestle absorbedly, through the complexities of the teletype, with computer-supplied arithmetic homework cannot help being struck by the motivating power of the interactive terminal.

So far, so good. Papert (1970) reports the same phenomenon when young children are introduced to the computer; they get "hooked" and very quickly learn the power of formal precision, a lesson of general educational value, as a consequence of their addiction. But then we read (Michie 1970):

What about even younger age-groups or mentally handicapped older children? Something can be done using the cathode ray display and voice output, permitting communication between child and machine in pictures and words.

The general impression given is that machines can already speak English; and the word "between" further suggests that they can even understand the child's own utterances. Nothing could be further from the truth, and one hopes that a justified enthusiasm for introducing children to computers at an early age will not cloud other important educational issues. One fact about teaching infants and mentally handicapped people is that the teacher must attend imaginatively to what *they* try to say and write—much of it unintelligible, illegible, or mis-spelt. It will be quite some time before any robot will know what to do—or even notice—when a child bursts into tears.

Conclusion—The Problems of Perception and Interpretation

If I have said rather little about the "ideal" problems of artificial intelligence, this is partly because they are less clearly related to cognitive psychology than are the "real" problems; for example, existing techniques for proving theorems automatically bear little or no relation to the way in which mathematicians discover proofs—moreover, the art of the mathematician consists largely in deciding what conjectures might be worth following up. But another reason for this emphasis has been my conviction that workers in the field have consistently and seriously under-estimated what are often dismissed as problems of "interfacing" but are really problems of perception and interpretation. It is one thing to write general-purpose planning programs in which the "states" of the problem are merely nodes on an abstract graph; it is quite another to take a "real life" problem in the form in which it is actually presented—as a visual, auditory, or tactile input—and transform it into an abstract representation upon which a planning program can then start work. It could be argued, indeed, that the problems of perception and interpretation are the only really challenging problems in the subject, and that when we have solved those we shall have peeled the onion right down to its non-existent core. It is no accident, surely, that the very word "intelligence" comes from the Latin for "I understand"?

References

Brindley, G. 1969. *Proc. R. Soc.* B 174: 173.

Clowes, M. 1971. In *Artificial Intelligence and Heuristic Programming*, ed. B. Meltzer and N. V. Findler (Edinburgh University Press).

Gregory, R. L. 1966. *Eye and Brain: The Psychology of Seeing*. London: Weidenfeld and Nicolson.

Holmes, J. N., I. G. Mattingly, and J. N. Shearme. 1964. *Lang. Speech* 7: 127.

Jardine, N., and R. Sibson. 1971. *Mathematical Taxonomy*. Chichester: Wiley.

Marr, D. 1969. *J. Physiol. (Lond.)* 202: 437.

Marr, D. 1970. *Proc. R. Soc.* B 176: 161.

Michie, D. 1970. *Nature* 228: 717.

Papert, S. 1970. In Proceedings of the International Federation for Information Processing World Congress on Computer Education, Amsterdam.

Pierce, J. R. 1969. *J. Acoust. Soc. Am.* 46: 1049.

Samuel, A. L. 1959. *IBM J. Res. Dev.* 3: 211.

Skinner, B. F. 1957. *Verbal Behavior*. New York: Appleton-Century-Crofts.

Steedman, M. J., and H. C. Longuet-Higgins. 1971. In *Machine Intelligence 6*, p. 221.

Willshaw, D. J., O. P. Buneman, and H. C. Longuet-Higgins. 1969. *Nature* 222: 960. [Chapter 29 in the present volume.]

Winograd, T. 1970. Procedures as a Representation for Data in a Computer Program for Understanding Natural Language. Ph.D. thesis, Massachusetts Institute of Technology.

4 Artificial Intelligence— A New Theroretical Psychology?

H. C. Longuet-Higgins

The phrase "artificial intelligence" tends to arouse passions and prejudices which endanger rational discussion. It suggests that computing science and advanced automation have now reached the point at which we can start to construct machines with superhuman faculties, and this idea has been seriously entertained by a number of computer scientists. In this note I shall try to dispel both the prejudices and the passions, and to propose that artificial intelligence, whatever its merits or defects as a technological aspiration, can provide us with ways of thinking about the human mind which are of great potential value in the formulation of cognitive theories.

It is necessary to begin by making two disclaimers. The first of these relates to the comparison often made between the human brain and the digital computer. In an obvious sense the brain—or rather the central nervous system as a whole—is the body's computing system; it has the formidable task of collecting and collating a mass of complex and detailed information from the outside world (and from inside the body) and controlling our movements and secretions in such a way as to meet our biological and social needs. But the structure of the central nervous system is profoundly different in almost all respects from that of a computer. Most existing computers possess just one central processor, which carries out, one at a time, every single logical operation demanded by the computation; in the central nervous system, on the other hand, we have a vast array of processors, all working in parallel and comparing notes only when it is necessary to do so. Another vitally important difference between the brain-body system and any computer-controlled machine is the astonishing versatility and sensitivity of our eyes, ears, and fingers; most of the sensors and effectors of existing robots are pathetically crude and clumsy by comparison. It would therefore be absurd to imagine that we can do justice to the information-processing abilities of humans—or even dogs—by a facile comparison with our own artefacts.

The second disclaimer is of a different kind: it concerns the level of abstraction at which it seems appropriate to compare our thoughts with the successive steps in a computer program. One of David Marr's most important contributions to theoretical psychology was to distinguish three levels of abstraction at which one might discuss a given cognitive skill. At the highest level one will need to examine the nature of the task itself, with a view to discovering the constraints which the nature of the task impose upon alternative methods of accomplishing it. An analysis of this sort will be equally relevant whether the task is to be carried out by a human being or a machine. At the next level, having adopted a particular method of solution, one will need to specify one or more effective procedures, or algorithms, for proceeding from the initial to the final state; such algorithms can most easily be specified as computer programs written in a high-level language such as ALGOL or LISP. Finally, if one is interested in the underlying physiology, one will need to make specific proposals about the way in which the successive steps in the program might be implemented in neural tissue; but what directly concerns the cognitive psychologist is the logic of mental processes, not their neurophysiological correlates. The analogy between the physical processes taking place in a computer and those which occur inside someone's head is likely to be remote in the extreme; and this is my second disclaimer.

But what justification might there be for attempting to describe the processes of human thought and perception in algorithmic terms? What reasons might there be for thinking that we can?

Everything hinges, I suggest, on what we take to be the goal of cognitive psychology. What the psychologist would like to do, surely, is to describe in logical terms the psychological events which mediate between our experiences and our actions. The question is: How would we recognize such an account if we were offered one? To this question artificial intelligence proposes the challenging answer: We should recognize an interpretation of some cognitive skill as a fully explicit theory if and only if it could *in principle* be used for the construction of an automaton which would simulate that skill. Such a criterion might well seem altogether too exacting, by making it virtually impossible to construct a fully explicit theory of any cognitive skill whatever. The idea of a fully explicit theory is, nevertheless, a valuable one, in that it induces a healthy dissatisfaction with cognitive theories which are avoidably imprecise or inattentive to detail.

At this point the question naturally arises: If and when someone advances a fully explicit theory of some cognitive skill—perhaps embodied in a computer program, perhaps not—how is one to tell whether the theory is right or wrong? There is, unfortunately, no easy answer to this question; but there are a number of relevant observations to be made. First, the process of constructing a fully explicit theory, in the form of an effective procedure, is itself illuminating; it invariably draws attention to important questions of detail which might otherwise have been overlooked. To take an example, the history of transformational grammar is littered with discarded hypotheses bearing witness to the progress of the subject; only a hypothesis which is sufficiently explicit to be possibly wrong is of any value in the progress of a science, and it is greatly to the credit of modern theoretical linguists that they have preferred a hazardous precision to a comfortable vagueness about matters of detail. Secondly, all that one can reasonably expect of a scientific theory is that it shall be clear, plausible, and suggestive of new experiments or observations, and, of course, that its predictions shall be firmly connected with its assumptions. Only then, if some of its predictions are eventually falsified, can one be sure that at least one of its premises was at fault and attempt to track down the offending assumption.

To repeat: The particular contribution that artificial intelligence can make to psychology is the concept of an effective procedure for the performance of a cognitive task. The concept of an effective procedure is general enough to cover such diverse cognitive skills as the acquisition, production, or comprehension of language, the perception of speech or music, and the mental reconstruction of the visual world. I mention these particular skills because they have actually been modelled, with varying degrees of sophistication, by workers in artificial intelligence, and they are tasks which human beings can actually perform reliably and reproducibly. And if one is able to discover an effective procedure for the accomplishment of a given task, then one can check whether or not it really is effective by translating it into a suitable programming language and running the program on a computer. One almost always finds, in real life, that the first few editions of a program are faulty in a number of respects: either the procedure fails to specify what should be done in one or more exceptional situations, or the processes to which it actually gives rise are not at all as planned, perhaps because one has overlooked some essential feature of the input or of the relevant cognitive states. When an AI program of any interest eventually reaches the journals, one can be quite sure that it has already been subjected to an extensive and ruthless series of revisions; if the final product seems unsatisfactory, that may be because constructing good theories is at least as difficult as designing good experiments.

One might compare the very short history of artificial intelligence with the very long history of alchemy, the ancestor of modern chemistry. The alchemists set themselves the task of finding elixirs which would turn base metals into gold, or prolong life indefinitely; modern chemistry has replaced such fantasies with a much deeper understanding of matter and its transformations. Artificial intelligence began with the ambition of constructing artificial people, but in its maturity is providing us with a new way of constructing theories of human cognition. The notion of an effective procedure is important in this connection for a number of reasons. First, it is a sufficiently abstract, though precise, idea to be applied to informational processes of virtually unlimited complexity—and we must be prepared to deal with such processes in studying human perception and cognition. Secondly, the description of cognitive processes as effective procedures does not commit one to any hypotheses about the physical nature of the central nervous system, and frees the psychologist to discuss the inner logic of mental processes independently of their neurophysiological correlates. Thirdly, a truly effective procedure can always in principle, and usually in practice, be embodied in a computer program written in an appropriate high-level computer language. Computer languages are designed for just this purpose: to enable us to write down with complete clarity and precision any conceivable sequence of logical processes. Fourthly, the exercise of expressing a procedure as a program reveals quite mercilessly any logical deficiencies in the procedure. And finally, when the program is actually run on a computer, the output will almost always surprise its author in one way or another. Such surprises are a source of new ideas. If they arise from gaps in the logic of the procedure itself, they usually point the way to a new and better theory, founded on more interesting or plausible premises.

It is, perhaps, time that the title "artificial intelligence" be replaced by something more modest and less provisional. Various alternatives have been offered at one time or another; "experimental philosophy", harking back to the seventeenth century, and "epistemics", suggesting a more practical pursuit than mere epistemology. Might one suggest, with due deference to the psychological community, that "theoretical psychology" is really the right heading under which to classify artificial-intelligence studies of perception and cognition? This suggestion seems to accord closely with the relation which commonly holds between the theoretical and the experimental branches of a science. The task of the theoretician is to formulate hypotheses and to elicit their logical implications as carefully as he can, with due attention to matters of internal consistency and predictive power; the duty of the experimenter is to confront the predictions of a theory with firm and relevant observations, and to suggest points at which the theory needs modifying in order to bring it into line with experiment—if that is indeed possible. The time has now come, it seems, when the task of theory construction is altogether too intricate to be consigned to spare moments away from the laboratory; it is at least as much of a discipline as good experimentation, and one is gratified to see that artificial intelligence is rapidly becoming a standard component of undergraduate courses in psychology.

5   Comments on the
Lighthill Report

H. C. Longuet-Higgins

To my mind Sir James Lighthill's most valuable contribution to the current debate on artificial intelligence has been to raise searching questions about the proper justification of the subject. We should, he suggests, ask about any piece of work whether its primary objectives are technological or scientific. If technological, such as the automatic exploration of the planets or the mechanical translation of Chinese into English, are such aims realistic in relation to our present knowledge and justifiable in economic terms? If scientific, then what science or sciences are likely to be enriched?

Sir James places in his category "C" all the artificial-intelligence work which he regards as scientifically promising, and refers to this category as "computer based studies of the central nervous system". This heading and some of his later remarks indicate that he attaches more significance to work on the "hardware" of the brain than to work on its "software". He is, of course, perfectly right in saying that anyone who is developing network models of the brain had better work within the constraints imposed by our knowledge of its anatomy and physiology; it would be foolish for an engineer to speculate about the circuitry of a computer when he could perfectly well open it up and look inside. But the hardware of computers is very far from being the only matter relevant to their functioning. In order to understand how a computing system works one must enquire into the logic of the system software and the semantics of the programming languages in which the system can be addressed. The corresponding questions about human beings are those asked by the science of psychology—though, admittedly, psychological theories seldom attain a degree of sophistication worthy of their subject matter. An outstanding exception to this stricture is the science of linguistics, and perhaps it is no coincidence that the most impressive achievement of artificial intelligence to date is a working model of the comprehension of natural language.

I would go further and hazard the prediction that for some time to come the most valuable work in artificial intelligence will be that which attempts to express, in the form of computer programs, abstract theories of our various cognitive faculties, rather than mathematical models of the brain itself—this in spite of some excellent recent work on the possible role of the neocortex as a classifying device. This view is based not only on the obvious vitality of current artificial-intelligence work on language and vision, but also on an evident dissatisfaction among psychologists with the naive stimulus-response theory of behaviour as it has been applied to human beings. It is now plain that a central problem in cognitive psychology is to understand how our knowledge is represented and deployed, and the computer program is the only medium which at present offers us the possibility of formulating adequately sophisticated theories of cognition. The elimination of inadequate theories is no longer the main problem; the defects of a programmed theory become immediately apparent as soon as it is run on a computer.

In short, whatever the technological prospects of artificial intelligence, its principal scientific value, in my view, is that *it sets new standards of precision and detail in the formulation of models of cognitive processes, these models being open to direct and immediate test.*

The question "What science or sciences are likely to be enriched by artificial-intelligence studies?" can now receive a provisional answer, namely "All those sciences which are directly relevant to human thought and perception". These "cognitive sciences" may be roughly grouped under four main headings:

(1) mathematical—including formal logic, the theory of programs and programming languages, and the mathematical theory of classification and of complex data structures,

(2) linguistic—including semantics, syntax, phonology, and phonetics,

(3) psychological—including the psychology of vision, hearing, and touch, and

(4) physiological—including sensory physiology and the detailed study of the various organs of the brain.

Perhaps "cognitive science" in the singular would be preferable to the plural form, in view of the ultimate impossibility of viewing any of these subjects in isolation; indeed artificial-intelligence studies are beginning to offer interesting suggestions as to how our various modes of experience might be logically related.

6

In Our Image?

H. C. Longuet-Higgins

tomorrow and tOMORROW aND tOMORROW creeps in tOMORROW/This
petty pETTY/Pace from day toMORROW TO dAY till thIS/THe last syllable **
PLEASE TYPE I FOR A FAIR COPY ... I
TOMORROW AND TOMORROW AND TOMORROW CREEPS IN THIS
PETTY PACE FROM DAY TO DAY TILL THE LAST SYLLABLE

Macbeth with a hangover? No. Shakespeare under the influence of LSD?
No. My secretary trying out her new typewriter? Wrong again. Then what
is this strange outpouring? I will tell you. It is the result of a brief collaboration between me and my CAT. No, not Felix—he is far too lazy to help
me with my literary jobs—I mean my Computer-Assisted Typewriter. You
thought computers just did sums, very fast? So they can, but much more
else besides, if you tell them exactly what to do. My CAT is not a computer, nor is it really a typewriter; it is a set of *instructions*. When people
think of computers they usually think of a black box filled with wires,
transistors, and things, and covered with little flashing lights; but this is less
than half the story. A computer is like a loom, and a loom will weave
nothing until the weaver comes along and supplies it with the *pattern* of the
carpet his client has ordered. But you still want to know about my CAT,
and what it does. To a computer programmer it is a very simple-minded
program—note the word "program" (meaning a set of instructions) rather
than "machine"—but perhaps you will not turn up your nose if I explain it
to you. So here goes:

When you are typing, someone looking over your shoulder can often
predict what letter you will type next, or even what word. If he were to
intervene and type the next letter or the next few letters correctly, this
would save you a little time—though if his predictions were wrong you
would find his help distinctly irritating. My CAT is like that person looking
over my shoulder. I sit at the typewriter and type (in lower case) the words
"tomorrow and". Nothing happens until I begin the next word, which

starts with t. The CAT has learnt just one word starting with t, so he fills in the rest of it (in block capitals, so that we can see who typed what). Result: "tOMORROW". I am satisfied, and proceed to the next word. The moment I type "a", the CAT supplies "ND", because "and" is the only word that it knows beginning with a. Again I am satisfied, and start the next word with a t. The CAT fills in "OMORROW". When I come to "creeps" I have to type the whole word myself, because the CAT doesn't know any words beginning with c. Likewise with "in". When I try and type "this" I am interrupted after the t with the letters "OMORROW". I smack the CAT with a stroke (/) and he gives me back a "T" so that I can type the rest of the word the way I want it; result: "This". And so on. The rules are simple; if I have typed one or more letters, and the CAT only knows one word starting with those letters, he fills in the rest of the word; if he does it wrong I smack him thus / and he realizes he has to learn a new word beginning with those letters, which he types out again to save me the trouble. At the end, on the signal ** from me, he asks if I would like a fair copy of our joint effort, and if I say "yes", or rather "ı", he provides it while I sit and watch.

You may have noticed—I only just have—that in telling you about the CAT I have sometimes spoken of "it", but more often of "he". Just a literary device? Yes and no. I could have used it on purpose, but actually I didn't; the word "he" simply slipped out. How ridiculous! Who in his right mind could imagine that my CAT is anything but neuter—a simple gimmick, an automaton, a mere mechanical artifice. Of course that's all it is, and a pretty elementary one at that. We humanists know better than to be deluded into imagining that computers "think"; they merely process information—to use the jargon of the experts. Human beings are different, utterly different. To begin with, computers have no souls. WHAT did I say? SOULS? Every good humanist knows that the soul is an outworn relic of religious super-stition. I'd better try again. Computers have no minds. That sounds less controversial, but perhaps we'd better make quite sure.

It would be an elementary philosophical blunder to suppose that the word "mind" has the same meaning as the word "brain". You might, if you were a cannibal, serve up my brain on a plate with Worcester sauce, but the best chef in the Congo could not cook my mind. The fact that we some-times say "There goes a first-class brain", meaning "That person has a first-class mind", does not alter my contention; people are incorrigibly sloppy about words—or poetic, if you prefer to put it that way. Of course if you removed my brain you would destroy my mind, but this is no reason to identify the two. Indeed it is only a few hundred years since it was firmly believed that the brain's function was merely to cool the blood. Nowadays we realize that mental activity depends upon the possession of a brain, but having a brain does not guarantee that one will be able to think clearly, or indeed to think at all, if one happens to be the victim of accident or disease.

One has to say these rather obvious things in order to avoid it being supposed that "Computers have no minds" means "Computers have no brains". It would be merely boring to point out that however hard you search inside a computer you will find nothing that would afford nourishment to a carnivore. Naturally you will find no such thing. But you will find something that might properly be called a brain, if we take that word to imply a physical system which can be—and is—used for processing information. So if I had said "Computers have no brains" you could have shot me down straight away by asking me to define the word "brain" in a non-trivial way, and then pointing out that the works of a computer ought to count as a perfectly good brain. Of course I could have tried to escape by saying that "brain" means not merely a system for processing information, but one which was enabling somebody or something to think. But that would have been cheating, and anyway it would have brought us back to the proposition which we have actually decided to discuss, namely that computers have no minds. (I shall treat this proposition as equivalent to the statement that they cannot think, without apology to any philosophically expert reader.)

The argument as to whether computers can "really think" or not has raged without interruption for twenty years and more. The only sensible way that I can find to approach this question is to consider how you and I would decide whether a person was "really thinking" or not. We would, I suggest, suspect him of *not* really thinking if he were to give apparently random or apparently automatic responses to questions or stimuli. When I was a schoolboy I often used to panic when asked a question in class, and give a silly answer. I can still hear my maths master's lisping reproof: "Think, Higginth! Think!" What upset him was not that my answer was wrong, but that it was apparently random, having no close connection with the question. But I had a friend who got into similar trouble in a subtly different way. The occasion was a Divinity lesson in which he was attempting to translate one of Pilate's utterances from the Greek, in front of the rest of us. The Greek words to be translated were "ὅ γέγραφα, γέγραφα" ("What I have written, I have written"), and quick as a flash my friend translated them as "O Jerusalem, Jerusalem!". Not completely thoughtless, but symptomatic of a somewhat parrot-like frame of mind; the appearance of the Greek sentence, particularly the "o" at the beginning, triggered off the one item in his memory that would fit this particular pattern. The reason why clichés are so tiresome is that when hearing them we have the horrid suspicion that the speaker's mind is out of action between the beginning and the end of the cliché; and if we are not careful our own minds go out of action too. This phenomenon is of immense value to politicians, salesmen, and ecclesiastics, but its exploitation is an insult to the human mind.

The only way of telling whether someone else is really thinking or not is to observe his responses, verbal or otherwise, to situations in which we can imagine ourselves being placed. If random or automatic responses are both signs of mental inactivity, then we must regard their opposites as signs of thought, even in non-biological systems, unless we are to be accused of a quite irrational anthropocentrism. We may, of course, discover that overt behaviour which seems thoughtful is in fact automatic; Grey Walter's artificial "tortoises", which explore their cage and make for the electric point when they run out of power, look as if they were thinking about what to do next, though of course they are "mere" automata. Conversely, we may discover that behavioural responses which are apparently random are actually systematic, that there is method in their madness, and we will then have to revise our opinion of the mental incapacity of the system under study. But we must be very careful about concluding that a system which *seems* thoughtful is in fact mindless just because we have reason to believe that its behaviour is automatic; this conclusion might ricochet on ourselves in a most embarrassing way. I know very well, and so do you, that my CAT is no more than a set of instructions which I have coded on to a piece of paper tape and fed into a computer; and we know that the computer itself is a mere automation obeying the laws of mechanics and electricity. It does not scratch, or bite, or mew, or produce KITTENs, so I need not be frightened of it, or feel that I have any obligation to look after it kindly. But ought I to say dogmatically that it doesn't think about what I give it to read? Its responses to what I type are certainly not random, and after it has read a few thousand words it responds in a way which I could certainly not predict in detail. If I didn't know that it is a mere automaton I might very well suspect that someone else was interrupting my laborious typing efforts.

The trouble is, you see, that I am more than likely to come under the same accusation as my CAT. It is fashionable nowadays to say that the Uncertainty Principle, or the complexity of the human brain, or the current state of ignorance about neurophysiology, lets me off the hook—lets me think of myself not as an automaton conforming slavishly to deterministic laws but as a free agent. In a sense this is true; but only in a sense. A necessary condition for me to behave intelligently and responsibly is that my brain should work "properly"—or so there is every reason to suppose—which means that its functioning is not subject to capricious interruption by "quantum jumps" in the atoms and molecules which compose it. I should feel most unhappy if I had reason to suppose that my brain were not working as smoothly and inevitably as I expect my digestion—or my CAT—to work. If my brain were diseased, or somehow excused from the laws of physics, I could not regard myself as a free and responsible agent; I should have to plead that my behaviour was not controllable, and expect to be treated accordingly.

So perhaps we are not going to find it so easy, after all, to make a hard and fast distinction between human beings and computers based on the assertion that we can think and computers cannot do so, even when they are programmed to carry out some non-trivial task. (My CAT is admittedly a rather trivial program. The triviality of a task is not an easy quality to assess, but simple arithmetic is certainly trivial compared with playing chess—an activity for which moderately successful programs are now being written, though a good player can still beat them without much difficulty.) Should we therefore explore some other tack, so as to establish to our satisfaction that we really are superior in some way to our artefacts and to any artefacts that our descendants might ever construct?

Most people who reach this point in their thinking stop and say to themselves: "I really can't see the point of trying to prove by philosophical argument something that is so patently true; why should I bother?" A reasonable enough attitude, if one is sure of the outcome. Some other people, who feel less sure where the argument might lead, think: "At the moment I feel reasonably secure in my position and that of my fellow human beings; please don't disturb me with worrying doubts". The good humanist ought to grasp the nettle, and see if it really is nettle or not. Does he really wish to emulate the dogmatic theologian, who starts with his conclusion and does everything he can to support it with ad hoc arguments of various kinds? So let us try to be good humanists for a moment, and see whether we have found a real bogey or a sham one.

Computers can do many jobs very fast and very efficiently, and they are going to get faster and more efficient. But this is not quite true. They don't work on their own; they have to be programmed, and intelligently programmed. In this respect a computer is like a car; it won't drive itself from London to Edinburgh; you have to drive it. But you would have a great deal of trouble in getting from London to Edinburgh without a car if there were a transport strike. The computer, in fact, puts a new kind of tool at the service of man, an extension of his intellect. If that were all to be said, the mountain would have given birth to an intellectual mouse, and you would be well justified in slamming this book with irritation. But we cannot avoid the lurking thought that machines which imitate our brains are for some reason to be taken rather more seriously than machines which imitate our arms or even our kidneys. Why do we have this feeling? Is it just a sense of competition? I suggest that there is more to it than that. It is because for the first time we have been made to think really hard about our own nature— what it is that entitles *us* to serious consideration. Let me, in the pages that remain, attempt to explain what I mean.

In the pre-scientific age—though its end is difficult to place exactly— the proper study of mankind was man. It was mildly eccentric, but quite harmless, to weigh bodies in water, to roll spheres down inclined planes, and to speculate on the motion of arrows; nobody minded very much unless, as sometimes happened, a natural philosopher went too far and encroached on the orthodox view of man's relation to the universe and its Maker. We like to think that that Golden Age is now over and has been replaced by an even better Platinum Age, in which our entire world view has been shaped (at least in outline) by the clean bright chisel of modern science. Nothing could be further from the truth. If man is the most significant phenomenon in the universe, and his own proper study, as most of us would like to think, then all the knowledge and insights of science have brought us only to the outer fortifications of our castle. We know, and the knowledge has been hard won, how oxygen is carried in the blood, how electrical impulses travel along nerves, and how it is that we can distinguish colours while most other animals cannot. But we have virtually no idea how we recognize a face or a tune, or attach meanings to words, or do the hundred-and-one other easy tasks that a worm, say, could never do however hard it tried. We can poke electrodes into people's heads and record their brain waves, but nobody has the slightest idea why some kinds of wave appear only when a person's eyes are shut and disappear when he opens them or when he is asked to do some mental arithmetic. We do not know what sleep is for—though there are plenty of hazy theories—and we haven't the faintest idea how we learn to ride a bicycle. And as to the writing of poems, or symphonies, or sermons. . . .

When one is faced with a really difficult problem in science a good thing to do is to sit back and ask oneself whether one has stated it correctly; stating a problem properly is half the job of solving it. Let us imagine ourselves as eighteenth-century naturalists trying to understand the flight of birds. What should we say to one another? What observations would we make? How should we attempt to piece together some plausible hypotheses? Argument by analogy, often a helpful dodge, would be useless, because apart from bats, which are equally remarkable, birds are the only things that fly. We might obtain some intuitive insight by comparing a bird in flight to a man swimming under water, but how would we set about testing our ideas? Without the resources of modern technology we would be fatally handicapped and could do no more than present our crude notions to the Royal Society in elegantly modulated prose.

What is the present state of affairs? Do we yet understand bird flight? Yes, fairly well. How has this come about? Through the development of modern aerodynamics. But aerodynamics did not come into existence by the unaided efforts of mathematicians; it evolved by a process of collaboration between mathematicians, engineers, and inventors. Nothing at all would have happened unless people had set themselves the formidable task of constructing heavier-than-air flying machines. As it is, we now have at hand some highly sophisticated aerodynamical concepts, and without these—in particular the concept of aerodynamical instability—we could never hope to have understood the remarkable manoeuvrability of a swallow on the wing. (I refer to the work of John Maynard Smith.)

The moral of this is that in order to understand our mental and perceptual processes in detail we may find it most profitable to try and make working models of them. By working models I do not mean just electronic devices, but carefully designed programs which express what we think may happen when we look, listen, speak, or act. Testing such programs demands, inevitably, some computing machinery, but it is not very useful to regard the machinery itself as the counterpart of the human brain. The fruitful analogy, it seems to me, is between the programs we write and the mental processes they are meant to simulate. Acceptance of this analogy allows us to reinstate the mind above its servant, the brain, because a program, unlike a computer, is a set of logical instructions, and the main interest of a computation lies in its logic rather than in the machine which carries out these instructions.

Now that our argument has come full circle, let us see where it has taken us. Computers and the programs which we feed into them are our own brainchildren. Some of these children are impressively precocious. Professor A. C. Aitken, probably the greatest human mental calculator in history, regarded their competition as thoroughly unfair. So we must not underestimate our artefacts, or adopt a holier-than-thou attitude towards them. Equally, there is no need to be frightened of them, any more than we need fear cranes or typewriters; they add power to our thoughts just as a mechanical digger adds power to our elbow. What we should do is to try and learn from them—to learn more about ourselves. Each of the great scientific revolutions of the last 500 years has given man a new view of himself. The Copernican revolution placed him in a much bigger universe, though not at its centre. The Newtonian revolution established the faithfulness and universality of natural law, so that he could feel secure against the arbitrary whims of supernatural forces. The Darwinian revolution placed him at the peak of a vast evolutionary development. Relativity and quantum mechanics re-established him as the observer who cannot be omitted from any complete account of matter and motion; and the computer revolution enables him to think of his own mind in a logical and systematic way, rather than in terms of dark nebulous concepts such as the Ego and the Id.

My CAT is mewing; I must go and see what is the matter.

II   Music

Prologue

Once upon a time St. Cecilia was giving a music lesson to two young geniuses, called George Frederick and Johann Sebastian.

"Boys," she said, "I want you to take your violins and play this scale together in unison." And she put on the music stand a piece of manuscript paper on which was written the descending scale

The youngsters picked up their bows and St. Cecilia raised her baton. The first six notes were beautifully together, in tempo and in pitch; but at the seventh note (E) the two boys stopped and frowned at one another.

"You're sharp!" said one.

"No I'm not; you're flat" said the other.

"Now, now," said St. Cecilia, "there's no need to quarrel; you were both right." And she explained what had happened.

Which of the two young musicians had accused the other of playing sharp?

We now come to the first set of essays on a special topic—the musical sense. The composition, the execution, and the appreciation of music are activities of the greatest interest to the cognitive scientist, not least because it is so difficult to think how to describe them "scientifically". Books on "science and music" often run aground on the physics of stretched strings, which has about as much relevance to Beethoven's quartets as it does to the squawk of the seagull. Perhaps it was natural for a chemist—for I was still a chemist when the first three essays were written—to realize that a piece of music is not just a succession of notes, any more than a molecule is just a collection of atoms; both are *structures*, in which the elements—be they atoms or notes—are connected together in a quite special way. Classically, the notes of a composition are related in two distinct ways: rhythmically and tonally. "The Three Dimensions of Harmony" (chapter 7) and the "Letters to a Musical Friend" (chapter 8) deal exclusively with tonal relations and how we conceptualize them, in terms accessible to the ordinary musician. The central idea—the fundamental theorem of harmony—is that the interval between two nearby notes in a tonal composition can be conceptualized in one and only one way as a combination of octaves, perfect fifths, and major thirds. (Similar ideas have recently been advanced by Sheppard and Balzano; but one could take the view that they were implicit in Alexander Ellis's appendix to his translation of Helmholtz's "Sensations of Tone".)

The prologue and the epilogue are the opening and closing passages of "The Three Dimensions". The "Letters to a Musical Friend" were written after some delightful conversations with the English composer John Gardiner. The second letter explores, in effect, the idea that we conceptualize tonal intervals not as mere differences in pitch but as *vectors* in a three-dimensional tonal space—though I did not say so in the letter for fear of frightening away the musically sensitive but mathematically diffident reader.

The joint essay "On Interpreting Bach" (chapter 9) broke new ground in maintaining that the listener to music is faced with a problem of interpretation no less demanding than that which faces the performer. Even the relatively lowly skill of the musical amanuensis raises, in fact, some of the central problems of musical cognition: By what kind of data structure is a piece of music represented in the composer's mind, and how are such conceptual structures recreated when one listens to a musical performance? This question pervades all the later chapters in this part of the volume.

Chapter 10, "The Perception of Melodies", may have caught the attention of some readers, when it was first published, by its quotations from

Tristan und Isolde—a subject not frequently encountered in the columns of *Nature*. An earlier version of the article, in which "Colonel Bogey" was used to illustrate the model, was politely returned with the suggestion that readers might expect an achievement more substantial than an accurate transcription of that well-known tune; what about something from Tristan, for instance? I am now glad that I was prompted to test the theory on such an interesting example. At the end of the article I said that a full account of the program and the underlying theory would be published elsewhere. I now honour this promise, somewhat belatedly, by appending the text of the program (translated into POP-11, the version of POP2 now current in the United Kingdom) and some comments on the various functions. I am glad to say that the translated program still correctly parses the performances described as "tris" and "stan".

"The Grammar of Music", written soon afterwards and originally published under the title "The Perception of Music", develops the concept (implicit in the *Nature* article) of a musical rhythm as a structure generated by a grammar, this grammar being none other than the musical metre specified by the time signature (e.g. $\frac{3}{4}$ or $\frac{6}{8}$). It was important to attempt to establish a link between the theory of music and the theory of language because ideas from each might enrich the other, and because without some repertoire of common concepts it would be well-nigh impossible to understand the relations between speech, melody, and song.

Chapter 12, "The Rhythmic Interpretation of Monophonic Music", represents an attempt to link the formal theory of metrical rhythms to the mental process of actually perceiving the rhythm of a piece of music. The link is the concept of syncopation, which is defined with formal precision but in a manner consonant with the way in which musicians actually use the term. It is no exaggeration to say that all monophonic sequences are infinitely ambiguous, rhythmically speaking; but this ambiguity can often be totally eliminated by the constraint that the rhythm be free of syncopation. Christopher Lee and I suggested that this is the principal constraint (analogous to the rigidity assumption in visual motion perception) that we unconsciously appeal to in identifying the rhythms of relatively straightforward pieces.

Chapter 13, "The Perception of Music", draws some of these threads together. Its literary style is that of the spoken word; there seemed little point in rewriting it in journalese. The only pity is that figure 12 cannot be "brought to life" for the reader of this book—that as he puts down simple chords on his own piano the squares of the display do not light up and make evident to his eyes the tonal relations between the notes he is playing.

The Three Dimensions of Harmony

H. C. Longuet-Higgins

Saint Cecilia, a woman of perspicacity, had noticed that George Frederick was particularly fond of the key of D major. Johann Sebastian, on the other hand, had a special affection for B minor, and some of his finest later works were written in that key. So when St. Cecilia put the music shown in figure 1 on the stand, George Frederick naturally saw a scale of D major, and Johann Sebastian a scale of B minor. The two scales look identical on paper, but they are not quite the same. The principal chords of D major are the major triads D–F♯–A, A–C♯–E, and G–B–D, while in B minor it is essential to tune correctly the three minor triads B–D–F♯, F♯–A–C♯, and E–G–B. Now the outer notes of a major or minor triad are spaced by a perfect fifth, and the interval between the two lower notes of a major triad, or the two upper notes of a minor triad, is a major third. One can therefore express the intervals relations between all the notes of D major and B minor as in figure 2, notes in the same row being spaced by perfect fifths and notes in the same column being a major third apart.

"But," asked George Frederick, "would it not be simpler to arrange all the notes in a single row, so that each is a perfect fifth from the next one?" And he wrote

G   D   A   E   B   F♯   C♯

"No," said St. Cecilia, "if you tune your notes like that your major thirds will be out of tune; for example, D and F♯ will be too far apart."

The notes of a perfect fifth, she went on to explain, have frequencies in the ratio 3 : 2, so that the sum of four perfect fifths is an interval with frequency ratio 81 : 16. Take away two octaves (frequency ratio 2 : 1) and you have an interval with frequency ratio 81 : 64. But the major third has the frequency ratio 5 : 4, or 80 : 64, and this is slightly smaller. The discrepancy is small—81 : 80 is about one fifth of a semitone—but large enough to offend a musical ear.

Returning to our puzzle, we are now in a position to say which of the

Figure 1

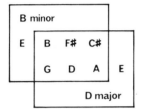

Figure 2

two pupils accused the other of playing sharp. To get from Johann Sebastian's E to George Frederick's one has to climb three perfect fifths, E–B–F♯–C♯, fall two octaves and a major third, C♯–A, and climb another perfect fifth. The last and first notes in this series have frequencies in the ratio 81 : 80, and it was therefore Johann Sebastian who accused George Frederick of playing sharp.

"So you see," said St. Cecilia, "you were both right all the time. That horrid noise was my fault; I didn't tell you whether to play in D major or B minor. If I had told you beforehand you would have played the same note. But when you grow up, boys, you will find that composers sometimes forget, as I did, to give clear directions to their performers, and then it is their own fault if their music is played out of tune. Let this be a lesson to you both."

The moral of this story is that ordinary musical notation, in spite of its complexity, is basically ambiguous; it does not tell the performer exactly what to play—unless, of course, he is playing on a fixed-note instrument such as the piano. For many purposes this does not matter; in classical music the harmonic relationships are usually obvious from the context, and in atonal music a discrepancy as small as a fifth of a semitone is neither here nor there. But any musician who likes to hear good music sung or played really well in tune will want to try and understand harmonic relationships properly, so that he can diagnose the source of trouble when it arises.

Tonal music is based on the ability of the ear to identify and to tune accurately certain intervals in the "harmonic series". The harmonic series is the set of notes with frequencies which are integral multiples of a particular frequency. As every brass-player knows, the harmonic series based on C is the following set of notes:

C(1), C(2), G(3), C(4), E(5), G(6), !(7), C(8), D(9), E(10),
!(11), G(12), !(13), !(14), B(15), C(16), etc.

The number after each note represents its frequency divided by that of the fundamental C. The exclamation marks indicate those harmonics which sound out of tune with the fundamental and are therefore to be avoided (though occasionally orchestral players are called upon to produce the 7th harmonic as a special effect).

Now it is a remarkable fact that Western musicians have no difficulty at all in tuning the 2nd, 3rd, 4th, 5th, and 6th harmonics, but that it requires a quite unusual degree of sophistication to tune the 7th, 11th, and 13th harmonics accurately. This state of affairs may be summed up by saying that we can tune without trouble the Nth harmonic if N has only 2, 3, and 5 as its prime factors; but that if N has a prime factor of 7, 11, 13, or higher, the Nth harmonic is rejected as being out of tune with the fundamental. Now if two harmonics can both be tuned with the fundamental, they can clearly be tuned with one another. It follows that we can tune the interval between the Nth and the Mth harmonic if the ratio M/N is of the form $2^x 3^y 5^z$, where x, y, and z are all whole numbers—positive, negative, or zero. For example the minor third, which is the interval between the 5th and the 6th harmonic, has a frequency ratio $6/5 = 2^1 3^1 5^{-1}$, so that for the minor third the values of x, y, and z are $(1, 1, -1)$.

Now in tonal music every pair of notes must be related by a musical interval that we can tune with reasonable accuracy. We are therefore led to the astonishing conclusion that every interval in tonal music has a frequency ratio of the form $2^x 3^y 5^z$, where x, y, and z are whole numbers. Table 1 gives, for illustration, the frequency ratios of some of the most important

Table 1

Interval	Frequency ratio	x	y	z
Octave	2:1	1	0	0
Perfect fifth	3:2	−1	1	0
Major third	5:4	−2	0	1
Perfect fourth	4:3	2	−1	0
Minor sixth	8:5	3	0	−1
Major sixth	5:3	0	−1	1
Minor third	6:5	1	1	−1

intervals used in tonal music, and the corresponding values of the "coordinates" x, y, and z.

Now there is a central theorem in number theory which states that every integer can be expressed in one and only one way as a product of prime factors; it is called the fundamental theorem of arithmetic. It implies that the ratio of two integers (the ratio M/N in our case) can be expressed in one and only one way in the form $2^x 3^y 5^z \ldots$, where x, y, z etc. are whole numbers. From it we deduce that any interval in tonal music can be assigned values of x, y, and z in one and only one way; we have already assumed this without proof in constructing the table. But the frequency ratio $2^x 3^y 5^z$ can also be written as $(2/1)^{x+y+2z}(3/2)^y(5/4)^z$, where the ratios in the brackets are the frequency ratios of the octave, the perfect fifth, and the major third. It follows that every interval in tonal music can be expressed *in one and only one way* as a combination of octaves, perfect fifths, and major thirds. It seems appropriate to call this the fundamental theorem of harmony.

The importance of the theorem is not that it prevents composers from writing impossible music, or performers from playing out of tune; it does neither of these things. What it does is to show that the three basic intervals of tonal music are incommensurable; it is impossible to equate the major third, or any combination of major thirds, to any combination of octaves and perfect fifths. This is why Johann Sebastian's E could not possibly have been the same as George Frederick's; for they could only have been the same if the sum of four perfect fifths had been equal to two octaves plus a major third, and this is impossible by the fundamental theorem of harmony.

Having assigned three small whole numbers (x, y, z) to each interval of tonal music, we can regard each interval as a vector connecting two points on a three-dimensional lattice. In this sense harmonic space has just three dimensions—no more and no less. Attempts to compress the notes of tonal music into two dimensions, by ignoring the major third, can lead only to confusion. If musical space were only two-dimensional—if all our intervals were derivable from the octave and the perfect fifth alone—music would be much duller than it is, as dull as many textbooks maintain that it is.

But what does it really *mean* to say that musical space is three-dimensional? What it means, surely, is that when we hear or imagine a sequence of notes, we regard their relative pitch as a relationship with not just one but three degrees of freedom. To see that there is more in relative pitch than meets the eye, let us consider the major third and the diminished fourth (figure 3).

The major third speaks for itself; it is one of our basic building blocks.

Major Third

Diminished Fourth

Figure 3

The diminished fourth, on the other hand, is far from primitive. It may be obtained by descending a major third, ascending an octave, and descending another major third (the intervening notes would be low G♯ and high G♯ in the quotation from the 48 Preludes and Fugues). Although the major third and the diminished fourth span the same number of semitones on the keyboard, and although we do not worry about the small difference in their magnitudes, the harmonic distinction between them is all-important: they represent moves in quite different directions in musical space. Regarded as vectors in our three-dimensional conceptual space, one of them has the components $(-2, 0, 1)$; the other is the vector $(5, 0, -2)$, corresponding to a much more remote interval. The very word "remote" confirms that we have some sort of space in mind when we talk of musical intervals, and every choirmaster knows that some intervals are much more difficult to sing than others, even though the number of semitones involved is just the same. A useful technique for tuning a remote interval such as a diminished fourth is to pass mentally from the first to the last note via one or more intermediate notes, between which the intervals are simple and easily judged. These simple intervals are the octave, the fifth, and the major third—the "unit vectors" in our lattice. Of course we quickly get used to cutting corners in the lattice and to jumping quite complex intervals directly; but beginners find it easier to use mental stepping stones on the way.

Finally, we look back at our earlier diagram of the keys of D major and B minor. What relation does this bear to our conceptual lattice of intervals? The answer is simple: if one note lies y places to the right of another and z places above it, then the interval between them has the frequency ratio $2^x 3^y 5^z$, where the value of x is indeterminate until we say in which octave each note lies. Our diagram is thus part of a projection of the three-dimensional lattice on to the plane $x = 0$. So our three-dimensional lattice is not quite so remote from musical thinking as it might have seemed to be.

8   Two Letters to a Musical Friend

H. C. Longuet-Higgins

My dear John,

You were kind enough to express an interest in what I was saying the other day about tonal harmony and musical intervals; so I thought I would put something on paper for my own benefit quite as much as for yours. Before plunging into technicalities I might remark that nowhere—*Grove's Diction-ary* not excepted—have I been able to find a coherent synopsis of harmonic principles; this is my excuse for adding one more straw to the already vast literature on musical theory. Perhaps, also, I should reassure you that though I am a scientist by profession my remarks will be couched entirely in musical terms. Harmony has, of course, attracted the attention of physicists and mathematicians, but it is not those aspects of music that I want to discuss. When you have read this letter I hope you will think that its contents have some real interest for the practical musician; if not, you would do well to consign it to the waste-paper basket.

The foundation of classical harmony is the major scale. We need not worry with the historical origin of this scale; let us take it as we find it in the post-Renaissance tradition of European music. The intervals between the notes of C major are most easily fixed by tuning three major triads, namely C–E–G, G–B–D, and F–A–C, these being respectively the chords of the tonic, the dominant, and the subdominant. In this way one relates all the notes of C major to one another in a definite manner, which may be expressed by the following little diagram:

```
A    E    B
F    C    G    D
```

Each note in the diagram is a fifth above the note to its left, and a major third below the note written above it. The notes of any major triad form an "L"-shaped constellation, and the constellations

```
A    E
     C
```

and

```
E    B
     G
```

represent minor triads.

You might well ask at this point why I adopt a two-dimensional array, rather than simply arranging the notes in a line as

```
F    C    G    D    A    E    B
```

where each note is a perfect fifth above the note to its left. This natural and important question can be answered in either of two ways: empirically, by saying that if one tunes the scale in this manner the major thirds C–E, G–B, and F–A all sound slightly sharp (for scientific reasons which we need not go into), or aesthetically, by pointing out that the musician regards the major third as a basic musical interval in its own right—he does not (unless perhaps he is a piano tuner) think of it as the difference between four perfect fifths and two octaves. Indeed, to think of the major third in this way is not only to commit a musical solecism but actually to make a mathematical mistake.

These remarks about C major clearly must apply to any major scale. In serial order the conventional "degrees" of the scale are the tonic, supertonic, mediant, subdominant, dominant, submediant, leading note, and upper tonic. Thus the three perfect major triads of the major scale are tonic–mediant–dominant, dominant–leading note–supertonic, and subdominant–submediant–tonic. The relations between the degrees of the major scale are therefore as follows:

submediant	mediant	leading note	
subdominant	tonic	dominant	supertonic

The "dominant region"—to steal Schönberg's language, but to use it a little differently—is on the right, the "subdominant region" on the left. Harmonically speaking, the remotest pair of notes in the major scale are the supertonic and the submediant; the interval between these is *not* a perfect fifth but a much more complex interval, the imperfect fifth. But I don't want to embark now on a detailed analysis of the various musical intervals; that can wait till we have examined key relationships more closely than is usually thought necessary.

In modulating from one key to another a composer relies on the fact that the two keys invariably have at least one note in common, usually several. An obvious example is the tonic major and the tonic minor, which have four important notes in common. We may therefore think of the various keys as overlapping regions of musical space. To determine the relations between different keys it is therefore helpful to begin by constructing a big map of notes; a particular key will then be recognizable as a certain cluster of notes on the map. The rules for making the map are based on our analysis of the structure of the major scale. The map must be a two-dimensional array of notes; each note is to be a perfect fifth higher than the note on its left and a major third higher than the note written underneath it. The result is as follows:

A♯	E♯	B♯	Fx	Cx	Gx
F♯	C♯	G♯	D♯	A♯	E♯
D	A	E	B	F♯	C♯
B♭	F	C	G	D	A
G♭	D♭	A♭	E♭	B♭	F
E♭♭	B♭♭	F♭	C♭	G♭	D♭

You will notice that there is a repeating pattern, so that one could extend the map indefinitely in both directions. But this repetition is, strictly speaking, illusory; it is merely that *we give different notes the same symbol.* Actually it would be just as wrong to confuse the two Ds as to confuse an F♯ with a G♭. Musical notation warns us not to fall into the latter error, but it conceals the former, equally real, distinction.

To show you that there is more in this business than meets the eye, let me pose the question: How many notes are there in common between the keys of C major and F major? Six, surely? No, in fact there are only five. The notes of C major comprise the block

A	E	B	
F	C	G	D

while the notes of F major are those of the following group:

D	A	E	
B♭	F	C	G

The notes A, E, F, C, and G are obviously common to both keys, but the D belonging to F major is a different note from that belonging to C major. It must be, because it is a perfect fifth below A, not a perfect fifth above G, and therefore it occupies a different place on the map. So the supertonic of a key has a quite different musical definition from the submediant of the subdominant key. Though the difference in pitch is scarcely perceptible, it is an artistic error to confuse the two.

Another question: How many notes are there in common between C major and A minor? The answer will depend of course upon how we care to define the scale of A minor. In the melodic form it consists of these notes:

D	A	E	B
	F	C	G

We must choose the D which lies to the left of A because that accords with the definition of the subdominant, which is indispensable to the scale. So there are not seven but only six notes in common between the two keys, though they have the same key signature. The subdominant of A minor is the D which belongs to F major, not that which forms the supertonic of C major. One must not, then, identify the supertonic of a major key with the subdominant of its relative minor.

It is about time to enliven the discussion with a musical example, so let me illustrate this last point with four bars from Purcell's *Faerie Queen* (example 1). The subtlety of the transition from bar 2 to bar 3 is, I suggest, that in the second bar the note C is manifestly the supertonic of B♭ major, whereas in the third bar it is transmuted into the subdominant of G minor, the relative minor.

One or two other points on the theory of key relationships. It is common to regard E major as more remote from C major than, for example, D major, which has fewer accidentals in its key signature. This is a mistake. C major

A	E	B	
F	C	G	D

and D major

	B	F♯	C♯	
	G	D	A	E

have only three notes in common (B, G, and D); E major

C♯	G♯	D♯	
A	E	B	F♯

also has three notes in common with C major (A, E, and B). Indeed, it is

Ex.1

Ex.2

very easy to modulate into the mediant major, whereas the supertonic major usually has to be reached in two steps.

But between C major and D *minor*

G   D   A   E
        B♭   F   C

we can find *four* notes in common (A, E, F, and C) provided we are prepared to leave G and D in the lurch. The key which one reaches by a direct modulation from C major to D minor is therefore *not* the minor form of the supertonic major, but a quite unrelated key, the relative minor of the subdominant. One may achieve intuitive certainty on this point by studying the opening five bars of Beethoven's String Quintet in C major (example 2).

Before concluding this letter I cannot resist analysing in these terms what to me is one of the most magical passages in all music—the opening section of the slow movement of Schubert's C major Quintet. In the first twenty-eight bars Schubert takes us on two successive excursions away from the tonic and back again. But where exactly, and how?

Bar 1 states the tonic key, E major, and bar 2 the chord of the dominant, B major. In bar 3 we suddenly find ourselves in F♯ minor. But this is not the true supertonic minor; it is the relative minor of the subdominant (A major). The first violin makes this plain by insisting on C♯, the submediant of E major. If we wanted to beat a cowardly retreat to the tonic the easiest way back would be via the subdominant, A major. But Schubert has us by the arm, and leads us further afield—upwards and to the left in our map of notes, not to the right. In bars 4 and 5 he transforms F♯ minor into its major form, in which C♯ and G♯ are the only notes that remain from the original tonic key. Bars 6–9 consolidate F♯ major with a pair of heavenly cadences, and in bar 10, after this refreshment, we set out for home by a more devious route. In bar 11 a remote chord of B minor has not a single note in common with the original tonic, but the first violin maintains that by holding to F♯ we may hope to find our way back. And so it turns out; in bars 12 and 13 we realize that the conspicuous F♯ was none other than the submediant of A major, the subdominant of the original tonic key. Having found our bearings again, we are back home in two strides (bars 14 and 15).

But Schubert gives us no rest. In bar 16 we find ourselves suddenly in the dominant minor, and a moment later in its relative major key—D major. Consulting our map we find we have travelled east-south-east, in the opposite direction to our first journey. But in bar 19 the first violin discovers a familiar note, B, in the chord of G major, and by harping on this note persuades the party to return home (bars 19–24), calling in at the subdominant on the way (bar 22). We are then allowed a few moments' respite (bars 25–28) before being buffeted by a south-westerly storm of flats.

I will leave the subject of musical intervals for another letter. Shall I try and summarize what I regard as the essential points of this one?

What I have tried to show is that harmonic relationships in general, and key relationships in particular, can be understood only by thinking in two dimensions, by recognizing the major third as a basic interval independent of the perfect fifth and the octave. But I have also attempted to convince you that (together with the octave) the perfect fifth and the major third provide the musician with a *sufficient* basis for connecting the notes of a given key with one another and with the notes of neighbouring keys.

It is perhaps unfortunate that our musical notation conceals the two-dimensional character of harmonic space, though in this respect it is not as seriously misleading as the keyboard. Conventional notation does at least distinguish the Neapolitan second (D♭ in C major) from the leading note of the supertonic (C♯ in C major); but it does not distinguish the supertonic of the dominant key from the submediant of the tonic—both are written as A if the tonic is C major. I am not proposing that we should complicate what is already an overburdened notation in order to bring out such distinctions; a notation which was good enough for Schubert ought to be good enough for you or me. But it shocks me a little that musical theorists should be, apparently, so ignorant of the two-dimensional nature of harmonic relationships. This remark must sound rather impertinent coming from a non-professional musician, but at least it may reassure you that I am not attempting to launch upon the musical world a private theory of my own. The whole thing follows relentlessly from first principles.

Yours ever,

Christopher Longuet-Higgins

My dear John,

I said I would write you another letter, on the subject of musical intervals, and here it is. What I propose to do is to try and bring out as clearly as possible the way in which the various intervals of classical music may be related to the map of notes which I drew in my last letter, and to translate them into musical experience with the help of some hand-picked illustrations.

It would be a labour of Hercules to try and list all the intervals which the classical masters have used, so to bring the problem within bounds I shall make an obvious simplification. This is to identify every interval greater than an octave with the corresponding interval which lies within the octave. Thus, the name "major third" is taken to cover not only the major third but also the major tenth, and the perfect twelfth is regarded as harmonically equivalent to the perfect fifth. With this convention in mind you will, I hope, not be puzzled by statements like "the sum of two perfect fifths is a major tone". Another convenience in discussion is to speak of two intervals as complementary if their sum is an octave. Thus, the major third and the minor sixth are complementary intervals, and the perfect fourth is the complement of the perfect fifth. You will appreciate the usefulness of these conventions as the discussion proceeds.

To start with the obvious, every musical interval is a relation between two notes, an upper and a lower note. But to define the interval precisely it is not enough to know merely the names of the notes; we must also know the musical *context*. Thus in G major, as we have already seen, D−A is a perfect fifth, but in C major it is a slightly smaller interval (the imperfect fifth). In classical music (I have nothing to say about atonal music) the context is a certain key, or a set of related keys. That is why it can be so disastrous to lose one's sense of key—an experience comparable with an acrobat losing his sense of balance. If this is agreed, then we should be able to use our map of the keys for enumerating all the intervals which we could ever hope or fear to meet in tonal music.

The idea is essentially simple. Starting at any note in the map

F♯	C♯	G♯	D♯	A♯
D	A	E	B	F♯
B♭	F	C	G	D
G♭	D♭	A♭	E♭	B♭

we may ask: What is the interval from this note up to any other which we might care to name? The interval can only depend on the position of the second note *relative to the first*, and is uniquely defined (within an octave) once their positions are given. To see how this procedure works, let us start from C and determine the upward intervals to its neighbours on the map. The note on the right (G) is a perfect fifth higher, that on the left (F) a perfect fourth higher. The note above is E, a major third higher; the note below is A♭, a minor sixth above C. To complete the scheme it is appropriate to regard C as being in unison with itself (or an octave higher). These statements are summarized compactly in figure 1.

This diagram constitutes the nucleus of a systematic table of musical intervals. To build up the table we simply apply the following rules of thumb: in the space on the right of any interval enter the name of the interval which is a perfect fifth greater; in the space above it write the interval obtained by adding a major third. (In moving to the left we must therefore add a perfect fourth, and in moving down the table we have to add a minor sixth at each step.) Figure 2 is the result. Let us look at it closely, and study some of its features.

First of all, it bears a very close relation to the map of notes on which it is founded. The relation is this: if we want to find the upward interval from a note X to a note Y, we superimpose the table of intervals upon the map of notes in such a way that the square marked "unison" lies over the note X. The square lying above the note Y then bears the name of the required interval. Conversely, if we wish to know the downward interval from X to

	major third	
perfect fourth	unison (octave)	perfect fifth
	minor sixth	

Figure 1

Augmented seventh	Augmented fourth	Small half-tone	Augmented fifth	Augmented second	Augmented sixth	Augmented third
$\dfrac{50}{27}$	$\dfrac{25}{18}$	$\dfrac{25}{24}$	$\dfrac{25}{16}$	$\dfrac{75}{64}$	$\dfrac{225}{128}$	$\dfrac{675}{512}$
Imperfect fifth	Minor tone	Major sixth	Major third	Major seventh	Diatonic tritone	Small limma
$\dfrac{40}{27}$	$\dfrac{10}{9}$	$\dfrac{5}{3}$	$\dfrac{5}{4}$	$\dfrac{15}{8}$	$\dfrac{45}{32}$	$\dfrac{135}{128}$
Imperfect third	Dominant seventh	Perfect fourth	Unison (octave)	Perfect fifth	Major tone	Imperfect sixth
$\dfrac{32}{27}$	$\dfrac{16}{9}$	$\dfrac{4}{3}$	1	$\dfrac{3}{2}$	$\dfrac{9}{8}$	$\dfrac{27}{16}$
False octave	Minor fifth	Diatonic semitone	Minor sixth	Minor third	Minor seventh	Imperfect fourth
$\dfrac{256}{135}$	$\dfrac{64}{45}$	$\dfrac{16}{15}$	$\dfrac{8}{5}$	$\dfrac{6}{5}$	$\dfrac{9}{5}$	$\dfrac{27}{20}$
Diminished sixth	Diminished third	Diminished seventh	Diminished fourth	Diminished octave	Diminished fifth	Great limma
$\dfrac{1024}{675}$	$\dfrac{256}{225}$	$\dfrac{128}{75}$	$\dfrac{32}{25}$	$\dfrac{48}{25}$	$\dfrac{36}{25}$	$\dfrac{27}{25}$

Figure 2

Y, we place "unison" above Y and discover the interval in question over the note X.

Secondly, as you will already have noticed, the two intervals of a complementary pair are situated in diametrically opposite positions relative to the centre of the table—the square marked "unison". Thus, the imperfect fifth and the imperfect fourth are complementary intervals.

Thirdly, the table can be used for a lightning calculation of the sum of any two intervals. We regard each of the two intervals as a displacement from the "unison" square and add the two displacements together. For example, the diminished fifth is the sum of two minor thirds, and the sum of a major seventh and a minor third is a major tone (actually a major ninth, but we have agreed to identify the two).

Fourthly, the commonest and most primitive intervals lie near the middle of the table, whereas those near the edges are the intervals which we instinctively regard as the most "remote" in a musical sense. This is a natural consequence of the way in which the table has been constructed, and gives the word "remote" an objectivity which we could scarcely have expected of it.

Fifthly, every interval normally recognized by the theorist finds its natural place in the table, and one or two others as well. (For the new ones I have invented names which I hope will seem inoffensive to you.) Indeed one could extend the table further outwards, to take in such recondite intervals as the Pythagorean third (the sum of two major tones) or the comma of Didymus (the difference between the major tone and the minor tone). But these intervals are so rare as to be a mere encumbrance to this discussion, and I feel that the edges of the table mark the boundaries of sanity. There is, actually, one class of intervals which the table does not recognize, namely intervals involving the natural seventh harmonic of a note. If this ever comes into common use we shall have to extend the table of notes, and of intervals, into three dimensions. But this is a digression.

To go through the whole table without stopping would be too exhausting for both of us, so let us consider the intervals in two groups: those which occur within the major scale and those which do not.

It is a commonplace that the major scale comprises two semitones and five tones; but this is a very superficial observation. The semitones are straightforward enough—they are both *diatonic semitones* according to the table of intervals—but the tones are of two distinct species. Thus in C major the intervals C–D, F–G, and A–B are *major tones*, but the intervals D–E and G–A are *minor tones*. The diatonic semitone is epitomized in the opening of Beethoven's First Symphony (example 1); as illustrations of the major and minor tones I can think of none better than examples 2 and 3.

Ex.1 (Diatonic semitones)

Ex.2 (Major tone)

Et in ter - ra   pax,   pax ho - mi - ni - bus

Ex.3 (Minor tone)

Ex. 4 (Major third)

Ex. 5 and 6 (Minor third and Imperfect third)

Ex. 7 (Imperfect fourth)

Three different thirds occur in the major scale: the *major third*, the *minor third*, and the *imperfect third*. The major third (C–E, G–B, and F–A in C major) is probably the least ambiguous interval in music, not excepting the perfect fifth (see example 4, but is an example really necessary?). The minor third, on the other hand, is relatively easily confused with the imperfect third, as ordinary notation does not make the difference plain. Thus in C major there are three minor thirds (E–G, B–D, and A–C), but the interval D–F is an imperfect third. Examples 5 and 6 illustrate the essential difference between the two.

The fourths of the major scale are also of three distinct kinds: the *perfect fourth*, the *imperfect fourth*, and the *diatonic tritone*. In C major there are five perfect fourths (C–F, D–G, E–A, G–C, and B–E) and one imperfect fourth (A–D). Because on paper it resembles the perfect fourth, the imperfect fourth is probably more often misconstrued than any other common interval, particularly by the composers of Anglican hymn tunes. Perhaps that is why it was hardly ever used melodically by the great masters. But here is one, from the first movement of Elgar's Cello Concerto (example 7). Elgar, by the way, seems to have had a liking for the imperfect fourth, and occasionally his good taste failed him (example 8). The diatonic tritone is the interval from the subdominant to the leading note (F–B in C major). It runs no risk of confusion with either the perfect or the imperfect fourth (example 9).

Ex. 8 (Imperfect fourth)

Ex. 9 (Diatonic tritone)

Ex. 10 (Perfect and Imperfect fifths)

Ex. 11 (Minor fifth)

Ex. 12 (Minor sixth)

Complementary to the three kinds of fourth are the *perfect fifth*, the *imperfect fifth*, and the *minor fifth*. The only imperfect fifth in the major scale is the interval from supertonic to submediant. It is as rare and treacherous as its complement, but immensely effective when correctly stated. Again Elgar provides us with a lovely one in the Cello Concerto (example 10); a nearby perfect fifth serves to stress the world of difference between the two intervals. The minor fifth is the interval from leading note to subdominant (example 11), and is the complement of the diatonic tritone. Nobody in his senses could mistake it for a perfect or imperfect fifth.

The three species of third have their complements in the *minor sixth*, the *major sixth*, and the *imperfect sixth*. The minor sixth belongs with the major third, and explains itself equally clearly (example 12). The major sixth (example 13) resembles on paper the imperfect sixth (example 14), but has

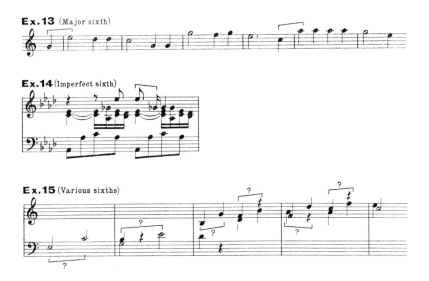

Ex.13 (Major sixth)

Ex.14 (Imperfect sixth)

Ex.15 (Various sixths)

an utterly different character. (Exercise for the reader: Identify the successive sixths occurring in example 15.)

There are three varieties of seventh in the major scale: the *minor seventh* (complementary to the minor tone), the *dominant seventh* (complementary to the major tone), and the *major seventh* (the complement of the diatonic semitone). It would be tedious to enumerate their occurrences in the major and minor scales—though one can do this simply enough with the table of intervals—so let me just give one classic example of the use of each (examples 16–18).

Before passing on to consider the so-called chromatic intervals—those which do not occur in the major or minor scales—it is worth noting that the four imperfect intervals all leave us with a feeling of dissatisfaction, and the same applies to the diatonic tritone and the minor fifth. This is essentially because the imperfect third and the imperfect sixth, like the tritone and the minor fifth, suggest the chord of the dominant seventh, to which these intervals all belong. Likewise, the imperfect fourth and fifth occur in the chord of the dominant ninth, to which they impart its special character. Which takes precedence, a chord or the intervals within it, is a barren question; but at least the designation "imperfect" is seen to have a musical as well as a technical meaning.

Now let us turn to the chromatic intervals—those which lie outside the heavy line in the table.

First of all there is the vexed question of nomenclature. Leaving aside for

Ex. 16 (Minor seventh)

Ex. 17 (Dominant seventh)

Ex. 18 (Major seventh)

Ex. 19 (Small half tone)

Ex. 20 (Small limma)

a moment the various semitones and their complementary intervals, on one rule at least all authorities agree: an interval is named a third, a fourth, a fifth, a sixth, or a seventh solely according to the distance apart of its two notes *on the stave.* Thus the interval between notes on adjacent lines or spaces of the stave is never called anything but a third. As to the qualifying adjectives "augmented" and "diminished", these serve to indicate how a chromatic interval is related to the corresponding diatonic interval. But to say any more without illustration would verge on pedantry, so let us now study the musical characters of some individual chromatic intervals.

The chromatic semitones are three in number: the *small half-tone*, which is the difference between a major and a minor third (example 19); the *small limma* (example 20), which separates the F of C major from the F♯ of G major, and the *great limma.* The notes of a small half-tone or a small limma are printed on the same line or space of the stave, so that they might be described as "augmented unisons". Thomas Morley seems to have been the first to distinguish between them. The notes of a great limma, on the other hand, like those of a diatonic semitone, are separated by one place on the stave; in this sense the great limma is a "diminished tone". Possibly because it is so difficult to distinguish musically from the diatonic semitone,

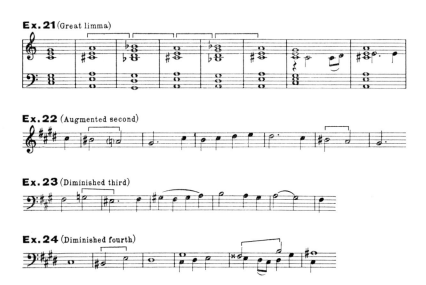

the great limma is exceedingly rare in melody. But here is one, from the slow movement of Vaughan Williams's Fifth Symphony (example 21). If you suspect it of being a diatonic semitone, consult the table of intervals in order to determine the relation between A and B♭ in the following constellation of notes:

C♯
A   E
        C   G   D
                        B♭

In contrast to the great limma, or diminished tone, the augmented tone, more often called the *augmented second*, is an interval of relatively wide occurrence in classical music. Beethoven has demonstrated once and for all its musical potentialities (example 22).

The *diminished third* (example 23) is a beautifully clear interval, even if something of a trial to choirs. The *augmented third* (flattened supertonic to leading note of dominant) is a real collector's piece, and I am still scouring the classical literature for a good example of its melodic use.

The *diminished fourth* speaks for itself (example 24). What I describe as the *augmented fourth* is the interval obtained by subtracting two minor thirds from an octave. It is not equal to the diatonic tritone, though some authorities use the two names synonymously. One might think that there were many augmented fourths worthy of quotation in Bach's *St. Matthew Passion*; but on close examination these all turn out to be diatonic tritones.

Ex. 25 (Augmented fourth)

Ex. 26 (Diminished fifth)

Ex. 27 (Augmented fifth)

Ex. 28 (Diminished sixth)

But Mozart uses a real augmented fourth at the end of the introduction to the first movement of his Thirty-Ninth Symphony (example 25).

The complement of the augmented fourth is the *diminished fifth*, the sum of two minor thirds. It is not to be identified with the minor fifth, which is the complement of the diatonic tritone. It is very much rarer than the minor fifth, but Mozart's Thirty-Ninth Symphony again provides an example (example 26), this time from the slow movement. The *augmented fifth* is the complement of the diminished fourth, and is equally self-explanatory (example 27). Mozart, by the way, seems to have had a fondness for chromatic fourths and fifths, just as Elgar had a taste for imperfect ones.

The *diminished sixth* is one of the most remote of all chromatic intervals. The best commentary on this interval is Schubert's Impromptu in G♭ major, which culminates in a diminished sixth to end all diminished sixths (example 28, transposed into G major for clarity). The *augmented sixth* is very easily degraded enharmonically into a dominant seventh, but Brahms, in the first movement of his Violin Concerto (example 29—the violin chord B♭–G♯) resists this temptation.

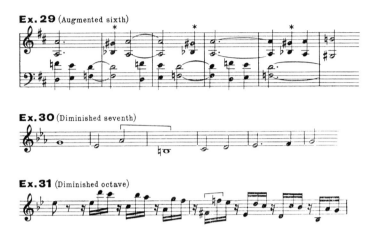

Ex. 29 (Augmented sixth)

Ex. 30 (Diminished seventh)

Ex. 31 (Diminished octave)

The complement of the augmented second is the *diminished seventh* (example 30). It needs no further description.

We have now given individual attention to all the intervals in the table except the complements of the chromatic semitones. Of these the only one which has found favour with composers is the *diminished octave*, the complement of the small half-tone (example 31). The other two are of no more musical importance than some of the intervals which lie beyond the frontiers of the table, so let us leave the matter there.

In conclusion, perhaps I should run over the essential points, as I see them. The most important generalization one can make about the intervals of tonal music is that every standard interval can be expressed *in one and only one way* as a combination of perfect fifths, major thirds, and octaves. Octaves and perfect fifths alone are not enough, but if we bring in the major third as well we can give a precise and unique definition to every interval, diatonic or chromatic. (Thus the diatonic tritone is two perfect fifths plus a major third minus an octave, whereas the augmented fourth is an octave plus two major thirds minus two perfect fifths.) Thanks to its specially primitive character, however, we can take the octave for granted, as I have done in this letter, and order the intervals systematically in an only two-dimensional array. The resulting table of intervals bears an intimate relationship to the map of notes: it simply embodies the relationships which are inherent in the latter. But, unlike the map of notes the table of intervals has no repeating pattern; this confirms what I asserted in my first letter: the map of notes does not really repeat itself; it is merely that we give different notes the same name.

Perhaps all the things I have said in these two letters are well known;

certainly a great many of them are. But all that I have tried to do is to stress the two-dimensional character of musical space (three-dimensional if one gives due respect to the octave) and to demonstrate the need to use two-dimensional maps for exploring it. Any attempt to understand harmonic relationships in simpler terms than these is bound, I maintain, to generate mystery and muddle. But ought one to expect the subtleties of classical harmony to yield to any less sophisticated analysis?

Yours ever,

Christopher Longuet-Higgins

9 On Interpreting Bach

H. C. Longuet-Higgins
and M. J. Steedman

The performance of a piece of music involves both the performer and the listener in a problem of interpretation. The performer must discern and express musical relationships which are not fully explicit in the musical score, and the listener must appreciate relationships which are not explicit in the performance. How the performer should convey his interpretation of the piece is an aesthetic question of the utmost delicacy; but the converse process, that of listening to a piece and discerning its structure, is partly amenable to objective investigation. This is because European classical music is written in a notation which conveys to the performer a considerable amount of information about its structure, and this information can be reconstituted by the educated listener from even a mediocre preformance. We refer particularly to the time signature and the key signature, of which the former indicates the metric grouping of the notes and the latter their harmonic relations with one another and in particular with the keynote. Any music student who scored the National Anthem as in example 1 would get very low marks for dictation, even though the note lengths, and their positions on the keyboard, are correctly indicated. The "correct" annotation of the melody in question is, of course, that shown in example 2, and even if he had never heard this melody before a competent musician would realize that this is how it ought to be scored.

Example 1

Example 2

As far as we are aware, no musical theorist has hitherto formulated the rules which generate the "correct" score of a simple melody, as opposed to any of the numerous incorrect scores which provide the same explicit information. This gap in musical theory is all the more glaring in view of the considerable effort which has been devoted to much more ambitious undertakings, such as programmed musical composition. We are cynical enough to believe that it is only the prevailing babel in contemporary classical music which saves most of these compositions from being treated with the derision which they merit, and that if any progress is to be made in this direction it will first be essential to formalize the most elementary facts about musical competence, such as those we have just mentioned.

The work which we describe in this paper may suggest a comparison with recent work in linguistics, and in some ways the comparison would be apposite. The close connection between music and language is evident in song, where the rhythm of the words is mirrored in the rhythm of the melody to which they are set and the rise and fall of the melody is to some extent constrained by the intonation pattern of the words. But to say this is only to prepare the ground for a linguistic approach to classical music. The main point of comparison between our work and modern grammatical theory is that we attempt to make a formally precise model of the cognitive processes involved in the comprehension of classical melodies—in particular the fugue subjects of *Das Wohltemperierte Klavier*. Our choice of these particular melodies was to some extent arbitrary, but we felt that the choice justified itself by the great variety, rhythmic subtlety, and harmonic sophistication of the 48 fugue subjects and the universal admiration in which they and their composer are held by educated musicians.

We might have attempted to formulate our model as a generative grammar, but we felt that such an attempt—even if it had been suited to the problem in hand—was clearly doomed to failure. It was unsuitable because those elements of structure in which we were interested, namely the more obvious metrical and harmonic relationships, were relatively superficial and were likely to be largely independent of the underlying architecture. In this respect our analysis was "phonological" rather than "syntactic", and was, furthermore, designed to describe the mental processes of the listener rather than the composer. A generative grammatical approach could hardly succeed, we felt, unless it were founded on musical insights as deep as, and more explicit than, those of Bach himself. Such an approach might be feasible for nursery tunes, or even for Anglican chants, but for the Forty-Eight it would be a monstrous impertinence.

What we have in fact done is to write two "parsing" programs, one for determining the metre and the other for explicating the harmonic relations between the notes of a Bach fugue subject. In writing these programs, which take account only of the note lengths and positions on the keyboard, we have attempted to make explicit our intuitive understanding of musical rhythm and harmony in general, and also to take account of one or two stylistic features which seem to distinguish Bach from some other classical masters. We do not claim that our parsing rules, or their discovery, have been informed by any methodological principles. Doubtless there are such principles, but we feel that they are more likely to become apparent after, rather than before, the formulation of rules to which they might apply. We have, however, attempted to make our programs mirror the progressive character of musical comprehension—by which we mean that as a fugue subject proceeds the listener's ideas about its metre and key become more and more definite, and may indeed crystallize well before the end of a long subject. The progressive nature of the listener's comprehension is made explicit in an assumption about the permitted order of musical events in an acceptable melody. This assumption we call the "rule of congruence", and it is fundamental to the operation of both our harmonic and our metrical rules.

Both the key signature and the time signature of a melody indicate underlying structures with which individual notes or musical features may not be superficially consistent. When some attribute of a note, such as its pitch, is consistent with the relevant underlying structure, we may describe the note as "congruent" in this attribute, and otherwise as "non-congruent". Thus a note which does not belong to the scale defined by the key signature—an "accidental"—is harmonically non-congruent; and a note carrying a rhythmic stress imparted by the context but not indicated by the time signature—a "syncopated" note—is metrically non-congruent. In adopting this definition of congruence we follow that introduced by Cooper and Meyer (1960) in the domain of rhythm, and extend it to harmony. We also follow their terminology in our use of the terms "rhythm" and "metre".

If our rules are to be able to decide the time signature and the key signature from the durations of the notes and their positions on the keyboard, some assumption must be made about how many of these data may safely be assumed congruent and may therefore be used as evidence in reaching the required decision. The rule of congruence is such an assumption. It states that until a metric or harmonic signature has been established, every note will be congruent with it in the relevant attribute, unless the note is non-congruent with all possible signatures. In other words, a non-congruence must not occur until it can be recognized as such. This is surely common sense. Music would be a dull affair if all notes had to be in the key and all accents on the beat, but it would be incomprehensible if the key and the metre were called into question before they were established.

The rule of congruence will be put to detailed use in the sections that follow. We should say at once that it will turn out to be an oversimplification, albeit a fairly successful one. Most of our rules are, furthermore, of reasonable generality, and we expect them to have validity outside the particular corpus which we have studied—and indeed to the music of other composers, though this remains to be seen.

The metrical program, which we describe first, is less sophisticated than the harmonic program, and leaves a great deal of room for further work, though the results of its application are not without interest. Its principal limitation is that it attends only to the relative durations of the notes (and rests), but not at all to their positions on the keyboard, so that it is unable to yield any significant information when applied to those fugue subjects in which all the notes are of equal length. In such melodies the metrical structure must be inferred from the harmonic information. As yet we have no specific ideas as to how this can be done, though a good musician can do it without the slightest difficulty.

The harmonic program, which has to decide as early as possible on the key and thereafter to place each note in its correct relation to the keynote, is further advanced. It is based on some earlier work by Longuet-Higgins (1962) in which the tonal relationships of classical music were exhibited as relations in a three-dimensional lattice, defined by the octave, the fifth, and the major third. This program attends only to the position of each note on the keyboard (identifying all notes separated by octaves) and disregards their durations. To disregard the note lengths in a harmonic analysis might seem as high-handed as to disregard their values in a metrical analysis; but the results strongly suggest otherwise.

There is nothing in our programs which does more than express our own provisional views as to how an educated musician makes sense of a melody which is played to him, note by note, on the keyboard. The programs do not discern any rules for themselves, if only because we have no idea how to write a program capable of forming a description of a composer's musical style. We hope, however, that our work may be of interest as a case study in which the discovery of a suitable representation is found to be essential for the formalization of a cognitive process.

The Metrical Algorithm

The problem to which we address ourselves in this section is that of grouping the notes and rests of each fugue subject into metrical units. The longest type of metrical unit which is explicitly indicated in the score is the "bar", and we would be very pleased to be able to place all the bar lines correctly on the basis of the notes of the subject alone. But even if we cannot identify whole bars we may hope to be able to identify the metrical units into which the bars are divided, or the smaller metrical units into which these in turn are subdivided; whether our identification is correct or not can be checked by inspecting the time signature which always appears at the beginning of the fugue and which indicates how the bar is to be metrically divided and subdivided. Thus the time signature "C" or "¢" (short for "common time") indicates that the bar is to be divided into two half-bars, which in turn are to be divided into two quarter-bars, and so on. But it is also possible for a metric unit to be subdivided into three lesser units, and when this happens it is indicated by a time signature such as 3/4, which means that the bar is divided into three crotchets (quarter-notes)—a situation which is to be distinguished from that signified by 6/8, which means that the bar is first divided in two and that each half-bar is further subdivided into three quavers (eighth-notes). In Bach's time every metrical unit less than or equal to a bar was subdivided, if at all, into two or three smaller units, but never, for example, five or seven; we have taken this for granted in our metrical analysis.

Before describing the analysis, we shall say a word or two about notation. The note durations which to an American musician are known as a whole note, a half note, a quarter note, an eighth note, a sixteenth note, and a thirty second note are to an English musician a semibreve, a minim, a crotchet, a quaver, a semiquaver, and a demi-semiquaver respectively; to increment any of these durations by one-half, one writes a dot after the symbol representing the note (or rest). As for time signatures, we use in table 1 a rather more explicit notation than the conventional one. Thus in table 1 the signature 3.2/8 (instead of 3/4) means that the bar is divided into three units, each of which comprises two quavers (eighth notes). An analysis yielding the signature 2/8 (with the right pairing of quavers) is then seen to be correct as far as it goes; but the result 2.2/8 would reveal a mistake at the second stage of grouping. If at any stage an analysis gives metrical units comprising the right number of smaller units, but incorrectly grouped together, then we indicate this fact by an asterisk against the corresponding number in the time signature. Thus the result 3*.2/8 means that the quavers were correctly grouped in pairs, but that the resulting crotchets were wrongly grouped in threes.

The rules which we develop below operate solely on the relative durations of the notes and rests, as they are given in the score. In an actual performance a player will "phrase" the music by altering slightly the time values, to help the listener perceive the metrical structure; but our algorithm is designed to operate on a "dead-pan" performance, in which even the pitch of each note is disregarded. Its limitations, which are quite severe, and the occasional wrong answer which it yields, may perhaps provide clues as to what extra information the performer should provide in carrying out his side of the business of "interpretation".

As one listens to a fugue subject, such as that of Fugue 2 in Book I, one gains the impression of certain notes being "accented". An accented note is one which is felt to fall at the beginning of a metrical unit of some length, which may be equal to the length of the note, or longer, or shorter. The simplest situation is that in which a metre has already arisen in the listener's mind, and a note is sounded at the beginning of a metrical unit; then the note, however short it is, automatically acquires an accent heavier than that of any other note in the same metrical unit. An example of this is Fugue 7 in Book II, where the listener adopts the initial semibreve as the unit of metre, and therefore feels a "semibreve accent" on the second note, the fourth note, and so on, though none of these notes is as long as a semibreve. This fugue subject illustrates, in fact, two general rules about the establishment of a metre. The first is that, whatever its length, the first note of a subject (or the first two notes, if the second is shorter than the first and third; see below) may always be taken to define a metrical unit at some level in the hierarchy—though usually at rather a low level. This may be seen as a manifestation of the rule of congruence, and would, for example, exclude the unlikely possibility that the first note of the subject occurred at the end of a bar and was tied over the bar line. The second rule is that once a metrical unit has been adopted it is never abandoned in favour of a shorter one, or another one which cuts across it. The only way, then, in which the metrical hierarchy can be built up is by the progressive grouping of metrical units into higher units. Any rules for doing this must clearly be framed with great circumspection, since any mistake, once made, will vitiate all that follows.

What, then, is good evidence for enlarging a metrical unit which has already been established? A natural suggestion would be that if a note falling at the beginning of a metrical unit lasts for two or three units, then the metrical unit should be doubled or trebled accordingly. This suggestion would account very neatly for our appreciation of the metre of Fugue 9 of Book I, which begins with a quaver, establishing a quaver metre, and continues with a crotchet, which lasts two quavers and therefore becomes the new metric unit. And stated thus cautiously the suggestion does not, in Fugue 8 of Book I, call upon us to abandon the crotchet metre established by the first note in favour of a dotted crotchet metre, for which the unit would be only $1\frac{1}{2}$ times as long. But it raises a serious problem in Fugue 2 of Book I. Here the semiquaver metre gives place to a quaver metre when the third note is reached, and no problem arises for a while. But eventually we come upon a crotchet, and the above suggestion would lead us to adopt this as establishing a crotchet metre which actually cuts across the bar lines in the score. In fact no musician would be so deceived; but how does he avoid deception, and come to realize that the crotchet is in fact a syncopation?

The answer, we believe, lies in the early occurrence, in this subject, of a rhythmic figure which seems to play a central role not only in Bach's music but in the music of every succeeding generation. We name this figure the "dactyl", after its counterpart in the metre of poetry. It consists—in its simplest manifestation—of a note followed by two equal notes of half the length, these being followed by a longer note. With no exceptions in the Forty-Eight, we find that if the first note of such a dactyl occupies one unit of an already established metre, then the metrical unit must be doubled so as to accommodate the dactyl. Thus in Fugue 2 of Book I notes 5, 6, and 7 form a dactyl, establishing a crotchet metre into which the dactyl 10, 11, 12 fits neatly; there is another dactyl 14, 15, 16 soon afterwards which cuts across the crotchet metre but is powerless to overthrow it.

There are, however, other sorts of dactyl to which we undoubtedly pay attention in discerning metre. In the first fugue of Book I, for example, we find a pair of demi-semiquavers preceded by a dotted quaver and followed by a quaver. It is difficult to resist the view that the dotted quaver and the two demi-semiquavers provide the same metrical information as would a quaver and two semiquavers, so we count this figure as a dactyl too. As a

result, the initially established quaver metre is doubled so as to accommodate the dactyl, and gives way to a crotchet metre.

We may define a dactyl in general terms as the first three notes in a
sequence of four, such that the second and the third are equal in length and
shorter than the first or the fourth. But we must then be very careful how
we state the metrical implications of its occurrence. Consider, for example,
Fugue 14 of Book I. The first two notes establish a crotchet metre, and are
followed by a dactyl consisting of a semibreve and two quavers (followed
by a minim). The dactyl is five crotchets long, but we are not allowed to
group metric units into fives. At this point we could of course draw in our
horns and say that only the figures described earlier count as dactyls, but
we prefer to restrict the range of the dactyl rule by a clause which says that
the general dactyl under consideration is to be adopted as the new metrical
unit only if it occupies a "reasonable" number of current metric units—a
"reasonable" number being an integer whose only prime factors are 2 or 3.
We shall see later what can be inferred when this condition is not satisfied.

Earlier we suggested that if a note falling at the beginning of a metrical
unit lasted for two or three such units, then the metrical unit should be
doubled or trebled accordingly. The natural generalization of this would be
to combine the metrical units into sets of 2, 3, 4, 6, 8, 9, 12, 16, and so on if
any note lasts for such a number of units. But then we run into immediate
trouble with Fugue 5 in Book I. After a flourish of eight demi-semiquavers
we come upon a dotted quaver, of six times the length. If we take the
dotted quaver as the new metrical unit, we make a mistake which is
apparent as soon as the following semiquaver is succeeded by another
dotted quaver. The root of the trouble, clearly, is that we did not wait long
enough to notice that the semiquaver following the dotted crotchet was an
isolated short note. For this particular fugue subject we should obtain a
correct result if we treated the semiquaver and the preceding dotted quaver
as a dactyl occupying eight demi-semiquaver units and thereby establishing a new crotchet metre. But this expedient would lead to trouble in other
connections—for example, in Fugue 8 of Book I. Perhaps erring on the side
of caution, we therefore rule that when a note falling at the beginning of a
metrical unit is followed by a single shorter note (which is followed by a
longer note), the metrical unit is to be doubled, trebled, etc., only if the
length of the first note *minus* that of the second is a reasonable number of
current metric units. Then in Fugue 5 of Book I the demi-semiquaver unit is
multiplied by 4 rather than by 6 on the evidence of the dotted quaver-
semiquaver pair.

At this point it is appropriate to return to the question of what conclusions can be drawn from the occurrence of an "unreasonable" dactyl. We propose the supplementary rule that when a dactyl occupies an "unreasonable" number of current metrical units, then the metrical unit is to be doubled, trebled, etc., only if the length of the first note *minus* the combined length of the two short notes is a reasonable number of current metric units. If we re-examine Fugue 14 of Book I we find that this rule leads to a correct inference—the metric signature that it finds is 3/4 consistent with the actual time signature 2.3/4.

We are now in a position to state more precisely the conditions under which a new metre can be inferred from the lengths of the incoming notes and rests. If a note is the first note of the subject or falls at the beginning of a unit of the most recently established metre, then various possibilities must be explored.

(1) The note may be the first note of a dactyl—a fact which can be established only by examining the durations of the following three notes. If the total length of the dactyl is a reasonable number of current metric units, then this must be adopted as the new metric unit. If not, but the length of the first note minus the combined length of the shorter notes satisfies this condition, then this difference in length is taken as the new metric unit (as in Fugue 14 of Book I). Otherwise (but there are no such cases in the Forty-Eight) things are left as they are.

(2) The note may be followed by a single shorter note (followed in turn by a longer note)—a fact which can be established only by examining the following two notes. If so, we subtract the length of the short note from the end of its predecessor. If the result is a reasonable number of current metric units, it is adopted as the new metric unit; otherwise (but again this does not occur) the previous metre is maintained.

(3) The note may be of neither of the above types, but may endure for two or more current metric units. If so, these units are combined together in groups of n, where n is the largest reasonable number of units which are filled by the note.

(4) If the note is not of type 1, 2, or 3, then the current metre is retained.

The above procedure enables us to take a step upwards in the metrical hierarchy whenever we encounter an accented note or dactyl of sufficient length, an accented note being one which falls at the beginning of a unit of the current metre. But when applied to a subject such as that of Fugue 15 of Book I, it fails to indicate the triple grouping of the quavers in the first bar—though this is quite obvious to the hearer—so that on reaching the crotchet in the second bar it incorrectly suggests a crotchet grouping of the quavers. To deal with such cases we need to extend the concept of an accent to metrical units as well as to individual notes. A metrical unit is "marked for accent" if a note or dactyl begins at the beginning of it and lasts throughout it. We can now state a new rule for establishing metre at a higher level, as follows: If in the current metre a unit which is marked for accent is followed by a number of unmarked units, and then by another marked unit, which in turn is followed by an unmarked unit, then the two marked units are taken to establish a higher metre, in which they occur on successive accents. In Fugue 15 of Book I the first two quavers of the subject are, according to this definition, both marked for accent, and the second is flanked by unmarked quaver units, as required for the application of the rule, so the rule establishes a higher metre, of dotted crotchets, in which the first and the fourth quaver units of the subject occur as the first two accents. But there is an important qualification to the rule, namely that if the higher metrical unit so defined is an unreasonable multiple of the lower one, it must not be adopted. With this qualification the new rule, which we call the "isolated accent rule", can be applied without absurdity.

We may illustrate the application of these rules in relation to Fugue 2 of Book I. The first note establishes a semiquaver metre, to which the second note conforms. The third note converts this into a quaver metre, fitting the fourth note. The fifth note is the first of a dactyl, lasting a crotchet, establishing a crotchet metre in which the dactyl is marked for accent. Notes 8 and 9 constitute an unmarked crotchet unit; notes 10, 11, and 12 constitute another dactyl, which is also marked for accent. Notes 13 and 14 make up an unmarked crotchet unit, so the isolated accent rule can be applied to the two marked crotchet units, revealing a minim metre, which is in fact the metre of Bach's half-bars. The fact that 14 is the first note of a dactyl does not disturb this analysis, since it is unaccented in the crotchet metre which has been established by the time it is sounded.

On the basis of these rules—which may seem complicated, but which are undoubtedly much less complicated than our perceptual processes—we have written a program for assigning metrical structures to the 48 fugue subjects; the results are given in table 1. By and large, the program avoids mistakes, at the cost of a rather incomplete analysis: for example, it is powerless to deal with any subject in which all the notes are of the same length, and where the musician would obviously rely on harmonic clues or skilful phrasing for discerning the metre. But there are some interesting mistakes. In Fugues 8, 14, and 19 in the second book the program makes just the sort of mistake a musician would probably make in performing the same task. In all three fugues the rhythm departs from the underlying metre

Table 1
Metrical analysis. > means that whole bars are grouped together; = means that notes are all equal in length; * indicates an erroneous result.

	Book I			Book II		
	Correct	Found	Comment	Correct	Found	Comment
1	$2^3/8$	$2/8$		$2^3/16$	$2^2/16$	
2	$2^4/16$	$2^3/16$		$2^3/8$	$2/8$	
3	$2^3/8$	$2/8$		$2^3/8$	$1/8$	=
4	$1/1$	$2/1$	>	$2^2.3/16$	$1/16$	=
5	$2^5/32$	$2^3/32$		$2^3/8$	$2/8$	
6	$3.2/8$	$2/8$		$2^3.3/16$	$2*.3/16$	*
7	$2^4/16$	$2^2/16$		$1/1$	$1/1$	
8	$2^2/4$	$1/4$		$2^3/8$	$2*.2/8$	*
9	$2^3/8$	$2/8$		$2/1$	$1/1$	
10	$3.2^2/16$	$2/16$		$2^2.3/8$	$2.3/8$	
11	$3/8$	$3/8$		$2.3/16$	$3.2/16$	*
12	$2^2/4$	$2/4$		$2^2/8$	$2/8$	
13	$2^3/8$	$2/4$		$2^4/16$	$2^5/16$	>
14	$2.3/4$	$3/4$		$2^3/8$	$2*.2^2/8$	*
15	$2.3/8$	$3/8$		$3.2/16$	$1/16$	=
16	$2^3/8$	$2/8$		$3/4$	$1/4$	
17	$2^3/8$	$2/8$		$2^3/8$	$2/8$	
18	$2^2/4$	$1/4$		$2.3/8$	$1/8$	=
19	$3^2/8$	$1/8$	=	$2^4/16$	$2*.2/16$	*
20	$2^4/16$	$2^2/16$		$2^2/4$	$1/4$	
21	$3.2/8$	$12/8$	>	$3.2/8$	$1/8$	=
22	$2/2$	$1/2$		$3/2$	$3*/2$	*
23	$2^3/8$	$2^2/8$		$2/2$	$1/2$	
24	$2^3/8$	$2^2/8$		$3/8$	$1/8$	

before the latter has been made explicit; by thus violating the rule of congruence, Bach plainly intends to throw the listener off the track. There are three other subjects for which the program gives a wrong result. In Fugue 6 of Book II it makes a mistake which would probably not be made by a musician who paid attention to the pitches of the notes. In Fugue 22 of Book II the program places accents on the second and fifth minim units rather than the first and fourth, and a musician might well make the same mistake. And in Fugue 11 of Book II it is misled by the semiquaver rests, which to a musician are merely indications of phrasing and are equivalent to staccato markings of dotted quavers. In three fugues (4 and 21 of Book I and 13 of Book II) the program actually carries its analysis beyond the bar; the resulting bar groupings seem quite acceptable, though they do not carry Bach's imprimatur. But one of these analyses (of Fugue 21, Book I)

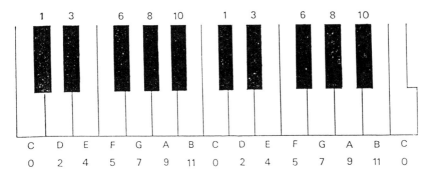

Figure 1

must be regarded as a fluke, because all the program does is to group quavers in twelves, without specifying whether the metrical structure is 2.2.3/8, or 2.3.2/8, or 3.2.2/8.

Our main reaction to these results was one of surprise that a program operating on so little information, and embodying such simple rules, could reveal so much metrical structure.

The Harmonic Algorithm

The problem for which our harmonic program is designed is to determine the key of a fugue from its subject, and, if there are any notes not belonging to the key, to determine their relation to those which do, and to the keynote in particular. Once this problem has been solved, it is a trivial matter to transcribe the solution into standard musical notation, so we shall eschew notational technicalities as far as we can in the following paragraphs.

Figure 1 depicts a short section of the keyboard, with each note lettered or numbered according to its position in the octave. The key of C major comprises the "white notes" 0, 2, 4, 5, 7, 9, and 11, and contains the three "major triads" (C E G), (G B D), and (F A C), that is, (0 4 7), (7 11 2), and (5 9 0). In each triad the first and third notes are separated by a "perfect fifth", which is one of the three basic intervals of music. The other two basic intervals are the octave—but we are treating two notes an octave apart as equivalent—and the "major third", which is the interval between the first and second notes of each major triad. These facts enable us to represent the harmonic relations within C major by the two-dimensional array shown in figure 2, where each note is a perfect fifth below the note on its right and a major third below the note written above it. A major triad

Figure 2

Figure 3

Figure 4

then forms an L-shaped cluster of three notes. One may set up a corresponding array of numbers, and extend it indefinitely in both dimensions (see figure 3) where a move to the right adds 7 modulo 12 and a move upwards adds 4. The key of 0 major then comprises the seven notes shown on the left. Notes other than these are conventionally denoted by "sharps" (♯) and "flats" (♭), as in figure 4.

It is important to observe that notes which have the same number in figure 3 do not necessarily have the same symbol in figure 4. For example, a note which lies a major third above an E in figure 4 is called G♯, and a note which lies a major third below a C is called A♭, but both notes are played in position 8 on the keyboard. And even figure 4 blurs the distinction between, for example, the A which lies immediately above F and the A which lies four places to its right. Strictly speaking, all of the notes in figure 4 should have different symbols because the octave, the perfect fifth, and the major third are incommensurable intervals. This incommensurability can be inferred from the fact that the frequency ratios of the intervals in question are 2/1, 3/2, and 5/4 respectively; but it is better to regard it as a musical rather than a mathematical fact, because the ear can be tricked by the keyboard into supposing that an octave equals three major thirds, and that two octaves plus a major third equals four perfect fifths. Indeed, it

```
 1  8  3
 9  4 11  6
```

Figure 5

is just this kind of trickery which our harmonic program is designed to expose; given the notes of a fugue subject played on the keyboard, it must decide how they should be related to one another on a two-dimensional lattice in which every point is properly distinguished from every other.

Armed with this two-dimensional representation of harmonic relationships, we are now in a position to see how to assign a particular fugue subject to a particular key. A convenient illustration is provided by Fugue 9 of Book I of the Forty-Eight, where the notes of the subject include 1, 3, 4, 6, 8, 9, and 11, but not 0, 2, 5, 7, or 10. Consulting figure 3, we would notice that a major-key-shaped box could be fitted round the notes of the subject in just one way (see figure 5) and we would conclude that the key was 4 major—that is, E major. In fact there are rather few fugues in which Bach uses all, and only, the notes of a major key, and a more sophisticated analysis will usually be called for. But before embarking on this let us discuss minor keys, where the situation is rather less straightforward.

Like the major key, the minor key of Bach's tradition comprises seven principal notes. Thus the key of C minor is composed of the seven notes, C, D, Eb, F, G, Ab, B, and C, the harmonic relations between them being fixed by the need to accommodate the major triad (G B D) and two "minor triads" (C Eb G) and (F Ab C). In a minor triad the outer notes are a perfect fifth apart, but the middle note is a major third below the highest note, rather than a major third above the lowest. These facts can be represented by enclosing the notes of a minor key within a box of the shape indicated on the right in figures 3 and 4; in these figures the notes of C minor are seen to differ from those of C major by the substitution of Ab and Eb for A and E. But there is an additional complication. In Bach's time, if a composer wished to write an ascending or a descending scale in a minor key he would use the *major* sixth in the ascending scale and the *minor* seventh in the descending scale. That is to say, in 0 minor (C minor) the upward scale 7, 8, 11 (G, Ab, B) would become 7, 9, 11 (G, A, B), and the downward scale 0, 11, 8 (C, B, Ab) would become 0, 10, 8 (C, Bb, Ab). This convention, which we shall call the "melodic convention", means that 9 may be regarded as belonging to 0 minor only if it occurs in the context 7,

Figure 6

Figure 7

9, 11, and that 10 may be so regarded only in the context 0, 10, 8. As an example of the melodic convention we may consider Fugue 4 of Book II. The notes of the subject are, in order, 1, 0, 1, 3, 1, 3, 8, 10, 0, 1, 3, 4, 6, etc. We observe from figure 3 that there is a minor key, namely 1 minor, which includes all these notes except one (see figure 6). But the note 10, which is the major sixth of 1 minor, occurs within the scale 8, 10, 0, and so can be understood to arise from the melodic convention. This note therefore provides no evidence that the subject is not in 1 minor—actually it is.

It is by no means uncommon, however, for the notes of a fugue subject to wander right outside the original key, even when allowance is made for the melodic convention. As an example we may cite Fugue 12 of Book I, where the first few notes are 0, 1, 0, 11, 4, 5, etc. Figure 3 reveals that no key, major or minor, will accommodate a 0, a 1, and an 11. After 0, 1, 0, the note 11 excludes all possible keys, and must therefore be outside the initial key. But there is one key which includes all of the first six notes *except* 11, namely the key of 5 minor (see figure 7). This should therefore be the key of the fugue—as it is.

In some cases, then, it is possible to decide the key after hearing only a few notes of the subject. A striking example is Fugue 4 of Book I, where the subject comprises just four notes, namely 1, 0, 4, 3. There are two keys which include 1, 0, and 4, namely 5 minor and 1 minor (see figure 8); but of these only 1 minor can also accommodate the fourth note. The key of the fugue is in fact 1 minor.

The above examples might suggest that the key of a fugue can always be determined by a process of elimination before the end of the subject, but this is not so. A simple example is Fugue 9 of Book II, where the notes of the subject are 4, 6, 9, 8, 6, 4. At the end of the subject (that is, before the

Figure 8

Figure 9

second 4, when another part enters) the key could be 4 major, or 9 major, or 1 minor (see figure 9).

To decide among these three possibilities we appeal to a musical intuition which is embodied in one of the standard rules of fugue. This rule demands that the first note of the subject be the tonic or the dominant (that is, the keynote or the note a perfect fifth above it)—though Bach actually breaks this rule in Fugue 21 of Book II. But to appeal directly to this rule of fugue would conflict with the spirit of our investigation, so we adopt instead a "tonic-dominant preference rule" to the following effect: When a dilemma of choice presents itself, first preference is given to a key whose tonic is the first note of the subject, and second preference to a key whose dominant is the first note of the subject. A dilemma of choice may arise in either of two ways. First, as above, one may reach the end of the subject without having eliminated all keys except one; secondly, one may meet a note which does not fit into any key at all. The dilemma illustrated in figure 9 is of the former kind; here the first note (4) is the tonic of 4 major and the dominant of 9 major, but is neither the tonic nor the dominant of 1 minor, so that 4 major is selected as first preference. The latter type of dilemma is illustrated by Fugue 14 of Book I, where the subject begins with the notes 6, 8, 9, 8, 10, 11, 10, 8, 10, 0, 1, and so on. The first four notes are compatible with several different keys, including 6 minor, 4 major, 9 major, and 1 minor. But the fifth note, 10, excludes all these possibilities, so a dilemma arises. But until that moment 6 minor was a possibility, a key whose tonic is the first note of the subject, so 6 minor is correctly selected as the key of the fugue.

Figure 10

A program embodying these rules—and no others—assigns all 48 of the fugues to their correct keys, on the basis of the notes of the subject alone. (The last note of the subject is taken, for definiteness, to be the last note sounded before, or at the same moment as, the first note of the second entry.) For most of the fugues the key is decided well before the end of the subject; in only 17 out of 48 cases is the tonic-dominant preference rule appealed to at the end.

The task of key assignment is, however, only part of the harmonic problem. As already remarked, a subject may contain "accidentals"—notes which lie outside the original key—and may indeed "modulate" into a new key. A fine example of this is the subject of Fugue 24 of Book I, shown in figure 10. The notes of the first bar correctly establish the key as 11 minor, but in the next bar there are three notes—3, 0, and 5—which do not belong to the key and are written as D♯, C♮, and E♯ respectively. In the third bar there are three more extraneous notes—0, 9, and 8—of which the 0 is now written as B♯. (The 9 and the 8 cannot be accommodated in 11 minor because they do not occur in the contexts demanded by the melodic convention.) The question arises: How can the listener tell that the six notes under consideration are to be interpreted as Bach wrote them, and in particular that the first 0 is a C♮ and the second a B♯?

For the first four of these notes the solution is provided by another rule, which seems to describe Bach's use of chromatic scales—note sequences of the form $(n, n + 1, \ldots, n + m)$ or $(n, n - 1, \ldots, n - m)$. We state this rule—the "semitone rule"—as follows: In a chromatic scale the first two notes are always related by a diatonic semitone, and so are the last two. By a "diatonic" semitone we mean the interval between B and C in C major—a move of one step to the left and one step downwards in a key diagram. Figure 10 shows that in the second bar of the above fugue subject there are

Figure 11

three chromatic scales, namely (4, 3), (0, 11), and (6, 5). But the notes 4, 11, and 6 all lie in the established key (11 minor—see figure 11). Therefore the 3, the 0, and the 5 are to be interpreted as D♯, C♮ and E♯ respectively. In the third bar the 0 is the last note of the chromatic scale (2, 1, 0) and the first note of the scale (0, 1). It must therefore be a diatonic semitone below 1 (which belongs to the key) and be interpreted (see figure 11) as B♯ rather than C♮. A problem arises, however, with the first 9 in the third bar. This lies outside 11 minor, but is not part of a chromatic scale. We therefore— and this is our last harmonic rule—place it in the closest possible relation to the notes which have already been heard. A convenient measure of closeness is the sum of its city-block distances, in figure 11, from all the positions at which earlier notes have been placed, and this identifies it as the lower right-hand A in figure 11, which is undoubtedly correct musically, as it must be a major third below the preceding C♯. Finally, the last note of the third bar has to be assigned a position in figure 11. If we disregard the trill, which involves the note a semitone above, and treat it as a plain unadorned 8, we find that there are two different readings of the note in figure 11 which give equal values for the sum of the city-block distances from already occupied positions. Either the left-hand or the right-hand G♯ in the figure would do equally well—though they would be annotated in the same way. This is the only case in which the city-block rule fails to settle the interpretation of an accidental—though it does indicate how it must be annotated. And even this single ambiguity would disappear if we took into account the upper note of the trill and demand that the two notes be inserted into figure 11 together at positions separated by a diatonic semitone.

We may summarize the operation of the harmonic algorithm as follows. Each major or minor key is represented by a box of appropriate shape superimposed on a two-dimensional lattice like that in figure 3. The first note of the subject lies in 14 of these keys, but not in the other ten, which are immediately eliminated. As each note comes in, it is tested in relation to each surviving key to see whether it lies in that key; if not, the key is eliminated unless the context of the note permits it to be assigned to the key on the basis of the melodic convention. If any note is found to have eliminated all the 24 possible keys, then their elimination must be reconsidered. First it must be asked whether one of the keys just eliminated was a key of which the first note was the tonic; if so, then that must be taken as the key of the fugue. If not, did one of the keys just eliminated have the first note as its dominant? If so, then that must be the key of the fugue. If the answer to both these questions is in the negative, then all the keys just eliminated must be reinstated and the following note tested in the same way. If at any stage a note eliminates all keys except one, then this is taken to be the key of the fugue. And if at the end of the subject two or more keys have survived elimination, then the tonic-dominant preference rule is used to decide between them.

In this part of the algorithm the operation of the rule of congruence is apparent; until the key of the fugue has been identified, any note which does not fit into a given key must be counted as evidence against that key unless it happens to eliminate all possible keys—which often happens. But after the key has been established, accidentals can be met with equanimity—provided that their relation to the established key can be clearly determined. The second part of the algorithm is designed for this purpose. It first invokes the semitone rule, which can be used for placing notes which belong to the first or the last pair in a chromatic scale, provided (as almost always happens) the other note of the pair belongs to the established key. If the semitone rule fails to place a note, then the algorithm resorts to the city-block distance rule for placing the note in the closest possible harmonic relation to the previous notes of the subject. In only one case does this rule also fail to place a note unambiguously; the program is designed to draw attention to such failures, so we can be sure that this case is unique in the Forty-Eight.

Space would not permit us to quote all the fugue subjects, or to give our analysis of them in detail, so we conclude by simply appending the main results (see table 2). Suffice it to say that every key is assigned, and every accidental notated, in accordance with Bach's score; and, furthermore, that the placing of the notes on each key diagram, which indicates how the subject would have to be played in "just intonation", rather than on the keyboard, seems to accord completely with our musical intuition. We know, however, that in at least one Bach fugue not belonging to the Forty-Eight, namely the second Kyrie of the Mass in B minor, our program would assign the fugue to the wrong key because the second note of the subject violates the rule of congruence. But such liberties are the very stuff of artistic creation.

Table 2
Key analysis (* tonic-dominant preference rule used).

Number of fugue	Key of fugue	Book I		Book II	
		Number of notes in subject	Decision at note number	Number of notes in subject	Decision at note number
1	0 major	16	16*	23	23*
2	0 minor	11	5	9	9*
3	1 major	22	16	4	4*
4	1 minor	5	4	22	12
5	2 major	15	15*	9	9*
6	2 minor	12	8	25	15
7	3 major	24	11*	20	20*
8	3 minor	12	12*	14	9
9	4 major	12	11	6	6*
10	4 minor	25	7*	46	18
11	5 major	19	6	21	17
12	5 minor	15	4*	27	7
13	6 major	17	8	28	12*
14	6 minor	18	5*	18	18*
15	7 major	31	15	43	16
16	7 minor	11	4	18	18*
17	8 major	7	7*	22	22*
18	8 minor	17	5	25	25*
19	9 major	7	7	20	20*
20	9 minor	31	5	10	5
21	10 major	38	14	24	9
22	10 minor	6	6*	27	5
23	11 major	14	11	12	12*
24	11 minor	22	7	25	6

Acknowledgements

We should like to record that our first attack on the metrical problem was made in collaboration with W. H. Edmondson, and to express our thanks to the Royal Society and the Medical Research Council for financial support.

References

Cooper, G., and L. B. Meyer. 1960. *The Rhythmic Structure of Music.* University of Chicago Press.

Longuet-Higgins, H. C. 1962. Letter to a musical friend. *Music Review* 23 (August): 244–248. [Chapter 8 in present volume.]

Longuet-Higgins, H. C. 1962. Second letter to a musical friend. *Music Review* 23 (November): 271–280. [Chapter 8 in present volume.]

Appendix 1: Some Fugue Subjects from Book I of the Forty-Eight

Appendix 2: Some Fugue Subjects from Book II of the Forty-Eight

10 The Perception of Melodies

H. C. Longuet-Higgins

A searching test of practical musicianship is the "aural test" in which the subject is required to write down, in standard musical notation, a melody which he has never heard before. His transcription is not to be construed as a detailed record of the actual performance, which will inevitably be more or less out of time and out of tune, but as an indication of the rhythmic and tonal relations between the individual notes. How the musical listener perceives these relationships is a matter of some interest to the cognitive psychologist. In this paper I outline a theory of the perception of classical Western melodies and describe a computer program, based on the theory, which displays, as best it can, the rhythmic and tonal relationships between the notes of a melody as played by a human performer on an organ console.

The basic premise of the theory is that in perceiving a melody the listener builds a conceptual structure representing the rhythmic groupings of the notes and the musical intervals between them. It is this structure which he commits to memory, and which subsequently enables him to recognize the tune, and to reproduce it in sound or in writing if he happens to be a skilled musician. A second premise is that much can be learned about the structural relationships in any ordinary piece of music from a study of its orthographic representation. Take, for example, the musical cliché notated in figure 1.

The way in which the notes are rhythmically grouped is evident from the disposition of the bar lines and the "beams" linking the notes of the first bar. The rhythm is, in this case, a binary tree each terminal of which is a note or a rest, but more generally such a tree may have ternary as well as binary nodes.

The tonal relations between the notes in figure 1 are also indicated by the symbolism, but more subtly. It is a common mistake to suppose that the position of a note on the five-line stave (and its prefix, if any) indicates

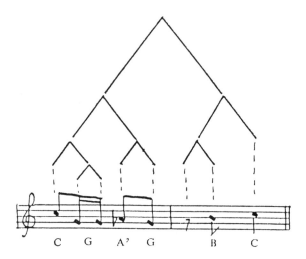

Figure 1

Figure 2

merely the approximate pitch of the note—where it would be located on the keyboard. If that were true, an equally acceptable alternative to figure 1 would be figure 2, in which the A♭ has been written as a G♯, with the same location on the keyboard. But a music student who offered figure 2 as his transcription would lose marks for having misrepresented the tonal relation of the fourth note to its neighbours (though he could hardly be imagined not to have perceived it properly).

The problems posed by melodic perception are not dissimilar to those which arise in perception of speech. The distinction between the A♭ in figure 1 and the G♯ in figure 2 is analogous to the difference between the homophones "here" and "hear" in English; though these words sound exactly alike, they are interpreted and spelt quite differently according to the context in which they are heard. Another problem in speech perception, which has its counterpart in the perception of melody, relates to the timing of successive acoustic events. The way in which the syllables of a poem are perceptually grouped into "feet" is largely unaffected by variations in rate of delivery, and the same applies to the rhythmic grouping of the notes of a melody. Notes which on paper are of equal length will in a live performance be sounded at quite unequal intervals of time, particularly in an "expressive" performance. A change of metre from duplets to triplets can, nevertheless, usually be distinguished quite clearly from a mere quickening of tempo, in a reasonably competent performance. Previous programs for the automatic transcription of music have required the performer to maintain a fairly constant tempo (Styles 1973; Askenfelt 1976); but human listeners have no difficulty in discerning the rhythms of melodies played by performers who are free from this constraint.

The third premise of the theory is that the perception of rhythm and the perception of tonal relationships can be viewed as independent processes. This strong claim (which is not to be misunderstood as referring to the process of musical composition) may be weakly supported by two observations. First, a given melodic sequence such as the ascending major scale will be heard as such by a Western musician regardless of the rhythm in which it is played. Conversely, a "dotted" rhythm, for example, will be clearly recognisable for what it is, regardless of the musical intervals between the successive notes. To say this is not, of course, to deny that higher cognitive processes can and will operate on the "surface structure" generated by rhythmic and tonal perception, to reveal musically significant relations between the rhythm and the tonality. But one may reasonably suppose that such processes of musical appreciation can begin only when some structure has been created on which they can get to work.

Rhythm

One might imagine that to discern the rhythm of a melody the listener must be able to perceive differences in loudness between successive notes. This may be true on occasion, but it fails as a generalization for two reasons. First of all, performers do not as a rule thump out every note which occurs on a beat or at the beginning of a bar; to do so would be as tiresome as to accent, in reading a poem, every syllable that occurred at the beginning of a foot. But more decisively, there are instruments, such as the organ and harpsichord, on which it is physically impossible for the performer to vary the acoustic intensity of each individual note; all he can control is the time of onset of the note and its temporal duration. It is nevertheless quite possible for a listener to perceive correctly the rhythm of a melody played on such an instrument; we conclude that temporal information alone is enough for the purpose, except in special circumstances.

The basic assumption underlying the rhythmic component of the program is that the first necessity in perceiving the rhythmic structure of a melody is to identify the time of occurrence of each "beat". Music in which the beat is irregular falls outside the scope of the theory, which therefore has nothing to say about the rhythmic perception of recitative or of music in which the beats alternate in length. The grouping of the beats into higher metrical units such as "bars" raises issues which have been discussed elsewhere (Longuet-Higgins and Steedman 1971; Steedman 1973); the principal concern of the present study is with the manner in which each beat should be subdivided, and with the problem of keeping track of the beat through unforeseen changes in tempo.

In Western music, by far the commonest subdivisions of the beat are into two and into three shorter metrical units; these in turn can be further subdivided into two or three. Whether a beat or a fraction of a beat is perceived to be divided depends, according to the theory, on whether or not it is interrupted by the onset of a note. What counts as an "interruption" is a matter of some delicacy to which I shall return in a moment.

After such a process of division and subdivision, every note will find itself at the beginning of an uninterrupted metrical unit. It is the relations between these metrical units which constitute the rhythm of the tune; the metrical units can be thought of as the nodes of a "tree" in which each non-terminal node has either two or three descendants. Every terminal node in the tree will eventually be attached either to a rest or to a note (which may be sounded or tied) in the manner of figure 1. The program does not actually draw such trees, nor print out a musical stave; it represents the rhythm in a nested bracketed notation. It also indicates the phrasing; if the offset of a note occurs earlier than half-way through its allotted time, or else appreciably before the end of that time, the note is marked *"stc"* standing for *"staccato"*, or *"ten"*, for *"tenuto"*.

We now return to the question: What counts as an interruption? By what criterion could a listener judge whether the onset of a note occurs "during" the current metrical unit rather than "at" its beginning or its end? Plainly there must be some upper limit to the temporal discrepancies he can disregard, just as there is a lower limit to those he can detect. The former limit—the listener's "tolerance"—must obviously exceed the latter. It must be small enough to permit the structuring of rapid rhythmic figures, but large enough to allow a reasonable degree of flexibility to the tempo. In the program the tolerance can be preset to any desired value. Experiments with the program indicate that for reasonably careful performances a tolerance of about 10 centiseconds meets both criteria, but that for more "expressive" performances of relatively sedate melodies a greater tolerance is needed if an obvious *rubato* is not to be misconstrued as a variation in rhythm.

In order to perceive the rhythm clearly a listener must, it is assumed, take account of the precise onset time of every note within any metrical unit in predicting when the unit could end. The rule eventually adopted for making such predictions was as follows: If, in the course of a binary metrical unit, a note which terminates the first subunit begins a little less than half-way through, then the expected further duration of the unit is reduced in magnitude to the mean of its original value and the value implied by the time of onset of the note in question. Corresponding remarks apply, of course, in cases where the note is slightly late or the current metrical hypothesis assigns a ternary rather than a binary structure to the metrical unit in question. In fact the program also allows for the termination of a metrical unit, not by the actual onset of a note, but by the anticipated end of a lower metrical unit which is itself interrupted by the onset of one or more notes. Such procedures are, unfortunately, much more difficult to specify precisely in English than in a suitably designed programming language; but this fact only underlines the value of casting perceptual theories in computational form.

Finally, it is necessary to commit oneself, in writing such a program, to a view as to what counts as good perceptual evidence for a change in metre. It is here assumed that the listener initially expects a pure binary metre, but is prepared to change his mind at any level in the metrical hierarchy. The evidence for a change in metre may be of two kinds: that the current metre implies a "syncopation", in which the beginning of the next beat, or higher metrical unit, is not accompanied by the onset of a note; or that it implies a "distortion" in which an excessively large change of tempo is required to accommodate the current metrical hypothesis. Each of these outcomes represents a flouting of the listener's expectations, and either may, according to the theory, lead him to change his opinion about the metre if the other possible division of the current metrical unit (ternary instead of binary, or vice versa) does not imply a distortion or a syncopation. Lastly, it is assumed that, once having changed his mind, the listener does not change it back again until he encounters positive evidence for doing so.

Tonality

In committing a melody to memory the listener must not only create a rhythmic structure of the kind depicted in figure 1; he must also identify the tonality of each note which is to be attached to it. This tonal information

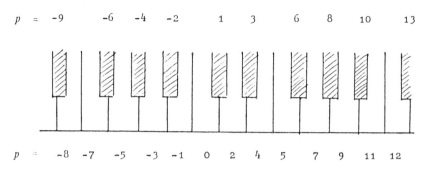

$p = $ −9   −6   −4   −2   1   3   6   8   10   13

$p = $ −8 −7 −5 −3 −1 0 2 4 5 7 9 11 12

Figure 3

x	0	1	0	1	.	1	0	(0)
y	0	0	−1	0	.	1	0	(2)
z	1	0	1	0	.	0	1	(0)
p	12	7	8	7	.	11	12	(8)
q	0	1	−4	1	.	5	0	(8)
N	C	G	A♭	G	.	B	C	(G♯)

Figure 4

should ideally suffice, not only for the transcription of the melody into standard notation, but also for the purpose of evaluating the intonation of a performance on, say, the violin, which permits fine distinctions of pitch which cannot be made explicit on a keyboard instrument. (See figure 3.)

To appreciate what is involved in this task it is necessary to formalize the classical theory of tonality developed by Rameau (1721), Bosanquet (1876), Helmholtz (1885), and other writers. In the formal theory (Longuet-Higgins 1962, 1972) every musical note is assigned coordinates (x, y, z) in a "tonal space" of three dimensions, corresponding to the perfect fifth, the major third, and the octave, respectively. (The ideal frequency ratios of these intervals are $3/2$, $5/4$, and $2/1$ respectively—involving the first three prime numbers—so that they are strictly incommensurable when not distorted by equal temperament.) Thus in figure 4, if the origin is taken as "middle C", the tonal coordinates of the various notes are as shown in the first three rows of the table. The following points may be noted:

(1) It is the relative values of the coordinates (x, y, z), not their absolute values, which characterise the melodic sequence. Thus, increasing all the z values by 1 would merely put the melody up one octave.

(2) The numerical values of the coordinates (x, y, z) are all small; this is evidently the result of having chosen middle C as origin.

(3) The "position" p of each note on the keyboard, that is, its distance above middle C in keyboard semitones, is given by $p = 7x + 4y + 12z$, so that there are arbitrarily many different notes (x, y, z) with the same value of p.

(4) The conventional name of any note is determined not by its keyboard position p but by its "sharpness" q, defined as $q = x + 4y$. The name N of the note is such that there are q sharps, or $-q$ flats, in the key signature of N major. Thus an "A" is a note with $q = 3$, and an "A♭" is one with $q = -4$.

The task of naming the notes of a melody played on the keyboard, or of notating them correctly on the five-line stave, therefore involves the apparently insoluble problem of determining the three coordinates (x, y, z) of each note from its keyboard position p, so as to be able to determine its sharpness q. The problem is analogous to the visual problem of adding an extra dimension to the two-dimensional image of a three-dimensional scene, except that a keyboard performance of a melody supplies the listener with only one directly audible dimension, to which he must add two more to identify each note uniquely.

There is in fact a short cut to the solution of this problem, arising from the mathematical fact that a given choice of p severely restricts the range of possible values of q. A little simple arithmetic shows that q must differ from $7p$ by a multiple of 12. If, therefore, we can find independent grounds for limiting q to one of a fairly small set of values, we can determine it uniquely from the remainder upon division of p by 12. A survey of the published scores of classical melodies reveals (Longuet-Higgins 1962, 1972) that the value of q (which can be directly determined from the notation) never changes from one note to the next by more than eleven units of sharpness. As a consequence, if δp is the "span" of any interval between two successive notes, then the "degree" δq of that interval is restricted to the following alternative values when δp lies in the range -11 to $+12$:

Figure 5

p	0	3	7	8	-1	7	6	5	4	3	2	1	0	-1	-3	-5	0	5	3	2	0
q	0	-3	1	-4	5	1	6	-1	4	-3	2	-5	0	5	3	1	0	-1	-3	2	0

Figure 6

$$\delta p = \quad 1 \quad 2 \quad 3 \quad 4 \quad 5 \quad 6 \quad 7 \quad 8 \quad 9 \quad 10 \quad 11 \quad 12$$
$$\text{or} \ -11 \ -10 \ -9 \ -8 \ -7 \ -6 \ -5 \ -4 \ -3 \ -2 \ -1 \quad 0$$

implies that

$$\delta q = \quad -5 \quad 2 \ -3 \quad 4 \ -1 \quad 6 \quad 1 \ -4 \quad 3 \ -2 \quad 5 \quad 0$$
$$\text{or} \quad 7 \ -10 \quad 9 \ -8 \quad 11 \ -6 \ -11 \quad 8 \ -9 \quad 10 \ -7$$

By far the commonest intervals occurring in classical and traditional melodies are "diatonic" intervals, with $|\delta q| < 6$. "Chromatic" intervals, with $|\delta q| > 6$, and "diabolic" intervals, with $|\delta q| = 6$, are relatively rare. If they were nonexistent, the degree δq of each interval would be uniquely determined by its span δp, and one could infer the sharpness of each note in any melody from its position relative to its immediate predecessor. Such a "Markovian" theory of tonal perception would, as it happens, correctly predict the q values in figure 4. It would, however, fail dismally for melodies containing chromatic scales, because each keyboard semitone in such a scale would be assigned the same value of δq, and this would lead to absurd tonal interpretations such as that shown in figure. 5.

An alternative, and musically much more plausible, hypothesis is that the listener identifies the sharpness of each note by placing it within a diatonic interval of the very first note (or perhaps an interval of degree 6 if the span indicates that the interval is diabolic). Such a rule would account equally well for the q values of the notes in figure 4. It would, furthermore, account very nicely for the sharpness of the notes in the theme of Bach's Musical Offering (figure 6). In this melody there are in fact four chromatic intervals—a diminished seventh between the fourth and fifth notes, of degree $\delta q = 9$, and three chromatic semitones, of degree -7. Such intervals

Figure 7

could not, for obvious reasons, be correctly identified by the "Markovian" procedure.

It will not do, however, to assume that the first note is invariably the "keynote" to which every other note should be referred in order to determine its sharpness, first because melodies very often begin on notes other than the keynote, or "tonic", and second because the tonic may very well seem to change in the course of a melody, when we speak of a "modulation" having occurred.

A good example of an indisputable modulation is to be found in the subject of the B minor fugue in the first book of Bach's *Wohltemperierte Klavier*. (See figure 7.) The first three notes clearly establish the tonic as B ($q = 5$), and all the other notes in bars 1 and 2 are related to it by nonchromatic intervals ($|\delta q| < 7$). But the first note of bar 3, though in the same keyboard position as the C in bar 2, is notated differently. To have written it as a C would have produced the sequence C♯ C C♯, calling for two chromatic semitones in succession. But in unaccompanied classical melodies such an event never seems to occur, for the very good reason that if X Y Z are three successive notes of a melody which, on paper, are separated by chromatic intervals X Y and Y Z, then there is always an alternative, simpler, interpretation of the middle note Y which transforms both intervals into diatonic ones. Generally speaking, then, the tonal identity of a note cannot be finally established until the following note is heard. In figure 7 the offending note has become transformed into a B♯, making both the neighbouring intervals into diatonic semitones, of degree 5 and -5 rather than -7 and 7 respectively. But a B♯ is too far from the old tonic B to belong to its key, so that a modulation is perceived to occur to a new key, that of F♯, such that the value of δq for the new note B♯ is only 6, which is just close enough for comfort.

There seem to be other general restrictions upon the contexts in which chromatic intervals occur in classical melodies. The most important of these relates to four-note sequences W X Y Z in which the middle interval is chromatic. In such a sequence not only must both W X and Y Z be nonchromatic, but at least one of the intervals W Y and X Z must be diatonic. If the interpretations of W, X, Y, and Z based on the current key violate this rule, then the tonality of the note Y is reinterpreted in such a way as to make $X Y$ a diatonic interval, and to force a modulation into a key to which Y belongs. As implied by what has been said, a note is regarded as belonging to a given key if its sharpness relative to the tonic lies in the range -5 to $+6$ inclusive.

Another rule which seems to be necessary in order to account for the notation of chromatic scales, particularly in music of the period following Bach, concerns the tonal interpretation of ascending semitones. If such a semitone ends on the note of a key whose sharpness relative to the tonic is 2, 3, 4, or 5, then its first note is to be assigned a relative sharpness 7, 8, 9, or 10. Though this reassignment places the note outside the key, it does not by itself precipitate a modulation; if it did, then an ascending chromatic scale of any length would trigger a whole sequence of modulations into progressively sharper and sharper keys.

Two further rules are necessary, and sufficient, for determining the relative sharpnesses of the notes in most classical melodies. The first is a rule to the effect that for the purposes of establishing tonality one may conflate repeated notes, or notes separated by an octave (the second and third notes in figure 4 provide an example). The other rule, which is theoretically less satisfactory, is that the tonic may be determined from the first two notes, and that it will be either the first note itself or the note a fifth below it. This rule, and the absence of any more delicate tests of modulation than those already described, are undoubtedly the weakest links in the tonal section of the program.

Before I describe the program in detail, a few words of caution may be in order. First, the tonal rules outlined above must not be expected to apply to accompanied melodies, where the accompaniment supplies tonal information which may not be implicit in the melody itself. Nor must it be supposed that the rules necessarily hold for covertly polyphonic melodies in which, for example, alternate notes really belong to two different melodies. Further, the contextual constraints on chromatic intervals will often be violated at phrase boundaries, marked by rhythmically prominent rests, though this is not always the case. And finally, one must allow for the possibility that in a musical score a radical change of notation (such as occurs between the first and second sections of Chopin's "Raindrop" Prelude) does not signify a real change in tonality, but merely an "enharmonic change" designed to simplify the reader's task. Only if such qualifications are borne in mind can the program safely be used to indicate how a melody performed on the keyboard should be transcribed into conventional notation.

The Program

The program accepts as input a list of sublists, each of which comprises three numbers. The first number is the keyboard position of the corresponding note and lies in the range 0 to 48, there being four octaves on the organ console. The second number is the time in centiseconds at which the note was depressed, and the third number indicates the time at which the note was released. The order of the notes on the list is the order of their times of onset. The list itself is generated from a live performance of a melody on an electronic organ connected, through an analogue-to-digital converter, to a high-speed paper-tape punch. The information on the paper tape is equivalent to the information which would be recorded on a player-piano roll, and no more. The preprocessing of the paper tape is an entirely automatic matter, which simply involves constructing the above-mentioned list from the paper-tape record and transferring it to disk storage.

The performer is required, by the present version of the program, to establish the initial tempo and the number of beats in a bar by prefacing his performance of the melody by a bar's worth of beats on some low note, which may conveniently be positioned an octave below the first note of the melody, so as not to prejudice the tonality.

The program itself is written in POP2, the high-level programming language designed and developed in Edinburgh by Burstall and Popplestone (Burstall et al. 1971). It is relatively short, and is structured as follows. First, the list of sublists is converted into a list of records, each of which has a "slot" indicating the pitch, onset time, and offset time of a particular note, and further slots which are to hold and span δp and the degree δq of the interval between the note and its predecessor. The keynote is then fixed by the positions of the first two notes, and the relative sharpnesses of all the notes are determined from their keyboard positions by an algorithm based on the theory of tonality outlined in the previous section. The next stage is a rhythmic analysis (which could have been carried out first, as it is indifferent to the results of the tonal routines). Each beat is examined in turn, by a combination of "top down" and "bottom up" analysis in which the time of onset of each note is used both for establishing the structure of the rhythmic hierarchy and for correcting the estimated tempo. In the course of this analysis the time of offset of each note is used for determining how the note was phrased.

The final stage in the operation of the program corresponds to the exercise of musical literacy; it consists of displaying, on paper, the essential

```
: printlist(cliche):

[ 12 154 227]
[ 36 285 294]
[ 31 322 327]
[ 31 336 341]      a
[ 32 349 383]
[ 31 384 407]
[ 35 445 453]
[ 36 484 527]
```

```
: 10->tolerance: notate(cliche):                                          b

[[[ 24 C STC] [[-5 G STC] [ 0 G STC]]] [[ 1 AB] [-1 G TEN]]]

[[[REST] [ 4 B STC]] [ 1 C TEN]]

:
```

Figure 8

features of the structure created by the rhythmic and tonal analyses as a sequence of nested lists of symbols. The innermost symbols name the individual notes as, for example, "D" (D natural), "DS" (D sharp), or "DB " (D flat); the word REST is self-explanatory. Each name is preceded by either the word TIED if the note is tied to its predecessor or a number indicating the span (not the degree, which is implicit in the name of the note) of the interval from the preceding note; this is needed for identifying the octave in which the note occurs. Finally, a note which is not tied may be followed by the abbreviation STC or TEN indicating that the note was played *staccato* or *tenuto*; the absence of either abbreviation implies that the note was played *legato*.

Figures 8, 9, and 10 provide examples of the program's performance. Each figure indicates (*a*) the "raw" input, in which each set of three numbers gives the keyboard position of a note and its times of onset and offset in centiseconds, (*b*) the output generated by the program from the input (*a*), and (*c*) the result of transcribing the output (*b*) by hand into ordinary stave notation.

The performance of the tune shown in figure 8 was prefaced by a single low C, and the time between the onset of this note and the next was arbitrarily taken as a "minim" in adopting the note values indicated in (*c*); it will be noted that in (*b*) the outermost brackets enclose a minim's worth of notes. The interpretation (*b*) was obtained from the input (*a*) with a tolerance of 10 cs; with a tolerance of 15 cs the program would assign the two semiquavers to the same node. The actual times of onset of the first four quaver units differed in the performance by 37, 27, and 35 cs respectively, the separation between the last two notes being 39 cs. The considerable discrepancy between these numbers clearly illustrates the acute difficulty which would confront any attempt to determine the rhythm without taking account of its hierarchical structure.

Figure 9 shows how the program handled a performance of part of the long cor anglais solo from the prelude to Act III of Wagner's *Tristan und Isolde*. This example is interesting in two particular respects. First, it involves the perception of a change from a binary to a ternary metre in the fifth bar; secondly, the published score indicates a grace note at the end of the seventh bar, to which it would be inappropriate to assign a separate place in the rhythmic structure. The program's output agrees fully with the score in its rhythmic and tonal indications. There are slight discrepancies in the marks of phrasing—Wagner marked all the triplet quavers as staccato—but for this the performer is clearly to blame, not the program.

Finally, figure 10 illustrates the program's handling of a later section of the same melody (prefaced, this time, by only one "cue" note, which is why each line of the output contains only one, not two, minim units). Again the rhythm is correctly represented, though there are minor discrepancies in phrasing. As for the tonality, the main point to note is the perceptual problem presented by the rapid succession of modulations beginning in the second bar. There is, nevertheless, only one note to which the program assigns a tonality at variance with that indicated by Wagner: He wrote the second C♯ in the second bar as a D♭.

Conclusions

The domain of competence of the program is, of course, very restricted; it cannot be expected to reveal significant tonal or rhythmic relations between the notes of "atonal" or "arhythmic" melodies, for example. But the perceptual theory on which it is based does seem worthy of serious consideration, in that up to the present time no detailed suggestions seem to have been offered as to how a listener builds an internal representation of a melody from a live performance. The most significant rhythmic hypothesis in the theory is that the rhythm of a melody is conceptualised as a structural hierarchy, and that the onset of each note provides important predictive information about the time of onset of the following note at every level in the hierarchy. The hypotheses underlying the tonal section of the program are presumably limited in application to the kind of music that has been developed in the West; but for such music one conclusion at least

```
: printlist(tris);

[ 12  24  114]
[ 12  148  238]
[ 24  274  399]
[ 31  400  554]
[ 34  551  587]
[ 32  586  671]
[ 27  669  711]
[ 32  707  794]
[ 26  795  831]
[ 31  829  860]
[ 24  863  895]
[ 29  895  989]              a
[ 31  987  1021]
[ 29  1020  1145]
[ 27  1140  1242]
[ 26  1268  1282]
[ 24  1289  1298]
[ 22  1308  1320]
[ 29  1332  1452]
[ 26  1450  1495]
[ 22  1508  1517]
[ 21  1528  1536]
[ 20  1546  1556]
[ 27  1570  1696]
[ 24  1692  1734]
[ 20  1752  1762]
[ 19  1774  1782]
[ 18  1792  1808]
[ 26  1815  1930]
[ 29  1928  1934]
[ 27  1932  2062]
[ 26  2059  2188]
[ 25  2183  2446]
[ 24  2491  2628]
```

```
: 13->tolerance; notate(tris);

[ 12 C][ 7 G]

[[[TIED G] [ 3 BB]] [-2 AB]][[[TIED AB] [-5 EB]] [ 5 AB]]

[[[TIED AB] [-6 D]] [[ 5 G] [-7 C]]][[ 5 F] [[TIED F] [ 2 G]]]

[-2 F][-2 EB TEN]                                              b

[[[-1 D] [-2 C STC] [-2 BB]] [ 7 F]][[TIED F] [-3 D TEN]]

[[[-4 BB STC] [-1 A STC] [-1 AB]] [ 7 EB]][[TIED EB] [-3 C TEN]]

[[[-4 AB STC] [-1 G STC] [-1 FS]] [ 8 D]][[TIED D] [ 3 F -2 EB]]

[[TIED EB] [-1 D]][[TIED D] [-1 DB]]

[TIED DB][TIED DB]

[-1 C]
```

Figure 9

```
: printlist(stan);
```

```
[ 19  148  190]
[ 31  280  287]
[ 29  302  309]
[ 27  322  329]
[ 34  347  466]
[ 31  474  518]
[ 27  538  548]
[ 26  559  566]
[ 25  578  586]
[ 33  605  648]
[ 30  646  657]
[ 26  669  678]
[ 25  687  696]
[ 24  707  714]
[ 32  729  760]
[ 29  769  777]
[ 25  791  801]
[ 24  811  820]
[ 23  830  839]
[ 31  856  987]
[ 27  986 1027]
[ 24 1049 1054]
[ 23 1068 1075]
[ 22 1087 1096]
[ 29 1111 1153]
[ 26 1152 1157]
[ 22 1174 1183]
[ 21 1194 1202]
[ 20 1211 1220]
[ 27 1232 1270]
[ 24 1272 1279]
[ 20 1295 1304]
[ 19 1316 1325]
[ 18 1336 1348]
[ 26 1360 1619]
```

a

```
: 13->tolerance; notate(stan);
```

```
[[[ 12 G STC] [-2 F STC] [-2 EB STC]] [ 7 BB]]
```

```
[[TIED BB] [-3 G TEN]]
```

```
[[[-4 EB STC] [-1 D STC] [-1 CS STC]] [[ 8 A] [TIED A] [-3 FS]]]
```
b

```
[[[-4 D STC] [-1 CS STC] [-1 C STC]] [[ 8 AB] [REST] [-3 F STC]]]
```

```
[[[-4 DB STC] [-1 C STC] [-1 B STC]] [ 8 G]]
```

```
[[TIED G] [-4 EB TEN]]
```

```
[[[[-3 C STC] [-1 B STC]] [-1 BB STC]] [[ 7 F] [TIED F] [-3 D STC]]]
```

```
[[[-4 BB STC] [-1 A STC] [-1 AB STC]] [[ 7 EB] [TIED EB] [-3 C STC]]]
```

```
[[[-4 AB STC] [-1 G STC] [-1 FS]] [ 8 D]]
```

c

Figure 10

seems secure, namely that the tonality of any note cannot in general be established unambiguously until the following note has been heard. It is perhaps surprising that such a limited amount of context should usually suffice for the purpose, but it should be remembered that it is really the key of the melody which creates the tonal context in the first place.

It seems altogether possible that the principles of operation of the program's rhythmic component will apply to other temporal processes, such as the perception of speech.

I thank D. C. Jeffrey, M. J. Steedman, B. C. Styles, O. P. Buneman, and G. E. Hinton for practical assistance and helpful discussions, and the Royal Society and the SRC for research support.

References

Askenfelt, A. 1976. *Quarterly Progress and Status Report, Speech Transmission Laboratory, Royal Institute of Technology, Stockholm* 1: 1.

Bosanquet, P. H. M. 1876. *Elementary Treatise on Musical Intervals and Temperament.*

Burstall, R. M., J. S. Collins, and R. J. Popplestone. 1971. *Programming in POP-2.* Edinburgh University Press.

Helmholtz, H. L. F. 1885. *On the Sensations of Tone* (tr. Ellis), second edition.

Longuet-Higgins, H. C. 1962. *Music Review* 23 (August): 244, 23 (November): 271. [Chapter 8 in present volume.]

Longuet-Higgins, H. C. 1972. *Proc. R. Inst.* 45: 87.

Longuet-Higgins, H. C., and M. J. Steedman. 1971. *Machine Intelligence 6*, p. 221.

Rameau, M. 1721. Traité de l'harmonie réduite à des principes naturels.

Steedman, M. J. Thesis, Edinburgh University.

Styles, B. C. 1973. Thesis, Cambridge University.

Appendix A: The Program "music.p"

```
recordclass note pitch onset offset span deg index;
function sift notefile = > notefile;
    maplist (notefile, lambda x;
    if x.tl.tl.hd − x.tl.hd < 5 then else x. close
    end) − > notefile;
end;
```

```
function takein notefile => nlist;
   maplist (notefile, lambda x;
      consnote (applist(x, identfn), undef, undef, undef)
   end) —> nlist;
end;

function res x;
   loopif x < 0 then x + 12 —> x close;
   erase (x//12);
end;

function int x;
   res(7*x + 5) — 5;
end;

vars flag k l m n;

function modulate;
   if m > 2 then y — 1 —> k
   elseif m < (— 1) then y + 6 —> k
   else exit;

   int(x — k) —> l; int(y — k) —> m; int(z — k) —> n;
end;

function hark;
   m —> l; n —> m; int(z — k) —> n;

   if flag and abs(n — l) > 6 then .modulate
   close; false —> flag;

   if abs(n — m) < 7 then return
   elseif abs(m — l) > 6 then .modulate
   elseif abs(n — l) > 6 and l < 7 then true —> flag
   elseif n — m = 7 and n < 6 then m + 12 —> m
   close;
end;

function simplify tune; vars y;
   tune.hd — 1 —> y;
   maplist (tune, lambda x;
```

```
      if res(x − y)>0 then x
      close; x −> y; end);
end;

function intervals tune; vars ints x y z;
   tune.simplify −> tune;
   false −> flag; nil −> ints;
   tune.hd −> y; tune.tl −> tune;
   if tune.null then return
   else tune.hd −> z; tune.tl −> tune
   close;

   y −> k; 0 −> m; int(z − k) −> n;

   if n = 3 or n < 0 and not(n = (− 3))
      then k + 5 −> k; 1 −> m; n + 1 −> n
   close;
   loopif tune.null.not
   then y −> x; z −> y;
      tune.hd −> z; tune.tl −> tune;
      .hark; (m − l)::ints −> ints
   close;
   rev((n − m)::ints);
end;


vars place;


function tuneup nlist; vars ints x0;
   maplist(nlist, pitch).intervals −> ints;
   nlist.hd −> x0; x0.pitch.int −> place;
   applist(nlist,lambda x;
      x.pitch − x0.pitch −> x.span;
      if res(x.span) = 0 then 0
      else ints.hd; ints.tl −> ints
      close −> x.deg;

      x −> x0;
   end);
end;


vars start beat position number group last metre nlist sequence;
```

```
function startup;
    nil —> sequence; nlist.hd.onset —> start;
    nlist.tl,hd.onset — start —> beat;
    nlist.hd.pitch —> position;
    nil —> group; nil —> last; 0 —> number;

    loopif nlist.hd.pitch = position then
        nlist.tl —> nlist; number + 1 —> number
    close;
end;

vars tol metre; 13 —> tol; nil —> metre;

function singlet —> stop —> fig;
    vars period mark;
    if group.null.not then
        if group.hd.offset < stop — period/2 then "stc"
        elseif group.hd.offset < stop — tol then "ten"
        else "leg"
        close —> mark;

        group.rev —> last; nil —> group; mark::last;
    else
        [%"tac",applist(last,lambda x;
        if x.offset > start + tol then x
        close end)%]
    close —> fig;
    if nlist.null or nlist.hd.onset > stop + tol then 0
    else nlist.hd.onset
    close —> stop;
end;

function rhythm start period —> stop —> fig; vars stop;
    start + period —> stop;
    if nlist.null.not and nlist.hd.onset < start + tol
    then nlist.hd::nil —> group; nlist.tl —> nlist;
    else goto label
    close;
    loopif nlist.null.not and nlist.hd.onset < stop + tol
        and nlist.hd.onset < group.hd.onset + tol
```

```
    then nlist.hd::group −> group; nlist.tl −> nlist;
    close;
    if group.hd.onset > stop − tol
    then group.hd::nlist −> nlist; group.tl −> group
    close;
label;
    if nlist.null or nlist.hd.onset > stop − tol
    then .singlet
    else .tempo
    close −> stop −> fig;
end;

function tempo −> stop −> figure;
    vars new old again pulse time count fig syncop;

    [%nlist,last,group%] −> old; 0 −> again;
loop:
    if metre.null then 2::nil −> metre
    close;

    metre.hd −> pulse; metre.tl −> metre;
    nil −> figure; period −> time;
    0 −> count; start −> stop;
    loopif count < pulse
    then
        count + 1 −> count;
        rhythm(stop,time/pulse) −> stop −> fig;
        fig::figure −> figure;
        if stop = 0 then start + count*time/pulse −> stop; true
        else stop − start + (pulse − count)*time/pulse −> time; false
        close −> syncop;
    close;
    again + 1 −> again;

    if not(syncop or stop > start + period + tol or stop < start + period − tol)
    then figure.rev −> figure; pulse::metre −> metre;
    exit;
    if again = 1 then
        [%nlist,last,group,figure.rev,stop,pulse::metre%] −> new;
        old.destlist −> group −> last −> nlist;
        (5 − pulse)::nil −> metre; goto loop;
    else
```

```
        new.destlist —> metre —> stop —> figure —> group —> last —> nlist;
     close;
end;

function tapout nlist —> sequence;
   vars start beat tol group last stop figure;

   loopif nlist.null.not
   then
      rhythm(start,beat) —> stop —> figure;
      figure::sequence —> sequence;

      if stop = 0 then start + beat
      else (stop — start + beat)/2 —> beat; stop
      close —> start;
   close;
   nil —> metre;
   sequence.rev —> sequence;
end;

vars max min; 17 —> max; — 13 —> min;

vars symbols: [Fbb Cbb Gbb Dbb Abb Ebb Bbb Fb Cb Gb Db Ab Eb Bb
   F C G D A E B Fs Cs Gs Ds As Es Bs Fx Cx Gx Dx Ax Ex Bx]
   —> symbols;

vars symbol; newarray([% — 15,19%],
   lambda x; symbols.hd; symbols.tl —> symbols end) —> symbol;

function name note:
   place + note.deg —> place;
   if place > max then "enh"; — 12
   elseif place < min then "enh"; 12
   else 0
   close + place —> place;

   place —> note.index;
   note.span; place. symbol;
end;

function describe fig; vars word;
   fig.hd —> word; fig.tl —> fig;
```

```
    if fig.null then [rest]
    elseif word = "tac" then
       "tied"::maplist(fig,index < > symbol)
    elseif word = "leg" then maplist(fig,name)
    else [%applist(fig,name),word%]
    close;
end;


function reveal figure;
    if figure.hd.isword
    then figure.describe
    else maplist(figure,reveal)
    close;
end;


function typeout seq; vars count;
    0 —> count; 1.nl;
    applist(seq, lambda x;
       if count = number then 1 —> count; 2.nl
       else count + 1 —> count
       close; x.reveal .pr
    end); 2.nl;
end;


function notate notefile;
    notefile.takein —> nlist;
    .startup;
    nlist.tapout —> sequence;
    nlist.tuneup;
    sequence.typeout;
end;


function printlist 1;
    2.nl;
    applist(1,lambda x; x.pr; 1.nl end);
    2.nl;
end;

$
```

Appendix B: Comments on the Program "music.p"

The program, which was originally named "music.pop", combines a number of hypotheses about melodic perception, most of which are highly provisional but all of which are readily falsifiable in principle (which is all one can ever expect of scientific theories). The following things are assumed:

a. The processes of rhythmic and tonal perception are independent, rhythmic perception being represented by the line

nlist.tapout —> sequence;

and tonal perception by the following line,

nlist.tuneup.

b. A tonal interval may be adequately characterized by its "span" (in keyboard semitones) and its "degree", which is the difference in the indices of the notes involved, the index of a note being the number of sharps in the key signature of its major key. Thus the upward diminished third from F$\sharp$ to A$\flat$ is of span 2 and degree -10 ($=(-4)-6$).

c. The tonality of the sequence $X\,Y\,Z$ is unaffected by repetition of one of its notes (say Y) at the unison or the octave. (See the note on *simplify* below.)

d. Melodic rhythms are parsed "bottom-up" (this is certainly an oversimplification), the precise time of onset of each note being taken into account in predicting the time of onset of the next metrical unit.

e. Our judgements of articulation are based not on the gaps between notes but on the gap between the end of a note and the start of the next metrical unit.

f. A rest is what separates the beginning of a metrical unit from the first note that interrupts it.

g. Rhythmic perception proceeds recursively (each of the functions *rhythm* and *tempo* calls the other) under the guidance of a structural preconception, the *metre*, which is changed only reluctantly. (The time signatures $\frac{3}{4}$ and $\frac{6}{8}$ correspond to the metres [3 2] and [2 3] respectively.) Only binary and ternary groupings are permitted by the program.

Now for some comments on the individual functions:

1. *sift* removes from a *file* all notes of duration less than 5 centiseconds. If this procedure is deemed necessary (to remove accidentally touched notes), *sift* must be called before *notate*.

2. The highest-level function is called *notate*; it takes as argument a *notefile* consisting of a list of lists. Each sublist gives the keyboard *pitch*, time of *onset*, and time of *offset* of a note played on the organ console; the times are measured in centiseconds. The output of the function is a sequence of lists, each of which represents the rhythm, tonality, and phrasing of the notes occurring in a single beat.

3. *sequence* is the data structure to be created from the file.

4. *nlist* is to be a list of notes, each being a record with six entries: a note's *pitch* (its position on the keyboard), its times of *onset* and *offset* (in centiseconds), the *span* and the *degree* of the interval from the preceding note, and the *index* (which is 0 for a C, 1 for a G and so on).

5. *takein* creates *nlist*.

6. *place* stores the index of the first note.

7. *tuneup* uses the musical intervals between the notes to assign a *span* and a *degree* to each note.

8. *intervals* takes as argument the pitches of the notes. It chooses a keynote *k*, studies each set of three notes in turn, and creates a list of the (non-zero) musical intervals between the notes (in the range -11 to $+11$ inclusive).

9. *simplify* removes any note separated from its predecessor by a whole number of octaves.

10. *res x* is the remainder on division of *x* by 12.

11. *int x* is the diatonic interval between two notes separated by *x* keyboard semitones.

12. *hark* studies a set of three successive notes and evaluates the intervals between them; *flag* indicates whether the third note seems remote from the first two.

13. *modulate* alters the keynote when appropriate and makes consequent changes in the positions of the three notes relative to the keynote.

14. *tolerance* is the permissible discrepancy between an observed and a predicted time (in centiseconds); it and *metre* can be preset as desired.

15. *tapout* studies each beat in turn, taking the beat length initially from the first two notes. At the end of each beat, the *beat* length is adjusted if necessary and a rhythmic *figure* is appended to *seq*.

16. *rhythm* does four things: (a) If its allotted *period* begins with the onset of a note, this note is placed in *group*. (b) If any more notes follow in rapid succession, these are added to *group*. (c) If the last such note might be the beginning of the next metrical unit, it is removed from *group*. (d) If the next

note begins before the end of the unit, *tempo* is called; otherwise *singlet* is called.

17. *singlet* places a *mark* of phrasing at the beginning of the current *group* if it is non-null; otherwise it harks back to any notes that may still be sounding (*tac* stands for "tacet"). It leaves on the stack a marked group and a finishing time (or zero). *mark* is taken as *stc* (staccato) if a note lasts less than half its allotted time, *ten* (tenuto) if it lasts nearly its allotted time, otherwise *leg* (legato).

18. *tempo* divides its time into *pulse* parts and uses the intervening notes to gauge the starting time of the next unit. If the unit fails to end with the onset of a note, or ends rather early or rather late, a different *metre* is tried; if this gives no better results, the original metre is accepted. It leaves on the stack a rhythmic figure and a finishing time, discovered or estimated.

19. *typeout* types out the sequence generated by *tapout*.

20. *reveal* is defined recursively, the lowest level being attended to by *describe*.

21. *describe* translates each figure composed of a word followed by a sequence of notes into a list of words and numbers.

22. *max* and *min* delimit the extremes of sharpness and flatness permitted in the output symbols, and may be preset at will. *place* may also be reset before any call of *typeout*; the effect is to make the tune start on the corresponding note.

23. *name* indicates the occurrence of an enharmonic change with the word *enh*, and gives (for non-tied notes) the keyboard interval up to the note from its predecessor, and the appropriate *symbol*. In the list of *symbols*, Eb stands for E flat, Fs for F sharp, Cx for C double sharp, Bbb for B double flat, etc.

11   The Grammar of Music

H. C. Longuet-Higgins

Recently I described a computer program that would transcribe quite sophisticated classical melodies from a live performance on an organ console into the equivalent of standard musical notation (Longuet-Higgins 1976). The program was intended, not as an aid to musical composition, but as a serious contribution to the theory of how Western musicians actually perform the same task. In the present article I shall try to describe the thoughts that led up to the writing of the program, and the psychological and aesthetic issues that are raised by such work. In so doing it will be necessary to refer to ideas in a number of disciplines, ranging from computing science to theoretical linguistics; at the end it may seem that the gulf between the sciences and humanities is not so wide as has often been supposed.

The idea of casting psychological theories in computational form is a relatively recent one. It stems in part from "artificial intelligence", which is the enterprise of programming computers to perform intellectually nontrivial tasks such as playing chess or proving mathematical theorems (Lighthill et al. 1973). The earliest attempts to do this relied on the discovery of heuristics, or "tricks", for the solution of problems, regardless of whether these tricks bore any relation to the intellectual processes of real people.

But at the same time, within psychology, it was becoming clear that a new paradigm would almost certainly be needed for handling theoretically the enormously complex processes of human perception and cognition (Neisser 1966). The outstanding problem was that of finding a suitable language for the formulation of new theories; a language comparable in power, say, to the differential calculus, in which virtually the whole of theoretical physics is expressed. Perhaps computing science could supply this new language. If the programmer could spell out, in ALGOL or LISP, "effective procedures" for the accomplishment of simple intellectual tasks, should it not be possible for the psychologist to describe human intelligence, at least up to a point, in the same medium? The possibility of doing so would not hinge upon the existence of any similarity, however remote, between the digital computer and the human nervous system; modern high-level programming languages enable one to specify complex sequences of logical operations without regard to their manner of implementation. The actual construction of cognitive theories must still, of course, be guided by observation and intuition; but the discipline of casting them in computational form would weed out vague or inconsistent hypotheses at the start. And above all, it would be possible, once a tentative theory had been programmed, to diagnose its failings immediately, by actually running the program on a computer, and to recast the theory and the program accordingly. It was this methodology that motivated me to write a program for the automatic transcription of music.

Theoretical Foundations

Though many scientists are musically gifted, and many musicians are mathematically inclined, the psychologist and the musicologist have tended to study music in quite different ways. The musicologist is concerned to describe the forms which music has taken in different cultures and periods, and the conventions which have dominated its performance and its written representations. The psychologist, on the other hand, has been mainly preoccupied with the overt responses of human beings to music and quasi-musical stimuli such as sequences of taps or tones (Deutsch 1977). As for the inner experiences evoked by music, and their relation to the music itself, only a few brave scholars—mostly practising musicians—have dared to pronounce on such intractable problems, realizing only too well the near impossibility of elevating their intuitions to the status of scientific discoveries. Donald Tovey (1949), Paul Hindemith (1942), Leonard Meyer (1956), and Deryck Cooke (1959), in varying styles and with varying degrees of cogency, have all attempted to define the relation between musical structure and experience; but they seem to leave untouched one central question: What *is* music, and how does it pass from one mind to another?

To suggest that music is a communicative art is to risk affronting those who maintain that the artist is his own master, answerable to nobody and ultimately indifferent to the reception of his work. But the risk seems to be justified by the observation that composers do as a rule offer their work for performance, and that other musicians are willing and eager to listen. What the listener actually hears, when a piece is played, is a sequence of tones whose timing and quality will never be quite the same from one performance to the next. But what he perceives, provided that he is familiar with the composer's language, is a piece of music—a composition of notes, organized into rhythmic figures and melodic phrases.

If he happens to be familiar with musical notation, he may, furthermore, be able to commit the music to paper; and if it is relatively straightforward, his transcription is likely to agree in detail with the score from which it was played. In this sense at least a process of communication has occurred, open to objective inspection; and we may speak of a musical composition having been communicated, through a performance, from one musician to another. So although it may be premature to enquire whether the listener's affective responses to music correspond in any sense to the feelings which inspired the composer, it is possible to examine with reasonable objectivity the question of how it is possible for a piece of music, realized in performance, to be encoded into a musical score by anyone versed in the same musical language.

In order to understand how musicians are able to compose, memorize, recall, recognize, and transcribe music, it is necessary to adopt some fundamental hypotheses about the way in which they conceptualize the relationships which distinguish one piece of music from another. It is natural to suppose that a person's memory of a piece of music is a conceptual structure of some kind, in which the elements are individual notes and the structure itself is defined by the rhythmic and tonal relationships between them. Such structures have been found indispensable to the description of natural language, where a sentence is regarded not as a mere sequence of words but as a structure held together by syntactic relations (Chomsky 1966; Lyons 1968). A commonplace example is the syntactic structure which one might assign to the sentence "Mary stroked the cat" (figure 1). In order to interpret a number of elementary facts about linguistic performance, it is necessary to suppose that a person considering such a sentence actually creates such a structure in his mind; otherwise he would be unable to appreciate the analogy between two sentences such as "Mary stroked the cat" and "A dog bit John" (figure 2)—an analogy which depends upon the presence, in both, of the structure illustrated in figure 3.

In classical music two kinds of structural relationship are pre-eminent: rhythm and tonality. Tonality is a concept with no obvious parallel in linguistic theory, but rhythm is, up to a point, susceptible to syntactic description. Fortunately for the musical theorist, standard musical notation provides powerful clues as to the nature of musical rhythm. It may be instructive to consider, as an elementary example, the musical cliché notated in figure 4. Disregarding for the moment the vertical positions of

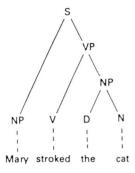

Figure 1

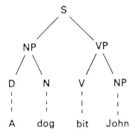

Figure 2

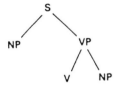

Figure 3

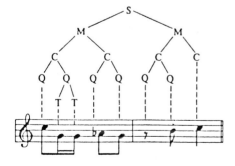

Figure 4

S (sentence) → NP + VP;
NP (noun phrase) → 'John', *or* 'Mary',
   or D + N;
D (determiner) → 'a', *or* 'the';
N (noun) → 'cat', *or* 'dog';
VP (verb phrase) → V + NP;
V (verb) → 'bit', *or* 'stroked';

Figure 5

S (semibreve) → o , *or* ⵁ, *or* M + M;
M (minim unit) → ♩ , *or* ⵁ , *or* C + C;
C (crotchet unit) → ♩ , *or* ⵡ , *or* Q + Q;
Q (quaver unit) → ♪ , *or* ⵎ , *or* T + T;
T (semiquaver unit) → ♪ , *or* ⵏ , *or* . . .

Figure 6

the notes on the stave, we observe that the rhythmic structure is clearly
indicated in the score by the disposition of the bar lines and the manner in
which the stems of the notes are linked by horizontal "beams". The two
shortest notes form a pair which together with the first note forms another
pair, and so on; the entire system of groupings is most simply represented
by a "tree" each of whose "nodes" either branches into two or supports a
note or a rest. Clearly there is a sense in which the rhythm is faithfully
represented by this tree; indeed one might suggest that the tree actually *is*
the rhythm.

The obvious analogy between figure 4 and figure 1 supplies the basis for
a "syntactic" theory of rhythm. To see why, we may return to the linguistic
examples. There is a precise sense in which the structures depicted in
figures 1 and 2 are "generated" by the simple "grammar" shown in figure
5. The grammar is not one which would be found in any textbook, if only
because the sentences it generates are very few in number. It does, however, serve as a model for the construction of a musical "grammar" which
generates the structure shown in figure 4; see figure 6. The symbols appearing on the right of each arrow are of two kinds, "terminal" and "non-
terminal". The terminal symbols stand for actual notes or rests; the non-
terminal symbols are to be interpreted more abstractly, as metrical units of
various kinds. The grammar represents, in formally precise terms, the *metre*
of the melody; since every metrical unit referred to is divided (optionally)
into two shorter metrical units, the grammar in figure 6 represents a pure
binary metre—the commonest metre in classical music. But there are other

DM (dotted minim unit) → $\downarrow$., *or* ⌐, *or* C + C + C;
C (crotchet unit) → $\downarrow$, *or* ⌐, *or* Q + Q;
Q (quaver unit) → $\downarrow$, *or* ⌐, *or* . . .

Figure 7

DM (dotted minim unit) → $\downarrow$., *or* ⌐., *or* DC + DC;
DC (dotted crotchet unit) → $\downarrow$., *or* ⌐, *or* Q + Q + Q;
Q (quaver unit) → $\downarrow$, *or* ⌐, *or* . . .

Figure 8

ways in which metrical units may be divided, and figures 7 and 8 are the grammars which underlie what the musician describes as $\frac{3}{4}$ and $\frac{6}{8}$ time respectively. The existence of such alternative grammars underlies the phenomenon of rhythmic ambiguity. A bar composed of six quavers is rhythmically ambiguous in the sense that it might be "in" either $\frac{3}{4}$ or $\frac{6}{8}$; the precise meaning of the word "in" is directly accessible within a theory which allows a given sequence of symbols to be generated by either of two distinct metres, but forbids a given rhythm to be generated by more than one of them. Figure 9 shows how the metres of figures 7 and 8 generate alternative interpretations of a sequence of six quavers; the distinction between the two rhythms would normally be made clear in a musical score by linking the stems of the quavers by beams in the manner shown.

As one might expect, musical grammars such as figures 7 and 8 have their limitations. First, they are powerless to deal with the problems raised by recitative, where the rhythm is determined by the words; this is an irremediable defect, which it would be pointless to discuss further. Second, they generate some absurdities, such as the structure illustrated in figure 10, which is not so much "ill-formed" as simply indistinguishable in performance from an undivided minim rest; we shall return to this point in a moment. (It is important, however, to notice that a succession of rests is by no means always absurd. Whenever at least one note descends from their lowest common ancestor it will be appropriate to assign them distinct symbols, as illustrated in figure 11.) Third—and this is a more revealing limitation—the metrical grammars so far described make no allowance for the possibility of a note being tied to its predecessor. What these grammars generate as they stand is really "percussive" rhythms in which each note has a defined time of onset but an indeterminate duration. The difference between the "percussive" rhythm $\uparrow$ ⌐ $\uparrow$ (generated by figure 6) and the "sustained" rhythm $\uparrow$ $\uparrow$ $\uparrow$ ($\uparrow$· $\uparrow$, for short) is that in the latter the first

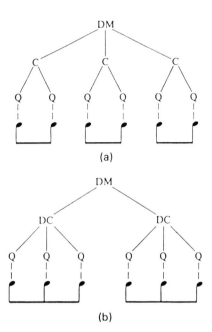

(a)

(b)

Figure 9

Figure 10

Figure 11

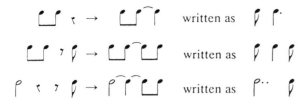

Figure 12

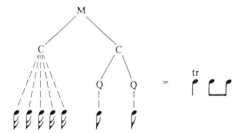

Figure 13

note has encroached upon the crotchet rest of the former. So to cover sustained rhythms one must supplement the grammar of figure 6 by a rule which permits any note followed by rests to be tied over into one or more of these rests. Other examples are illustrated in figure 12. Fourth, the metrical grammars of figures 6–8 make no provision for differences in phrasing, especially differences in the conceptual durations of notes which are not tied. A plausible interpretation of the difference between *staccato* and *legato* is that, at least in fairly rapid rhythms, a note is heard as *staccato* *if it occupies less than half the unit represented by its terminal node, but otherwise as legato*. This account of the matter implies, in agreement with musical intuition, that a note tied to its successor cannot be regarded as *staccato*. Finally, there is the question of ornaments, in particular grace notes and trills. The fact that a trilled minim, say, is usually written as a minim rather than as a sequence of semiquavers supports the hypothesis that trills are heard as rhythmically undivided, and that sufficiently rapid sequences of notes should all be attached to the same terminal node of the rhythmic tree—in the right order, of course (figure 13).

Supplemented in these ways, the grammatical theory of rhythm outlined at the beginning of this section enables one to describe, in formally precise terms, the significance of the temporal symbolism in which most classical music is notated. It does, however, contain one or two minor flaws (such as the generation of pointless sequences of rests, and a certain awkwardness in the handling of tied notes) which suggest that it fails to reach the best attainable level of explanatory power. As will now be shown, such imperfections can be eliminated by considering its perceptual basis, that is, by considering the way in which a listener might actually assign a rhythm to a melody that he hears for the first time.

The Perception of Rhythm

The perception of rhythm owes its psychological interest to the fact that no two performances of the same piece of music will ever be identical in the timing and the dynamics of the individual notes. We infer that there must be a one-to-many mapping of rhythmic structures on to performances, and consequently a many-to-one mapping of performances on to rhythmic interpretations. But even if musical rhythms were invariably performed in "strict" time, the listener would not necessarily assign to a particular sequence the same rhythmic structure as that indicated in the score from which the performer was playing. If the composer were so bold as to present the performer with a sequence of notes whose theoretical durations were 8, 7, 6, ... semiquavers (figure 14), then the listener would be most unlikely to hear the sequence as such; he would perceive a sequence of equivalent note values with an imposed *accelerando*. If, on the other hand, the performer were to tap out, with no variations in loudness, a sequence such as that shown in figure 15, the listener would be more than likely to perceive an alternation of duplets and triplets, rather than a succession of notionally equal note values distorted by a sequence of alternating *accelerandi* and *rallentandi*. Clearly, then, the listener must be exercising some unconscious judgement in making such discriminations; the problem for the psychologist is to bring such judgements into the open—to discover what criteria are employed in distinguishing one rhythmic structure from another.

Figure 14

Figure 15

The most obvious fact about rhythmic perception is that in listening to metrical music one perceives a more or less regular succession of pulses or "beats" (though the word "beat" is also used to mean the period between two successive pulses). If every note of a piece of music occurred on the beat, and if every beat were accompanied by the onset of a note, the listener's perceptual problem would be relatively straightforward. At any given moment he would have predicted the time of occurrence of the next beat, and would then listen for a note occurring close to that time. The words "close to" indicate the existence of a certain "tolerance", t, determining the maximum allowable discrepancy between the note's expected and perceived times of onset; the value of t appears, in fact, to be one or two tenths of a second.

Hearing the new note, the listener will update his estimate of the beat length, and in this way he will be able to keep track of the beat, provided that the tempo does not change too rapidly. But in most melodies notes occur between beats. If T_1 and T_2 are the actual time of one beat and the expected time of the next beat, then a note may well occur at a time between $T_1 + t$ and $T_2 - t$. Such a note calls for a division of the beat into a number of parts determined by the listener's current hypothesis about the metre; but in addition, its precise time of onset provides the listener with evidence which may lead him to revise his estimate of T_2. In this sense there is "feedback" between the rhythm and the tempo; each note is assigned a node of its own on the basis of the metre and the estimated tempo, but the time of onset of the note provides further evidence about the tempo and may actually suggest a change in metre. Ideas such as these must of course be worked out in full detail before they can be embodied in a computer program; the exercise of doing so ensures that the resulting theory is at least logically coherent, even if it does not withstand subsequent empirical testing.

The hypothesis that a node on the rhythmic tree is perceived to divide only if a note interrupts the corresponding metrical unit accounts nicely for the rarity, in published musical scores, of beats divided into equal rests; if no note begins on or during such a beat, there is no audible evidence that the beat should be divided at all. As for ornaments such as grace notes and trills, the concept of a tolerance t suggests naturally how these may be distinguished from rhythmically structured sequences; if the onset times of two or more successive notes are separated by times less than t, then they are treated as constituting an ornament rather than a rhythmically structured figure. Similar ideas inform the theory of how we perceive changes of metre, but to discuss them would, unfortunately, take us too far afield.

Tonality

The word "tonality" is commonly used to signify all those relationships which hold between different notes by virtue of their relative pitch. At least this may serve as a provisional definition—provisional, because it appears that the tonal relationships between the notes of a chord or a melodic phrase cannot be adequately specified by merely indicating their relative pitch (the number of keyboard semitones, for example, by which they are separated). Musical intervals are, apparently, conceptualized not simply as "distances" but as *vectors* in a tonal space of precisely three dimensions (Longuet-Higgins 1962). To see why this is so, it is necessary to refer to certain facts in musical acoustics—facts which Helmholtz (1885) clearly expounded in his classic book *On the Sensations of Tone*, but without fully developing their implications for tonality.

The relevant facts are these. A musician who is asked to tune two notes so that they are separated by a simple musical interval will adjust their relative frequencies to be in the ratio of two small integers, m and n. But not all simple rational numbers m/n correspond to musical intervals, only those which can be expressed as products of low powers (positive or negative) of the first three prime numbers, namely 2, 3, and 5. The most familiar intervals whose frequency ratios can be so expressed are the octave (2/1), the perfect fifth (3/2), and the major third (5/4). It follows directly that any interval of tonal music can be expressed in one and only one way as a combination of octaves, perfect fifths, and major thirds. When two intervals are added together, their frequency ratios are multiplied, so that for example the perfect fourth, which is an octave minus a perfect fifth, has the frequency ratio $(2/1)/(3/2) = (4/3)$.

The three-dimensionality of tonal space follows directly from the fact that just three basic intervals are necessary, and sufficient, for the construction of all others. Given any note such as middle C, we may place it at the origin in tonal space and relate all other notes to it by assigning them coordinates (x, y, z) which represent the numbers of perfect fifths, major thirds, and octaves by which one must move in order to get from middle C to the note in question. In principle, then, the notes of tonal music lie at the points of a discrete three-dimensional space which extends infinitely in all directions away from any starting point. Viewed in this way, the notes of a melody perform a "dance" in an abstract conceptual space; the appreciation of tonality depends upon the ability to discern the direction and the distance of each step in the dance.

Contrary to appearances, the tonal space defined in this way bears a

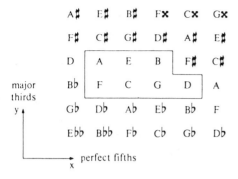

	A♯	E♯	B♯	F✕	C✕	G✕
	F♯	C♯	G♯	D♯	A♯	E♯
	D	A	E	B	F♯	C♯
major thirds	B♭	F	C	G	D	A
y	G♭	D♭	A♭	E♭	B♭	F
	E♭♭	B♭♭	F♭	C♭	G♭	D♭

perfect fifths
x

Figure 16

close relation to the concepts and conventions of standard musical theory. A key appears as a neighbourhood in tonal space, and modulation amounts to passing from one such neighbourhood to another. As for the symbols (such as C, F♯, and B♭) which are customarily used to name the notes of a piece, these stand for columns of notes in tonal space, the notes in each column having the same values of the coordinates x and y and being separated by octaves. (The z dimension corresponds to the octave.) One can therefore relate the points of tonal space to the ordinary names of the corresponding notes by projecting the space on to the (x, y) plane; the result is figure 16, in which each note is a perfect fifth above (or a perfect fourth below) the note to its left, and lies a major third above (or a minor sixth below) the note printed directly underneath. (Strictly, of course, each symbol stands for a whole set of notes spaced by octaves, but the musician is quite used to thinking in this way.)

Any closely related set of notes, such as those which constitute the scale of C major, will form a compact group in figure 16. The notes of C major are actually those which lie inside the frame shown; this is evident from the fact that the major triads FAC, CEG, and GBD all form compact L-shaped patterns lying inside the frame. But the observant reader will notice that there is another D which lies outside the frame, immediately to its left, and he may wonder why this note should be excluded from the key of C major. The reason is that it is, strictly speaking, a different note from its namesake; it must be, because of the incommensurability of the three basic intervals which define the tonal space. (It is in fact a slightly flatter note if played strictly in tune, the difference in pitch amounting to 80/81, which is about 1/5 of a keyboard semitone.)

The existence, in principle, of such "homophones" (Lyons 1968)—notes which sound much alike but are conceptually distinct—is an inevitable consequence of the fact that tonal space has infinitely many points, but the human ear cannot make infinitely fine discriminations of pitch. The history of the keyboard bears witness to the compromises musicians have had to make in order to map the notes of tonal music on to a finite number of divisions of the octave. Equal temperament as we know it depends upon the fact that the perfect fifth is close to 7/12 of an octave, and the major third is nearly 1/3 of an octave. However, earlier systems of tuning the keyboard did not divide the octave into equal parts, but exploited the fact that most pieces of music were confined to a relatively small neighbourhood in tonal space, so that the notes of the key could be tuned with good accuracy, though this entailed an unsatisfactory tuning of notes lying outside the key.

In "mean tone" temperament (Lloyd and Boyle 1963), for example, one might tune a harpsichord in such a way that the notes we describe as E♭, B♭, . . . , C♯, G♯ were connected by slightly imperfect fifths, of such a magnitude that four of them were exactly equal to two octaves plus a major third. Major thirds such as CE and EG would therefore be exactly in tune, but G♯C would not be a proper major third—as indeed it should not be according to the relation of these notes in tonal space. But in mean-tone tuning the same note on the keyboard served equally well for both the Ds in figure 16, just as in equal temperament the same black note serves to represent both G♯ and A♭. It was therefore natural to give them the same name and place them in the same position on the stave; as a consequence, the conceptual distinction between homonyms such as the two Ds was obscured, and the tonal space of figure 16 was replaced by a "curved" space in which such homonyms were treated as if they were the same note.

To digress for a moment, it may be worth remarking that mean-tone temperament is very closely approximated by a division of the octave into 31 equal parts (Bosanquet 1875), since the major third is almost exactly equal to 10/31 of an octave and the perfect fifth is close to 18/31 of an octave. Thirty-one-note temperament also accommodates very accurately the natural seventh, with frequency ratio 7/4, this interval being very close to 25/31 of an octave. It is interesting to speculate how tonal music might have developed if it had been practicable to construct a keyboard in which the octave was divided into 31 rather than 12 equal "semitones". First, on such a keyboard the notes G♯ and A♭ of figure 16 would have had different positions, the former lying one "semitone" below the latter; as a consequence, the conceptual distinction between such pairs of notes would probably have been more secure than it has proved to be in recent musical history. But more significantly, perhaps, the very good intonation of the natural seventh on the 31-note keyboard might have led to its recognition as a basic interval in its own right. Tonal space would then have had four rather than three dimensions—a possibility which is, of course, still open to the future development of tonal music.

The Perception of Tonal Relations

We are now in a position to appreciate more clearly the problem of tonal interpretation which confronts a musician listening to a classical melody played on an ordinary keyboard. The problem arises from the fact that the notes of tonal space are related to the notes of the keyboard by a many-to-one mapping, so that a given keyboard interval has more than one interpretation as a vector in tonal space. The multiplicity of the mapping is illustrated in figure 17, in which the upper block is a replica of figure 16 and the lower block indicates the serial number of each note within the keyboard octave (depicted at the foot of the figure). A fuller representation of

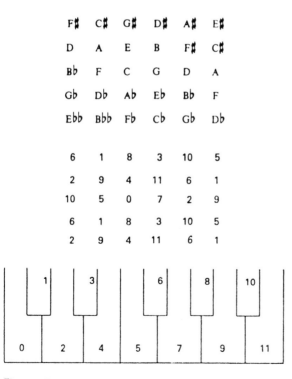

Figure 17

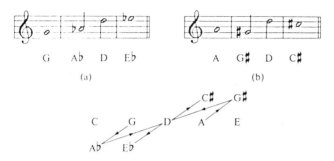

Figure 18

the mapping would take the form of a three-dimensional diagram in which each note (x, y, z) of tonal space is allotted a keyboard position $p = 7x + 4y + 12z$ semitones above middle C. The listener is supplied, in a keyboard performance, with the relative p values of successive notes, but each keyboard interval δp might, in principle, be perceived as any one of a number of tonal vectors $(\delta x, \delta y, \delta z)$. Thus a keyboard interval with $\delta p = 6$ might represent either the tritone $(2, 1, -1)$ or the minor fifth $(-2, -1, 2)$. Nevertheless, as figure 18 illustrates, the context will usually provide enough information to decide between such possibilities. The keyboard positions of the middle two notes are the same in both sequences, but the interval between them is more naturally interpreted as a tritone in figure 18a and a minor fifth in figure 18b; the arrows in the accompanying diagram indicate the tonal movements. So is it possible to understand, in general, how tonal ambiguities can be resolved by reference to the context?

One way of approaching the phenomenon of tonal ambiguity and its contextual resolution would be to attempt to discover a grammar which generated (see below) all and only those melodies which we regard as tonally well formed. But even if agreement could be reached, in general, on the well-formedness or otherwise of any given tonal sequence, the discovery of such a grammar would not necessarily explain why so few classical melodies seem tonally ambiguous even when played on an equally tempered keyboard. For if T were the set of all well-formed sequences in tonal space and K were the set of all keyboard sequences, then we should have no guarantee that two distinct members of T did not map on to the same member of K.

For these reasons it seemed preferable to look for rules which would describe how a listener does in fact assign a tonal interpretation in T to a given sequence in K. On the entirely reasonable assumption that not only listeners but also composers regard two or more melodies as tonally iden-

 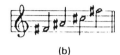 

(a) (b) (c)

Figure 19

tical if they map on to the same sequence of keyboard intervals, one might then be able to understand why classical composers notated their melodies as they did. Tonal sequences such as that implied by figure 19a would be ruled out, not on "grammatical" grounds, but simply because no listener hearing such a sequence would be able to resist perceiving it as figure 19b or 19c.

This shift of viewpoint from a "grammatical" to a "perceptual" view of tonal sequences allows us to withhold judgement as to whether a particular *keyboard* sequence is well formed or not, and to focus attention on the way in which such a sequence will actually be perceived, taking evidence from the way in which it was notated by the composer. It is not unreasonable to suppose that a composer of the stature of Bach or Brahms is at least as reliable an informant about the tonal relationships implicit in his music as any randomly selected group of musicians; if this is admitted, the harshest test of any theory of tonality is whether it can account for his actual choice of symbols when there is, superficially, a choice between homophones such as G♯ and A♭.

It is at this point that the musical concept of a key becomes crucial. Without doubt the most important single factor influencing the tonal interpretation of any note is the perceived key of the passage in which the note occurs. Three questions immediately arise: (1) How do we perceive the key in the first place? (2) How does the perceived key influence the interpretation of each note? (3) What kinds of tonal sequence lead us to perceive a change of key?

These questions are, of course, much more easily asked than answered. But in order to address question 2 in particular it proves convenient to extend the concept of a key in the following manner. The extended key of C is to be regarded as embracing the keys of C major and C minor, and as comprising all those notes whose projections in figure 16 lie in the rectangle shown in figure 20. The "tonic" (C) and the "dominant" (G) lie in the middle, and every note on the keyboard is represented exactly once in the key. On this extended definition every keyboard note receives a unique interpretation in any given key, so that once a key has been established there exists a unique *prima facie* interpretation for each subsequent note.

A	E	B	F♯
F	C	G	D
D♭	A♭	E♭	B♭

Figure 20

Figure 21

Question 1 is altogether more challenging. But if melodies are not to be tonally ambiguous, the key must presumably be established, or at least suggested, by the first few notes. In many melodies (and in all classical fugue subjects) the first note is either the tonic or the dominant, and the first two different notes are close together in tonal space. It is therefore natural to associate with the first interval a vector of minimal length in figure 16; if this vector points to the right (or directly upwards) the first note was probably the tonic; otherwise it was probably the dominant (Longuet-Higgins 1972). Thus in figure 18a the first interval is heard as the diagonal vector $(\delta x, \delta y) = (-1, -1)$, suggesting the first note (G) as the dominant and the key as that of C; in figure 18b, on the other hand, the initial vector is $(1, 1)$, favouring the first note as the tonic and the key as that of A.

As for question 3, we are far from a complete understanding of the way in which the successive notes of a melody may precipitate a change of key. All one can be sure of is that in certain contexts the listener finds it impossible to interpret every note as lying within the previously estab-lished key, even though there always exists, in principle, such an interpreta-tion. More specifically, it seems that he is led to perceive a change of key whenever the old key imposes on a keyboard sequence LMN an interpreta-tion in which LM and MN are both "remote" intervals in the space of figure 16. In such a situation, modulation is felt to occur to a new key which assigns to the note M a tonal position nearer to that of L and N. This is undoubtedly what happens towards the end of the subject of the B Minor Fugue in Book I of the Forty-Eight, where the three notes marked with asterisks in figure 21 would receive the unacceptable interpretation C♯CC♯

in the key of B minor but the much more natural interpretation C♯B♯C♯ in the key of F♯, to which the subject plainly modulates.

There are, without doubt, many other "rules" describing the way in which keyboard sequences guide the listener through tonal space, and some of them have been formulated and incorporated into the program. Whether or not these particular rules survive more careful investigation, the existence of such rules can no longer be doubted. Otherwise it would be impossible to understand how Western musicians succeed in recreating the tonal information which is inevitably lost in a keyboard performance, just as one can recreate imaginatively the three dimensions of a world which has been reduced to a two-dimensional photograph.

Conclusions and Implications

The view may now have become plausible that a listener committing a piece of music to memory is an "information-processing system" altogether different from a machine cutting a pianola roll. In writing down a piece of music which is played to him, he is giving overt expression to his capacity for interpreting it as a conceptual structure similar to that which originated in the mind of the composer.

The musical transcription program which I described elsewhere is, of course, only a first step towards the modelling of musical perception. The input to the program is not an acoustic waveform, but a mere specification of the precise times at which the performer depressed and released each note, and the output is a typed sequence of symbols which only just suffices for the specification of a musical score. There is nothing in the operation of the program corresponding to a listener's awareness of the higher-level relationships implicit in the music or to an appreciation of its quality. The program is, furthermore, bound by the prejudice that any sequence of notes presented to it is a melody with a more or less regular beat whose length is determined by the first few notes which are sounded; for this reason its transcription of a random sequence of notes bears little or no relation to the perceptions of a musical listener, who would be more than likely to abandon the attempt to discern any significant rhythmic or tonal relationships within such a sequence.

But is spite of all these limitations, the program succeeds in reconstructing with remarkable fidelity the rhythmic and tonal features of classical melodies, including the marks of phrasing, from reasonably competent keyboard performances. It transcribes, into a notation essentially equivalent to that of their published scores, unaccompanied melodies by composers as widely separated in time as Bach, Beethoven, Schubert, Wagner, Brahms, Debussy, and Britten.

Possibly the most advanced exercise on which it has yet been tested is the long cor anglais solo at the beginning of the Prelude to Act III of *Tristan und Isolde*; but an almost equally sophisticated passage, in view of its chromatic subtlety, is the opening bars of *L'Après-Midi d'un Faune*. Unfortunately, the capacity of a computer program to perform any such task is easily interpreted as implying that the task itself is essentially trivial; or perhaps any phenomenon may be classified as trivial once we succeed in giving a precise account of it.

But it must surely be a matter of some interest that the perception of music, at least in its more superficial aspects, seems to be a sufficiently orderly process to be modelled in this way. If, in this review, I have dwelt at much greater length on the concepts of rhythm and tonality than on the actual operation of the transcription program, that is only because, in the last analysis, no working model of musical perception can be of greater theoretical interest than the concepts and schemata upon which it is founded.

References

Bosanquet, P. H. M. 1875. *Elementary Treatise on Musical Intervals and Temperament.* London: Macmillan.

Chomsky, N. 1966. *Syntactic Structures.* The Hague: Mouton.

Cooke, D. 1959. *The Language of Music.* London: Oxford University Press.

Deutsch, D. 1977. Memory and attention in music. In *Music and the Brain*, ed. M. Critchley and R. A. Henson (London: Heinemann).

Helmholtz, H. L. F. 1885. *The Sensations of Tone.* London: Longmans.

Hindemith, P. 1942. *The Craft of Musical Composition.* London: Schott.

Lighthill, M. J., et al. 1973. *Artificial Intelligence—A Paper Symposium.* London: Science Research Council.

Lloyd, L. S., and H. Boyle. 1963. *Intervals, Scales and Temperaments.* London: Macmillan.

Longuet-Higgins, H. C. 1962. Letter to a musical friend. *Music Review* 23 (August): 244. Second letter to a musical friend. Ibid. 23 (November): 271. [Chapter 8 in present volume.]

Longuet-Higgins, H. C. 1972. Making sense of music. *Proc. R. Inst.* 45: 87.

Longuet-Higgins, H. C. 1976. The perception of melodies. *Nature* 263: 646. [Chapter 10 in present volume.]

Lyons, J. 1968. *Introduction to Theoretical Linguistics.* Cambridge University Press.

Meyer, L. B. 1956. *Emotion and Meaning in Music.* University of Chicago Press.

Neisser, U. 1966. *Cognitive Psychology.* New York: Appleton-Century-Crofts.

Tovey, D. F. 1949. *Essays and Lectures on Music.* London: Oxford University Press.

12

The Rhythmic Interpretation of Monophonic Music

H. C. Longuet-Higgins and C. S. Lee

When a listener hears a tune played or sung without accompaniment, he does not merely perceive the relative pitches and durations of the notes; he becomes aware, to a greater or lesser extent, of the tonal and rhythmic relations between them—for example, whether the tune is in a major or a minor key, and whether its rhythm is that of a march or a minuet. In assigning a rhythmic interpretation to a particular passage, the listener will generally be influenced by clues of many different kinds. The notes of the passage may be differently accented, some of them may be played *staccato* and others *legato*, rhythmic clues may be supplied by the tonal relationships between the notes, and in vocal music the words may exert a dominant effect. But there is one source of evidence that is always available, even when there are no words, when the notes are of indefinite pitch, and when the performance is devoid of accent, phrasing, or rubato: even in such improverished conditions the listener may still arrive at a rhythmic interpretation of the passage based solely on the relative durations of the notes. It was, we believe, Simon (1968) who first recognized the need for an account of how listeners perform this lowly perceptual task, and since that time Longuet-Higgins and Steedman (1971), Longuet-Higgins (1976), and Longuet-Higgins and Lee (1982) have suggested partial solutions of the problem. In this article we take a step back and consider the criteria that might lead a listener to favor a particular rhythmic interpretation of a given sequence of notes.

The article falls roughly into three parts. In the second and third sections we develop a generative theory of musical rhythms in the spirit of Lindblom and Sundberg (1972), but focusing particularly on the rhythms of individual bars and their relationship to the underlying meter. We pay special attention to the concept of syncopation. In the fourth section—the middle of the article—we suggest that in assigning a rhythmic interpretation to a sequence of notes the listener tends to avoid interpretations that demand either syncopations within bars or syncopations across bar lines.

Figure 1

The fifth section sketches some hypotheses about the perception of higher-level rhythmic structure. In the sixth section we consider the role of the performer in clarifying for the listener what might otherwise be rhythmically ambiguous sequences; in this section we pay special attention to the grouping of notes into phrases by the device of slurring together adjacent notes.

Our data and predictions, like those of Lindblom and Sundberg (1972), refer in the first instance to written music, just as the data and predictions of the theoretical linguist usually refer in the first instance to printed text. The reader may feel that this restriction evades a number of important issues connected with the live performance of real music; but the expressive qualities of live performances vary so widely that we have felt it essential to restrict the discussion in some way, and we have done this by concentrating on those directions about a performance that a composer customarily indicates in a musical score, such as whether a particular note is to be played *staccato* or *legato*. Our appeal is therefore not to the auditory sensibilities of the reader but to that part of his musical intuition that is engaged when he reads a musical score that indicates the values of the notes and the way in which they are meant to be phrased; in a sense we appeal to him as a potential performer, who has to decide how the musical listener is likely to interpret the music if it is performed according to the composer's directions.

We start, then, by considering unadorned sequences of note values and how a listener might assign them rhythmic interpretations. The following examples may convince the reader that the problem is more subtle than it might seem:

a. An isochronous sequence of notes such as the chimes of a clock has no obvious rhythmic structure, in that the notes might be felt to be grouped in twos or in threes, with or without "upbeats" (figure 1). But, at least if heard in isolation, the sequence is most unlikely to receive any of the theoretically possible rhythmic interpretations given as examples 1–3 in figure 2.

b. If the relative values of the notes are as shown in example 4 of figure 2, the sequence has the obvious rhythmic interpretation shown in example 5 rather than that shown in example 6 or that in example 7.

Figure 2

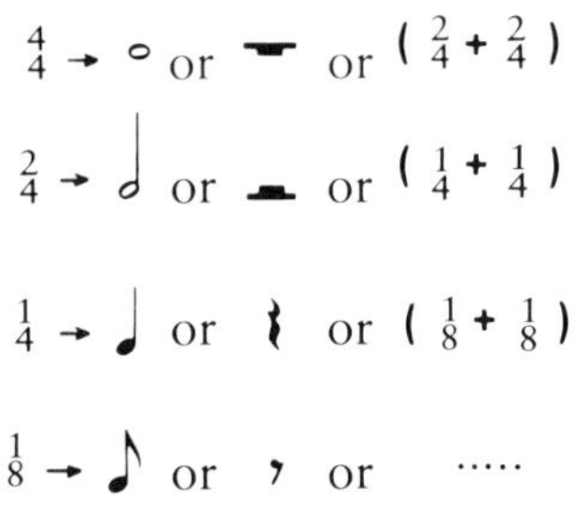

$\frac{4}{4} \rightarrow$ ○ or ▬ or $(\frac{2}{4} + \frac{2}{4})$

$\frac{2}{4} \rightarrow$ ♩ or ▬ or $(\frac{1}{4} + \frac{1}{4})$

$\frac{1}{4} \rightarrow$ ♩ or 𝄽 or $(\frac{1}{8} + \frac{1}{8})$

$\frac{1}{8} \rightarrow$ ♪ or 𝄾 or ⋯⋯

Figure 3

c. If, on the other hand, the relative note values are as shown in example 8, the obvious interpretation is that shown in example 9 rather than that shown in example 10 or that in example 11.

These particular facts (assuming the reader to accept them as such) are, of course, uninteresting in themselves; what is of interest is whether they exemplify any generalization about the perceptual propensities of musicians. We suggest that they do, and in the following paragraphs we attempt to formulate such a generalization as precisely as possible and to show that its implications accord with common musical intuition.

The Theory of Metrical Rhythms

In recent years it has been recognized (Martin 1972; Lindblom and Sundberg 1972; Longuet-Higgins 1976) that there is a close parallel between metrical rhythms (as opposed to the "free" rhythms of plainchant or recitative) and the syntactic structures of sentences. A metrical passage is one that could be assigned a "time signature" such as $\frac{4}{4}$, $\frac{3}{4}$, or $\frac{6}{8}$; what such a signature specifies is actually a grammar consisting of a set of context-free realization rules such as those illustrated in figure 3. In such a set of rules the symbols $\frac{4}{4}$, $\frac{1}{8}$, etc. (which have been adopted here for their appeal to musical intuition) are not themselves notes or rests, although they may be realized as such; they correspond to entities such as bars and beats and may be said to designate "metrical units" at various levels in a metrical hierarchy. In the commonest meters each bar or shorter metrical unit is divisible into either two or three metrical units at the next level down; if this is the case, the meter may be described as a "standard" meter and represented by a list consisting entirely of twos and threes. Thus the $\frac{4}{4}$ meter specified above would be represented by the list [2 2 2 . . .], indicating that the bar—the top-level unit—is divisible into two, the half-bar is also divisible into two, and so on.

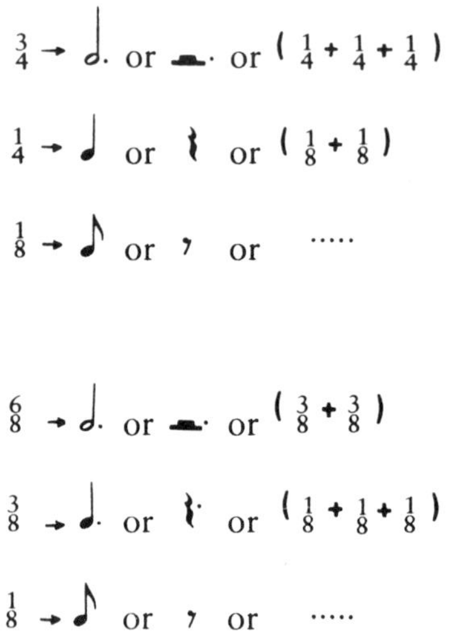

$\frac{3}{4} \rightarrow$ ♩. or ▬· or $(\frac{1}{4} + \frac{1}{4} + \frac{1}{4})$

$\frac{1}{4} \rightarrow$ ♩ or 𝄽 or $(\frac{1}{8} + \frac{1}{8})$

$\frac{1}{8} \rightarrow$ ♪ or 𝄾 or ·····

$\frac{6}{8} \rightarrow$ ♩. or ▬· or $(\frac{3}{8} + \frac{3}{8})$

$\frac{3}{8} \rightarrow$ ♩. or 𝄽· or $(\frac{1}{8} + \frac{1}{8} + \frac{1}{8})$

$\frac{1}{8} \rightarrow$ ♪ or 𝄾 or ·····

Figure 4

The time signatures $\frac{3}{4}$ and $\frac{6}{8}$ indicate meters with different realization rules, namely those illustrated in figure 4. The time signatures commonly used for specifying such meters usually imply only the first one or two divisions of the bar; in the notation that we are proposing the $\frac{3}{4}$ and $\frac{6}{8}$ meters would be symbolized as [3 2] and [2 3] respectively. (We will not enter here into the detailed description of "context-sensitive" meters, in which, for example, the first beat of a bar is divisible into two and the second into three, or of "variable" meters, in which the bar, or any subunit thereof, is optionally divisible into either two or three units at the next level down.)

By the progressive application of the realization rules of a given meter we generate a "tree" structure, in which the "root" node represents the whole bar and the other nonterminal nodes represent lower-level metrical units. At this point the terminal nodes of the tree are all either (sounded) notes or rests. In order to allow for tied notes (notes that are tied back to their predecessors, rather than being separately sounded), a further rule is now invoked: If any note N, sounded or tied, is immediately followed by a rest R, then R may be replaced by a note that is tied back to N (figure 5). Finally, in order to avoid meaningless sequences of rests or tied notes, it is stipulated that any divided metrical unit consisting entirely of rests, or of notes that are tied together, is replaced by an undivided unit composed of a single rest, or of a single note that is sounded or tied according to whether the first note of the replaced unit was sounded or tied (figure 6).

Figure 5

Figure 6

Figure 7

Any tree that results from the application of a set of metrical realization rules and the meter-independent replacement rules just stated is a possible rhythm that accords with the given meter. The relationship between the rhythm and the meter may be simply stated: The former is one of the structures that is generated by the grammar associated with the latter. On this view, a rhythm is much more than just a sequence of note values; it is a syntactic structure in which the note values are implicit in the terminal symbols, but do not by themselves define the rhythm; if they did, then no sequence of note values could be rhythmically "ambiguous"—open to alternative rhythmic interpretations—as such sequences undoubtedly are.

To show that the formal theory just described accounts quite naturally for the phenomenon of rhythmic ambiguity, one example should suffice. A bar consisting of a dotted crotchet (quarter note) followed by three quavers (eighth notes) might be, in common parlance, "in either $\frac{3}{4}$ or $\frac{6}{8}$". In the terms of the present theory, such a bar is generated both by the meter [3 2] and by the meter [2 3] (figure 7). The relative note values are the same for both, but the structures to which they belong are quite different, and it is the existence of these alternative structures that constitutes the rhythmic ambiguity of the sequence.

This example might suggest that rhythmic ambiguity is a merely sporadic occurrence, like syntactic ambiguity in sentences; but in fact it is an all-pervasive musical phenomenon. As the reader will already have noticed in examples a–c of the first section, even the most innocuous

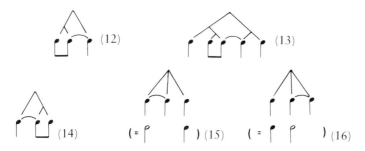

Figure 8

sequences of note values permit an unlimited number of rhythmic interpretations. Hence, insofar as listeners agree on the rhythms of given sequences
of note values, we can infer that the process of rhythmic perception must
be tightly constrained by some tacit assumption as to what counts, or does
not count, as a "natural" interpretation. In the following sections we are
largely concerned with the uncovering of just such an assumption, but in
order to state the assumption precisely, it is first necessary to clarify
another rhythmic concept—that of syncopation.

Syncopation

Informally, most musicians would agree that the rhythms illustrated in
examples 12 and 13 of figure 8 are syncopated, whereas those in examples
14 and 15 are not; example 16 is perhaps a marginal case. What is the
difference? Surely that, in examples 12 and 13 at least, a "heavier" note is
tied back to a "lighter" sounded note, whereas in examples 14 and 15 the
"heavier" note is the first of the tied pair. This observation suggests that in
order to pin down the concept of syncopation we need to define the
"weight" of a note or a rest. The following definition seems to accord with
intuition: The weight of a given note or rest is the level of the highest
metrical unit that it initiates. (The level of the topmost metrical unit is
arbitrarily set equal to 0, and the level of any other unit is assigned the
value $n - 1$, where n is the level of its "parent" unit in the rhythm.)

On this definition, the weights of the notes in examples 12–16 are as
shown in figure 9.

We are now in a position to define a syncopation:

If R is a rest or a tied note, and N is the next sounded note before R, and
the weight of N is no greater than the weight of R, then the pair (N, R) is
said to constitute a syncopation. The "strength" of the syncopation is the
weight of R minus the weight of N.

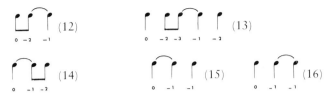

Figure 9

Thus in examples 12 and 13 we have syncopations of strength 1 and 2 respectively, and in example 16 a syncopation of strength 0, but examples 14 and 15 contain no syncopations—as musical intuition demands.

So far our discussion of rhythmic structure has been confined to the individual bar, for which the entire rhythm descends from a single node, the level of this node being arbitrarily set to zero. But many monophonic passages consist of sequences of bars which may or may not be grouped into higher metrical units. The concepts of level and weight may nevertheless be applied to such passages; the level of any metrical unit in a sequence of bars can still be defined as zero if the unit is a full bar, and can otherwise be assigned the value that it would have if the bar containing the unit were considered in isolation. The same applies to the concept of weight; the weight of a note or rest can still be defined as the level of the highest metrical unit that it initiates. Then it will be appropriate to describe a sequence of bars as syncopated if and only if one of the bars contains a syncopation, or some bar begins with a rest or a tied note that follows a sounded note of lesser weight.

Regular Passages

At this point the reader is invited to reconsider the note sequences a, b, and c of the first section. In each case, the "natural" interpretations of the sequence are the only ones that are entirely unsyncopated; in all the alternative interpretations there are notes that are tied back to sounded notes of equal or lesser weight. We may suspect that this is a general characteristic of "natural" interpretations: that when a sequence of notes can be interpreted as the realization of an unsyncopated passage, then the listener will interpret the sequence in this way. But the question immediately arises: If a note sequence is indeed the realization of an unsyncopated passage, how can the listener arrive at such an interpretation of it, using no more information than the relative durations of the notes? This is the problem to which we now turn.

We define a regular passage as a sequence of bars satisfying the following conditions:

1. Every bar, except possibly the first, begins with a sounded note. (This ensures that there are no syncopations across bar lines.)
2. All the bars are generated by the same standard meter.
3. There are no syncopations within any of the bars.

We now show that if a sequence of notes is indeed the realization of a regular passage, then the durations of the sounded notes (defined as the times between their onsets) supply useful evidence about the rhythmic structure. More precisely, we show that if D is the duration of the metrical units at level L, then the sounded notes whose durations exceed D must be spaced by time intervals that are multiples of D', where D' is the duration of the units at level $L + 1$. So by considering notes of progressively greater duration we can, as it were, build up the meter from the bottom, until we reach the lowest metrical unit that accommodates the longest sounded notes. We will now present the steps in the demonstration as a series of lemmas with accompanying proofs.

Lemma 1: Let N be a sounded note, and let U be the highest metrical unit that N initiates. Then the duration of N cannot exceed that of U.

Proof: Let N be any sounded note except the last one in the sequence, and let S be the next sounded note after N; let U be the highest metrical unit that N initiates. Suppose, contrary to the lemma, that the onset of S occurs later than the end of U. Then the end of U must coincide with the onset of a rest or tied note R; let V be the highest metrical unit initiated by R. Since the beginning of V coincides with the end of U, the level of V must be at least as high as the level of U. Hence the weight of R is no less than the weight of N, and so (N, R) constitutes a syncopation. But by hypothesis the rhythm is unsyncopated, and so the onset of S must occur no later than the end of U, as the lemma asserts.

Lemma 2: If D is the duration of the metrical units at level L, then every sounded note of duration greater than D must be of weight at least $L + 1$.

Proof: By lemma 1, no sounded note of weight L can have a duration greater than D. Therefore any sounded note of duration greater than D must be of weight at least $L + 1$.

Lemma 3: If L is any level in the meter, and if D is the duration of the units at that level, then the time intervals between the onsets of sounded notes of weight L or greater must be multiples of D.

Figure 10

Figure 11

Proof: The duration of any metrical unit of level higher than L must be a multiple of D, because when a metrical unit is divided, its daughter units are of equal duration. But the sounded notes under consideration all initiate metrical units of level L or greater, so the lemma follows.

The task of determining the meter of a regular passage, and thus revealing its rhythmic structure, may therefore be broken down into the following steps:

First one must locate the shortest metrical units, and these will have the same durations as the shortest sounded notes. (This is not true for syncopated passages, such as that shown in figure 10, where the crotchet does not delimit the shortest metrical unit, which is at the quaver level.) The next step is to consider the set of all sounded notes of duration longer than the shortest metrical unit. By lemma 3, the times of onset of these notes must be spaced by multiples of the next shortest unit. So if the shortest metrical unit is of duration D, and the highest common divisor of the spacings between sounded notes longer than D is D', we shall find that D'/D is an integer whose only prime factors are 2 and 3. (This conclusion rests, of course, on the assumption that the meter is standard.) If D'/D turns out to be a power of 2, then we can conclude that the metrical unit at the next level is of duration $2D$, and if D'/D is a power of 3, the duration of the unit must be $3D$. But if D'/D is a multiple of 6, then the next unit up might have a duration equal to either $2D$ or $3D$; in this case the meter, and consequently the rhythm, will be ambiguous (figure 11). If D'/D has any other value, such as $\frac{1}{2}$, 1, $\frac{3}{2}$, or 5, we can infer that there is no interpretation of the sequence as the realization of a regular passage.

The remaining stages in the determination of the meter follow exactly the same lines. D is multiplied by 2 or 3, as the case may be, and we form the set of all sounded notes whose durations are greater than the new value of D. If at any stage there is just one such note in this set, then the procedure fails to provide a regular interpretation of the sequence, since we need at least two notes of duration greater than D in order to determine D'. But if, for a given value of D, there are no sounded notes of duration greater than D, then the process comes to an end, and the metrical units of duration D can be identified as the bars of a regular passage.

To show how the procedure works in practice, we can apply it to note sequence 4 of figure 2. The shortest notes are the quavers, and these reveal the lowest level of the meter. The sounded notes that exceed a quaver in length are the crotchets and the dotted crotchets; the highest common divisor of their spacings is a crotchet, so that $D'/D = 2$. The next metrical unit above the quaver is therefore a crotchet unit. The only notes longer than a crotchet are the dotted crotchets, and their spacing is a dotted minim, equal to three crotchets, so that the duration of the next metrical unit is a dotted minim. There are no notes longer than a dotted minim, so the process terminates, and we obtain a rhythmic interpretation of the sequence as the realization of a regular passage in which the value of each bar is a dotted minim, and the meter is [3 2]. This is the interpretation given in example 5.

Note sequence 8 of figure 2 supplies another example. The shortest notes are the quavers, and the notes longer than a quaver are spaced by dotted crotchets, so that the quaver units must be grouped in threes forming dotted crotchet units. There are no notes longer than a dotted crotchet, so the process terminates, yielding an interpretation of the sequence as the realization of a regular passage consisting of dotted crotchet bars as shown in example 9. The associated meter is simply [3].

For the isochronous sequence discussed in example a of the first section, the procedure finds the shortest metrical unit—of value, say, one crotchet. But as there are no sounded notes longer than a crotchet, the process immediately halts, implying that every bar contains just one note. Although this interpretation is rather uninteresting, it does at least preclude the implausible interpretations shown in examples 1–3 of figure 2.

As a final example we may consider the note sequence that consists of a single crotchet followed by several quavers. The quaver immediately establishes itself as the shortest metrical unit, but now there is only one note longer than a quaver. The presence of this note indicates that if the passage is regular there must exist metrical units above the quaver level. But we need at least two notes longer than a quaver to delimit this higher metrical unit, and only one note is available. This shortage of evidence corresponds to the fact that the quavers might indeed be grouped in either twos or threes (figure 12).

In short, there exists a parsing algorithm for note sequences which, when

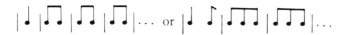

Figure 12

Figure 13

it succeeds, delivers an interpretation of the sequence as the realization of a regular passage. When the algorithm fails at any stage, its failure is evident from the fact that either D' is not computable (because there is only one sounded note of duration greater than D) or the computed value of D'/D is not a power of 2 or a power of 3.

We can now return, with a clearer insight, to the question why listeners regard some rhythmic interpretations of note sequences as so much more plausible than others. We propose the following answer: If the parsing algorithm just described succeeds in interpreting a note sequence as the realization of a regular passage, then this interpretation will be implicit in the listener's interpretation of what he hears. We may describe one interpretation as being "implicit" in another if all the metrical units of the former are present in the latter; thus an interpretation that specifies the rhythmic structures of all the bars of a regular passage is implicit in a richer interpretation that goes further and groups the bars together in twos or threes. Thus, the first of the two interpretations shown in figure 13 is implicit in the second.

We close this section with a pair of real musical examples, to illustrate how the rhythmic ambiguity inherent in the first few notes of a sequence can be resolved by later notes, on the assumption that the sequence is the realization of a regular passage. The examples are taken from the second movement of Beethoven's Piano Sonata Op. 109 and the second subject of the first movement of Brahms's Symphony No. 2. The relative note values (which in the first example disguise the rhythmic structure) are as shown in passages 17 and 18 of figure 14. The first six notes have the same relative values in these two passages.

For both sequences the parsing algorithm yields a quaver as the shortest metrical unit; the question then arises how the quavers are grouped. In

Figure 14

passage 17 the notes longer than a quaver are spaced by the following numbers of quavers: 6, 6, 3, 3, and 3; the highest common divisor of these numbers is 3, so the next metrical unit is of value 3 quavers, equal to one dotted crotchet. There are two notes longer than a dotted crotchet, and these are spaced by two dotted crotchets, so that the highest metrical unit accessible to the algorithm has a value of one dotted minim. In decreasing order of size, the metrical units are therefore a dotted minim, a dotted crotchet, and a quaver, and the meter is [2 3]. Parsing the sequence according to this meter, we obtain the regular passage shown in passage 19, which agrees with Beethoven's score.

In passage 18 the notes longer than a quaver have the following spacings: 6, 6, 2, 2, 2, 2, of which the highest common divisor is 2, so that the quavers must be grouped in pairs, forming crotchets. There are just two notes longer than a crotchet, and these are spaced by three crotchets, so that in descending order the metrical units must be a dotted minim, a crotchet, and a quaver, yielding the meter [3 2]. The sequence is thus interpreted as the realization of a regular passage in $\frac{3}{4}$ time, namely passage 20. Our analysis of the Beethoven example differs somewhat from that of Simon (1968), but he also made the point that the full meter of monophonic sequence may not become clear until after a few bars have been heard.

Higher-Level Rhythms

Our discussion has so far been confined to monophonic passages in which all the bars are generated by the same standard meter, but the bars are not necessarily grouped together into higher-level metrical units. In many passages, however—particularly complete melodies—higher-level groupings are musically apparent. In most folk tunes, for example, there is rhythmic structure at all levels, so that the whole passage may be assigned a rhythmic structure with a single root node (Lindblom and Sundberg 1972). In this section we consider how such higher-level rhythms might be perceived by the listener on the basis of the durations of the notes.

The problem of discerning higher-level structure arises, in the present context, from the fact that if every bar (except possibly the first) begins with a sounded note, then the bar itself is the highest-level metrical unit that is accessible by the parsing algorithm described in the preceding section. The reason is that no note can then have a duration longer than a single bar, so that if D is the duration of a bar, the duration D' of the units at the next level up cannot be computed from the highest common divisor of the spacings of notes with duration greater than D. For example, if the note durations are as shown in passage 21 of figure 14, only two metrical levels can be discovered by the algorithm, namely the crotchets and the quavers; this impasse corresponds to the fact that both passage 22 and passage 23 are possible regular interpretations of passage 21, satisfying conditions 1–3, but in these two interpretations the crotchets are grouped in different ways. One does feel, however, that 22 is a more natural interpretation than 23; one therefore looks for perceptual reasons why this might be so.

An obvious property of passage 21 is that the notes of duration greater than a quaver are spaced by minims (half notes), so that $D'/D = 4$, and since this is a power of 2, the algorithm adopts $2D$ as the duration of the metrical unit at the next level. But it might seem more natural to adopt D' itself, namely $4D$, as a higher metrical unit. If this idea is in fact adopted,

Figure 15

then one obtains not merely a grouping of the quavers into crotchets but also a grouping of the resulting crotchet units into minim units, with the result shown in passage 22, and perhaps this is one reason why 22 seems a more natural higher-level interpretation than 23. (The resulting rhythmic repetition will undoubtedly reinforce this interpretation, as against passage 23, but repetition cannot be the whole story, because for the note sequence 24, shown in figure 15, the natural interpretation is still that shown in passage 25 rather than that shown in 26.)

We are suggesting, in short, that although higher-level rhythms cannot be inferred from the regularity assumption as it stands, the listener may nonetheless perceive such higher-level groupings even if the notes of duration greater than D are quite widely spaced, provided that D'/D is still a power of 2 or a power of 3. But we must stress that this conjecture is logically independent of the assumption that the passage is regular in the precise sense defined in the preceding section.

The Role of Phrasing

So far our discussion has been confined to extremely impoverished musical material, in which the only information accessible to the listener is that which can be derived from the times of onset of the notes. In real musical performances, however, the performer will not be content merely to sound the notes at appropriate moments; he will accent some notes more than others, advance or delay the onsets of some of the notes, and play some notes *staccato* and others *legato*. In this section we will sketch a theory of the communicative function of such devices and will suggest that, in some cases at least, they supply essential clues to the rhythmic structure. In particular we will be concerned with the device of "slurring", although doubtless similar considerations would help one to understand the effects of accent or *rubato*.

Figure 16

In a musical performance of any interest there will be occasional gaps between consecutive notes. If, in a given sequence of notes, the offset of every note coincides with the onset of its successor, then we may describe the sequence as "slurred" or as constituting a single "phrase"; it follows that any sequence whatever can be partitioned into phrases, with a gap between the end of each phrase and the beginning of the next. We propose that phrasing, so defined, is not merely an ornamental device but can serve an essential function in making clear to the listener the rhythmic structure of a passage. The examples given in figure 16 should make clear the basis for this view. Thus a sequence of quavers phrased as shown in 27 is likely to be assigned the same meter as the unphrased sequence 28, whereas if the quavers are phrased as shown in 29 the natural rhythmic interpretation will be closely related to that of 30. The effect of the phrasing seems to be to create "virtual" notes of duration equal to the individual phrases; if these durations are sufficiently long, they may reveal metrical units of duration greater than the longest notes of the unphrased sequence. To illustrate the role that phrasing can play in the rhythmic clarification of note sequences, we may consider just one simple rule for phrasing the notes of a passage, whether regular or not: If any metrical unit is divided (into two or three), then slur together all the sounded notes that belong to it except those that descend from its rightmost node.

For a passage in which every bar begins with a sounded note, the effect of this phrasing rule is to replace the sounded note by a virtual note which lasts for at least half the bar, or two-thirds of the bar if the meter is ternary at the highest level. It is not difficult to see, furthermore, that the resulting sequence of virtual notes will be regular even if some of the bars of the unphrased sequence were originally syncopated; see figure 17. So if a

Figure 17

passage is phrased according to the rule in question, then the resulting sequence will be amenable to the parsing algorithm of the fourth section, and it becomes possible for the listener to establish its meter on the basis of the virtual sequence and to use this meter (assuming it does not change from bar to bar) for parsing the individual notes of each phrase and thereby arriving at a rhythmic interpretation in which not necessarily all the bars are unsyncopated.

To illustrate the use of phrasing for revealing the rhythmic structures of even syncopated passages we may consider a final pair of examples (derived from the opening of Bach's D Minor Klavier Concerto). The note values are as shown in passage 31 of figure 18. If the passage is slurred according to the given phrasing rule, the result is as shown in 32. The corresponding virtual sequence 33 leads to the rhythmic interpretation indicated by 34, which is of course the interpretation that Bach intended. If, however, Bach's own bar lines are moved forward by one quaver, then the application of the phrasing rule leads to the slurring given in 35, corresponding to the virtual sequence 36. Applying the parsing algorithm to this sequence, we obtain the quite different rhythmic interpretation indicated in 37. The reader will, perhaps, agree that such an inappropriate phrasing of the passage in question is liable to quite mislead the listener as to its rhythmic structure. The phrasing rule that we have used for illustration is not, of course, intended as an infallible guide to musical performance, but merely an illustration of our thesis that phrasing is not merely an ornamental device but can have a crucial role to play in the elucidation of rhythmic structure.

Conclusions

• Any given sequence of note values is in principle infinitely ambiguous, but this ambiguity is seldom apparent to the listener.

• It appears that in choosing a rhythmic interpretation of such a sequence the listener is guided by a strong assumption: If the sequence can be interpreted as the realization of a regular passage in the sense of the fourth section, then that is how it is to be interpreted.

Figure 18

• The listener may well group the bars of this passage into higher-level metrical units.

• Phrasing can make an important difference to the way in which the listener perceives the rhythm of a sequence. Even syncopated sequences which would otherwise be difficult to interpret can be rhythmically clarified by slurring the notes appropriately.

Acknowledgements

We are indebted to the Royal Society of London and the Nuffield Foundation for financial support.

References

Lindblom, B., and J. Sundberg. 1970. Towards a generative theory of melody. *Svensk Tidskrift for Musikforskning* 52: 71–88.

Lindblom, B., and J. Sundberg. 1972. Musical Acoustics and Music Theory. STL-QPSR 4.

Longuet-Higgins, H. C. 1976. The perception of melodies. *Nature* 263: 646–653. [Chapter 10 in present volume.]

Longuet-Higgins, H. C. 1978. The perception of music. *Interdisciplinary Science Rev.* 3: 148–156. [Chapter 11 in present volume.]

Longuet-Higgins, H. C. 1979. The perception of music. *Proc. R. Soc. Lond.* B 205: 307–322. [Chapter 13 in present volume.]

Longuet-Higgins, H. C., and C. S. Lee. 1982. The perception of musical rhythms. *Perception* 11: 115–128.

Longuet-Higgins, H. C., and M. J. Steedman. 1971. On interpreting Bach. In *Machine Intelligence* 6, ed. B. Meltzer and D. Michie (Edinburgh University Press). [Chapter 9 in present volume.]

Martin, J. G. 1972. Rhythmic (hierarchical) versus serial structure in speech and other behaviour. *Psychological Rev.* 79, no. 6: 487–509.

Simon, H. A. 1968. Perception du pattern musical par AUDITEUR. *Sciences de l'Art* 5, no. 2: 28–34.

Simon, H. A., and R. K. Sumner. 1968. Pattern in music. In *Formal Representation of Human Judgment* (New York: Wiley).

Steedman, M. J. 1977. The perception of musical rhythm and metre. *Perception* 6: 555–569.

Sundberg, J., and B. Lindblom. 1976. Generative theories in language and music descriptions. *Cognition* 4: 99–122.

13 The Perception of Music

H. C. Longuet-Higgins

You are browsing, let us imagine, in a music shop, and come across a box of faded pianola rolls. One of them bears an illegible title, and you unroll the first foot or two, to see if you can recognize the work from the pattern of holes in the paper. Are there four beats in the bar, or only three? Does the piece begin on the tonic, or some other note? Eventually you decide that the only way of finding out is to buy the roll, take it home, and play it on the pianola. Within seconds your ears have told you what your eyes were quite unable to make out—that you are now the proud possessor of a piano arrangement of "Colonel Bogey".

Music presents the psychologist with a variety of problems, ranging from the auditory discrimination of tones to the emotive effects of different kinds of music. I shall say nothing in this lecture about audition as such, except to remark that if the perception of music were limited by the acuity of the ear, then we would be unable to tell when a musical performance was out of time or out of tune. Nor shall I say anything about musical aesthetics; the subject is far too difficult and too controversial. The question I shall consider is simply this: given that a listener can distinguish time intervals differing by a few hundredths of a second, and can tell the difference between two notes separated by a keyboard semitone, how does he use this information in discerning the rhythmic and tonal structure of a piece of music? How, in short, does the brain solve the problem you were unable to solve in the music shop? Can we construct a precise and plausible theory of the cognitive processes that must be involved?

In order to understand the nature of musical perception, one must distinguish clearly between a piece of music as such and any performance of it. A performance is a temporal succession of sounds, whereas a piece of music is a composition of notes linked together by rhythmic and tonal relations. In Western classical music—which is the only sort of music I am competent to discuss—the rhythmic relationships have to do with the way

Figure 1

in which the notes are grouped conceptually in the time dimension: into duplets, or triplets, or duplets of triplets, or what you will. Thus a regular succession of six notes may be thought of as a duplet of triplets or as a triplet of duplets, but this distinction is mental, not physical. A competent performer can help the listener recreate whichever rhythm the composer had in mind, but in the last resort the listener must supply the interpretation himself, on the basis of his familiarity with the composer's language. The same applies to tonal relations; the conceptual structure created by the listener contains more information than the actual sounds that enter his ears. In one context he will interpret an interval of six keyboard semitones as an augmented fourth, in another as a diminished fifth (figure 1). The paradox—if it is a paradox—disappears if one remembers that information that is lost in transmission can be made good by the recipient if he has inside knowledge about the signal. For the kind of music we are discussing, this will be a knowledge of the principles of construction of rhythmic figures and tonal sequences.

However, if the perception of music requires the listener to impose rhythmic and tonal relations on the sounds that enter his ears, how are we to tell what relations he has actually imposed, and whether they correspond with those intended by the composer or the performer? This might well be an embarrassing question were it not for the existence of stave notation, which makes fully explicit the rhythmic and tonal relations between the notes of a classical composition. Every music student is taught not only to read from a score, but also to transcribe into stave notation music which is played to him on the piano. If his transcription agrees closely with the score from which the music was played, we can hardly doubt that he perceived the music in the way intended by the composer. If there is disagreement, no immediate conclusion can be drawn: his attention may have wandered; he may not have mastered the notation completely; he may have misperceived the music, perhaps because it was incompetently played; there might even be a notational mistake in the score itself. But if he can consistently reproduce the scores of the passages played to him by his teacher, this is an acceptable guarantee of the musical competence of all concerned, and it becomes a matter of great interest exactly how he does it.

Figure 2

Later, I shall describe a computer program which transcribes classical melodies played on a keyboard into the equivalent of stave notation (Longuet-Higgins 1976). The writing of the program has been an attempt to spell out, precisely and in detail, the steps by which a musical listener—whether literate or not—arrives at a rhythmic and tonal interpretation of a tune that is played to him (Longuet-Higgins 1978). The program is deficient in many respects, but I hope that some of the underlying ideas may be of interest. The kind of information that it is designed to deal with is shown below:

[12 154 227]
[36 285 294]
[31 322 327]
[31 336 341]
[32 349 383]
[31 384 407]
[35 445 453]
[36 484 527]

This input is encoded on a pianola roll, produced by connecting the organ to a high-speed paper-tape punch; it supplies the keyboard position of each note that was played, and its time of onset and time of offset in centiseconds. The corresponding output is

[[[24 C STC][[−5 G STC][0 G STC]]][[1 AB][−1 G TEN]]]
[[[REST][4 B STC]][1 C TEN]]

Each bar is represented on a new line, and the nested brackets indicate its rhythmic structure. A number indicates the keyboard position of a note relative to its predecessor. The name of the note is indicated by a letter or a pair of letters—"AB" means "A flat", to be distinguished from "GS", meaning "G sharp". In certain cases there is a mark of phrasing such as "STC" for *staccato* or "TEN" for *tenuto*. It is then a purely automatic matter to transcribe the symbols by hand into stave notation; the result is figure 2, which seems quite unexceptionable.

If we assume that our listener can tell a jump of n keyboard semitones from a jump of $n + 1$, the numbers in the output need not detain us. But the indications of rhythm and phrasing are remarkably straightforward if we realize just what liberties the performer took with the tempo: the times of onset of the first four quaver units differed by 37, 27, and 35 cs respectively. As for the tonal relations between the notes, even this apparently trivial example illustrates the fact that the choice of a name for a note is not determined merely by its keyboard position; one must also take account of its tonal relation to its fellows. The educated musician will agree that the fourth note is indeed an A♭; to have identified it as a G♯ would have misrepresented its relation to the other notes.

The theory underlying the program falls naturally into two parts, which I shall deal with separately. The first part is concerned with rhythm and phrasing, the second with tonality. Many of the basic concepts will be familiar to musical theorists, but those having to do with the perception of music, as opposed to its acoustic realization, are my own. At the end I shall return to the program, with further examples, and consider some of the important problems that it leaves unsolved.

Rhythm

Let us look again (figure 3) at the score of the little cliché shown in figure 2, disregarding the vertical positions of the notes on the stave. The bar lines and the "beams" joining the notes indicate the temporal structure quite clearly. The second and third notes form a duplet, and this combines with the first note to form a duplet at a higher level. The fourth and fifth notes form a duplet at the same level; and so the bar contains two equivalent metrical units, as required by the time signature. The same applies to the second bar; here the first unit is a rest paired with the following note, and the second is filled by the last note. Pairing the two bars together we obtain a binary tree, and this represents the rhythm as concisely as we could hope to. Its nodes correspond to metrical units at successively lower levels—the whole piece, the bars, the beats, and so on. Contrast this with the worm's-

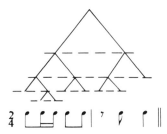

Figure 3

eye view, which regards the rhythm merely as a succession of note values —crotchets, quavers, and so on. Such a view, all too common, fails to capture the fact that a given sequence of note values may well admit two or more different rhythmic interpretations. Take, for example, a sequence of six quavers; in $\frac{3}{4}$ time the quavers form three duplets, whereas in $\frac{6}{8}$ time they make up two triplets. The two rhythms are shown in figures 4 and 5; they can be represented either as trees or by bracketing the notes together. (Each pair of matched brackets corresponds to one node of the tree.)

In the language of modern linguistic theory (Lyons 1968), one may associate the rhythmic ambiguity of a six-quaver sequence with the existence of two distinct ways of "generating" such a sequence from an underlying grammar. The grammar that generates classical rhythms is unusually simple in that it contains only one basic rule. The rule says, in effect, that a metrical unit at a given level may be directly realized as a note or a rest; alternatively, it may be divided into n equal metrical units at the next level down. The value of n is usually 2, and sometimes 3, but seldom any other value such as 5 or 7. When the value of n depends only on the level of the metrical unit, we obtain a "pure" metre such as $\frac{3}{4}$ time or $\frac{6}{8}$ time, though mixed metres are also quite common in classical music.

The rule needs to be supplemented in two particular respects. First, to allow for "tied" notes, in a rhythm containing one or more rests, a given rest may be encroached upon by the preceding note if this overflows its own metrical unit; the rest must then be replaced by a note tied to its

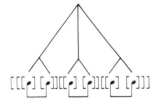

Figure 4

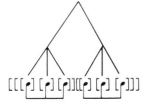

Figure 5

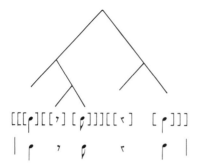

Figure 6

Figure 7

predecessor. Secondly, trills and other ornamental clusters of notes are most naturally viewed as being all attached to the same node of the tree; we shall meet examples later.

A final point in favour of defining a rhythm as a tree is that it helps us to see what distinguishes a "syncopated" rhythm from an ordinary one. Figure 6 gives an example—the rhumba rhythm. There are two rests. Between the first rest and the preceding note there is just one closing bracket, indicating that the first note initiates a higher metrical unit than the following rest. However, between the second rest and the preceding note there are no fewer than three closing brackets, and a heavy syncopation is felt at this point. It seems that whenever a rest or a tied note follows a sounded note which initiates a metrical unit at a lower level, we perceive a syncopation, and that its strength can be estimated by counting the closing brackets that intervene and subtracting 1. Syncopated rhythms are, as a matter of experience, more confusing perceptually than unsyncopated ones: they are more likely to precipitate a revision of the metrical hypothesis from which the rhythm was derived. This point is illustrated by figure 7, which is taken from the last movement of the Sibelius Violin Concerto. The passage in question makes us revise our opinion about the metre in every single bar. The reason, surely, is that a $\frac{3}{4}$ metre implies a

Figure 8

Figure 9

syncopation in every odd-numbered bar, whereas a $\frac{6}{8}$ metre implies that every even-numbered bar is syncopated, and given the choice we opt for a metre which assigns a nonsyncopated rhythm to the notes that we actually hear.

In perceiving the rhythm of a piece, the listener's primary task, I shall assume, is to keep track of the beat. (The word "beat" may be used to refer either to a metrical unit at the appropriate level or to the time at which that unit begins; here I am using the word in the latter sense.) If the listener can identify two notes which occur on successive beats, he is in a position to predict when the next beat will occur; if another note is sounded at about that time, he will tend to identify its time of onset with the next beat and to update, if necessary, his current estimate of the tempo. Here is a simple electronic device, built by D. C. Jeffrey, which makes just this sort of prediction. I give it two beats by pressing this button, and it ticks away happily at the same tempo until switched off.

Exactly what clues a listener attends to in locating the first few beats is a largely unsolved problem, though Steedman (1977) has suggested rules which can be exploited when the first few notes differ in length. We can, at least, be reasonably sure that notes occurring on the beat are not necessarily louder or longer than others; on the organ or the harpsichord, for example, the performer has no control over the relative loudness of successive notes. Much can be achieved with careful phrasing, but the way in which a particular choice of phrasing affects the perception of rhythm is still largely mysterious. Here is just one example of the obvious importance of phrasing, taken from the opening of Bach's D minor Harpsichord Concerto (figures 8 and 9). The first time I play it, you will, I hope, hear it as figure 8, which is what Bach wrote; the second time you may well hear it as figure 9. The only difference is in the phrasing of each note—whether it was played *staccato* or *legato*—though you will have to take my word for this.

However, it is not enough for the listener merely to identify the notes and rests that fall on the beat; he must also create a node on the rhythmic tree for every note that falls between two beats. The word "between" immediately raises a problem. If a note is sounded very slightly before or very soon after a predicted beat, we want to regard it not as falling between two beats but as signalling a slight change of tempo. So we must introduce a time constant, which I shall call the "tolerance", into the theory. A note is deemed to fall between two beats if and only if its time of onset differs from the times of the two beats by more than the tolerance. In advance of experiment, one can only guess at the magnitude of the tolerance (which turns out, in fact, to be about a tenth of a second); all that one can be sure of is that it must safely exceed the temporal resolution of the ear, so that we are able to perceive changes of tempo without losing track of the beat.

If a note falls between beats, or interrupts any lower metrical unit, then that unit must be divided into n equal subunits, where the value of n is determined by the metre which the listener has in mind. In general, it seems, the listener is conservative in his expectations, and interprets what he hears in terms of a pure metre; he is prepared to revise it from time to time, but only when necessary. In the program, the initial choice of metre is pure binary, but a change in metre is called for if the current metre implies a syncopation or a "distortion" of tempo which can be avoided by adopting an alternative metre. Thus if a triplet of notes is encountered when a duplet might have been expected, the duplet hypothesis, applied to the first two notes of the triplet, will imply an inordinate quickening of the tempo, and will therefore be rejected in favour of a metre that interprets the group as a triplet.

The details of the theory are unavoidably complicated, but the idea is quite simple. A node of the rhythmic tree sprouts n daughter nodes if, and only if, the corresponding metrical unit is interrupted by the onset of a note. Since a unit that is shorter than twice the tolerance cannot, in principle, be interrupted, there is a built-in restriction to the amount of ramification that can possibly occur; when this is complete, every note finds itself close to the beginning of some metrical unit and becomes attached to the corresponding node. Every unoccupied node is then supplied with a rest, which may later be transformed into a tied note.

Once the rhythmic tree has been constructed, it is a relatively simple matter to determine the phrasing. Every note will have been assigned to a metrical unit, but in general its time of offset will not coincide with the end of that unit. If the note lasts for less than half the unit, it is classified as *staccato*. If it extends into the following rest—by more than the tolerance—that rest is converted into a tied note. If it lasts for more than half but appreciably less than the whole unit, it is classified as *tenuto*; otherwise as *legato*. Ornaments such as trills, in which the times of onset of successive notes differ by less than the tolerance, are treated as if they were unitary musical events, with no internal rhythmic structure.

In the present version of the theory the tolerance plays three different but related roles. First, it limits the extent to which the tempo may accelerate or decelerate without causing the rhythm to disintegrate; secondly, it determines the perceptual distinction between notes played *staccato*, *tenuto*, or *legato*; and thirdly, it decides whether a rapid succession of notes will be heard as an ornament or as a rhythmically structured figure. It may be that three different time constants should be introduced for these three purposes, but to do so would considerably complicate the rhythmic component of the program. As things are, a value of 10–15 cs for the tolerance seems to serve all three purposes quite well, judging from an extensive series of experiments with the program.

But time presses, and we must now turn to our other main problem—the perception of tonality.

Tonality

The word "tonality" covers those aspects of a composition that depend on the musical intervals between the notes. In a century when music has fallen under the tyranny of the keyboard, it is customary to regard musical intervals as mere differences in pitch, to be measured in fractions of an octave. But this doctrine begs a number of questions. First, what is so special about the octave, anyway? Secondly, why should one wish to divide it into twelve equal parts rather than thirteen? And thirdly, can people actually divide musical intervals into equal parts, except with the help of log tables and frequency meters?

These questions are not difficult to answer, but the answers are important for the perception of music. First, the octave is special because any musician can tune an octave to the satisfaction of any other musician, and the same applies to the fifth and the major third, for example. Secondly, the keyboard divides the octave into twelve rather than thirteen equal parts because the fifth is very nearly a whole number of twelfths of an octave, but not a whole number of thirteenths; and the same applies to the major

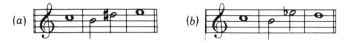

Figure 10

third. And thirdly, there is no evidence worth quoting that Western musicians can divide such intervals accurately into equal parts; I would be astounded if anyone in this room could tune a violin so that its strings were accurately one fifth of an octave apart, or if anyone else could tell whether or not he had succeeded in doing so.

A simple thought experiment will indicate the subtlety of tonal perception. Suppose that you are an expert violinist, and that I ask you to reproduce a simple melody that I play on the organ. Then you will probably play it better in tune than I do; what is more, you will vary the magnitudes of the keyboard intervals in accordance with the context. If I play the sequence shown in figure 10(*a*) you will slightly reduce the interval between the second and third notes so that it becomes an accurate major third; but if I play the one shown in figure 10(*b*) you will slightly stretch the interval between the second and third notes, so that it becomes a diminished fourth. We can only conclude that you are imposing some tonal interpretation upon the notes, over and above their actual sounds.

A slightly different thought experiment points to exactly the same conclusion. This time I merely ask you to name the notes that I play, telling you that the first one was a C. If you are familiar with standard notation, you will name them in the first case as C, B, D♯, and E, but in the second case as C, B, E♭, and D, despite the fact that the first three notes have the same keyboard positions in both sequences. What is the distinction that you are making, and what is the evidence on which you base it?

In order to understand such phenomena we must get behind standard musical notation and consider the perceptual basis of tonality. The frequency ratios of tonal intervals have, of course, been fully discussed by a number of authors, notably Helmholtz (1885), but purely acoustic questions are not our present concern. The only fact we need is that musical intervals, although they cannot be created by division, can certainly be formed by addition and subtraction. We shall then find that all the intervals of Western classical music can be created in this way from just three basic intervals—the octave, the fifth, and the major third (Longuet-Higgins 1962a, b). Thus an octave minus a fifth gives a fourth, a fourth plus a major third gives a major sixth, and so on.

It is helpful to visualize the situation geometrically. We construct a

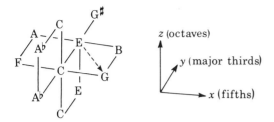

Figure 11

three-dimensional array of notes in the following way. At the origin we put middle C, and above it the C which lies an octave higher (figure 11). On the right we put the G which lies a fifth above middle C, and in front the E which lies a major third above middle C. Continuing in this way, we obtain an array in which the note at the point (x, y, z) lies x fifths, y major thirds, and z octaves above middle C. The coordinates (x, y, z) may have negative as well as positive values, and in principle the array extends to infinity in all six directions. I shall refer to it as "tonal space". It has a number of useful properties.

First, the tonal coordinates of a note determine its keyboard position, but the converse is not true. The keyboard position of the note (x, y, z) in semitones above middle C is simply

$$p = 7x + 4y + 12z,$$

because the fifth spans seven keyboard semitones, the major third spans four, and the octave twelve. Secondly, the intervals of tonal music now appear as vectors in tonal space. Thus the interval from E to G, for example, is simply the dotted vector, with components $(1, -1, 0)$. But a given keyboard interval corresponds, in general, to a number of different intervals in tonal space. A keyboard interval of four semitones, for example, might be either a major third, with components $(0, 1, 0)$, or a diminished fourth, with components $(0, -2, 1)$, meaning one octave minus two major thirds. The two intervals are noticeably different when accurately tuned; but the important point is that a violinist can mark the acoustic distinction between them only if he has the relevant conceptual distinction in mind.

Finally, the concept of tonal space makes it possible to clarify the important notion of a key, in the following way. We start by reducing tonal space to two dimensions, by treating notes separated by an octave as equivalent. The result is shown in figure 12, and I shall refer to it as "harmonic space" (Longuet-Higgins 1972). The symbol at the point (x, y) stands for all those notes which lie x fifths, y major thirds, and any number

$y = 3$	D♯	A♯	E♯	B♯	F×	C×	G×	D×
2	B	F♯	C♯	G♯	D♯	A♯	E♯	B♯
1	G	D	A	E	B	F♯	C♯	G♯
0	E♭	B♭	F	C	G	D	A	E
−1	C♭	G♭	D♭	A♭	E♭	B♭	F	C
−2	A♭♭	E♭♭	B♭♭	F♭	C♭	G♭	D♭	A♭
$x =$	−3	−2	−1	0	1	2	3	4

Figure 12

of octaves above middle C. A key may then be defined as a neighbourhood in harmonic space similar to the one bordered by the black rectangle. In the experimental arrangement, there are lights behind the panel, and I will now connect the notes of the keyboard to the lights behind the black rectangle. The keyboard note at position p is connected to the light bulb at position (x, y) if and only if p differs from $7x + 4y$ by a multiple of 12. As a result, every note on the keyboard is now connected with just one note inside the rectangle. If I now play a few chords in the key of C, we will see what happens. If I play a chord of C major, F major, or G major we get an L-shaped pattern which correctly indicates the tonal relations within these chords. If I play a chord of C minor, F minor, or G minor the patterns are different, but still compact. However, a chord of F♯ major gives a disjointed pattern bearing no relation to its tonal structure. The reason is that the black rectangle frames a region of tonal space to which the chord of F♯ major does not belong. Let us call this region the "extended key" of C, since it includes all the notes of C major and of C minor in the correct tonal relations to one another, and two extra notes as well. The tonic, C, and the dominant, G, are safely buried in the middle of the rectangle.

If a piece of music, played on the keyboard, lies entirely within one extended key, then once the listener has identified that key his tonal problems are solved, because it will allow exactly one interpretation of each note that he hears. To illustrate, let me play the subject of Bach's Musical Offering, which happens to lie entirely within the extended key of C. The symbols that light up are just those indicated by Bach in his score; F♯, not G♭, and D♭, not C♯, for example. He uses, in fact, all the notes of the extended key except B♭. But how are we to identify the key in the first place? What counts as evidence that the melody is in one key rather than another?

No one, as far as I know, has ever suggested a general answer to this question; but the great majority of unaccompanied melodies, and almost all fugue subjects, begin on either the tonic or the dominant and move, more or less immediately, towards the other side of the extended key. Therefore, one may start by assuming the first note to be the tonic, and setting up the extended key accordingly. If the second note lies to the right of the first, or directly over it, the original hypothesis is supported; otherwise the first note was more likely the dominant, and the extended key should be moved one place to the left in harmonic space. Later notes may well cast doubt on either choice of extended key; but that will happen in any case, if the melody modulates. This simple-minded algorithm is actually the one used in the program; it plainly leaves much to be desired.

However, if, as we have seen, every note played on the keyboard can be accommodated within any extended key, then what evidence could possibly lead a listener to abandon his original choice of key? This is a deep question, but if one studies the scores of classical melodies, focusing attention on the tonal intervals between successive notes, one finds that these intervals are usually rather short vectors in harmonic space. From time to time we do find consecutive notes lying in non-adjacent rows of the extended key, but when such a "remote" interval occurs it is almost always preceded, and followed, by a less remote interval in the opposite direction. (In this context the word "direction" refers to the direction of movement in harmonic space, not the direction of pitch movement.) Let us go back to the two sequences considered earlier, shown in figure 10. The first two notes suggest, in both cases, that one should identify the first note as the tonic, because the second note does indeed lie to its right on this assumption. But then there is a large jump, of two rows. In the second sequence this is followed by a smaller opposite movement, so there is reason to doubt that the third note was an E♭, but the first sequence seems to call for two large jumps in succession, and is correspondingly difficult to perceive as such. The difficulty can, however, be neatly avoided by reinterpreting the third note as a D♯, which is harmonically much closer to both the B and the E. But at a price: since D♯ does not belong to the original key, the rectangle must be moved one level upwards, and we find ourselves in the extended key of E.

In order to convert these observations into general rules for the tonal interpretation of melodies, one has to formalize the concept of the "remoteness" of an interval. To do this we begin by defining the "sharpness" of a

G♭	D♭	A♭	E♭	B♭	F	C	G	D	A	E	B	F♯	C♯	G♯	D♯	A♯
−6	−5	−4	−3	−2	−1	0	1	2	3	4	5	6	7	8	9	10

Figure 13

note as the quantity $q = x + 4y$ (figure 13), where (x, y) are its harmonic coordinates. On this definition the sharpness of a note is closely related to the signature of its major key; thus A, with three sharps in its key signature, has a sharpness of 3, while A♭, with four flats, has a sharpness of −4. The "remoteness" of an interval is then just the difference in sharpness between the two notes it connects. Thus the interval from B to D♯ has a remoteness of 4, while the interval from B to E♭, a diminished fourth, has a remoteness of 8. At this point the theory merges with the standard classification of intervals. Intervals with a remoteness less than 6 turn out to be those usually described as "diatonic"; intervals of remoteness greater than 6 are "chromatic". In keeping with mediaeval tradition, the word "diabolic" seems appropriate for intervals such as the tritone which have a remoteness equal to 6. No interval used in melody has a remoteness as great as 12, though intervals of remoteness 11 are occasionally found.

The distinction between diatonic and chromatic intervals is just what we need in order to account for the tonal interpretation of melodies. At any time after the first two notes have been sounded, the listener will have a certain extended key in mind, Let L, M, and N be the tonal interpretations which that key assigns to any three consecutive notes of the melody. Then the following rules seem to hold with fair generality:

1. If the intervals LM and MN are both chromatic, then M is assigned a new interpretation M', which makes both intervals diatonic, and the key is felt to change so as to take in M'. We have already seen this rule at work.

2. If K, L, M, and N are four successive notes, and the three intervals LM, KM, and LN are all chromatic, then M is again reinterpreted, and the key is changed accordingly. This rule captures the difficulty of perceiving an interval as chromatic in a context where it is neither adequately prepared nor adequately resolved.

3. Otherwise, if N is a note of the *major* key and MN is a rising chromatic semitone, then M is reinterpreted so as to make $M'N$ a diatonic semitone; but no change of key is precipitated. This rule accounts, among other things, for the perceptible difference in tonality between descending and ascending chromatic scales.

To recapitulate briefly: The main assumption is that the listener inter-prets each note as lying within the extended key suggested by the first two notes; but if this interpretation requires the notes to jump about too violently in harmonic space, then he is forced to select a new key in which the offending intervals give place to less remote ones. Thus the perception of tonality, no less than the perception of rhythm, involves an interplay between the sounds themselves and the frame of reference created by the listener. In the perception of rhythm the frame of reference is the tempo and the metre; in the perception of tonality it is the extended key.

The Program

The program is, of course, no more than an embodiment of these ideas in computational form; and the ideas themselves are very far from complete. First, the tonal rules which I stated cannot possibly be applied as they stand to anything but unaccompanied melodies, where the notes are sounded one at a time. Secondly, if a melody is covertly polyphonic, again the rules may well fail, because the melodically significant intervals are those between alternate, not successive, notes. Thirdly, even in purely melodic music the contextual constraints on chromatic intervals should really be applied only to intervals between notes in the same phrase, and we still lack any formal theory of the musical phrase and its scope.

I mentioned earlier the tricky problem of finding where the beat falls, and the number of beats in the bar. This problem is finessed in the program by requiring the performer to preface his performance of the melody by a bar's worth of beats on some low note, preferably an octave below the first note of the melody, to avoid biasing the initial choice of key.

The paper tape generated by the performance is dealt with by the program as follows. First, there is a tonal analysis, which ignores any octaves or repeated notes in the melody. Each note is assigned a place in the current key, and if a chromatic interval is found, the context is examined to see if a change of key is called for. The next stage is a rhythmic analysis. Each beat is examined in turn, and the onset time of each note is used both for constructing the rhythmic hierarchy and for correct-ing the estimated tempo. In the course of this analysis the offset time of each note is used for determining the phrasing.

The final stage corresponds to the exercise of musical literacy; it consists of displaying on paper the structure created by the rhythmic and tonal analyses. As we have seen, this output is not exactly easy to read, but it can be transcribed quite automatically into stave notation.

```
[ 12 24     114]          [ 22 1308 1320]
[ 12 148    238]          [ 29 1332 1452]
[ 24 274    399]          [ 26 1450 1495]
[ 31 400    554]          [ 22 1508 1517]
[ 34 551    587]          [ 21 1528 1536]
[ 32 586    671]          [ 20 1546 1556]
[ 27 669    711]          [ 27 1570 1696]
[ 32 707    794]          [ 24 1692 1734]
[ 26 795    831]          [ 20 1752 1762]
[ 31 829    860]          [ 19 1774 1782]
[ 24 863    895]          [ 18 1792 1808]
[ 29 895    989]          [ 26 1815 1930]
[ 31 987   1021]          [ 29 1928 1934]
[ 29 1020 1145]           [ 27 1932 2062]
[ 27 1140 1242]           [ 26 2059 2188]
[ 26 1268 1282]           [ 25 2183 2446]
[ 24 1289 1298]           [ 24 2491 2628]
```

```
[ 12 C] [ 7 G]
[[[ TIED G] [ 3 BB]] [–2 AB]] [[[ TIED AB] [–5 EB]] [ 5 AB]]
[[[ TIED AB] [–6 D]] [[ 5 G] [–7 C]]] [[ 5 F] [[ TIED F] [ 2 G]]]
[–2 F] [–2 EB TEN]
[[[–1 D] [–2 C STC] [–2 BB]] [ 7 F]] [[ TIED F] [–3 D TEN]]
[[[–4 BB STC] [–1 A STC] [–1 AB]] [ 7 EB]] [[ TIED EB] [–3 C TEN]]
[[[–4 AB STC] [–1 G STC] [–1 FS]] [ 8 D]]] [[ TIED D] [ 3 F –2 EB]]
[[ TIED EB] [–1 D]] [[ TIED D] [–1 DB]]
[ TIED DB] [ TIED DB]
[–1 C]
```

Figure 14

Figure 14 shows how the program handled two excepts from the cor anglais solo in the Prelude to Act III of *Tristan und Isolde*. The input from the organ is shown above, followed by the output, which is transcribed by hand.

Two points are worth noting. First, the listener is called upon to perceive a change from duplets to triplets in bar 5, and the program spots this change; secondly, the published score indicates a grace note at the end of bar 7, and the program does attach this grace note to the same node as the following note. The rhythm and tonality agree in all details with Wagner's score; there are a few discrepancies in phrasing—Wagner marked all the triplet quavers as *staccato*—but for these the performer must accept the blame.

Finally, the input from the organ and the output for a later section of the same melody are shown, followed by the transcription, in figure 15. Again, the rhythm is correctly specified, though there are a few discrepancies in phrasing. As for the tonality, the main perceptual problem is that of following the rapid succession of modulations beginning in the second bar. There is, none the less, only one note with a tonality at variance with that indicated by Wagner: he wrote the second C♯ in the second bar as a D♮.

Conclusion

I hope it is clear that the perceptual theory on which the program is based is far from complete. It assumes, for example, that the perception of rhythm and the perception of tonal relations can be treated as independent processes; concepts such a repetition, variation, progression, and resolution are conspicuous by their absence from the theory. It is powerless to deal with the perception of atonal or arhythmic music, and it passes no judgements about the musical acceptability of arbitrary sequences of tones. Its intellectual distance from a theory of musical appreciation is therefore as great as the distance between a theory of speech perception and a theory of poetry, whatever form such a theory might take. But one may reasonably suppose that the processes of musical appreciation can only begin after the creation of a conceptual structure on which they can get to work.

In closing, I must express my warmest thanks to Mark Steedman, Peter Buneman, Geoffrey Hinton, and David Jeffrey for many useful discussions and much practical help.

[19	148	190]	[23	830	839]
[31	280	287]	[31	856	987]
[29	302	309]	[27	986	1027]
[27	322	329]	[24	1049	1054]
[34	347	466]	[23	1068	1075]
[31	474	518]	[22	1087	1096]
[27	538	548]	[29	1111	1153]
[26	559	566]	[26	1152	1157]
[25	578	586]	[22	1174	1183]
[33	605	648]	[21	1194	1202]
[30	646	657]	[20	1211	1220]
[26	669	678]	[27	1232	1270]
[25	687	696]	[24	1272	1279]
[24	707	714]	[20	1295	1304]
[32	729	760]	[19	1316	1325]
[29	769	777]	[18	1336	1348]
[25	791	801]	[26	1360	1619]
[24	811	820]			

[[[12 G STC] [–2 F STC] [–2 EB STC]] [7 BB]]
[[TIED BB] [–3 G TEN]]
[[[–4 EB STC] [–1 D STC] [–1 CS STC]] [[8 A] [TIED A] [–3 FS]]]
[[[–4 D STC] [–1 CS STC] [–1 C STC]] [[8 AB] [REST] [–3 F STC]]]
[[[–4 DB STC] [– 1 C STC] [– 1 B STC]] [8 G]]
[[TIED G] [–4 EB TEN]]
[[[[–3 C STC] [–1 B STC]] [–1 BB STC]] [[7 F] [TIED F] [–3 D STC]]]
[[[–4 BB STC] [–4 A STC] [–1 AB STC]] [[7 EB] [TIED EB] [–3 C STC]]]
[[[–4 AB STC] [–1 G STC] [–1 FS]] [8 D]]

Figure 15

References

Helmholtz, H. L. F. 1885. *The Sensations of Tone*. London: Longmans.

Longuet-Higgins, H. C. 1962a. Letter to a musical friend. *Music Rev.* 23 (August): 244. [Chapter 8 in present volume.]

Longuet-Higgins, H. C. 1962b. Second letter to a musical friend. *Music Rev.* 23 (November): 271. [Chapter 8 in present volume.]

Longuet-Higgins, H. C. 1972. Making sense of music. *Proc. R. Inst. G.B.* 45: 87.

Longuet-Higgins, H. C. 1976. The perception of melodies. *Nature* 263: 646. [Chapter 10 in present volume.]

Longuet-Higgins, H. C. 1978. The perception of music. *Interdisc. Sci. Rev.* 3, no. 2: 148. [Chapter 11 in present volume.]

Lyons, J. 1968. *Introduction to Theoretical Linguistics*. Cambridge University Press.

Steedman, M. 1977. The perception of musical rhythm and metre. *Perception* 6: 555.

Epilogue

"I see," said Johann Sebastian, "but mayn't I, just sometimes, write notes which people won't be able to tell whether I'm in D major or B minor just for a bar or two?"

Saint Cecilia raised her eyebrows ever so slightly. "I expect you will, my dear, whether I say yes or no. But if you do it too often people will begin to wonder whether you understand harmony any better than you seem, from the words of your question, to understand ordinary grammar."

"I like that!" said Johann Sebastian. "You understood perfectly well what I meant, grammar or no grammar. Anyway, your beastly old organ's out of tune."

And he ran away and invented Equal Temperament.

III Language

For such a brash intrusion into linguistics as is made in these chapters, some apology is called for. Mine is that language is too rich a source of insight to be left out of account in studying the human mind. Most of these papers were written at a time when theoretical linguists were preoccupied with the syntax of natural language, to the virtual exclusion of semantics. Questions about the processes underlying the actual production and comprehension of utterances were relegated to the category of "performance"; psycholinguists might wish to attend to such matters, but the proper study of the linguist was the native speaker's "competence"—his ability to decide whether a string of words did or did not belong to his language.

Into this deserted area marched the artificial-intelligentsia, headed by Terry Winograd with his program SHRDLU. Here for the first time was a computational model of what might be actually happening when a person is addressed in his or her own language and is moved to reply. The psychological community greeted the program with blank incomprehension, and the linguists declared it to be "of no linguistic interest". I was working on similar problems at the time and had been invited by my patron, the Royal Society, to review my current work. "The Algorithmic Description of Natural Language" (chapter 14 here) was the outcome—an essay in what would now be described as computational linguistics. Two issues were uppermost in my mind at the time: the psychological processes accompanying the use of tense and aspect, and the way in which we handle fragmentary sentences such as "Will Harry?" or "Just after?". The program that Anthony Kenny later nicknamed "Waiting for Cuthbert" was informed by an unashamedly *ad hoc* theory, but that was because there was no existing theory to be adopted or amended.

A natural language, is, however, a seamless robe, and once one had embarked on a study of English verb forms it was inevitable that one would soon be faced with the problem of modality. "Modal Tic-tac-toe" (chapter 15) and "Question-Answering in English" (chapter 16) are included here because they were the best Stephen Isard and I could do to relate our ideas about modals and quantifiers to current logical and linguistic orthodoxy. I suspect there are still insights to be gleaned from reflecting upon the various ways in which a person might deploy the resources of tense, aspect, and modality in discussing the progress of a game of chess, or even "noughts and crosses".

The idea of adopting a simple game as a scenario for the use of tense, aspect, and modality also inspired the work of Anthony Davey, described in chapter 17. In the course of a game a sentence such as "If you had ... I would have ..." has an absolutely clear meaning in relation to the moves already made and the strategies of the two players, so the production of appropriate comments is at least free from unresolved semantic issues. The most obvious feature of Davey's program is that is produces spontaneous discourse, rather than merely responding to factual questions; but it raises a number of other interesting problems that have been largely neglected. The naturalness of the program's prose, which was *not* stored as a repertoire of useful phrases, is a classic case of *ars celare artem*.

The grammatical knowledge built into Winograd's SHRDLU and Davey's PROTEUS was language-specific, having to do with the way in which ideas are expressed in English. But a major problem in the theory of language is how it is acquired in the first place, and this is the issue addressed in "Learning to Count" (chapter 18). Almost every human infant succeeds in picking up its parents' language; could one hope to construct a plausible theory of how this was possible? The concept of a "language-acquisition device" had received much disussion among the Chomskian linguists, but there seemed to be acute difficulties in constructing a device which would learn a human language—or any well-defined part of a language—from textual information alone. Richard Power and I doubted the realism of such a task and decided to explore the idea that the most natural way to learn a language is from a set of instances of its use. The resulting program learns the numeral grammars of a wide variety of languages in a pleasingly realistic manner; perhaps in due course it will be extended to other semantic domains.

The last chapter in this part, "Tones of Voice", is the only one which deals specifically with the spoken word. It is a lecture that I gave at a workshop on the computer processing of speech held in Cambridge in 1984. A preoccupation with the written word often deafens us to the extraordinary variety and subtlety of audible speech—until we consider the problem of designing a machine that could tell the difference between admiration and sarcasm on the basis of the speaker's tone of voice. In the lecture I attempted to circumnavigate the prevailing disagreements about the very foundations of the theory of prosody—for example, whether the elementary units of intonation are pitches, pitch variations, or pitch differences. Perhaps not surprisingly, the lecture adopts a typically English view of the matter.

14

The Algorithmic Description of Natural Language

H. C. Longuet-Higgins

The subject of this lecture, natural human language, is one about which we have an immense amount of knowledge, but hardly any precisely formulated knowledge. All of us in this room can speak at least one language with fluency, but are at a loss to tell where our words come from or how we string them together. And when others address us in our own tongue, not only do we understand them immediately and without effort, but we can distinguish delicate shades of meaning from their tone of voice and choice of construction. For this reason the faculty of language undoubtedly qualifies—to borrow a phrase from Freeman Dyson—as something sufficiently obvious never to have been investigated scientifically. Or at least it did until recently, because it is commonly agreed that linguistics, although a very old subject, is still a very young science.

Ultimately language is a biological phenomenon, and its study belongs among the B sciences rather than the A sciences, to adopt the Royal Society's standard classification. As a form of social behaviour it concerns the sociologist and the anthropologist; as a manifestation of cognitive activity it falls within the province of the psychologist. Language offers us an incomparable window into the mind—one which is denied to even the most patient observer of non-human animals. Through language we are able to communicate our thoughts and experiences, and to make our wishes known to one another. A great deal is to be learned about the way in which we perceive the world and organize our knowledge of it by studying closely the way in which we talk about it and the things which we say to one another. And if we can formulate an adequate theory of language in psychological terms, there are bound to be important implications for neurophysiology. In so far as the neurophysiologist is concerned to understand "how the brain works", he must equip himself with a non-physiological account of the tasks which the brain and its peripheral organs are able to perform; only then can he form mature hypotheses as to how these tasks are carried out by the available "hardware"—to borrow a phrase from computing science.

There are many obvious differences between the brain and man-made computers, but one thing at least is clear: that the human brain is by far the most powerful and versatile computer in existence. In this chapter I shall try to develop this comparison in relation to human language. One must not imagine, of course, that the hardware of present-day computers bears any resemblance at all to the neuronal circuitry of our own thinking machines; but there are good reasons for thinking that at least some of our mental processes can be usefully described in algorithmic terms. Though native speakers of English, for example, differ widely in their linguistic performance, one can idealize the "competence" of a native English speaker in a systematic and orderly fashion. This idea was first given precise expression by Noam Chomsky in his now classic book *Syntactic Structures* (Chomsky 1957), which brought into existence the subject of transformational grammar. The transformational grammarian attempts, broadly speaking, to characterize the program which converts a meaning, or "deep structure", into a well-formed sentence in a natural language, and, conversely, to characterize the logical processes which are involved in the assignment of meaning to such a sentence. But, as I shall hope to show later, the concept of a program has further applications in the theory of language. In the first place, language is but one of the activities of an animal whose general behaviour is much too complex to be amenable to anything less than an elaborate algorithmic description. Secondly, human utterances are not produced *in vacuo*, but in response to the needs or wishes of the speaker in a particular real-world situation, a particular conversational context, and a particular set of beliefs about the state of mind of the hearer. Any theory of the manner in which all these factors combine to determine the form of the utterance is bound to be exceedingly complex, and to be virtually inexpressible without ambiguity except in the logically foolproof terms of a formal algorithm. And thirdly, what is an utterance in a natural language but a message to the hearer; and how can we understand its effect upon him unless we regard it as a piece of program which his knowledge of the language enables him to interpret, much as a computing system equipped with a suitable compiler is able to interpret a set of instructions supplied to it in, say, Fortran? (Longuet-Higgins 1969)

I shall be suggesting, then, not only that we should think of the production and comprehension of natural utterances as processes describable in algorithmic terms, but that our utterances themselves should be thought of as pieces of program whose effect is to modify one another's behavioural predispositions in a manner dependent on the circumstances of the conversation; and finally that, to be fully coherent, consistent, and testable against the commonly available facts about natural language, our linguistic theories now can, and should, be realizable as computer programs with which we can actually converse. Anyone who has tried to represent a process of any complexity in programmatic form will know how difficult it is to cover all logical possibilities and to be quite sure of the outcome when the program is put to the test. The discipline of doing so not only clears the mind wonderfully; it raises all kinds of questions of detail which otherwise would almost certainly escape attention.

Existing Conversational Programs

The idea of casting a theory of conversation in the form of a program with which one can hold a conversation is no longer new. The most famous early program of this sort was Eliza (Weizenbaum 1966), designed to simulate the activity of keeping a conversation going without attending in any real sense to its substance. There is a story of a salesman visiting the headquarters of Project MAC at the Massachusetts Institute of Technology, where Eliza was invented. He sat down at a teletype and switched it on, thinking he was connecting himself to one of the professors there. The following conversation took place:

Salesman: Do you think I can use the computer this morning?
Teletype: WHY DO YOU ASK?
S: I might be able to make some additional telecomp sales.
T: WHY AREN'T YOU SURE?
S: My prospective customers have never seen a demonstration of the system.
T: DOES THIS MEAN VERY MUCH TO YOU?
S: Of course it does.
T: YOU SEEM VERY POSITIVE ABOUT THAT.
S: This is ridiculous.
T: WHAT DO YOU MEAN THIS IS RIDICULOUS!
S: Is there any reason why I can't use the computer now?
T: TELL ME MORE ABOUT YOUR PROSPECTIVE CUSTOMERS.
S: Please dial me up on 491-1850.

It is not difficult, being wise after the event, to see roughly how the program works; it is designed to hold on to the conversational initiative at all costs, by changing the subject if necessary, in order to hide its inability to answer any of the operator's questions. To do this it must be able to recognize the difference between statements, commands, and questions; to identify noun phrases in the remarks of the operator, and certain constructions which permit a standard response; and to interchange the first and the second person in a grammatically correct fashion. The strong points of the program are its conversational strategy and its grammatical tactics; its weaknesses, from the point of view of linguistic theory, are in its semantics: in no sense does it understand what is said to it, or mean what it says. Nevertheless, Eliza does demonstrate what can be done with quite limited computational resources in modelling particular aspects of the use of language; and her example has inspired others to be more ambitious. Without doubt the most impressive achievement in this area to date has been a program written by Winograd, also of MIT, and described at moderate length in his recent book (Winograd 1970, 1972). The distinctive feature of this program is its possession of a well-defined universe of discourse, consisting of an imaginary table top bearing a box and a set of blocks of various shapes and colours, which can be rearranged by a crane-like "arm", the current state of the world being displayed all the time on the screen of an oscilloscope. The operator can issue instructions and ask questions in simple English, and the program will obey such instructions as it can, and answer in good English all those questions which it "understands", indicating what commands it cannot obey and which of the operator's utterances strike it as unintelligible, ambiguous, or misconceived. Here is an extract from a conversation between Dr. Winograd and his program:

Man: Had you touched any pyramid before you put the green one on the little cube?
Computer: YES, THE GREEN ONE.
M: When did you pick it up?
C: WHILE I WAS STACKING UP THE RED CUBE, A LARGE RED BLOCK AND A LARGE RED CUBE.
M: Why?
C: TO GET RID OF IT.
M: Why did you do that?
C: TO CLEAN OFF THE RED CUBE.
M: Why did you clear off that cube?
C: TO PUT IT ON A LARGE GREEN CUBE.
M: Why did you do that?
C: TO STACK UP THE RED CUBE, A LARGE RED BLOCK AND A LARGE GREEN CUBE.

M: Why did you do that?
C: BECAUSE YOU ASKED ME TO.
M: How did you do it?
C: BY PUTTING A LARGE RED BLOCK ON THE TABLE; THEN LETTING GO OF IT; THEN PUTTING A LARGE GREEN CUBE ON IT; THEN LETTING GO OF THAT CUBE; THEN PUTTING THE RED CUBE ON THAT CUBE; THEN LETTING GO OF THAT CUBE.

One is immediately struck by the program's extraordinary virtuosity in the use of the pronouns "one", "it", and "that". But the main interest of the program is its capacity to understand, in a non-trivial sense, what the operator says to it; to form plans with a hierarchical structure of goals and subgoals; and to remember not only the current state of the "universe" and the actions leading to it but also, for each action which it took, the state of its plans at the time.

It would be quite impossible to do justice to this achievement in a few minutes, so I shall confine myself to a few relevant observations about it. First, it is an essential part of Winograd's thesis that the responses of a hearer to utterances in natural language cannot be understood unless we suppose the hearer to be able to interpret them in relation to a universe of discourse. One is reminded, naturally, of the semantics of formal languages (Tarski 1931), where it would be impossible even to state the central problems without the concept of an interpretation—of a universe in which a well-formed symbolic formula can be assigned a meaning. But whereas in formal logic one can separate quite cleanly matters of syntax from matters of interpretation, one may have serious doubts (McCawley 1968) as to whether the well-formedness of an utterance in a natural language is a matter which can be decided, in general, without reference to the circumstances in which it is actually employed.

The second main point which Winograd makes explicitly, and which has been the guiding principle of our own work (Isard and Longuet-Higgins 1972), distinguishes natural language from formal declarative languages such as the first-order predicate calculus: that the elements of natural utterances—and indeed the utterances themselves—represent not just individuals and logical relations but *procedures* for implementation by the hearer. For commands and questions this proposal has an immediate appeal, because in logical languages we do not normally deal with anything but declarative statements; but in natural language even statements are readily amenable to interpretation as procedures. If we are playing blindfold chess, and I say "My king's pawn takes your queen's pawn", I am specifying a brief procedure by which you are to bring your mental chess-board up to date; you should first identify the two pawns in question by their relations with my king and your queen respectively, and then take the latter pawn off the board, replacing it by the former. If these remarks seem to labour the obvious, let us bear in mind that the obvious is often too close for us to see it clearly; as Chomsky has remarked, the problem of "psychic distance" is one of the biggest obstacles to the formal description of natural language.

The Forms of Simple Utterances

In order to give body to some of these general assertions, I will now describe some simple programs of our own, much smaller and less complex than those of Weizenbaum or Winograd but illustrating, I hope, one or two points of general linguistic interest.

The first of these programs is designed to produce simple English sentences in which the main verb is transitive and the subject is in the third person singular; the latter restriction is for convenience only. Figures 1, 2, 4, and 5 show some exchanges with the program as they took place on the teletype. Each exchange is initiated by the operator typing ".sentence;", which is in effect the instruction to produce a sentence. The program types back "question:" and the operator types "1" or "0" for yes or no respectively. Thereafter, the first word on each line is typed by the program, and what follows the colon is typed by the operator. (For those whose formal grammar is rusty, the "progressive" and "perfective" aspects are those expressed by the constructions "to be doing something" and "to have done something" respectively.) I have used the words "agent" and "patient" to differentiate these concepts from those of "subject" and "object"; thus in an active sentence the subject is the agent and the patient the object, whereas in a passive sentence the patient is the subject, and there is no object.

The grammar incorporated into the program is but a small part of the grammar of English verbs; how small a part is indicated by the program's restricted repertoire of questions to the operator. Even so, its construction calls for considerable care and attention to the details of English syntax; for example, to the fact that the emphatic negative "not" attaches itself to the beginning of the verb, whereas the non-emphatic form "nt" is attached to the end of the auxiliary.

Having asked all its questions, the program prints a colon, and the operator then has the choice of typing ".surface =>", in which case the fully formed sentence is printed out within a single pair of brackets, as in figure 1; or of typing simply "=>", in which case the sentence appears

```
   .SENTENCE;
QUESTION: ∅
EMPHATIC: ∅
SUBJECT: STEPHEN;
PASSIVE: ∅
VERB: SEE;
PROGRESSIVE: 1
PERFECTIVE: 1
PAST: ∅
NEGATE: ∅
PATIENT: PETER;
:  .SURFACE=>

** [STEPHEN HAS BEEN SEEING PETER],
:
```

Figure 1

```
   .SENTENCE;
QUESTION: 1
EMPHATIC: ∅
SUBJECT: JOHN;
PASSIVE: ∅
VERB: HAVE;
PROGRESSIVE: 1
PERFECTIVE: ∅
PAST: ∅
NEGATE: 1
PATIENT: LUNCH;
: =>

** [[IS NT] [JOHN] [[HAVING] [LUNCH]]],
:
```

Figure 2

with its full set of nested brackets, as in figure 2. The nested brackets betray
the manner in which the program constructed the sentence; a more complete description of the surface structure would, of course, indicate the
grammatical category of each bracketed string of words. Thus the final
output in figure 2 is a condensed version of the more complete phrase
marker given in figure 3. Orthodox transformational grammarians may be
uneasy about the precise form of figure 3—in particular about the absence
of the word "nounphrase" from the figure, and the absence of any indication of the composite character of the strings [IS NT] and [HAVING].
Perhaps I may deflect such criticisms by remarking that figure 3 represents
only the surface structure of the utterance, and conceals some of the steps by
which the various phrases were constructed. A more substantive departure
from transformational grammar should, however, be mentioned; namely

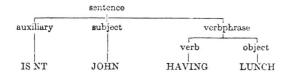

Figure 3

```
   .SENTENCE;
QUESTION: Ø
EMPHATIC: 1
SUBJECT: FRED;
PASSIVE: Ø
VERB: HAVE;
PROGRESSIVE: Ø
PERFECTIVE: 1
PAST: 1
NEGATE: 1
PATIENT: SUPPER;
:  .SURFACE= >

** [FRED HAD NOT HAD SUPPER],
:
```

Figure 4

```
   'TAUGHT'– >'TEACH'.EN;
:  .SENTENCE;
QUESTION: Ø
EMPHATIC: 1
SUBJECT: HARRY;
PASSIVE: 1
VERB: TEACH;
PROGRESSIVE: Ø
PERFECTIVE: 1
PAST: 1
NEGATE: 1
AGENT: PETER;
:  .SURFACE= >

** [HARRY HAD NOT BEEN TAUGHT BY PETER],
:
```

Figure 5

that this question was actually constructed, not by applying an interrogative transformation to the corresponding statement "John isn't having
lunch", but by using a rule to the effect that whereas a statement has the
form [subject, auxiliary, verbphrase], in a question the order is [auxiliary,
subject, verbphrase]. Such a rule can of course be implemented if and only if
grammatical categories like "subject" can be identified otherwise than by
their place in any pre-existing ordered set; and the program which produces figures 1–5 expresses the idea that, in so far as a characteristic
ordering is associated with a feature such as "interrogative", this feature
produces the required ordering on an unordered set, rather than altering a
pre-existing ordering of the set in question.

Figures 1–5 call for some other detailed comments. In figure 1 the word
"has" is the present tense form of the progressive aspect, whereas in figure
2 the word "having" is the present participle of the main verb. In figure 4
both sorts of "have" appear in the appropriate syntactic variants. Figure 5
captures a detailed fact about English (and many other languages), namely
that many verbs are irregular in their conjugation, but that we can learn
irregular forms independently of our general grammatical knowledge. The
first line of the figure, typed by the operator, informs the program that the
past participle of "teach" is "taught"—which, incidentally, is not the same
as saying that "taught" is the past participle of "teach".

My main purpose in writing this program was to express the idea that
grammatical categories such as "sentence", "auxiliary", and so on are not
just class names but functions which call for an input of some kind and
deliver an appropriate output. Whether the input to this particular program
may be properly described as "semantic" is a moot point; but at least the
supplier of the information need know nothing of the syntax of English—
only that the verb he puts in is the English word for the action he has in
mind. A foreigner equipped only with a dictionary could use the program
to produce sentences as impeccable as those in figures 1–5, provided he
was possessed of the semantic ideas represented by words such as "question", "subject", and "agent".

But we may well ask: Can one demonstrate in a more clear-cut fashion
the generation of a natural utterance in response to a semantically significant input? The following programs attempt to do this.

The English Names of the Natural Numbers

Rather early in life we learn the names "one", "two", "three", ..., "eighty-
five", ..., "three thousand seven hundred and two", and so on. Each of
these words or strings of words (of which there is an unlimited number)

```
: [TWO HUNDRED AND FIFTY THREE].VALUE= >

** 253,
:
  45678.NAME= >

** [FORTY FIVE THOUSAND SIX HUNDRED AND SEVENTY EIGHT],
:
  36789.NOM= >

** [TRENTE SIX MILLE SEPT CENT QUATRE VINGT NEUF],
:
  [QUARANTE NEUF].VALEUR= >

** 49,
:
```

Figure 6

conforms to certain grammatical rules, which, for example, are violated by the string "two and hundred seven thousand three". The rules are not very difficult (or very easy) to formulate precisely. Of more interest is the fact that each grammatical word string of this class *means* something, namely one of the natural numbers. And conversely, for every natural number there is a string of words which is its English name. So we should be able to write a program which will accept any grammatical number name as input and deliver the named number as output. In practice, of course, the numbers cannot to handled entirely abstractly, and it will be convenient to employ a decimal representation; but we may regard this representation as adequately expressing the value of the number.

Figure 6 shows four such programs at work. The first, called "value", takes a well-formed English number name and produces the number in decimal form; the second, called "name", performs the reverse process. The third and fourth are the corresponding programs for French.

In writing these programs (and my colleague Stephen Isard has written a more sophisticated one which can cope with non-standard forms such as "nineteen hundred and seventy two"), one begins to understand more clearly why the grammatical rules for forming number names have the form that they do. The reason seems to be that a number name is essentially a sequence of instructions for producing a number. If I enunciate slowly the words "one...hundred...and...twenty...three...thousand...four... hundred...and...fifty...six", you will build up, by stages, a decimal representation of the number I am naming; and it is not difficult to formulate reasonable hypotheses as to how people do so. Likewise with the process of naming a number, rather than making sense of a name; the way

```
: [FIVE HUNDRED AND EIGHTY FOUR].VALUE.NOM= >

** [CINQ CENT QUATRE VINGT QUATRE],
:
  [CINQUANTE SIX MILLE SEPT CENT QUATRE VINGT NEUF].VALEUR.NAME= >

** [FIFTY SIX THOUSAND SEVEN HUNDRED AND EIGHTY NINE],
:
```

Figure 7

in which we place the power words "hundred", "thousand", and "million" is an obvious clue to the manner in which we take a decimal number to pieces in our minds and pass the pieces over to the hearer for re-assembly.

Figure 7 shows how the operations of the English and French number programs may be combined for the purposes of translating number names between the two languages. Application of "value" and then "nom" translates a name from English into French; the reverse process is achieved by applying first "valeur" and then "name". This simple example illustrates the usefulness of "comprehension" as an aid to translation; a word-for-word transcription would produce such gibberish as "fifty six thousand seven hundred four twenty nine".

Natural and Programming Languages

I now want to press further the analogy between natural languages and the languages which have been developed for programming computers. To this end figures 8–10 show the entire text of a program for playing noughts-and-crosses written in POP-2, the high-level language designed and developed in Edinburgh by my colleagues Burstall and Popplestone (1971). Figures 8 and 9 are primarily for the connoisseur, but even to the unpractised eye figure 10 will, I think, seem to mean something. What it says, in effect, is this: "To move: if some squares are valuable to you, then you take any one of the squares which are valuable to you; otherwise if some squares are valuable to me, then you take any one of the squares which are valuable to me; otherwise you take any one of the squares which are vacant."

Inspection of the earlier functions "valuable" and "useful" reveals that a square is valuable if it is vacant and lies on a line the other two squares of which are already in the player's possession; in other words, if it is a winning square for the player. With this knowledge we can understand the strategy of the program, and very feeble it is; but that is by no means the end of the matter. I have already drawn attention to the fact that the last

```
[TICTAC]  16.Ø5  24  4  1972

VARS A B C D E F G H K ME YOU; [ME]– >YOU; [YOU]– >ME;
[A]– >A; [B]– >B; [C]– >C; [D]– >D; [E]– >E; [F]– >F; [G]– >G; [H]– >H; [K]– >K;

OPERATION 1 SQUARES; [%A, B, C, D, E, F, G, H, K%]; END;
FUNCTION R1; [%A, B, C%]; END; FUNCTION R2; [%D, E, F%]; END;
FUNCTION R3; [%C, H, K%]; END; FUNCTION C1; [%A, D. G%]; END;
FUNCTION C2; [%B, E, H%]; END; FUNCTION C3; [%C, F, K%]; END;
FUNCTION D1; [%A, E, K%]; END; FUNCTION]D2; [%G, E, C%]; END;
OPERATION 1 LINES; [%.R1,.R2,.R3,.C1,.C2,.C3,.D1,.D2%]; END;

FUNCTION START;
  APPLIST([%A, B, C, D, E, F, G, H, K%], LAMBDA X; NIL– >X.TL; END;);
END;

FUNCTION WHICH XS RY;
  [%APPLIST(XS, LAMBDA X; IF X.RY THEN X CLOSE; END;)%]
END;

FUNCTION HOWMANY XS RY; LENGTH(WHICH(XS, RY)); END;

FUNCTION SOME XS RY;
  IF XS.NULL.NOT AND XS.HD.RY OR SOME(XS.TL, RY)
    THEN TRUE ELSE FALSE CLOSE;
END;
```

Figure 8

```
FUNCTION ANYONEOF XS;
  VARS EENY MEENY; ERASE(POPTIME//1Ø)– >EENY; XS– >MEENY;
  L: IF MEENY. NULL THEN XS– >MEENY CLOSE; IF EENY=Ø THEN MEENY.HD EXIT;
    EENY–1– >EENY; MEENY.TL– >MEENY; GOTO L;
END;

FUNCTION CONTAIN LIST ITEM;
  IF LIST.NULL.NOT AND EQUAL(LIST.HD, ITEM) OR CONTAIN(LIST.TL, ITEM)
    THEN TRUE ELSE FALSE CLOSE;
END;

FUNCTION TAKE HIM SQUARE; HIM– >SQUARE.TL; SQUARE= >2.NL; END;

FUNCTION BELONG SQUARE HIM; SQUARE.TL=HIM; END;

FUNCTION VACANT SQUARE; SQUARE.TL.NULL; END;

FUNCTION USEFUL XS HIM; HOWMANY(XS,BELONG(%HIM%))=2; END;

FUNCTION BOTH X RY RZ; IF X.RY AND X.RZ THEN TRUE ELSE FALSE CLOSE; END;

FUNCTION VALUABLE SQUARE HIM;
  IF SQUARE.VACANT AND SOME(LINES, BOTH(%CONTAIN(%SQUARE%),
    USEFUL(%HIM%)%)) THEN TRUE ELSE FALSE CLOSE;
END;
```

Figure 9

```
FUNCTION MOVE;
  IF SOME(SQUARES,VALUABLE(%YOU%))
  THEN YOU, TAKE(ANYONEOF(SQUARES,WHICH(VALUABLE(%YOU%))))
  ELSEIF SOME(SQUARES, VALUABLE(%ME%))
  THEN YOU, TAKE(ANYONEOF(SQUARES,WHICH(VALUABLE(%ME%))))
  ELSE YOU, TAKE(ANYONEOF(SQUARES,WHICH(VACANT))); CLOSE;
END;
```

Figure 10

part of the program reads very much like English. It might be supposed that this is merely because, like Humpty Dumpty, one is allowed in POP-2 to use English words however one likes; and in a sense this would be true. But it would miss the main point, which is far from obvious, namely that in order to achieve such a degree of resemblance to English—not only in the vocabulary but in the actual word order—all the key words must be introduced as the names of very carefully considered functions—or, if you will, procedures.

Two examples will help to make this point clear. In figure 8 appears the incantation: "function which XS RY; ... end;", which can be read casually as "Which Xs are Y", and defines the word "which". The definition is this; "which" takes a list (of) XS and a predicate RY as its arguments, and delivers another list, comprising just those XS *which* satisfy the predicate. (We shall see the function at work in figure 11.) The quantifier "some" is also defined as a function of a list (of) XS and a predicate RY which can be applied to them. The output of this function is a truth value—true if and only if some member of the list satisfies the predicate (though this meaning is not transparent from figure 8 unless one knows POP-2).

To return to the capabilities of the program: It doesn't just play a rather poor game; it can be engaged in "conversation" at the same time. Figures 11–14 show a game which actually took place between me and the program. The board has its squares lettered in the following way:

A   B   C
D   E   F
G   H   K

Every symbol from each double asterisk to the following colon, inclusive, was typed by the computer, and all the remaining symbols by me. The conversation began by my asking how many squares were vacant, in almost so many words. The answer was "9". The next line uses the function "which" interrogatively, the question mark being represented by the double symbol => , which causes the result of the function to be printed out

HOWMANY(SQUARES,VACANT) = >

** 9,
:

WHICH(SQUARES,VACANT) = >

** [[A] [B] [C] [D] [E] [F] [G] [H] [K]],
:

.MOVE;

** [C ME]
: ME, TAKE(E);

** [E YOU]

Figure 11

.MOVE;

** [B ME]
: HOWMANY(LINES,USEFUL(%YOU%)) = >

** 1,
:

WHICH(LINES,USEFUL(%YOU%)) = >

** [[[A] [B ME] [C ME]]],
:

WHICH(SQUARES,VALUABLE(%YOU%)) = >

** [[A]],
:

Figure 12

ME, TAKE(A);

** [A YOU]
: WHICH(SQUARES,BELONG(%ME%)) = >

** [[A YOU] [E YOU]],
:

.MOVE;

** [K ME]
: WHICH(SQUARES,VALUABLE(%YOU%)) = >

** [[F]],
:

Figure 13

```
    ME, TAKE(F);
** [F YOU]
:  .MOVE;

** [D ME]
:  WHICH(SQUARES,VALUABLE(%ME%))= >

** NIL,
:
    ME, TAKE(G);

** [G YOU]
:  .MOVE;

** [H ME]
```

Figure 14

on the following line. Then I instruct it to move, and it replies in its own dialect "I take C". Next I indicate that I am taking E, and it echoes my remark with the response "[E YOU]". (The interchange of first and second person is achieved by the simple device in the first line of figure 8.) And so on. The rest of the conversation should be self-explanatory, including all the remarks passed in POP-2.

The program has no game-theoretical interest whatever, nor has it any pretensions to computational elegance. It is simply designed to reinforce the idea that strong comparisons are possible between natural languages and programming languages, particularly in their semantics. This ought not to be in the least surprising, because programming languages, like natural languages, are designed to elicit responses from other beings, albeit non-human beings, and should therefore permit the expression of at least some of the ideas which we habitually express in natural language. But I may seem to have digressed too far from real human language; so let me now describe some work which brings us a little closer to the realities of human conversation.

The Modelling of Discourse

The program that I shall describe in a moment began as an attempt to produce a working model of the use of tense and aspect in English. Much thought has been given to the semantics of the present, past, and future tenses, and of the progressive and perfective aspects, notably by Prior (1967) and Reichenbach (1966); and Winograd's program makes effective use of at least some of the commonest tense constructions, though the underlying logic is not made fully explicit. We were anxious to clear our minds on these matters, if only because every complete English sentence has tense, and a large proportion have aspect as well. It should surprise no one that we have made only a small inroad into the extensive problems involved; but in the course of doing so we have obtained some insight into matters relating to connected discourse.

There would not be time, nor would I be competent, to review the complexities of English tense; all I shall therefore do is to make some remarks about the manner in which we speak of events ("Mary arrived an hour ago") as opposed to states of affairs—either temporary ("The sun is shining") or permanent ("Two plus two equals four"). In speaking of past events we use either the past tense or the perfective aspect, or both. There is an interesting difference between "Has Mary arrived?" and "Did Mary arrive?". Whereas the former seems completely clear as it stands, the latter is incomplete unless some definite past time is already in the hearer's mind. In short, non-present-tense sentences demand a stated or implied time of reference; in present-tense sentences the moment of speech serves as the time of reference. The function of the perfective aspect is to place the event time before the reference time; the use of the past tense is appropriate if and only if the reference time precedes the moment of speech. The sentence "When I arrived, he *had* already left" illustrates the functions of both past and perfective, incorporated into the word "had".

Similar remarks apply to the way in which we refer to future events; we may use either the "future tense"—whose status is a matter of doubt among linguists (Boyd and Thorne 1969), but never mind—as in "John will take his examination tomorrow"; or the progressive aspect, as in "Are you going to the party?".

It soon became clear, in thinking about these and many other facts concerning English tense and aspect, that the best way of testing one's understanding would be to write a program with which one could converse about a model world in which events occurred in a definite order known to the program but not to the operator. The model adopted was that of a party, beginning and ending at prescribed times, with the guests arriving in alphabetical order. Al is the first to arrive, then Bob, then Charlie, then David and Derek, then Ed, then Fred, then George, and finally Harry. Another gentleman, called Cuthbert, is not expected and does not turn up. Figures 15–19 show some pieces of conversation with the program; let us study them in detail.

Since the meaning of an utterance, and the appropriate response to it, will depend on the time at which the utterance is made and the state of

: IS HARRY COMING:

YES

: IS AL:

YES

: IS CUTHBERT:

NO; HE NEVER WILL

: DID AL ARRIVE SAFELY:

EH

: WHEN DAVID GETS HERE WILL BERT HAVE ARRIVED:

YES

: WILL ED:

NO, NOT BY THEN

:

Figure 15

affairs prevailing at that time, we must specify the time of utterance before starting the conversation; the time of utterance for figures 15 and 16 was initially set to the very beginning of the party. The first two questions asked by the operator are in the progressive aspect (recognized by the program through the occurrence of "is"). I should explain at once that the program assumes, when anyone is mentioned, that his arrival is under discussion, and passes over such words and word strings as "arrive", "coming", "gets here", and "turned up", so that the sentence "When David gets here will Bert have arrived?" is actually treated as if it were simply "When David will Bert have?" In a sense this is cheating, but perhaps it is not without interest that one can cheat so extensively without losing the thread of the conversation. How often, in trying to understand a foreign language, do we not clutch at the few words we are sure of, leaving the rest to guesswork!

Returning to figure 15, we notice that the reply to the third question employs the pronoun "he" in an appropriate way, to refer to the subject of the immediately preceding sentence. The fourth question receives the answer "eh?", because nothing has happened yet to provide a time of reference for the interpretation of the past tense. The next question is syntactically and semantically complete, and receives a monosyllabic answer; but the following question "Will Ed?" could not possibly stand on its own. You and I realize that in the context the question is equivalent to

: WILL CHARLIE JUST HAVE:

YES

: WILL HARRY TURN UP AFTER GEORGE:

YES

: JUST AFTER:

YES

: WILL AL:

NO

: WHEN CUTHBERT GETS HERE WILL ED HAVE ARRIVED:

CUTHBERT NEVER WILL

:

Figure 16

"When David gets here *will Ed* have arrived?", but the program has to figure this out. It does so by holding on to the conjunction "when", the reference time indicated by "David", and the aspect "have" until the questioner changes the tense, when they cease to be of any further utility. Since "Will Ed"? is in the same tense as the previous question, its deficiencies can thus be made good, and the question answered in the negative; the extra phrase "not by then" appears because Ed is known to be going to arrive eventually.

Figure 16 continues where 15 left off, the first sentence being equivalent to "When David gets here will Charlie just have?", and the adverb "just" is taken to modify the aspect word "have". Something similar happens two questions later, where the fragment "just after" is put in place of the word "after" in the preceding question, the structure of which must of course have been saved for the substitution to be performed. The following question "Will Al?", being in the same tense, is interpreted as "Will Al turn up just after George?", the elements of which derive from the question itself and the *two* preceding questions. The final question of figure 16 alters the time of reference, but in so doing reveals a wrong presupposition in the mind of the questioner, namely that Cuthbert is coming. The only possible response is to question the presupposition; but here it would be misleading to say "*He* never will", because the subject of the question was Ed, not Cuthbert; hence the mention of Cuthbert in the answer.

The clock is now advanced to a time between the arrival of Charlie and Derek, and the conversation is resumed in figure 17. The question "Is Al

:

  IS AL COMING:

NO; HE ALREADY HAS

: IS ED:

YES

: WHEN FRED GETS HERE WILL GEORGE HAVE ARRIVED:

NO, NOT BY THEN

: HAS FRED ARRIVED SINCE DEREK:

DEREK HASNT YET

:

Figure 17

coming?" now receives a different answer, as indeed it should; but the one-word reply "No" would plainly be misleading, if not actually false, because it would fail to draw attention to the fact of which the questioner is obviously unaware, namely that Al has already arrived. Hence the addendum "he already has". This question and its answer illustrate the frequent necessity not only of detecting those false presuppositions which people make explicit—such as that embodied in "When Cuthbert gets here, ..."—but also of discerning the misconceptions of a speaker from remarks which, superficially at least, are quite unexceptionable.

The last question in figure 17 exemplifies the use of a time clause in a sentence in the present tense. Whereas clauses beginning with "when", "before", and "after" specify the reference times of past and future sentences, a "since" clause can occur in a sentence of any tense, provided it has perfective aspect. In this particular question, of course, the words "since Derek" reveal a false presupposition, so the response draws attention to it. In figure 18 we see the first and second questions receiving different answers, though the second relies very heavily on the first for its interpretation. The question "Did Derek?" reveals, if not a false presupposition, at least a probable misconception—hence the addendum "he still hasn't". The following question incorporates the pronoun "he", which the program takes to indicate the subject of the prceding sentence; and the last question is a chatty variant (in which, as already remarked, the words "gets here" and "turned up" are actually ignored). Figure 19 shows what happens when we put both a "when" clause and a "since" clause into a question and the presupposition embodied in the "since" clause fails. Note the different forms of words in the first and third replies, and the fact that in the reply to

DID CHARLIE ARRIVE AFTER AL:

YES

: JUST AFTER:

NO

: DID DEREK:

NO; HE STILL HASNT

: IS HE COMING:

YES

: WHEN CUTHBERT GETS HERE WILL HARRY HAVE TURNED UP:

CUTHBERT NEVER WILL

:

Figure 18

WHEN BOB ARRIVED HAD CHARLIE GOT HERE SINCE DEREK:

DEREK HADNT BY THEN

: HAD HE COME SINCE AL:

NO, NOT BY THEN

: WHEN FRED GETS HERE WILL AL HAVE COME SINCE GEORGE:

GEORGE WONT HAVE BY THEN

:

Figure 19

the second question neither the word "hadn't" nor the word "won't" is present. As a matter of fact, the program as it stands interprets the "he" of the second question as referring to Charlie rather than to Derek, because it is unable to remember its own replies—only the questions put to it; this is a undoubted weakness, from which Winograd's program does not suffer.

The program in its present form is, needless to say, extremely limited in scope. It responds only to questions, its world is restricted to a succession of point events, and its replies are constructed from excessively large linguistic units (such as "hadn't", "by then", and so on) by rules which bear no simple relation to those which it uses for interpreting the questions put to it. To improve on this linguistically unsatisfactory expedient is perhaps the biggest problem confronting students of natural language—the problem of modelling the speaker of a language, as opposed to the hearer.

```
2   9   4

7   5   3

6   1   8
```

Figure 20

The Semantics of Modals and Hypotheticals

The last program I shall discuss was written by my colleague Stephen Isard (in whose company many of the above ideas were also refined and elaborated). We were both discontented with existing modal logic as a vehicle of expression for assertions such as "Jones *must* have committed the murder", "No, he *couldn't* have", and various other assertions involving modal verbs. We decided to think up a universe of discourse in relation to which modal sentences would have as clear a meaning as possible, and which would, furthermore, permit a straightforward interpretation of hypothetical sentences such as "If I do such-and-such what will you do?", and even of counterfactual ones such as "If I had done such-and-such, what would you have done?". The problem was not so much one of finding a logical notation in which to express modal and hypothetical assertions as one of discovering what logical processes would be needed for determining the appropriate responses to such questions and assertions about the universe under discussion.

The model universe we finally chose was, as in a previous section, a game of noughts and crosses (Isard and Longuet-Higgins 1972). The particular virtue of games in this connexion is that their course is not fully predictable, so that there is a natural set of "possible worlds" associated with any given state of play; and, furthermore, that worlds which were once possible, but are possible no longer, also have a role to play, in sentences of the type "If I had . . . " .

Isard chose to represent the board as a magic square, as shown in figure 20; a player then wins if he succeeds in taking three numbers which add up to 15. Figure 21 shows the state of a typical game, which we join as the human player, playing "X", is about to make his second move. He indicates his move with the English sentence "I take 6". The board is then displayed (see figure 22), and the human issues the instruction "Move". The program (see figure 23) takes square 4, in the top right-hand corner; and the human asks "How can I win?". (Unfortunately we have no question mark on our teletype.) In order to answer such questions the program has been supplied

```
0  9  4

7  X  3

6  1  0
```
: I TAKE 6.

Figure 21

```
0  9  4

7  X  3

X  1  0
```
: MOVE.

Figure 22

```
0  9  0

7  X  3

X  1  0
```
: HOW CAN I WIN.
YOU CANT. IF YOU TAKE 7 I TAKE 3. IF YOU TAKE 3 I TAKE 7.
  IF YOU TAKE 1 I TAKE 3. IF YOU TAKE 9 I TAKE 1.
: I TAKE 9.

Figure 23

with the meaning of the word "can", namely that "X can Y" is true if and only if there is a strategy for X which leads to the result "X Ys" whatever the opponent does. In the situation of figure 23, "Human can win" is actually false, so the question "How?" does not arise. The program says so, and explains why. Undaunted, the human announces "I take 9"; the resulting state of play is shown in figure 24. The human's next question "How can you win?" embodies a correct presupposition, and receives a straight answer—as does the next question. The following question is much more tricky. In order to answer it the program has to rack its memory of the moves made, to find whether the human actually did take 9, and if so on which move. It then has to alter that move to the taking of 3, creating a hypothetical state of affairs in which it now has to decide what it will take, and tell the operator. The fuller reply "I would have taken 9" would necessitate returning from the hypothetical to the actual state of affairs, and recognizing the former as such, so as not to make the mistake of answering

```
0  X  0

7  X  3

X  1  0
```
: HOW CAN YOU WIN.
BY TAKING 3
: WHAT WILL YOU TAKE.
  3:
: IF I HAD TAKEN 3 WHEN I TOOK 9 WHAT WOULD YOU HAVE TAKEN.
  9:
: MOVE.

Figure 24

```
0  X  0

7  X  0

X  1  0
```

Figure 25

"I will take 9". All these details must be attended to in order to produce a plausible model; any simpler account of the matter could not possibly be faithful to our own thought processes.

On the final command to move, the program takes 3 and wins.

Concluding Remarks

Language is not only an object of interest in its own right, but an incomparable window into the mind, through which we can study the processes of thought which our utterances reflect and provoke.

Although our brains are constructed very differently from electronic computers, and comparisons at the level of "hardware" are pathetically inadequate, there are powerful analogies between natural languages and the languages which we use for programming computers. In particular, natural utterances have an obvious parallel with the messages which we type into suitably prepared computing systems, and once this analogy is recognized it becomes possible not merely to describe the phenomena of language, but actually to make working models of linguistic processes.

Although one can never satisfy oneself that any such model faithfully describes the phenomena which it simulates, one will very quickly discover those respects in which it falls short. The main problem, in linguistics as in other sciences, is not so much one of choosing between alternative, equally plausible theories, as it is one of constructing any theory at all which will harmonize with the vast range of observable phenomena.

I would like to thank my colleague Mr. S. Isard for invaluable discussions during the progress of this work, and also to thank the Royal Society and the Science Research Council for generous financial support.

References

Boyd, J., and J. P. Thorne. 1969. The semantics of modal verbs. *J. Linguistics* 5 : 57.

Burstall, R. M., and R. J. Popplestone. 1971. *Programming in POP-2*. Edinburgh University Press.

Chomsky, N. 1957. *Syntactic Structures*. The Hague: Mouton.

Isard, S. D., and H. C. Longuet-Higgins. 1973. In Proceedings of the Fourth International Conference for Logic, Methodology and Philosophy of Science. [Chapter 15 in present volume.]

Longuet-Higgins, H. C. 1969. *Bull. Inst. Math. Applic.* 6 : 8.

McCawley, J. D. 1968. The role of semantics in a grammar. In *Universals in Linguistic Theory*, ed. E. Bach and R. Harms (New York: Holt, Rinehart and Winston).

Prior, A. N. 1967. *Past, Present and Future*. Oxford: Clarendon.

Reichenbach, H. 1966. *The Elements of Symbolic Logic*. New York: Free Press.

Tarski, A. 1931. The concept of truth in formalised languages. In *Logic, Semantics, Meta-mathematics* (Oxford: Clarendon).

Weizenbaum, J. 1966. *Comm. Am. Computer Monthly* 9 : 1.

Winograd, T. 1970. Ph.D. thesis, Massachusetts Institute of Technology.

Winograd, T. 1972. *Understanding Natural Language*. New York: Academic.

15 Modal Tic-Tac-Toe

S. D. Isard and
H. C. Longuet-Higgins

The work we are doing began as an attempt to find a formal definition of truth for a limited class of English sentences. Guided by Tarski's definition of truth for formalized languages and by Chomsky's conception of natural-language syntax, we wanted to take a subset of English suitable for discussing a model universe and to define in an intuitively satisfying way what it would mean for a sentence *to be true of that universe*, in terms of the syntactic structure of the sentence and the referents of the individual words. We did not feel committed to any specific grammar of English, but we were—and are—strongly prejudiced to the view that English syntax must serve some purpose in the process of communication, and we wanted our scheme to assign some function to as much as possible of the syntax we would use.

Our desire to do justice to English usage has, in fact, led us to modify our original goal. Instead of pressing the analogy between truth in English and truth in a formalized predicate language, we have chosen to view English as an *imperative* language, analogous to the languages which are used for programming computers. According to this view, English sentences are to be treated not as formulas (in the predicate-language sense) but as terms whose domain of interpretation is a set of instructions to the hearer. In this setting our analogue of a truth definition becomes a way of deriving from a sentence a set of instructions for determining an appropriate response. For a well-posed question the appropriate response will be its answer; for a command it will be the execution of the command; for a statement it will be a modification of the hearer's state of knowledge (which will be part of the logical system upon which the set of instructions operates). This view is sufficiently general to accommodate sentences which fail to convey meaning to the hearer, for example those which incorporate erroneous presuppositions. In such a case the set of instructions for determining the response may be incomplete or impossible to carry out, and the sentence must be regarded as inappropriate. Allowing for this shift in viewpoint, our semantics has some features in common with those studied by modal and tense logicians, although our treatment of a number of locutions—in particular, those involving modal verbs—is quite different.

"Must"

Consider the difference between the following in ordinary English usage:

It is raining   (1)
It must be raining   (2)

Informally, we might say that it is the difference between the rain's being entirely obvious to the speaker and his having to infer it from other facts. A man who comes in out of a downpour and announces "It must be raining" is a rather comic figure; while Sherlock Holmes, when he sees a footprint and immediately says "The man who made this has a tattoo on his left arm", is showing off. In fact, all the English modal verbs can be used to signify that the speaker does not have direct knowledge and has to figure something out. They can, of course, be used in other ways too—"You may go now"—but here we have in mind such usages as "It may rain tomorrow" and "He cannot have committed the murder". It would be quite unreasonable to claim that example 2 is "stronger" than example 1; if anything it is weaker, expressing less certainty on the part of the speaker. How could we capture this formally?

A formalism to deal with this use of "must" might involve a language, a distinguished subset of "axioms" of the language, and a method of computing a "follows from" relation on sentences. An "indicative" predicate would hold of those sentences which were axioms, and a "must" predicate of those sentences, not themselves axioms, which followed from the axioms. This formalism would not, however, be expressing our intuition for "truth" so much as our intuition for "an appropriate thing to say". We have, in fact, opted for formalizing this notion of "appropriateness" (though not with the formalism just outlined) because it seems more likely to lead to a theory of the performance of English speakers, and because we feel that a clear intuition for what it is appropriate to say in given circumstances will extend to more sentences than those whose "truth" is beyond dispute, making it easier to test such a formalism. It is, in any case, difficult to handle sentences other than statements within the confines of a conventional theory of truth; and a very large part of ordinary discourse consists of questions, commands, and fragmentary utterances including exclamations.

Presuppositions

A class of sentences over which intuitions about truth tend to clash is that involving unacceptable presuppositions. Using a computational setting, and going for acceptability instead of truth, allows us to dispose of these in a rather natural way. Roughly speaking, a presupposition represents a condition which must be satisfied in order for the hearer to carry out his instructions. If the presupposition is false, he is unable to perform some step in his computation. If asked whether the present king of France is bald, he is unable to find a referent for "the present king of France". Notice that exactly the same view may be taken of presuppositions, whether they are embodied in statements ("the king of France is bald"), in questions, or in commands ("Go and assassinate the king of France!").

Context

Another feature of English that fits naturally into a computational setting is the fact that sentences and fragments of sentences are interpreted according to context. The interpreter can be put, so to speak, into a variety of different states, and will treat the same sentence in different ways according to which state he is in. Extreme examples are the single-word utterances "yes" and "no", where the interpreter's state is partly revealed by the question to which these sentences are addressed; but even complete sentences which would be ambiguous in isolation are usually disambiguated by context—otherwise the speaker would not do well to employ them. Of course, pronoun reference depends heavily on context; a pronoun may refer back to an individual who was last mentioned many sentences ago.

A Model Language User

As a means of expressing, clarifying, and testing our ideas, particularly about English tenses and modal verbs, we are attempting to actually construct a model language user, in the form of a computer program. It is to be able to play a game of tic-tac-toe against a human opponent and discuss with him the progress of the game in ordinary if simple English. At present we are concentrating on getting the program to answer questions about the game; it is not clear to us yet how to motivate it to ask questions itself.

A "situation" for this machine consists of a board position, together with the sequence of moves leading to it. These essentially play the role of "possible worlds". The machine knows its own strategy, but makes no assumptions about that of its opponent. Thus it should be able to answer questions beginning "What would you have done if ...", but not, in general, questions of the type "What would I have done if ...".

Our treatment of tense is broadly in accord with that of Reichenbach (1966). In particular, we distinguish between the time at which the sentence is uttered, the time of reference, and the time of occurrence of events mentioned in the sentence. For instance, in the sentence

When I arrived, he had already left   (3)

my arrival gives the time of reference, which is before the time of utterance and after the time of his departure. If we restrict ourselves to present and past tenses, and to sentences dealing only with moments of time, not intervals, then a good rule of thumb is that the past tense will be used when and only when the time of reference precedes the moment of speech, the present tense indicates that the two moments coincide, and the presence of "have" signifies that the time of the event precedes the reference time whereas its absence indicates coincidence of these two times. In symbols, this is written as follows:

past tense $\Rightarrow$ time of ref $<$ time of speech,
present tense $\Rightarrow$ time of ref $=$ time of speech,
presence of "have" $\Rightarrow$ time of event $<$ time of ref,
absence of "have" $\Rightarrow$ time of event $=$ time of ref.

Every sentence must, in fact, be interpreted with respect to some reference time, although this time may not be mentioned in the sentence itself. Thus,

Was he there when you arrived? No, he had already left.   (4)

In general, a time clause in a sentence (but not one introduced by the word "since") will indicate its time of reference; but if this has already been determined, for instance by a question to which the sentence is an answer, then the time clause can indicate the event time. An example of this is the following:

He had left at 8 o'clock.   (5)

Reichenbach (1966, p. 294) claims that 8 o'clock must be the reference time in this sentence; but if sentence 5 is the answer to

Why wasn't he there when you arrived at 8.30?   (6)

then the "8 o'clock" in sentence 5 is clearly the event time.

We have written a number of pilot programs, just dealing with tense, to work out our ideas in this area. One of these is designed to deal with questions about the arrival of guests at a party, and is supplied in advance with the information that Al, Bob, Bert, Charlie, David, Derek, Ed, Fred, George, and Harry arrive in alphabetical order; a non-guest, Cuthbert, has not been invited and is not going to show up. Here is a sample of actual output; the time of speech was initially set to just before the party, the questions are the operator's, and the answers are the program's:

Q: Will Fred arrive before Harry?
A: Yes.
Q: Just before?
A: No.
Q: When Fred arrives will Bob have come since Cuthbert?
A: Cuthbert never will.
Q: When Bob arrives will Harry have come since David?
A: David won't have by then.

The time of speech is now moved to just after the arrival of Charlie.

Q: Has David turned up?
A: No, not yet.
Q: Has Cuthbert?
A: No, he never will.
Q: Will Bob arrive before Bert?
A: Bert already has.

The machine works by first "parsing" the question in a primitive way to determine the time of reference, the event in question, and any other time-adverbial information provided. Any essential gaps are then filled by reference to what has been said already. In the subsequent process of interpretation, the reference time is first determined, and if the tense is "inappropriate", revealing a false presupposition, then the reply has to indicate the fact. The details are somewhat complex, but the main point is to derive from the question a systematic procedure for answering it, taking account not only of the words of the question itself and the knowledge available but also of the conversational context and allowing for the possibility that the question may not be well posed, in which case attention must be drawn to the erring presuppositions.

Analogous problems arise with hypothetical and subjunctive clauses; they call for the construction of situations within which other sentences are tested. The construction of the "subjunctive situation" begins from the reference point of the "if" clause, which is the present moment in

If I go here, what will you do?   (7)

and which is some point in the past in

If I had gone here when I went there, what would you have done?   (8)

Subjunctive reference situations can persist for several sentences, in the same way that past situations can. If

I would have done this.   (9)

is used as an answer to question 8, its reference situation is the same.

Modal verbs are connected with possible games which are continuations from the reference situation. "May" asks whether something is true in some such possible game, "must" whether it is true in every such game. Our provisional interpretation of "will" is that it asks about all games which are consistent with the machine's strategy. This works well in the specific context we have chosen, but is clearly less general than it might be. The same applies to our use of "can". We say that a player "can" achieve something if there is a strategy for him that leads to this result no matter what the opponent does. Thus,

I can win.   (10)

is taken to mean that I have a winning strategy, not necessarily that I will use it.

In general we regard "could", "would", and "might" as those forms of "can", "will", and "may" which appear when there is reference to a past or subjunctive situation. We accept, but do not attempt to explain, the fact that "might" can also be used when the reference time is the present, as in

Will you go here? I might.   (11)

Conclusion

In summary, we have found it impossible to give a satisfactory account of the use of English entirely in terms of any concept which can reasonably be called "truth". This is because the appropriateness of a natural utterance depends heavily on the states of the speaker and hearer, and the nature of this dependence is such that it distinguishes sentences like 1 and 2 in cases where no one would want to call one "true" and the other "false". And in any case it could be argued that questions and commands are likely to require for their explication basic categories additional to those of truth and falsehood. But there does seem to exist, for natural language, a useful analogue to the truth definitions offered by the formal logician, namely a set of meta-rules for constructing from a natural utterance a set of instructions to be followed by the hearer. Winograd (1971) has shown that much light can be thrown on English sentences by viewing them as representing such sets of instructions, and one of the merits of this proposal is that one can test one's intuition as to the relation between utterances and the programs they represent by expressing the relationship in the medium of a programming language and then holding a conversation with one's theory.

References

Reichenbach, H. 1966. *Elements of Symbolic Logic*. New York: Macmillan.

Winograd, T. 1971. Procedures as a Representation for Data in a Computer Program for Understanding Natural Languages. Project MAC report MAC-TR-84, Massachusetts Institute of Technology.

16   Question-Answering in English

S. D. Isard and
H. C. Longuet-Higgins

In this chapter we shall consider the problem of when an English sentence, or a series of sentences, provides enough information to answer a question, also posed in English.

The sentence

John kissed Mary   (1)

obviously enables the question

Did John kiss Mary?   (2)

to be answered in the affirmative, and transformational grammar partly accounts for this by giving formal criteria by which a declarative sentence and a question can be recognized as having the same underlying structure. But transformational grammar does not explain why

John saw a flying saucer   (3)

and

Mary saw it too   (4)

provide an affirmative answer to

Did John see the flying saucer that Mary saw?   (5)

whereas sentence 3 and

Mary saw one too   (6)

fail to provide an answer to this question.

Neither does transformational grammar concern itself with the notion of logical consequence, whereas we want to understand why "Socrates is a man. All men are mortal." enables us to answer the question "Is Socrates mortal?".

Various systems of formal logic raise an analogous problem—at least for "yes/no" questions—within their own languages, and solve it by formalizing the concept of logical consequence. Thus in the first-order predicate calculus, we could say that a set of sentences Σ "contains enough information to answer the question posed by" the sentence ϕ if either ϕ or its negation is derivable from Σ. The formalization may be either in "syntactic" terms, involving derivations, or in "semantic" terms, which appeal to the interpretation of sentences in a particular set theory; and in many cases we may not have an algorithm which will enable us to decide whether Σ answers ϕ. But at least there is a definition of what it means for Σ to answer ϕ; we know what task there is no algorithm for.

It would seem that we might make substantial progress if we could translate English into the language of some logical system, and there is a widespread feeling that such a translation ought to be possible, for at least a large and important subset of English. Indeed, the applicability of theorems in mathematical logic to the rest of mathematics depends largely on the assumption that mathematics could, if necessary, be conducted in the language of first-order predicate calculus. And, indeed, people familiar with logical notations—and with English—can become very adept at this sort of translation. What they cannot do, however, is to give a formal description of how they go about it. Quine (1959), after outlining some useful hints for his reader, says: "... in the main we must rely on our good sense of everyday idiom for a sympathetic understanding of the statement, and then re-think the whole in logical symbols".

The problem of translating English into another representation, one in which we hope to be able to formalize the concept of logical consequence, is our main concern in what follows. We have been taking a "syntactic" approach to this problem; our aim is to operate directly on the strings of words presented, rather than on our "understanding" of them. While we do not yet have a fully specified candidate for the representation into which we should translate, the need for one which can be related to English by formal rules has led us to structures very similar to those of the transformational grammarian.

Some English Quantifiers

We begin by describing a method for translating a modest subset of English into a slightly modified first-order predicate calculus—modified just enough to provide a representation for questions. We can then go on to investigate the difficulties which arise when we attempt to treat more of the language, not the least of these being that the first-order predicate calculus is not adequate to express the whole range of meanings of English sentences.

The statements and questions which we shall consider now may be exemplified by the following:

Not everyone met John. (7)

Someone didn't meet everybody. (8)

No one told anybody anything. (9)

Did anyone meet John? (10)

Did anyone meet everybody? (11)

Did anyone tell anybody anything? (12)

More precisely, we consider

- declarative sentences

$$D \rightarrow NP'(\text{didn't}) V(NP)(NP)$$

containing a noun phrase, possibly followed by "didn't", followed by a verb, possibly followed by one or two noun phrases, and

- questions beginning with the word "Did"

$$I \rightarrow \text{Did } NPV(NP)(NP)?$$

followed by a noun phrase, then a verb, then possibly one or two noun phrases.

A noun phrase is either a proper name or a word formed by combining one of the quantifiers "some", "any", "every", and "no" with one of the variables "one", "body", and "thing":

$$NP \rightarrow \begin{cases} \text{John} \\ QX \end{cases} \qquad Q \rightarrow \begin{cases} \text{some} \\ \text{any} \\ \text{every} \\ \text{no} \end{cases} \qquad X \rightarrow \begin{cases} \text{one} \\ \text{body} \\ \text{thing} \end{cases}$$

Furthermore, the first noun phrase of a declarative may be "not every X":

$$NP' \rightarrow \begin{cases} NP \\ \text{Not every } X \end{cases}$$

Let us emphasize that we are not claiming that every string of words produced by these rules is an English sentence (e.g., Anybody saw John). It is just that we are restricting our attention to those sentences which can be so produced.

We would like to have rules which transcribe such declarative sentences into predicate calculus formulas, such as

$$\sim \forall x M x j, \tag{7'}$$

$$\exists x \sim \forall y M x y, \tag{8'}$$

$$\forall y \forall z \sim \exists x T x y z, \tag{9'}$$

where Mxy stands for "x met y" and $Txyz$ stands for "x told y z". We would also like, for reasons which will become apparent, rules for transcribing questions into modified formulas of the type

$$\forall x? M x j, \tag{10'}$$

$$\forall x? \forall y M x y, \tag{11'}$$

$$\forall x \forall y \forall z? T x y z. \tag{12'}$$

In every formula there appears a matrix consisting of a predicate symbol corresponding to the verb, followed by a string of variables and constants; these are understood to correspond to the "variables" and proper nouns appearing in the sentence, and in the same order. The matrix will be preceded by a string of quantifiers and negations, and possibly a question mark; we have found that the transcription rules which appear below produce unique and acceptable orderings of these symbols from unambiguous sentences of the specified type.

If, as we hope to demonstrate, there is any unique transcription of "some", it must surely be into an existential $\exists$ rather than a universal quantifier; and "every" must surely become a universal quantifier, $\forall$. "No one did so-and-so" seems to be the direct contradiction of "Someone did so-and-so", so that there is a *prima facie* case for transcribing "no" as $\sim \exists$. The word "any" is much trickier to deal with. In sentences of the type under consideration it can appear only after a "not", a "no", or a "did". "Anyone met John" and "anyone didn't meet John" are not English, although we can say "John didn't meet anyone". One could take the line that "John didn't meet anyone" should be transcribed as $\sim \exists x M j x$ (like "John met no-one"). This would be in accord with the approach of those linguists who view "any" as a variant of "some" which appears in "negative contexts"; see, for instance, Klima 1964. It is possible to write a set of rules which transcribe "any" as "∃" and which are as good for the purpose at hand as our rules which follow. However, the fact that "any" behaves in other connections as a universal quantifier ("Anyone can do that") leads us to prefer the transcription $\forall x \sim Mjx$, in which "any" becomes a universal quantifier immediately preceding the "$\sim$". Quine (1960, p. 139), among others, discusses the behaviour of "any" viewed as a universal quantifier.

The following rules enable us to construct the string of quantifiers and negations (and possibly a question mark) which are to precede the matrix in the transcription of an English sentence of the specified type.

(a) We define a "transcription function" T which takes occurrences of words into occurrences of logical symbols:

"not"   ⎫
           ⎬ → $\sim$
"didn't"   ⎭
"some"   → ∃
"every"   → ∀
"any"   → ∀
"no"   → $\sim$∃
"did"   →?

(b) If an occurrence of a quantifier Q precedes an occurrence of "not" or "no", then $T(Q)$ must precede $T(\text{not})$ or $T(\text{no})$.

(c) $T(\text{any})$ must directly dominate $T(\text{not})$ or $T(\text{no})$ or $T(\text{did})$ for some occurrence of "not", "no", or "did" which precedes the occurrence of "any".

(d) If an occurrence of "not" or "no" or "did" precedes an occurrence of "every", then $T(\text{not})$ or $T(\text{no})$ or $T(\text{did})$ precedes $T(\text{every})$.

(e) If an occurrence of "not or "no" precedes an occurrence of "some", then $T(\text{not})$ or $T(\text{no})$ must *not* directly dominate $T(\text{some})$.

(f) ? must precede any occurrence of ∃.

(g) The transcriptions of occurrences of "not" or "did" must appear in the same order as the occurrences themselves.

When we say that a symbol σ directly dominates a symbol τ, we mean that σ precedes τ and either there are no intervening symbols (not counting variables) or all the symbols in between are identical with each other and with either σ or τ.

The above rules were in fact used to generate formulae $7'-12'$ from sentences $7-12$. Confining our attention to declarative sentences for the moment, we claim that any unambiguous sentence from our subset of English can be transcribed in exactly one way without violating rules b–e, and that this transcription represents the meaning of the sentence. For an ambiguous sentence, rules b–e will allow two or more transcriptions, corresponding to the various interpretations of the sentence. Consider, for example, the sentence

Not everyone saw somebody. (13)

The $\forall$ representing "everyone" must follow the $\sim$ representing "not", by rule d, but the only restriction on the placing of the $\exists$ representing "somebody" is that it should not immediately succeed the $\sim$, which would then directly dominate it (rule e). Two readings are therefore possible:

$$\sim \forall x \exists y Sxy \qquad (13')$$

and

$$\exists y \sim \forall x Sxy, \qquad (13'')$$

either of which is a possible interpretation. (Actually the former, in which the order of the quantifiers is the same in the formula as in the sentence, is the preferred reading, and we believe this to be true of ambiguous sentences in general.) Or consider

Everyone didn't see somebody. (14)

Here rule b dictates that $\forall x$ must precede $\sim$, and, by rule e, $\exists y$ must not immediately follow $\sim$. This leaves open the two interpretations

$$\exists y \forall x \sim Sxy \qquad (14')$$

and

$$\forall x \exists y \sim Sxy, \qquad (14'')$$

of which the latter is perhaps preferable. But one could also interpret the sentence in either sense of sentence 13, and this suggests that rule b *might* be relaxed by adding "unless $\forall$ is 'every' and is the first word of the sentence". Whether one allows this exception or not is, of course, a matter of personal linguistic style.

There are a number of "sentences" produced by our little grammar, including double-negative sentences and negative questions, which sound a bit strange, and which some people might reject as not belonging to English; for example, "Everybody gave nobody something". We do not wish to argue here over whether these "really" are sentences. In as far as such sentences are amenable to interpretation, our rules yield their interpretations, with one exception:

Not everyone met anybody,   (15)

which is, so it seems, interpretable as either or both of the following:

$\forall y \sim \forall x M x y$,   (15′)

$\sim \forall x \exists y M x y$.   (15″)

   Our rules predict only the former reading. If we had written them to transcribe "any" as $\exists$, we would have got only the latter. Together with a number of other examples, this suggests that the proper treatment of "any" might be to write it *either* as an existential quantifier inside the scope of a "negative word" *or* as a universal quantifier outside the scope. (E.g., "Few students solved any of the problems" can mean either that, given any problem, few students solved it, or that there were few students who did any problem-solving.)

   Sentences involving more than one negation also fall into the "marginal" category. An interesting case is

No one didn't see anybody   (16)

which according to rules b and c may be written as either

$\forall y \sim \exists x \sim S x y$ (16′)

or

$\sim \exists x \forall y \sim S x y$.   (16″)

But if more than one occurrence of "not" or "no" precedes an occurrence of "any", the preferred interpretation seems to be that in which T(any) directly dominates the transcription of the "not" or "no" to which it is closest.

   In general our rules interpret double-negative sentences in the "proper" rather than the "vulgar" fashion; for example, they interpret "Nobody saw nothing" as a paraphrase of "Everybody saw something" rather than "Nobody saw anything".

   Our transcription of a question gives a predicate-calculus formula with a "?" in its prenex. To every such formula there corresponds another, in which the "?" is replaced by a "$\sim$", and which can be obtained by transcription of a negative declarative sentence.

   Consider, for example, the question

Did John tell anyone everything?   (17)

which our rules transcribe into

$\forall x ? \forall y$ (John told x y).   (17′)

Replacement of "?" by "$\sim$" in question 17 gives

$$\forall x \sim \forall y \ (\text{John told } x \ y), \tag{18'}$$

which is the transcription of

John didn't tell anyone everything. (18)

On the basis of sentence 18 we would undoubtedly wish to reply "no" to question 17. So if a question differs from a (single-negative) declarative only by the presence of "?" rather than "$\sim$" in its transcription, we can answer "no" to the question on the basis of the declarative. More generally, we shall obtain a "no" answer if a declarative is available from which can be deduced the negative formula which matches the question. Thus in the above situation we might have been told

John told no one everything (19)

i.e.,

$$\sim \exists x \forall y \ (\text{John told } x \ y) \tag{19'}$$

This implies 18', so on the basis of 19 we could answer 17 in the negative.

To obtain a "yes" answer to a question we may proceed by erasing the "?" and converting any universal quantifiers which precede it into existential quantifiers. The answer is "yes" if the resulting declarative formula is available, or follows logically from other available formulas. Thus question 17, i.e.,

$$\forall x ? \forall y \ (\text{John told } x \ y), \tag{17'}$$

is answered "yes" if the formula

$$\exists x \forall y \ (\text{John told } x \ y) \tag{20'}$$

is available, as it is if we have been told

John told someone everything. (20)

Given this way of interpreting questions, we wish to make the same claims about the way our rules operate on ambiguous questions that we made about the way they operate on ambiguous declaratives. There is one additional point, however, relating to questions containing negations. If we were to ask someone "Did no one meet anybody?" and he were to answer simply "yes", it would not be clear whether he meant "Yes, no one met anybody" or "Yes, someone met somebody". For this reason, we might not want to give "yes" and "no" answers to questions containing negations, but the procedure of replacing the "?" with a " $\sim$ " or erasing it still indicates what information the questioner has asked for.

Extensions

Plainly, the only interesting thing that this translation procedure purports to do is to get the order of the prenex right. Keeping this in mind, we can see that there will be a number of ways of enlarging the class of sentences treated without seriously altering our rules. First of all, we can introduce noun phrases consisting of "the" followed by a noun, and treat these in the same way as we treat proper nouns. Slightly more ambitiously, we could let ordinary nouns appear in the places where "variable" words appear, and then, instead of writing ordinary quantifiers, we would write "relativized quantifiers" in the sense of Tarski, Mostowski, and Robinson (1953): $(\forall x^{Man})$, $(\exists y^{Dog})$. Formulae with relativized quantifiers could later be converted to ordinary formulae, if this seemed convenient, by the standard method of rewriting $(\forall x^{Man})\psi$ as $(\forall x)(\text{Man}(x) \rightarrow \psi)$ and $(\exists y^{Dog})\psi$ as $(\exists y)(\text{Dog}(y) \wedge \psi)$. This same trick can be used to represent sentences which have relative clauses attached to nouns (for example, "Every man that I know is here"), putting the whole relative clause inside the relativized quantifier. This will work as long as no quantifiers appear inside the relative clause itself. If quantifiers do appear inside a relative clause, the situation may become more complicated. To begin with, we must decide whether the quantifiers in a relative clause should come into the prenex of the main formula or stay with the clause. Then, how do we account for "Everyone who met anyone enjoyed the party", where there is no negation present, and why is there no sentence "Someone who met anyone enjoyed the party"?

The failure of these rules to handle relative-clause sentences actually points to a more general failure to cope with sentences having any subordinate clauses at all. But for simple sentences, those without subordinate clauses, the rules do get quantifier order right, even if the sentences are, say, passives, or involve a preposition, as in "No one gave anything to everybody".

Grammar and Scope

If we are to take advantage of this and extend our rules to cover more than simple active sentences, we should introduce rules relating "active" and "passive" matrices in our formulae. The most sensible way to do this would

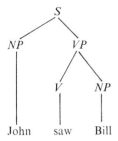

Figure 1

appear to be to retain the actual words rather than introduce constants and predicate symbols, and then use grammatical transformations. Of course, these transformations are not properly stated in terms just of strings of words, but rather in terms of strings with their grammatical structure indicated. (That is, if we view a transformation as an instruction to do something, it might be an instruction to move, say, a noun phrase to the end of the sentence; in some situations this would amount to moving the word "John", in other cases, the word "Bill". But a grammar would never have an explicit instruction "Move the word 'John' to the end of the sentence". Thus we must not only keep the words of the sentence, but we must indicate their structure as well, for example by indicating that "John" is a noun phrase.)

The structure of a sentence is normally expressed in "tree" form, and we wish to adopt this form. (Figure 1 represents a conventional parsing tree.)

There are a number of ways in which the concept of quantifier scope might be incorporated into syntactic trees. We do not want to discuss the merits of particular ways here, but simply note that some device must be adopted which will indicate which quantifiers fall within the scopes of which others.

In fact, it will be necessary to indicate the scopes of some other words besides quantifiers: "not" certainly, and also some verbs. There is, for instance, the notorious sentence

Mary wants to marry a Norwegian.   (21)

This is ambiguous, one reading being that Mary has a particular man in mind and the other that she does not. We think that the best way of expressing the difference is to say that in the latter case the existential quantifier falls within the scope of the verb "want", while in the former case it does not. A proposal to this effect appears in Bach 1969. This represents an extension of predicate calculus where quantifiers cannot appear within the arguments of predicate symbols, but notice that the interpretation on which there is no particular Norwegian does not have a natural predicate-calculus representation.

It is, of course, difficult to assess the rightness or wrongness of such a notational device unless we can point out some consequences of adopting it. One consequence is that we have two ways of representing a sentence which has two different meanings, and this is desirable, but there are surely many other ways of achieving it.

Earlier in the chapter we introduced a new bit of notation, the question mark in the modified predicate calculus, and justified it in two ways. We displayed rules linking it with English, and we gave rules for manipulating it which produced appropriate "yes" and "no" answers. We are not prepared, at this point, to do either of these things for the present "scope" notation, but we can produce some justification for it beyond saying that it "feels right". This is that the notation partitions existentially quantified variables according to the verbs within whose scope their quantifiers fall. English makes a similar partition, which shows itself when we try to make further references to these variables, using pronouns such as "he" or "it". Notice that the question "How tall is he?" as a reply to sentence 21 is appropriate only if we understand sentence 21 as "There is a Norwegian that Mary wants to marry". Otherwise we have to say something like "How tall does she want him to be?" In general, we will not be able to use "he" or "it" to refer to a variable whose quantifier falls within the scope of a verb without repeating the verb, or at least using a modal or subjunctive construction ("How tall should he be?") to indicate that the referent does not exist "in reality" but only within some understood context such as "What Mary wants". Things which "really exist" are those whose existential quantifiers do not fall within the scope of any other operator, and only they can be directly referred to as "he" or "it". Further discussion along these lines appears in Karttunen 1970.

Banyans

Supposing that we have a case where a pronoun in one sentence makes reference to an object introduced in a previous sentence, we must be able to express this in our notation. We have decided to do it by letting the trees representing the two sentences share the node representing the object. Thus,

John saw a flying saucer. Mary saw it, too.   (22)

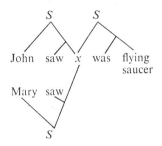

Figure 2

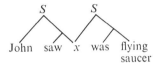

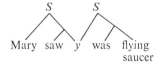

Figure 3

would be represented by linked trees which (omitting details) would look something like figure 2. But "John saw a flying saucer; Mary saw one too." would receive the different representation shown in figure 3. We have adopted the word "banyan" for such sets of linked trees.

Using these banyans we can see a way of generalizing our question-answering procedure to more than "yes-no" questions. The procedure described for predicate calculus, when transferred to trees, amounts to trying to find in the information store a tree which corresponds exactly to the question except for the question mark itself. The answer is then determined by what on the information tree corresponds to the question mark on the question tree. Thus figure 4 represents a situation in which we get the answer "no". Now we can do essentially the same thing to answer "who-what-where"-type questions if we replace the "question word" with a question mark. If we do this, as in figure 5, the information "John saw Mary" will provide the answer "Mary" to the question "Who did John see?"

Of course, in the predicate-calculus case we did not actually have to find one of the two sentences corresponding to the question, but just infer one

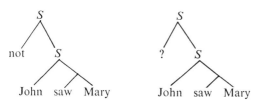

Figure 4

Information:

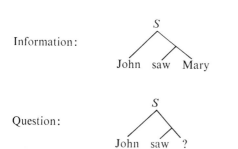

Question:

Figure 5

of these sentences from the given information. The same will be true here if we introduce rules, corresponding to axioms of modal logic, which allow us to deduce trees from one another. In saying this we are not, however, claiming that any existing logical system will prove adequate for elucidating completely the semantics of natural language.

Acknowledgements

We are grateful to the Royal Society and the Medical Research Council for financial support in the course of this work, and S.D.I. would like to thank the National Science Foundation for the opportunity to attend the 1969 Advanced Research Seminar in Mathematical Linguistics at the University of Illinois.

We both express our warmest thanks to Professor Michael Geis for a great deal of helpful advice and constructive heckling.

References

Bach, E. 1968. Nouns and noun phrases. In *Universals in Linguistic Theory* (New York: Holt, Rinehart and Winston).

Karttunen, L. 1970. Discourse referents. In Proceedings of the International Conference on Computational Linguistics, Stockholm, 1969.

Klima, E. S. 1964. Negation in English. In *The Structure of Language* (Englewood Cliffs, N. J.: Prentice-Hall).

Quine, W. V. O. 1959. *Methods of Logic*. New York: Henry Holt.

Quine, W. V. O. 1960. *Word and Object*. Cambridge, Mass.: MIT Press.

Tarski, A., A. Mostowski, and R. M. Robinson. 1953. *Undecidable Theories*. Amsterdam: North-Holland.

17

A Computational Model of Discourse Production

A. C. Davey and
H. C. Longuet-Higgins

A central problem in the psychology of language is to explain as precisely as possible how the speaker of a natural language expresses himself in words. The problem is really twofold. In the first place, how does the speaker decide what to say? Secondly, how does he find the words in which to say it? Existing grammatical theories (Chomsky 1965; Lakoff 1971) address the latter problem by positing a semantic representation for each sentence and attemptir.g to prescribe, for a given language, a set of rules for mapping such semantic representations onto syntactic structures, or vice versa. This approach, however, does not cast any light upon the first problem, namely how the semantic representations are created in the first place; the main difficulty here is in specifying the message which is to be conveyed independently of the linguistic structures which must be created in order to express it.

This chapter describes an attempt to deal with both aspects of the problem by specifying effective procedures for the production of whole paragraphs of English in response to a well-defined communicative need. These procedures have been cast in the form of a computer program (Davey 1974) which generates a post mortem, in English, on any given game of noughts and crosses (tic-tac-toe). The choice of this particular universe of discourse was motivated by the desire to keep the subject matter of the message as simple as possible without reducing it to complete triviality; as will be seen later, even for such a simple universe quite subtle linguistic problems arise about the choice and ordering of the words in which the messages are couched. The present enterprise complements, in a sense, the work of T. Winograd, whose book *Understanding Natural Language* (1972) describes a computer program capable of understanding and responding to quite a wide range of English sentences typed in by a human operator. In Winograd's work the main emphasis was on linguistic comprehension, the sentences produced by the program itself being of relatively limited syntactic complexity and being closely constrained in form by the operator's own questions. It therefore seemed worthwhile to try to develop a program which would produce coherent discourse spontaneously, without prompting by a human operator. In the following sections we outline the way in which the program works, and the general implications of the ideas on which it is based.

An Overview of the Program

In order to give the program something to talk about, the operator begins by playing a game of noughts and crosses with the program, whose grasp of the tactics of the game was made relatively unsophisticated, so that occasionally it loses. Once the game is over a suitable instruction will then cause the program to type out a paragraph of English describing the progress of the game and its outcome. An example of such a game (in which the program's moves are symbolized by noughts and its opponent's moves by crosses) is shown in figure 1. The commentary which was subsequently typed out was the following:

I started the game by taking the middle of an edge, and you took an end of the opposite one. I threatened you by taking the square opposite the one I had just taken, but you blocked my line and threatened me. However, I blocked your diagonal and threatened you. If you had blocked my edge, you would have forked me, but you took the middle of the one opposite the corner I had just taken and adjacent to mine and so I won by completing my edge.

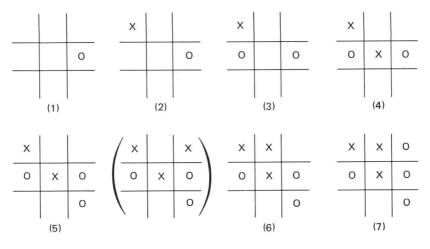

Figure 1

It is important to realize that none of the sentences or phrases in the above commentary had any previous existence in the program's memory; they were all constructed *de novo* by the systematic application of pragmatic and syntactic procedures to the situation in hand. It will be convenient to comment first on the grammatical component of the program.

The grammatical theory embodied in the program is basically the same as that used by Winograd, namely a systemic grammar in the tradition of Halliday (1961, 1967, 1968) but owing a particular debt to work by Hudson (1972a,b). Essentially, the grammar specifies the program's linguistic resources, by enumerating systematically the various constructions which are available in the relevant subset of English. The grammar is generative in that it has complete and explicit rules of formation, which are here used to govern the production of grammatical items. One part of the grammar specifies the options which may or must be selected for a given grammatical item; a major clause, for example, must be past or present tense but cannot have gender or number. These options are set out in the network of "systems" in which each system is a set of simultaneous exclusive alternatives, and the network structure exhibits the logical relation of each system with the rest. The systems network thus sets out exactly what grammatical decisions must be taken in order adequately to characterise any item under construction. The other part of the grammar comprises sets of rules which state how the available options may be constrained by the role of the item in the grammatical environment. For example, the grammar contains a rule which constrains a pronoun such as "I" to have the accusative form "me" in an environment in which the pronoun is dominated by a preposition.

By itself, however, the grammar is powerless to determine what sentences should actually be produced, as it merely lays out the options which are available to the speaker and controls the production of sentences in accordance with those options which he selects. The selection of the options is made by the pragmatic component of the program, which has the task of specifying how to decide what has to be put into words, how to divide this information into sentences, how to arrange each sentence so that its parts fit their context and are easy to understand, and then how to pick words and combine them into phrases to mean the right things. It also specifies—and this is perhaps the most interesting pragmatic problem— what can be left unsaid: it attempts always to avoid telling the hearer anything he knows already, anything more than he needs to know, or anything he might reasonably be expected to work out for himself.

The general principle underlying the design of the pragmatic component was that a speaker must accommodate his remarks to the hearer's presumed state of knowledge, and that any speaker who ignores this maxim runs the risk of baffling or boring his addressee. One reason for selecting a simple game as subject matter was that a game offers a suitable context in which the speaker can keep up to date with the hearer's presumed state of knowledge—presumed because, in the absence of responses from the hearer, the program must assume that he both understands the rules and the point of the game and follows the developing description of the particular game in hand. The program's discourse is thus accommodated to what the hearer's state of knowledge ought to be, rather than to what it actually is.

It is impossible in such a brief space to explain the workings of the program in detail, so we shall content ourselves with analysing the commentary quoted above, in the hope that this example will illustrate the problems which the program has to face and the manner in which it handles them. It should, however, be pointed out that there are about 20,000 tactically distinct games of noughts and crosses upon which the program might be asked to report, and that for any one of these it should produce an equally coherent description, so that our observations on this particular commentary are of general application.

An Example

The first obvious point to note about the game commentary quoted above is that it consists of a number of sentences each of which reports upon one or more actual or possible moves. In order to construct such a paragraph the program must decide how to allocate the semantic material to individual sentences in a sensible fashion. The general principle adopted was to group together the descriptions of moves which are tactically related—with certain qualifications to be mentioned in a moment. The first two moves are tactically neutral and can be conveniently described in a single sentence of coordinate construction:

I started the game by taking the middle of an edge, and you took an end of the opposite one.

(i)

Moves 3 and 4 of figure 1 belong together tactically in that 4 is, among other things, a reply to 3. For this reason the description of 3 is associated, in a new sentence, with that of 4 rather than being appended to the sentence describing moves 1 and 2. A coordinate conjunction is again appropriate, but since the expectations raised by describing 3 as a threat are deflated by learning that 4 was a defence, the required conjunction is contrastive:

I threatened you by taking the square opposite the one I had just taken, but you blocked my line and threatened me.

(ii)

Because move 4 has an offensive as well as a defensive aspect, and the same applies to move 5, one might be tempted to add an additional "but" clause to sentence ii. The result would, however, be somewhat confusing—

Move 3, but move 4, but move 5.

—because the hearer would not receive a clear signal from the second "but" as to the element with which move 5 is to be contrasted. The program therefore places move 5 in a fresh sentence, prefaced by "however" to make it plain that expectations aroused by the description to date are not to be fulfilled:

However, I blocked your diagonal and threatened you.

(iii)

Moves 6 and 7 call for special treatment, because the threat posed by move 5 was not countered by move 6. The program can recognize this fact by referring to its own game-playing routines, which assign a tactical evaluation to any move made in any board position. This way of integrating the move-making and move-describing functions is designed to suggest a way of thinking about semantic representations. The effect here is to treat move 6 as a mistake, in that the program would not have made move 6 in the situation created by move 5. In such circumstances the program draws attention to the mistake by first describing, not what actually happened, but what would have happened if the operator had adopted the program's own tactics. For this purpose a counter-factual hypothetical construction is appropriate:

If you had blocked my edge you would have forked me. . . .

(iva)

The actual course of events, however, contrasts with the previously favourable position of the operator, and so the appropriate conjunction is "but":

. . . but you took the middle of the one opposite the corner I had just taken and so I won by completing my edge.

(ivb)

As the winning move was the immediate consequence of the operator's mistake, the causal connective "so" prefaces the description of the final move.

The hypothetical construction just illustrated is used by the program when the hypothetical move has both an offensive and a defensive aspect, requiring two separate clauses. If the best available alternative were merely defensive, the program would produce

You could have blocked my edge, but you ...

(va)

or

Although you could have blocked my edge, you....

(vb)

In both cases, as in ivb, there is a contrast between the favourable hypothetical move and the less favourable actual one. In va the contrast is signalled by "but"; in vb the hypothetical is expressed in a subordinate clause and the expectations thereby aroused are disappointed in advance by the introductory "although".

In setting about the construction of each sentence, the program makes a tactical evaluation of the next few remaining moves in deciding how many of them to describe in the forthcoming sentence. Its next task is to distribute the move descriptions between major and minor clauses. Normally each move is described in one or more major clauses, linked by conjunctions in the ways just explained. This is appropriate where the moves are of comparable interest, but when a move is futile or vacuous its description may be relegated to a subordinate clause. For example, if the program had posed a double threat—a "fork"—the operator cannot defend himself, and his final move is of no avail. The program may then produce

... I forked you. Although you blocked my edge, I won by completing my diagonal.

The subordination of the operator's final move is appropriate only if the program did in fact go on to win; otherwise the operator's move is tactically important, and is therefore described in a main clause. This resource of the program is no more than a hint at one of the many ways in which clause subordination may be motivated in richer universes of discourse.

Within each major clause describing a move, there may be major and minor clauses conveying the various tactical aspects, if any, of the move. If there is both an offensive and a defensive aspect, both aspects are likely to be significant, and so a coordinate structure is appropriate:

I blocked your line and forked you

while a subordinate structure is distinctly odd:

I forked you by blocking your line

or even odder:

I blocked your line by forking you.

If, furthermore, a coordinate structure is employed, the program must conform to the likely train of thought of the hearer and must mention the defensive aspect of the move before indicating its offensive aspect. It would not do to say

I forked you and blocked your line,

both for this reason and because the second clause is necessary for the identification of the move referred to in the first clause.

Sometimes two clauses are required to describe a move, but one is plainly not as significant as the other. For example "taking a square" is tactically noncommittal, while "threatening" is not. In such a case it seems equally acceptable either to subordinate the less significant clause:

You threatened me by taking a corner

or to present the less significant clause first and then enlarge upon it:

You took a corner and threatened me.

The alternatives

You took ... by threatening

and

You threatened ... and took ...

are plainly unacceptable as confounding the end in view and the means adopted for achieving it.

Referring Expressions

A noteworthy feature of the program is the way in which it identifies the moves of the game. As the procedures for doing this illustrate several important aspects of the use of English, it seems worthwhile to draw attention to some of the underlying principles.

First, it may not even be necessary to identify explicitly the square which was taken in a particular move; clauses such as "I blocked your line" or "by completing my edge" serve to identify unambiguously the square which was taken provided the hearer follows the commentary.

Secondly (a point which is implicit in what has just been said), the construction of the commentary takes for granted that the description of each event is to be interpreted in the light of what has been said so far. In order to achieve this effect of "a train of thought" the program must tacitly replay the game which it is describing, so that the identity of the square can be established with reference to the board position which has been defined by all the statements so far enunciated. In order to achieve this, the program must arrange the sentences, and the main clauses within them, in an order corresponding to that of the events which they describe. This necessity is not, we suggest, a peculiar feature of the chosen universe of discourse, but a direct reflection of the way in which, in any ordinary situation, the hearer's state of mind is progressively modified by each sentence or clause the speaker utters.

Thirdly, the reader will notice the subtle—and correct—distinctions which the program makes in its use of indefinite as opposed to definite noun groups. The use of indefinite referring expressions is appropriate for identifying certain moves because of the symmetry of certain board positions, and the corresponding tactical equivalence of some alternative moves. Thus in sentence i it is of no consequence which of the four edges had its middle square taken in the first move, or which end of the opposite edge was taken in the second move. By contrast, a definite noun phrase such as "the one I had just taken" or "my line" is used when the entity referred to is in a class by itself, and is uniquely indentifiable by such a description.

Fourthly—and this is a pervasive feature of natural language use—the program identifies squares, edges, and so forth by the relations in which they stand to other identifiable entities. The program has a repertoire of such relationships (defined by such words as "opposite", "middle", "end", and so on) and works through these systematically in deciding which one to use for specifying any particular move. According to which relation is chosen, it will construct an appropriate qualifier, which may take the form of a relative clause, a prepositional phrase, or a relational adjective; the relevant grammatical decisions are again governed by the principle of economy of expression, though the details are too complex to describe in this account.

In employing the device of relational reference, the program sometimes relies on its assumption that the hearer is keeping abreast of events. For example, if a particular square has just been mentioned and the program now needs to refer to the only one of its neighbours which is free, it produces

... took the adjacent square.

The referent is unambiguous despite the fact that more than one square is adjacent.

Fifthly, the program leans heavily on anaphoric reference, especially on the use of pronouns. The program's use of the pronoun "one" is of special interest. In contrast to "it", which is co-referential with a definite noun phrase, "one" refers to a *type* of entity previously specified by a noun of appropriate significance. In the given universe of discourse, "types" include such entities as edges and corners; the use of the word "one" is deemed appropriate if reference has recently been made to such a type and there is need to refer to it again. There is a "pronoun specialist" which has to decide, in the light of what has been referred to so far, what type of entity will be uppermost in the hearer's mind on the basis of both its recency of mention and its depth in the existing constituent structure.

The pronoun specialist must not be thought of as operating solely within given constraints arising from the existing context. Just as the part of the program which allocates conjunctions to major clauses does so by manipulating sentence content in order to make the fullest use of the conjunctions available, so too the pronoun specialist may manipulate the planned output to make full use of its anaphoric resources. Consider in particular the construction "one of ... the other" occurring in the sentence "although you blocked one of my edges, I won by completing the other". By the time the hearer reaches "... completing the other", one of the two equivalent edges referred to in the "although" clause has been eliminated from consideration by the operator's blocking move (see figure 2). Nonetheless, "other" implicitly refers to a pair of items, so that the program must suspend its usual practice of replaying each move as soon as it is

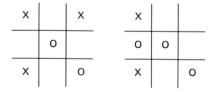

Figure 2

described and treat the two moves in question as a composite event. The point of general interest to emerge from this is that the pragmatic procedures involved in the production of discourse must be sensitive to the grammatical resources of the language.

Discussion

Our main purpose in developing this particular model of discourse production was not to demonstrate (which would be impossible) that human beings do produce language in the way described, but to present a fully explicit theory of how this task might conceivably be accomplished in a limited universe of discourse. The suggestion which the program explores is that the generation of discourse is an ongoing process in which, far from merely translating a pre-existing structure into words, the speaker must proceed in a stepwise fashion, first deciding what requires to be said and then creating a succession of linguistic structures whose interpretation by the hearer may be presumed to depend upon exactly what has been said so far. It is of course essential for the speaker to have a working knowledge of the language in order to make himself clear to the hearer, and this knowledge must be expressed, at least in part, in the form of a generative grammar of some kind. A crucial question, which remains open, is how, given a particular language and a particular universe of discourse, the speaker's pragmatic knowledge is to be related to the one and to the other. Our program was designed in such a way that its pragmatic component would be fully adequate for describing games of noughts and crosses in English, but we hope that our suggested solutions to some of the problems we encountered may have application to richer universes of discourse. But whatever the merits or demerits of our detailed suggestions, we feel that a full understanding of discourse production is likely to require the formulation of psychological hypotheses at least as detailed as those which our program offers and, furthermore, hypotheses which specify, in full procedural detail, the logical processes which may occur in a speaker's mind when he is engaged in the production of an intelligible and informative utterance or sequence of utterances.

Acknowledgements

We are specially indebted to Stephen Isard, who jointly supervised this project, for invaluable suggestions and criticisms, and would also like to thank the Royal Society and the Science Research Council for financial support and computing facilities.

References

Chomsky, N. 1965. *Aspects of the Theory of Syntax*. Cambridge, Mass.: MIT Press.

Davey, A. C. 1972. A Computational Model of Discourse Production. Ph.D. thesis, Edinburgh University.

Halliday, M. A. K. 1961. Categories of the theory of grammar. *Word* 17: 241–292.

Halliday, M. A. K. 1967. Notes on transitivity and theme in English, parts 1 and 2. *Journal of Linguistics* 3: 37–81, 199–244.

Halliday, M. A. K. 1968. Notes on transitivity and theme in English, part 3. *Journal of Linguistics* 4: 179–215.

Hudson, R. A. 1972a. Systematic Generative Grammar. Privately communicated.

Hudson, R. A. 1972b. *English Complex Sentences*. Amsterdam: North-Holland.

Lakoff, G. 1971. On generative semantics. In *Semantics*, ed. D. D. Steinberg and L. A. Jakobovits (Cambridge University Press).

Winograd, T. 1972. *Understanding Natural Language*. Edinburgh University Press.

18 Learning to Count: A Computational Model of Language Acquisition

R. J. D. Power and
H. C. Longuet-Higgins

Perhaps the most remarkable feat that a person ever accomplishes is that of learning to speak. From the most fragmentary evidence, and with no formal instruction, the child succeeds in discovering the grammar of his parents' language, and is soon able to express his own thoughts in grammatically well-formed sentences. A central problem in the theory of language is to understand the mental processes which are involved in its acquisition. In what terms should one formulate the grammatical rules which the learner derives from his observations, and what general principles must he be taking for granted in inducing the grammar of an unfamiliar language from a severely limited set of instances of its use?

In approaching these questions theoretically it is useful to distinguish two senses of the word "grammar", since the phrase "grammar induction" is otherwise unclear. We here use the term "simple grammar" to denote a set of rules which generate all, and only, the well-formed sentences of a language, and reserve the term "extended grammar" for a set of rules which pair sentences with their meanings. (An extended grammar therefore contains a simple grammar. If, for example, the semantic component is removed from a transformational grammar, what remains is a simple grammar.) Although a human learner plainly acquires an extended grammar, most of the formal work that has been done on language acquisition has been concerned with the induction of simple grammars. This work is not necessarily misdirected, of course, since it is conceivable that human learners proceed by first inducing a simple grammar and then converting it into an extended grammar by the addition of an interpretive semantic component. But the theoretical results of Gold (1967) on the induction of simple grammars make this view seem implausible, and Anderson (1975) has cogently argued that the language learner must have access to semantic clues even in order to learn to distinguish well-formed from ill-formed sentences. To show that this view can be elaborated in detail, Anderson describes a language-acquisition system (LAS) partly implemented as a computer program, which actually uses semantic information in acquiring an extended grammar. But Anderson's LAS program, impressive as it is, leaves something to be desired in that the only grammars which it has been able to acquire are either artificial ones or highly simplified versions of natural grammars, and that the semantic networks by which it represents the meanings of sentences are not related to those sentences by any formally precise theory.

Prompted by ideas similar to Anderson's, we decided to undertake a theoretical study of the acquisition of natural numeral systems. How, we asked ourselves, could a person learn to name the numbers 1, 2, ..., 99, ... in an arbitrary natural language, and to understand their names, on the basis of no more information than a mere list of representative numerals, and the numbers for which they stand?* We undertook this study for four reasons. First, we were particularly interested in natural languages as opposed to artificial languages, and in the preconceptions which people bring to their acquisition. Secondly, most languages seem to possess numeral systems, but these systems are sufficiently diverse to make the problem of identifying their common characteristics non-trivial. Thirdly, much linguistic research has been done on natural numeral systems, and many significant generalizations have already emerged from this work (Hurford 1975; Stampe 1976). Fourthly, the semantics of numerals is exceptionally clear: it is beyond dispute that *soixante-dix* in French and *seventy* in English both denote the number which is symbolized by the Arabic numeral 70, and it is intuitively obvious that *soixante-dix* realizes a semantic representation of this number as the sum of the number named *soixante* and the number named *dix*.

Since our principal aim was to find effective procedures for the acquisition of a natural numeral system from a limited set of number/numeral pairs, we regarded it as essential to check the adequacy of our ideas by embodying them in a computer program which would actually acquire a given numeral system in this way. We describe such a program, and report on its performance; it will, in fact, learn numeral systems as diverse as those

---

*We shall follow standard linguistic practice in using the word "numeral" to refer to a string of words such as *five hundred and three*, and the word "number" for the abstract entity which is referred to by such a word string. Symbols such as the Arabic 503 are, strictly speaking, numerals, but we shall use them when we wish to refer to numbers, or to specify the numbers which are referred to by verbal numerals. With these points in mind, the reader should have no difficulty in understanding sentences such as "the value of *five hundred and three is* 503" and "the English name for 503 is the numeral *five hundred and three*".

of English, French, Japanese, Mixtec, Suppire, and Biblical Welsh, given a little good-will in relation to variations of word form. It demonstrates, as Anderson's program does, how useful semantic information can be in the task of grammar induction. Whether the semantic ideas which inform the program will find application to other parts of natural language remains to be seen.

Linguistic Considerations

Our starting point is *The Linguistic Theory of Numerals* (Hurford 1975). In this useful and thought-provoking book Hurford treats the numerals of a natural language as surface structures generated by a transformational grammar. The base of this grammar is a set of context-free rewriting rules, which correspond to the various ways in which a number can be expressed arithmetically as a combination of two other numbers. The only trouble with such a base is that the vast majority of structures which it generates are linguistically ill formed; anomalous numerals such as *six thousand hundred* are profusely generated along with acceptable ones such as *six hundred thousand*. Hurford deals with this problem by introducing a number of "well-formedness constraints" to separate the wheat from the chaff. As he points out, however, these constraints do not supply any effective procedure by which the well-formedness of a numeral can be established solely on its own merits; *forty nineteen* is rejected only because *fifty nine* is an alternative way of naming the same number and 5 is greater than 4. As criteria which one linguist might offer to another for deciding whether a given numeral is or is not well formed, such constraints may be unexceptionable; but no one could imagine that in order to produce a well-formed numeral the speaker must first call to mind a large number of possible candidates. It appears, therefore, that the knowledge which a speaker actually deploys in using a numeral system cannot be coextensive with the set of all "linguistically significant" generalizations that can be made about the system; part, at least, of his apparent "competence" is no more than an account, by the linguist, of certain observable regularities which owe their origin to the evolutionary history of the language and the way in which it is normally used. But if part of the speaker's competence is apparent rather than real, how are we to specify what he really has learned at any stage in the acquisition of a numeral system? In the following section we attempt to answer this question, in a way which does justice both to the recursive nature of numeral systems, as emphasized by Hurford, and to the central role of semantics in the generation of well-formed numerals. If in reformulating the theory of numeral systems we miss a number of significant generalizations, especially about the morphology of number-words, this is in order to arrive at a psychologically plausible, if incomplete, account of the learner's developing knowledge, and of the grammatical preconceptions which enable him to extend it.

The Translation of Numbers into Numerals

Figure 1 shows, in a slightly modified form, the structure that Hurford assigns to a typical English numeral. We shall want to discuss it in terms rather different from his, since we are primarily interested in the mental processes by which the speaker translates the number at the top into the string of words at the bottom.

We suppose that the speaker's internalized grammar comprises three components: a semantic component, a syntactic component, and a lexicon.

Reference to the lexicon enables the speaker to decide whether any number occurring in the structure is to be realized directly, by a single word, or is to be further elaborated by the semantic component. This decision will depend, in general, upon the context in which the number occurs. Thus the number 100 standing on its own cannot be realized by a

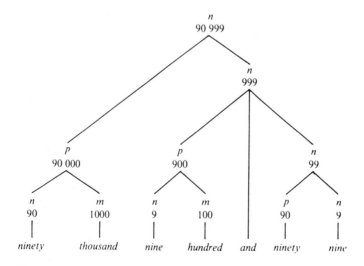

Figure 1
The structure of a typical English numeral. A number is marked with the symbol m if it is the major term (multiplicand) in a product, with n if it is the minor term in an expression or if it stands alone, and with p if it is the major (principal) term in a sum.

single word, but in its role as the multiplicand m in a product it is realized by the word *hundred*.

The semantic component of the speaker's grammar supplies, for every number which cannot be named by a single word, an arithmetic expression—possibly more than one—by which that number may be semantically represented. Such a "well-formed" expression* may be the *sum, difference,* or *product* of two unequal numbers, which we shall call the *major term* and the *minor term*. We use the symbol p to denote the major term in a sum or difference, and the symbol m to denote the major term of a product; the symbol n is used for the minor term in any expression, or for a number standing on its own.[†] In contrast to the constituents of numerals, the two terms of an expression are to be thought of as occurring in any left-to-right order; they are distinguished solely by their semantic roles. This is an important point of departure from Hurford, whose symbols NUMBER, PHRASE, and M designate not semantic roles but syntactic categories.

The minor term in any expression is always a number, but the major term requires further discussion. In a product the major term is always a number, directly realized by a single word (Stampe 1976). Such numbers, which we describe as *multiplicands*, are few and far between, the only multiplicands in the English numeral system being 100, 1000, 1 000 000, etc. In a sum or difference, on the other hand, the major term may be either a number which is realizable by a single word, or a product whose major term exceeds the minor term of the sum or difference in which the product occurs. It is convenient to have a name for numbers, as opposed to products, which can play the role of major term in a sum or a difference; we shall refer to such numbers as *constants*.

The syntactic component of the speaker's grammar consists, we suggest, of a set of rules for the realization of expressions by syntactic forms. Thus in English there is a rule to the effect that any expression of the type $(20 + n)$, where n lies in the range 1–9, can be realized by the syntactic form $\langle p \rangle \langle n \rangle$, which means the name of the major term, in this case *twenty*, followed directly by the name of the minor term. The form of these rules depends upon the validity of two principles which seem to apply to all numeral systems. The first principle concerns expressions in which the major term is a number rather than a product:

---

*In the following paragraphs the word "expression" is to be taken to mean "well-formed expression".

[†] The symbols n, p, and m correspond superficially to Hurford's categories NUMBER, PHRASE, and M (see text).

If two such expressions, having the same major term and the same arithmetical operation, are both realized by a given syntactic form, then any expression involving the same major term, the same operation, and an intermediate value of the minor term, is well formed, and is also realized by that form.

Thus, knowing that *twenty one* and *twenty nine* realize the expressions $(20 + 1)$ and $(20 + 9)$ respectively, we may infer that $(20 + 5)$ is well formed and can be realized by the numeral *twenty five*. This fact suggests that one should group such allied expressions together into semantic *formulas* such as $20 + (1 \ldots 9)$, in which the minor term is a sequence of consecutive numbers, and should associate the relevant syntactic form with the formula itself, rather than with the expressions that it generates.

But there is a further principle which seems to apply to the syntactic forms of sums and differences in which the major term is not a constant but a product:

If a sum or difference has a product as its major term, then the syntactic form or forms by which it can be realized are left unchanged by replacing that product by any other product which is generated by the same formula.

Thus, the existence of a product formula which generates all the expressions $(100 \times 1), \ldots, (100 \times 9)$ ensures that the syntactic form by which $((100 \times 5) + 13)$ is realized must be the same as that which realizes, say, $((100 \times 1) + 13)$; the corresponding English numerals are, of course, *five hundred and thirteen* and *one hundred and thirteen*.

In summary, we may think of the speaker's knowledge of a numeral system as comprising, apart from the lexicon, a set of formulas each of which generates a set of sums, differences, or products by which numbers may be semantically represented. A number may be representable by more than one such expression, but no two formulas can generate the same expression. The syntactic realization rules associate syntactic forms, not with the expressions themselves, but with the formulas which generate them. Tables 1 and 2 illustrate the application of these ideas to the English and French numeral systems for numbers up to 999 999.

The Interpretation of Numerals

To use a numeral system effectively the speaker must be able not only to produce the numeral corresponding to a given number, but also to identify the number referred to by a given numeral. The interpretation of numerals calls for two logically distinct but intimately related procedures: the assignment of a syntactic structure to the numeral, and the determination of the

Table 1
The English numeral system for numbers up to 999 999.

Lexicon

Word	Number	Roles
one	1	n
two	2	n
⋮		
nineteen	19	n
twenty	20	n, p
⋮		
ninety	90	n, p
hundred	100	m
thousand	1000	m

Rules

Formula	Form
$20 + (1 \dots 9)$	$\langle p \rangle \langle n \rangle$
⋮	
$90 + (1 \dots 9)$	$\langle p \rangle \langle n \rangle$
$100 \times (1 \dots 9)$	$\langle n \rangle \langle m \rangle$
$1000 \times (1 \dots 999)$	$\langle n \rangle \langle m \rangle$
$[100 \times (1 \dots 9)] + (1 \dots 99)$	$\langle p \rangle$ and $\langle n \rangle$
$[1000 \times (1 \dots 999)] + (1 \dots 99)$	$\langle p \rangle$ and $\langle n \rangle$
$[1000 \times (1 \dots 999)] + (100 \dots 999)$	$\langle p \rangle \langle n \rangle$

number and semantic role to be associated with each node of the structure. We shall use the word "parsing" for the former procedure, and "evaluation" for the latter.

We believe that numerals are actually parsed and evaluated by a "bottom-up" procedure in which nodes at a lower level are progressively conjoined to form higher-level nodes. A clue as to how this may be done is provided by the fact that from every branching node there descends just one node with the role n; the other node is of type p or m. Conversely, in the conjoining of two lower-level nodes, every m at the lower level is replaced by a p or an n at the higher level, and a p at the lower level gives rise to an n at the higher level.

The interpretation of a well-formed numeral consisting of two number-words (and possibly a conjunction) is a relatively straightforward matter. It must be possible to interpret one of the number-words as referring to a number in the role n and the other as referring to a number in one of the

Table 2
The French numeral system for numbers up to 999 999.

Lexicon

Word	Number	Roles
un	1	n
deux	2	n
$\vdots$		
seize	16	n
vingt	20	n, p, m
trente	30	n, p
$\vdots$		
soixante	60	n, p
cent	100	n, p, m
mille	1000	n, p, m

Rules

Formula	Form
$20 + 1$	$\langle p \rangle$ *et* $\langle n \rangle$
$20 + (2 \ldots 9)$	$\langle p \rangle \langle n \rangle$
$\vdots$	
$60 + 1$	$\langle p \rangle$ *et* $\langle n \rangle$
$60 + (1 \ldots 19)$	$\langle p \rangle \langle n \rangle$
20×4	$\langle n \rangle \langle m \rangle$
$[20 \times 4] + (1 \ldots 19)$	$\langle p \rangle \langle n \rangle$
$100 + (1 \ldots 99)$	$\langle p \rangle \langle n \rangle$
$100 \times (2 \ldots 9)$	$\langle n \rangle \langle m \rangle$
$[100 \times (2 \ldots 9)] + (1 \ldots 99)$	$\langle p \rangle \langle n \rangle$
$1000 + (1 \ldots 999)$	$\langle p \rangle \langle n \rangle$
$1000 \times (2 \ldots 999)$	$\langle n \rangle \langle m \rangle$
$[1000 \times (2 \ldots 999)] + (1 \ldots 999)$	$\langle p \rangle \langle n \rangle$

roles m and p, and there must exist in the grammar a rule which associates the corresponding syntactic form with a formula whose major term is the number labelled m or p and whose minor term includes the other number. If these conditions are all satisfied, then the evaluation of the numeral can immediately be carried out: the numbers in question must be added, subtracted, or multiplied according to the arithmetical operation involved in the relevant formula. If the conditions cannot be met, the numeral is ill formed.

In the parsing of a numeral containing three or more number-words, it is necessary to find a sub-string of words which is itself a well-formed numeral and can be evaluated by the grammar. Here we appeal to a principle which follows from the way in which numerals are generated, namely that the number associated with any node N of type p or m is always less than the number associated with any p-type node from which N descends. In building the structure from the bottom upwards it is therefore advisable to search for well-formed numerals in which the major term of the underlying expression is as small as possible, and to give such numerals precedence over others having bigger major terms. Thus in the French numeral *deux cent mille*, both *deux cent* and *cent mille* are well formed,* but the first of these has a smaller major term than the second and is therefore to be evaluated first; the final result is figure 2. If, furthermore, two overlapping well-formed numerals within the original numeral have the same major term, then if either realizes a product, it should be given precedence over the other (Stampe 1976). For example, in *deux cent trois* both *deux cent* and *cent trois* are well formed, but now the major terms are equal, so that *deux cent*, being a product, takes precedence over *cent trois*, which is a sum (figure 3).

A fully effective parsing procedure must also make allowance for the possibility that two overlapping well-formed numerals with the same major term may *both* realize products, or expressions which are not products. Numeral systems in which this happens seem to be rare, but when it does happen our parser gives precedence to the left-hand numeral. We have been able to find *sufficient* conditions, satisfied by many numeral systems, which ensure that the system will not generate ambiguous numerals and

---

*Actually, the conventions of written French pluralize the word for "hundred" when it occurs in such expressions as *deux cents* but leave it unpluralized in such expressions as *deux cent deux*. But, as already remarked, we have not thought it worth while to enter into questions of word-level morphology; the reader will notice one or two similar morphological simplifications in the pages that follow.

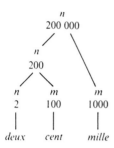

Figure 2

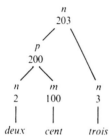

Figure 3

that our parsing algorithm will assign the correct structure to any well-formed numeral generated by the system.* But the ambiguity of certain numerals in, for example, Biblical Welsh shows that these conditions cannot be satisfied by all numeral systems; all we can say is that, when applied to systems which do not satisfy them, our parsing algorithm seems to select, in ambiguous cases, that structure for a given numeral which corresponds to it most "natural" interpretation.

The Acquisition of a Numeral System

So far we have been concerned exclusively with the way in which a numeral system may be represented in a person's mind, and with the use

---

* A particularly simple set of sufficient conditions consists of the following: (i) The semantic component generates only sums and products, never differences, for the representation of non-primitive numbers. (ii) All the syntactic forms by which sums are realized place the names of the major and minor terms in the same order, and the same is true of the forms which realize products; but these two orders are opposite. The above conditions are violated, for example, in German: *vier und zwanzig* and *hundert und zwanzig* display their major and minor terms in opposite orders. But, as already remarked, the conditions are not necessary, only sufficient.

that he makes of his grammatical knowledge in translating numbers into numerals and vice versa. We now turn to the problem of how he can induce this knowledge from a limited succession of well-formed numerals presented in association with their numerical values.

In order for him to learn the system at all, it is clearly necessary that the teacher should present him with relatively simple examples first, including all the single-word numerals by which numbers may be directly named. If a newly presented numeral contains more than one unfamiliar word, the learner can hardly be expected to make sense of it; we allow him to assume that, in a numeral containing just one unfamiliar word, that word is a conjunction if two or more other words are present, and otherwise a constant or a multiplicand—the latter if the stated value of the numeral is divisible by the known value of the other number-word. This convention is the only obvious alternative to suspending judgement in the hope that the meaning of the unfamiliar word will ultimately become clear from later presentations; such suspensions of judgement do not fit comfortably into a formal theory of language acquisition.

To illustrate the process of grammatical induction, let us imagine that the learner has acquired the English names for the numbers $1, \ldots, 20$, and that he is now presented with the number/numeral pair (*twenty one*, 21). Knowing the numerical values associated with *twenty* and *one*, he can infer that the given numeral is the syntactic realization of a sum, that in this sum 20 must be the major term p and 1 the minor term n, and that the syntactic form by which the sum is realized is therefore $\langle p \rangle \langle n \rangle$. Next he is introduced, let us suppose, to the pair (*twenty nine*, 29). This is clearly the syntactic realization of $(20 + 9)$ by the same form; using the first of the two principles enunciated above, he can now construct a formula $20 + (1 \ldots 9)$, and associate with this the syntactic form $\langle p \rangle \langle n \rangle$. Now, when invited to name the number 25, for example, he can consult his grammar and produce the numeral *twenty five*, or given this numeral he can interpret it as meaning 25. In making these inductions he has used semantics in two ways: first, in inferring, by arithmetic, that *twenty one* and *twenty nine* both realize sums rather than products or differences; and secondly, in conflating the corresponding expressions into a formula, by arithmetical interpolation between the values of their minor terms.

Proceeding in this way he succeeds, let us suppose, in learning the English numeral system up to 99, and is then presented with (*one hundred*, 100). *Hundred* is an unfamiliar word occurring in a two-word numeral, so it must stand for the major term in some expression with minor term 1; since 100 is divisible by 1, he interprets *hundred* as the word for 100 in the role m and enters it as such in the lexicon. The syntactic form of *one hundred* is therefore $\langle n \rangle \langle m \rangle$. Presentation of (*nine hundred*, 900) now enables him to establish the existence of a product formula $100 \times (1 \ldots 9)$ and to associate the form $\langle n \rangle \langle m \rangle$ with this formula.

At this point he meets his first many-word numeral, in the pair (*one hundred and one*, 101). A parsing problem arises and is dealt with in much the same way as when he knows the full grammar. The word *and* is unfamiliar, and is diagnosed as a conjunction because there are more than two words in the complete numeral. There is only one well-formed composite numeral in the given string, namely *one hundred*, so this must be evaluated first, giving 100. The problem is now much the same as that of interpreting the numeral *twenty one*; *one hundred and one* must be the realization of the sum $(100 + 1)$, by the form $\langle p \rangle$ and $\langle n \rangle$. But the major term in this sum was the product (100×1), and this product is generated by a formula with which the learner is already familiar. He is therefore in a position to name all the numbers $201, \ldots, 901$, or to interpret the corresponding numerals, even though he has never met them before. Finally, he is introduced to the pair (*nine hundred and ninety nine*, 999). This contains two well-formed substrings, namely *nine hundred* and *ninety nine*, of which the latter has a smaller major term (90) than the former (100) and so should be evaluated first (though in this case the order is immaterial). Only addition of 900 and 99 will give 999, so again the numeral must stand for a sum, realized by the form $\langle p \rangle$ and $\langle n \rangle$. By interpolation he thus arrives at the general formula $((100 \times q) + r)$, where q ranges from 1 to 9 and r ranges from 1 to 99; any expression generated by this formula can safely be realized by the syntactic form $\langle p \rangle$ and $\langle n \rangle$.

In English the only types of expression used for representing numbers semantically are sums and products, and the only conjunction used in the English numeral system is the word *and*, which always appears between the numerals which it conjoins. In some other languages subtraction is employed, and also extraposed conjunctions; in Biblical Welsh, for example, the numeral for 39 is *onid un dau ugain*—literally "subtract one two twenty". This presents a minor problem for the parser, but one which may be easily circumvented provided that only single-word numbers are ever subtracted from other numbers and that extraposition only moves the conjunction across the corresponding word. The details are not worth entering into, as they raise no points of linguistic or psychological interest.

In the preceding discussion we have made use of the idea that a formula which generates sums or differences may have as its major term a product formula rather than merely a product. In computational terms, one may think of the major term in a sum or difference formula as "pointing to" the product formula in question, and as continuing to point to that product formula even when the range of the latter has been extended. We think it quite possible that this idea (which is actually implemented in the program) corresponds with the way in which grammatical rules are actually stored in a person's memory; if so, it would account naturally for the second principle of induction to which we drew attention above.

Reasoning by Syntactic Analogy

We saw above how semantic inference, based on the two inductive principles stated, can enable a learner to acquire a numeral system from a restricted set of well-formed numerals, provided that each is presented in association with its numerical value. Having acquired the system, he can then name with confidence an arbitrary number, or evaluate any well-formed numeral. But it is also possible for someone who has learned or partly learned a language to make plausible guesses as to the meaning of a sentence which, though not actually generated by the grammar, would be if the grammar were extended in a "natural" way. Thus an English speaker, hearing a foreigner ask for "twenty and four envelopes", would naturally suppose him to be wanting 24 envelopes, rather than 80, 16, or any other number. Is it possible to understand such analogical reasoning in terms of the present theory of numeral systems?

Even to someone who knows the entire numeral system of English, the ill-formed numeral *twenty and four* is not entirely nonsensical. Up to a point it is amenable to parsing: *twenty* is the word for 20 in the role p or n, and *four* realizes 4 in the role n. From a purely syntactic point of view, $\langle p \rangle$ *and* $\langle n \rangle$ is an acceptable form to be associated with a sum or difference formula and, furthermore, a form which is actually associated with two of the sum formulas present in the grammar. The only trouble is that the putative major term 20 in *twenty and four* is not the major term of either of these formulas; but apart from this, everything points to the numeral's being the realization of the sum 20 + 4 by the syntactic form $\langle p \rangle$ *and* $\langle n \rangle$, so that the most reasonable value to assign to it is 24.

Similar reasoning might lead a person learning the French system to guess correctly the meaning of *deux cent*, having acquired the system only as far as 199. In this slightly different case, *cent* has appeared hitherto only in the roles n and p, so that the apparent syntactic form of *deux cent* is $\langle n \rangle \langle p \rangle$, which is not present in the grammar. But the form $\langle n \rangle \langle m \rangle$ is present, having been encountered in the numeral *quatre-vingts*, and this would match the given numeral if *cent* were able to serve as the major term m in a product. So a good guess would be that *deux cent* realizes a product, and thus has the value 200.

Syntactic analogy is, however, an unreliable guide to the well-formedness of numerals, or to the names of numbers which are not representable by any formula yet present in the speaker's grammar. A person who had learned the English numeral system up to 100 might be tempted to suppose, by syntactic analogy with *twenty one*, that *one hundred one* was a well-formed numeral, and that it was the name of the number 101; but he would be wrong in drawing either conclusion. On its own, therefore, reasoning by syntactic analogy is only useful in the formulation of plausible hypotheses about the grammar; it can only suggest, not confirm, how the grammar should be extended.

A Program which Learns to Count

The surest way of finding logical flaws in any cognitive theory such as that proposed here is to attempt to implement it as a computer program. For this reason we decided to compose a program that would actually learn to name the numbers in a natural language, and to evaluate well-formed numerals in that language, upon presentation of a representative set of number/numeral pairs. In this section we describe the external aspects of the program, as seen by the operator; an actual session with the program is described, with comments, in appendix A.

At any stage in the training session the operator may type in a number, a numeral, or a number/numeral pair, followed by a question mark or a full stop. (The order of the number and the numeral in a pair is immaterial.) He may also, if he wishes, inspect the current state of the program's grammar, by typing appropriate instructions, but the development of the program's knowledge will, in any case, be evident from its output. If he types in just a number (in Arabic notation) followed by a question mark, then the corresponding numeral (or numerals, in systems which permit paraphrase) will be typed out if and only if it is generated by the grammar in its current form; otherwise the program will respond with the word UNKNOWN.

If a numeral is presented on its own, there are three possible types of response. If the grammar permits the reliable interpretation of the numeral, then the corresponding number will be printed, followed by a full stop. Otherwise, if the value of the numeral can be guessed by syntactic analogy (see above), then this value will be printed out, followed by a question mark. If the operator then types Yes, the program will extend its grammar accordingly and will indicate the nature of the extension; if he types No, then the program may make another guess, but ultimately it will give up and output the word UNKNOWN. Finally, if the numeral cannot even be parsed by analogy, the word UNKNOWN will be printed out immediately.

Presentation of a number/numeral pair may also evoke a variety of responses. If the numeral is a single word, then this word will be entered in the lexicon as the name of the number, overwriting any name which may have already been assigned to that number. The new lexical entry is displayed, and the word ACCEPTED is printed. Otherwise, if the numeral can be reliably evaluated according to the current grammar, the program will print either TRUE or SURELY NOT according as the value found does or does not agree with the number presented. Two other possibilities remain, according as the program can or cannot "nearly" parse the numeral according to the grammar. A numeral may be said to have been "nearly" parsed when it has been expressed as the concatenation of two interpretable numerals and possibly a conjunction. If the values of these numerals can be combined by addition, subtraction, or multiplication to give a result equal to the presented number in a way which conforms with the general principles outlined above, then the grammar can be correspondingly extended; the consequent changes in the grammar are typed out, followed by the word ACCEPTED. Otherwise the program responds with the word UNINTELLIGIBLE.

By typing Why? the operator can cause the program to display, as an indented tree, the structure of any numeral that it has produced or evaluated successfully. Such a tree, representing the structure of the Suppire numeral for 376, is exhibited near the end of appendix A. Apart from the three nodes associated with the conjunction *and*, every node is associated with a number, a role for that number, and either a number word or an expression generated by one of the formulas in the grammar.

A word may be said about the way in which the program actually stores the grammar. Every rule of the grammar points directly to a formula and a syntactic form; the major term of every formula points either to a lexical entry or to a product formula. This device is not only convenient when it proves necessary to correct misinformation with which the program has inadvertently been supplied; it also captures the idea that a speaker's internalized knowledge of a numeral system is a highly connected data structure in which an entity such as a lexical number is not represented by several tokens of the same type, but by a single token which can be accessed in a number of different ways. The language POP 10 (a descendant of POP 2; see Burstall, Collins, and Popplestone 1971), in which the program is written, lends itself naturally to the implementation of this idea.

Finally, though perhaps it needs no emphasis, the program illustrates the fact that the effectiveness of any procedure for learning a language rests upon the cooperation of the teacher. If the training set is presented in a random order, the grammar may take a very long time to acquire.

Discussion

In this chapter we have attempted to explore the idea that a learner makes essential use of semantic information in acquiring the syntax of a natural language. The experiments of Miller (1967), Moeser and Bregman (1972, 1973), and Anderson (1975) on grammatical induction have already shown that human learners have great difficulty in inducing artificial grammars unless supplied with relevant semantic information; we have offered detailed suggestions as to how such information can actually be brought to bear on the task. For the limited and admittedly rather special domain of number-names, we have shown, first, that an effective procedure for inducing a numeral system from a set of number/numeral pairs can actually be specified, and, second, that semantic information can be powerfully employed in acquiring that component of the grammar which generates underlying structures. So far as we know, no effective procedure for inducing a grammar from purely syntactic data has ever been proposed, either for the numerals or for any other domain.

It is worth reviewing the main ways in which our program uses semantic information, since they resemble those used by Anderson in his LAS program, and may well apply more generally. First, the inductive rules used in our program can only be stated in semantic terms. For example, the training sequence (*one*, 1), (*two*, 2), ..., (*twenty*, 20), followed by (*twenty one*, 21) and then (*twenty nine*, 29), enables the program to construct the formula 20 + (1 ... 9), thereby adding the numerals *twenty two*, ..., *twenty eight* to the set generated by the grammar. Such a generalization, which admits, for example, *twenty two* but excludes *twenty ten*, must of necessity be semantically based, since the actual words *two* and *ten* have the same syntactic distribution in the training sequence. The general idea exemplified by this rule is that the substitution class of a constituent is most reliably extended by identifying some natural class of semantic entities to which the meanings of the current substitution class all belong.

The second important use of semantic information is in assigning a syntactic structure to a novel word string. If the learner can assign meanings to possible constituents of a string, then knowing its meaning will often help him to assign a syntactic structure to the string as a whole. Thus if the training sequence begins with the pairs (*deux*, 2), (*cent*, 100), (*cent deux*, 102), and (*deux cent*, 200) he can infer not only that *cent deux* must be the realization of a sum, and *deux cent* the realization of a product, but also that if *deux cent deux* means 202, then it should be bracketed as [(*deux cent*) *deux*] rather than as [*deux* (*cent deux*)], though there would be no purely distributional reason for preferring the former to the latter.

Although our program may have some relevance to the way in which an adult learns the numeral system of a foreign language (as witnessed by the resemblance between the optimal training sequence for the program and the information typically supplied in dictionaries), it is not intended as a model of how children first learn to count. Nor do the grammars which the program induces capture all the significant generalizations which a linguist might wish to make about numeral systems. But if they fail to recognize a number of regularities, especially about the relations between different number-words in a language, that is because they are designed to accommodate those generalizations which are of most help to the language user, rather than those which arise from the evolutionary history of the language.

Our attempt to understand how numeral systems could be acquired by induction has led us to describe them in terms which do not fit neatly into any theory of grammar with which we are acquainted. The base grammar of a numeral system, in our theory, is a set of semantic formulas which generate unordered arithmetic expressions for the representation of non-primitive numbers. These expressions are converted into syntactic structures by rules which order the terms in an expression according to their semantic roles; the lexicon attaches words to the terminal nodes. Thus the base grammar generates semantic structures, reminding one of generative semantics; simple arithmetic supplies the semantic interpretation rules, postulated in the standard theory (Chomsky 1965); and the use of semantic roles, referred to by realization rules, puts one in mind of the concept of a "function" in Systemic Grammar (Halliday 1961; Hudson 1972). Whether such an eclectic approach to linguistic theory will prove helpful in other domains remains, of course, to be seen.

Acknowledgements

Our thanks are due to G. Gazdar, J. Hurford, S. Isard, P. Johnson-Laird, S. Sutherland, A. Zwicky, and W. G. Evans for useful discussion, and to the Royal Society and the Science Research Council for financial support and computing facilities.

References

Anderson, J. R. 1975. Computer simulation of a language acquisition system—a first report. In *Information Processing and Cognition*, ed. R. L. Solso (Hillsdale, New Jersey: Erlbaum).

Burstall, R. M., J. S. Collins, and R. J. Popplestone. 1971. *Programming in POP-2*. Edinburgh University Press.

Chomsky, N. 1962. Explanatory models in linguistics. In *Logic, Methodology and Philosophy of Science*, ed. E. Nagel, P. Suppes, and A. Tarski (Stanford University Press).

Chomsky, N. 1965. *Aspects of the Theory of Syntax*. The Hague: Mouton.

Gold, E. M. 1967. Language identification in the limit. *Inf. Control* 10: 447.

Halliday, M. A. K. 1961. Categories of the theory of grammar. *Word* 17: 241.

Hudson, R. A. 1972. *English Complex Sentences*. Amsterdam: North-Holland.

Hurford, J. R. 1975. *The Linguistic Theory of Numerals*. Cambridge University Press.

Miller, G. A. 1967. *The Psychology of Communication*. London: Penguin.

Moeser, J. D., and A. S. Bregman. 1972. The role of reference in the acquisition of a miniature artificial language. *J. Verbal Lang. Verbal Behav.* 11: 759.

Moeser, J. D., and A. S. Bregman. 1973. Imagery and language acquisition. *J. Verbal Lang. Verbal Behav.* 12: 91.

Stampe, D. 1976. Cardinal number systems. In Proceedings of the 12th Annual Conference of the Chicago Linguistics Society. University of Chicago Press.

Welmers, W. E. 1973. *African Language Structures*. Berkeley: University of California Press.

Appendix A

In the following session with the operator, the program acquired the numeral system of Suppire, in Anglicized form. The data on which the number/numeral pairs are based are from Welmers 1973. The symbols typed by the operator are those which appeared on the lines prefaced by a colon, and include all the words typed in lower case. Everything else was printed by the program, including the upper-case symbols. The following notes refer to stages in the session, which are indicated by bracketed lower-case letters.

(*a*) The lexical entry for a number word consists of a word, a list of roles, and a number. The entry indicates that if the number appears in one of the listed roles, it should be represented by the word.

(*b*) If a new word is introduced in a numeral more than two words long, the new word is assumed to be a conjunction. The major term of the formula $10 + 1$ is actually a pointer to the lexical entry for the word TEN.

Similarly, the second term in the form ⟨P⟩ AND ⟨N⟩ is a pointer to the lexical entry for the conjunction AND.

(*c*) A solitary number or numeral, followed by a question mark, is taken as a request to produce the corresponding numeral or number. If the operator presents a number for which no numeral is generated by the program's language model, the program always replies UNKNOWN. If, however, the operator presents a numeral which is not generated by the program's language model, the program is sometimes able to guess the meaning of the numeral by syntactic analogy. When this happens, the program types back a number and then a question mark to show it is guessing. The operator must then reply Yes or No. If the answer is Yes, the program updates its language model; if No, it guesses again, and so on until its guesses are exhausted.

(*d*) The program's language model now generates every numeral from TEN AND ONE to TEN AND NINE. The program can therefore evaluate any of these numerals without needing to guess.

(*e*) When it produces or evaluates a numeral, the program constructs a tree which represents both the syntactic structure of the numeral and the underlying semantic structure. This tree is printed out in response to Why? Each node on the tree consists of a numerical value (unless the node represents a conjunction), a role, and a third item, which is either a word (in the case of a terminal node) or an arithmetic expression (in the case of a non-terminal node). Daughter nodes are indented several spaces to the right of their parent.

(*f*) The program can find no arithmetic operation which produces 22 when applied to 20 and 1.

(*g*) The program is able to guess a numeral if it can evaluate it to two trees, or three trees including a conjunction, and can match the resulting list of trees to a syntactic form in the language model. After a guess has been confirmed, Why? is taken as a request to print out this list of trees.

(*h*) Since 2 exactly divides 40, the new word SCORE is assumed to symbolize a multiplicand.

(*i*) The major term [20 * 2] is actually a pointer to that product formula, and thus any subsequent extension of the product formula automatically extends the major term as well.

(*j*) The rule added before note *h* has now been extended to [20 * (2 3)] + (1 19), ⟨P⟩ AND ⟨N⟩, and the program can therefore give definite answers to the next two questions.

```
    : .lesson:
  : one 1.
   NEW LEXICAL ENTRY: [ONE [N] 1]                              (a)
  * ACCEPTED.
  : two 2.
   NEW LEXICAL ENTRY: [TWO [N] 2]
  * ACCEPTED.
  : three 3.
   NEW LEXICAL ENTRY: [THREE [N] 3]
  * ACCEPTED.
  : four 4.
   NEW LEXICAL ENTRY: [FOUR [N] 4]
  * ACCEPTED.
  : five 5.
   NEW LEXICAL ENTRY: [FIVE [N] 5]
  * ACCEPTED.
  : six 6.
   NEW LEXICAL ENTRY: [SIX [N] 6]
  * ACCEPTED.
  : seven 7.
   NEW LEXICAL ENTRY: [SEVEN [N] 7]

  * ACCEPTED.
  : eight 8.
   NEW LEXICAL ENTRY: [EIGHT [N] 8]
  * ACCEPTED.
  : nine 9.
   NEW LEXICAL ENTRY: [NINE [N] 9]
  * ACCEPTED.
  : ten 10.
   NEW LEXICAL ENTRY: [TEN [N] 10]
  * ACCEPTED.
  : ten and one 11.
   NEW LEXICAL ENTRY: [AND [C] AND]
   NEW RULE: 10 + 1, <P>AND<N>
   LEXICAL ENTRY CHANGED: [TEN [N] 10] => [TEN [P N] 10]      (b)
```

```
*  ACCEPTED.

:  seven?

*  7.

:  11?

*  TEN AND ONE.

:  19?

*  UNKNOWN.

:  ten and nine?

*  19?

:  yes.

   NEW RULE:  10 + 9,  <P>AND<N>
   INTERPOLATION WITH 10 + 1,  <P>AND<N>
   RESULT:  10 + (1 9),  <P>AND<N>

:  ten and five?

*  15.

:  why?

   [15 [N] 10+5]
       [10 P TEN]
       [AND C AND]
       [5 N FIVE]

:  twenty 20.

   NEW LEXICAL ENTRY:  [TWENTY [N] 20]

*  ACCEPTED.

:  twenty and one 22.

*  UNINTELLIGIBLE.

:  twenty and one 21.

   NEW RULE:  20 + 1,  <P>AND<N>
   LEXICAL ENTRY CHANGED:  [TWENTY [N] 20] => [TWENTY [P N] 20]

*  ACCEPTED.

:  twenty and ten and nine?

*  39?

:  yes.

   NEW RULE:  20 + 19,  <P>AND<N>
   INTERPOLATION WITH 20 + 1,  <P>AND<N>
   RESULT:  20 + (1 19),  <P>AND<N>

:  why?

   [20 [P N] TWENTY]
```

(c)

(d)

(e)

(f)

[AND [C] AND]

[19 [N] 10+9]   (g)
    [10 P TEN]
    [AND C AND]
    [9 N NINE]

: twenty and ten and four 34.

* TRUE.

: twenty and ten 37.

* SURELY NOT.

: score two 40.

NEW LEXICAL ENTRY: [SCORE [M] 20]   (h)
NEW RULE: 20 * 2, <M><N>

* ACCEPTED.

: score two and one 41.

NEW RULE: [20 * 2] + 1, <P>AND<N>

* ACCEPTED.

: score two and ten and nine 59.

NEW RULE: [20 * 2] + 19, <P>AND<N>
INTERPOLATION WITH [20 * 2] + 1, <P>AND<N>
RESULT: [20 * 2] + (1 19), <P>AND<N>

* ACCEPTED.   (i)

: score three 60.

NEW RULE: 20 * 3, <M><N>
INTERPOLATION WITH 20 * 2, <M><N>
RESULT: 20 * (2 3), <M><N>

* ACCEPTED.   (j)

: 76?

* SCORE THREE AND TEN AND SIX.

: score three and four?

* 64.

: eighty 80.

NEW LEXICAL ENTRY: [EIGHTY [N] 80]

* ACCEPTED.

: eighty and one 81.

NEW RULE: 80 + 1, <P>AND<N>
LEXICAL ENTRY CHANGED: [EIGHTY [N] 80] => [EIGHTY [P N] 80]

* ACCEPTED.

: eighty and score three and ten and nine?

* 159?

▪ yes.

```
 NEW RULE: 80 + 79, <P>AND<N>
 INTERPOLATION WITH 80 + 1, <P>AND<N>
 RESULT: 80 + (1 79), <P>AND<N>
```

▪ eighty two?

★ 160?

▪ yes.

```
 NEW RULE: 80 * 2, <M><N>
 LEXICAL ENTRY CHANGED: [EIGHTY [P N] 80] => [EIGHTY [M P N] 80]
```

▪ eighty four 320.

```
 NEW RULE: 80 * 4, <M><N>
 INTERPOLATION WITH 80 * 2, <M><N>
 RESULT: 80 * (2 4), <M><N>
```

★ ACCEPTED.

▪ eighty three and one 241.

```
 NEW RULE: [80 * (2 4)] + 1, <P>AND<N>
```

★ ACCEPTED.

▪ eighty four and score three and ten and nine 399.

```
 NEW RULE: [80 * (2 4)] + 79, <P>AND<N>
 INTERPOLATION WITH [80 * (2 4)] + 1, <P>AND<N>
 RESULT: [80 * (2 4)] + (1 79), <P>AND<N>
```

★ ACCEPTED.

▪ 275?

★ EIGHTY THREE AND TWENTY AND TEN AND FIVE.

▪ eighty four and score two and ten and six?

★ 376.

▪ why?

```
[376 [N] (80*4)+56]
    [320 P 80*4]
            [80 M EIGHTY]
            [4 N FOUR]
        [AND C AND]
        [56 N (20*2)+16]
            [40 P 20*2]
                    [20 M SCORE]
                    [2 N TWO]
                [AND C AND]
                [16 N 10+6]
                        [10 P TEN]
                        [AND C AND]
                        [6 N SIX]
```

▪ eighty two and score two?

★ 200.

```
ı stop.

ı .prlexiconı
LEXICON
  ONE [N] 1
  TWO [N] 2
  THREE [N] 3
  FOUR [N] 4
  FIVE [N] 5
  SIX [N] 6
  SEVEN [N] 7
  EIGHT [N] 8
  NINE [N] 9
  TEN [P N] 10
  AND [C] AND
  TWENTY [P N] 20
  SCORE [M] 20
  EIGHTY [M P N] 80

ı .prrulesı
RULES
  10 + (1 9), <P>AND<N>
  20 + (1 19), <P>AND<N>
  20 * (2 3), <M><N>
  [20 * (2 3)] + (1 19), <P>AND<N>
  80 + (1 79), <P>AND<N>
  80 * (2 4), <M><N>
  [80 * (2 4)] + (1 79), <P>AND<N>

ı
```

Appendix B

We here record, in brief, five more training sessions in which the program learns (or partly learns) the numeral systems of English, French, German, Mixtec, and Biblical Welsh. We have taken a few liberties with these systems to allow for the program's inability to do morphology; for instance, the French numeral for 80, usually written *quatre-vingts*, is presented as *quatre vingt*, and the German numeral for 13, usually *dreizehn*, is changed to *drei zehn*. In each session, the training sequence is optimal (i.e. the shortest sequence from which the program can learn the specified part of the numeral system). To save space we give just the following data:

the sequence of number/numeral pairs presented,

literal translations of foreign numerals, and

the language model which the program constructed from the training sequence.

English, below 1 000 000

Number	Numeral
1	one
2	two
3	three
4	four
5	five
6	six
7	seven
8	eight
9	nine
10	ten
11	eleven
12	twelve
13	thirteen
14	fourteen
15	fifteen
16	sixteen
17	seventeen
18	eighteen
19	nineteen
20	twenty
21	twenty one
29	twenty nine
30	thirty
31	thirty one
39	thirty nine
40	forty
41	forty one
49	forty nine
50	fifty
51	fifty one
59	fifty nine
60	sixty
61	sixty one
69	sixty nine
70	seventy
71	seventy one
79	seventy nine
80	eighty
81	eighty one
89	eighty nine
90	ninety

Number	Numeral
91	ninety one
99	ninety nine
100	one hundred
101	one hundred and one
199	one hundred and ninety nine
900	nine hundred
1 000	one thousand
1 001	one thousand and one
1 099	one thousand and ninety nine
1 100	one thousand one hundred
1 999	one thousand nine hundred and ninety nine
999 000	nine hundred and ninety nine thousand

```
! [engl sh].readmodel! .prmodel!        RULES
LEXICON                                   20 + (1 9), <P><N>
ONE [N] 1                                 30 + (1 9), <P><N>
TWO [N] 2                                 40 + (1 9), <P><N>
THREE [N] 3                               50 + (1 9), <P><N>
FOUR [N] 4                                60 + (1 9), <P><N>
FIVE [N] 5                                70 + (1 9), <P><N>
SIX [N] 6                                 80 + (1 9), <P><N>
SEVEN [N] 7                               90 + (1 9), <P><N>
EIGHT [N] 8                               100 * (1 9), <N><M>
NINE [N] 9                                [100 * (1 9)] + (1 99), <P>AND<N>
TEN [N] 10                                1000 * (1 999), <N><M>
ELEVEN [N] 11                             [1000 * (1 999)] + (1 99), <P>AND<N>
TWELVE [N] 12                             [1000 * (1 999)] + (100 999), <P><N>
THIRTEEN [N] 13
FOURTEEN [N] 14
FIFTEEN [N] 15
SIXTEEN [N] 16
SEVENTEEN [N] 17
EIGHTEEN [N] 18
NINETEEN [N] 19
TWENTY [P N] 20
THIRTY [P N] 30
FORTY [P N] 40
FIFTY [P N] 50
SIXTY [P N] 60
SEVENTY [P N] 70
EIGHTY [P N] 80
NINETY [P N] 90
HUNDRED [M] 100
AND [C] AND
THOUSAND [M] 1000
```

French, below 1 000 000

Number	Numeral	Translation
1	un	one
2	deux	two
3	trois	three
4	quatre	four
5	cinq	five
6	six	six
7	sept	seven
8	huit	eight
9	neuf	nine
10	dix	ten
11	onze	eleven
12	douze	twelve
13	treize	thirteen
14	quatorze	fourteen
15	quinze	fifteen
16	seize	sixteen
17	dix sept	ten seven
19	dix neuf	ten nine
20	vingt	twenty
21	vingt et un	twenty and one
22	vingt deux	twenty two
29	vingt neuf	twenty nine
30	trente	thirty
31	trente et un	thirty and one
32	trente deux	thirty two
39	trente neuf	thirty nine
40	quarante	forty
41	quarante et un	forty and one
42	quarante deux	forty two
49	quarante neuf	forty nine
50	cinquante	fifty
51	cinquante et un	fifty and one
52	cinquante deux	fifty two
59	cinquante neuf	fifty nine
60	soixante	sixty
61	soixante et un	sixty and one
62	soixante deux	sixty two
79	soixante dix neuf	sixty ten nine
80	quatre vingt	four twenty
81	quatre vingt un	four twenty one
99	quatre vingt dix neuf	four twenty ten nine
100	cent	hundred

Number	Numeral	Translation
101	cent un	hundred one
199	cent quatre vingt dix neuf	hundred four twenty ten nine
200	deux cent	two hundred
201	deux cent un	two hundred one
299	deux cent quatre vingt dix neuf	two hundred four twenty ten nine
900	neuf cent	nine hundred
1 000	mille	thousand
1 001	mille un	thousand one
1 999	mille neuf cent quatre vingt dix neuf	thousand nine hundred four twenty ten nine
2 000	deux mille	two thousand
2 001	deux mille un	two thousand one
2 999	deux mille neuf cent quatre vingt dix neuf	two thousand nine hundred four twenty ten nine
999 000	neuf cent quatre vingt dix neuf mille	nine hundred four twenty ten nine thousand

```
 ! [french].readmodel! .prmodel!
LEXICON
UN [N] 1
DEUX [N] 2
TROIS [N] 3
QUATRE [N] 4
CINQ [N] 5
SIX [N] 6
SEPT [N] 7
HUIT [N] 8
NEUF [N] 9
DIX [P N] 10
ONZE [N] 11
DOUZE [N] 12
TREIZE [N] 13
QUATORZE [N] 14
SEIZE [N] 16
QUINZE [N] 15
VINGT [M P N] 20
ET [C] ET
TRENTE [P N] 30
QUARANTE [P N] 40
CINQUANTE [P N] 50
SOIXANTE [P N] 60
CENT [M P N] 100
MILLE [M P N] 1000
```

```
RULES
10 + (7 9), <P><N>
20 + 1, <P>ET<N>
20 + (2 9), <P><N>
30 + 1, <P>ET<N>
30 + (2 9), <P><N>
40 + 1, <P>ET<N>
40 + (2 9), <P><N>
50 + 1, <P>ET<N>
50 + (2 9), <P><N>
60 + 1, <P>ET<N>
60 + (2 19), <P><N>
20 * 4, <N><M>
[20 * 4] + (1 19), <P><N>
100 + (1 99), <P><N>
100 * (2 9), <N><M>
[100 * (2 9)] + (1 99), <P><N>
1000 + (1 999), <P><N>
1000 * (2 999), <N><M>
[1000 * (2 999)] + (1 999), <P><N>
!
```

German, below 1 000 000 (Slightly Modified)

Number	Numeral	Translation
1	eins	one
2	zwei	two
3	drei	three
4	vier	four
5	funf	five
6	sechs	six
7	sieben	seven
8	acht	eight
9	neun	nine
10	zehn	ten
11	elf	eleven
12	zwolf	twelve
13	drei zehn	three ten
19	neun zehn	nine ten
20	zwanzig	twenty
21	eins und zwanzig	one and twenty
29	neun und zwanzig	nine and twenty
30	drei zig	three tens
31	eins und drei zig	one and three tens
39	neun und drei zig	nine and three tens
90	neun zig	nine tens
100	hundert	hundred
101	hundert und eins	hundred and one
199	hundert und neun und neun zig	hundred and nine and nine tens
200	zwei hundert	two hundred
201	zwei hundert und eins	two hundred and one
299	zwei hundert und neun und neun zig	two hundred and nine and nine tens
900	neun hundert	nine hundred
1 000	tausend	thousand
1 001	tausend und eins	thousand and one
1 999	tausend und neun hundert und neun und neun zig	thousand and nine hundred and nine and nine tens
2 000	zwei tausend	two thousand
2 001	zwei tausend und eins	two thousand and one
2 999	zwei tausend und neun hundert und neun und neun zig	two thousand and nine hundred and nine and nine tens
999 000	neun hundert und neun und neun zig tausend	nine hundred and nine and nine tens thousand

```
  ! [german].readmodel!. .prmodel!          RULES
LEXICON                                     10 + (3 9), <N><P>
  EINS [N] 1                                20 + (1 9), <N>UND<P>
  ZWEI [N] 2                                10 * (3 9), <N><M>
  DREI [N] 3                                [10 * (3 9)] + (1 9), <N>UND<P>
  VIER [N] 4                                100 + (1 99), <P>UND<N>
  FUNF [N] 5                                100 * (2 9), <N><M>
  SECHS [N] 6                               [100 * (2 9)] + (1 99), <P>UND<N>
  SIEBEN [N] 7                              1000 + (1 999), <P>UND<N>
  ACHT [N] 8                                1000 * (2 999), <N><M>
  NEUN [N] 9                                [1000 * (2 999)] + (1 999), <P>UND<N>
  ZEHN [P N] 10
  ELF [N] 11                                !
  ZWOLF [N] 12
  ZWANZIG [P N] 20
  UND [C] UND
  ZIG [M] 10
  HUNDERT [M P N] 100
  TAUSEND [M P N] 1000
```

Mixtec, below 8000 (Source: Hurford 1975)

Number	Numeral	Translation
1	ii	one
2	uu	two
3	uni	three
4	kuu	four
5	usu	five
6	inu	six
7	uha	seven
8	una	eight
9	ee	nine
10	usi	ten
11	usi ii	ten one
14	usi kuu	ten four
15	siaku	fifteen
16	siaku ii	fifteen one
19	siaku kuu	fifteen four
20	oko	twenty
21	oko ii	twenty one
39	oko siaku kuu	twenty fifteen four
40	uu siko	two score
41	uu siko ii	two score one
59	uu siko siaku kuu	two score fifteen four
380	siaku kuu siko	fifteen four score
400	ii tuu	one four-hundred
401	ii tuu ii	one four-hundred one
799	ii tuu siaku kuu siko siaku kuu	one four-hundred fifteen four score fifteen four
7 600	siaku kuu tuu	fifteen four four-hundred

```
 ! [mixtec].readmodel! .prmodel!     RULES
LEXICON                               10 + (1 4), <P><N>
  II  [N]  1                          15 + (1 4), <P><N>
  UU  [N]  2                          20 + (1 19), <P><N>
  UNI [N]  3                          20 * (2 19), <N><M>
  KUU [N]  4                          [20 * (2 19)] + (1 19), <P><N>
  USU [N]  5                          400 * (1 19), <N><M>
  INU [N]  6                          [400 * (1 19)] + (1 399), <P><N>
  UHA [N]  7
  UNA [N]  8                          !
  EE  [N]  9
  USI [P N] 10
  SIAKU [P N] 15
  OKO [P N] 20
  SIKO [M] 20
  TUU [M] 400
```

Biblical Welsh, below 10 000 (Source: Hurford 1975)

The reader is warned that the following forms of the Biblical Welsh
numerals, as taught to the program, are in some cases not strictly correct,
because of our decision to use only a single morphological variant of each
number word. Among the variants which actually occur are the following
words *dau/ddau, tri/thri/dri, pedwar/phedwar/bedwar, pump/phump/bump,
deg/ddeg/deng/ddeng, pymtheg/phymtheg/bymtheg/pymtheng/bymtheng/phy-
mtheng, ugain/hugain, cant/chant/gant, mil/fil*, the choice between these
forms being determined by rules of consonantal variation that pervade the
whole language (Hurford 1975, p. 139). But at the present time we can
offer no detailed suggestions as to how rules of this kind might be induced
from the available evidence.

Number	Numeral	Translation
1	un	one
2	dau	two
3	tri	three
4	pedwar	four
5	pump	five
6	chwech	six
7	saith	seven
8	wyth	eight
9	naw	nine
10	deg	ten
11	un ar deg	one on ten
14	pedwar ar deg	four on ten
15	pymtheg	fifteen
16	un ar pymtheg	one on fifteen
19	pedwar ar pymtheg	four on fifteen
20	ugain	twenty
21	un ar ugain	one on twenty

Number	Numeral	Translation
39	pedwar ar pymtheg ar ugain	four on fifteen on twenty
40	dau ugain	two twenty
39	onid un dau ugain	subtract one two twenty
36	onid pedwar dau ugain	subtract four two twenty
41	un ac dau ugain	one and two twenty
59	pedwar ar pymtheg ac dau ugain	four on fifteen and two twenty
180	naw ugain	nine twenty
61	tri ugain ac un	three twenty and one
79	tri ugain ac pedwar ar pymtheg	three twenty and four on fifteen
200	dau cant	two hundred
201	un ac dau cant	one and two hundred
299	pedwar ugain ac pedwar ar pymtheg ac dau cant	four twenty and four on fifteen and two hundred
900	naw cant	nine hundred
1 000	mil	thousand
1 001	un ac mil	one and thousand
1 999	pedwar ar pymtheg ac pedwar ugain ac naw cant ac mil	four on fifteen and four twenty and nine hundred and thousand
2 000	dau o mil	two of thousand
2 001	un ac dau o mil	one and two of thousand
2 999	onid un pump ugain ac naw cant ac dau o mil	subtract one five twenty and nine hundred and two of thousand
9 000	naw o mil	nine of thousand

```
   : [welsh].readmodel: .prmodel:        RULES
LEXICON                                  10 + (1 4), <N>AR<P>
UN [N] 1                                 15 + (1 4), <N>AR<P>
DAU [N] 2                                20 + (1 19), <N>AR<P>
TRI [N] 3                                20 * (2 9), <N><M>
PEDWAR [N] 4                            [20 * (2 9)] - (1 4), ONID<N><P>
PUMP [N] 5                             [20 * (2 9)] + (1 19), <N>AC<P>
CHWECH [N] 6                           [20 * (2 9)] + (1 19), <P>AC<N>
SAITH [N] 7                            100 * (2 9), <N><M>
WYTH [N] 8                            [100 * (2 9)] + (1 99), <N>AC<P>
NAW [N] 9                             1000 + (1 999), <N>AC<P>
DEG [P N] 10                          1000 * (2 9), <N>O<M>
AR [C] AR                            [1000 * (2 9)] + (1 999), <N>AC<P>
PYMTHEG [P N] 15                      1000 * (2 9), <N><M>
UGAIN [M P N] 20
ONID [C LEFT] ONID                        :
AC [C] AC
CANT [M] 100
MIL [M P N] 1000
O [C] O
```

19

Tones of Voice:
The Role of Intonation
in Computer
Speech Understanding

H. C. Longuet-Higgins

What I want to discuss is not so much the things we say to computers or to one another as the way we say them—what people commonly mean when they use the phrase "tone of voice".

You might wonder, at first thought, whether it would ever be desirable, necessary, or even possible for a speech-understanding system other than a human being to pay intelligent attention to a person's tone of voice. Surely it is something of a weakness in human beings that we often pay more attention to someone's tone of voice than to what he or she actually says; the computer bids fair to be the first conversational saint, unmoved by expressions of irritation, anxiety, or sarcasm and prepared to answer every question patiently and precisely. So let us consider in detail what it is that distinguishes different ways of uttering the same words, and whether the information that is conveyed by the choice of one mode of utterance rather than another is indeed worthy of the attention of our new conversational partners.

Phoneticians customarily classify the features of an utterance under two headings, segmental and suprasegmental. The segmental features are those that are associated with individual speech sounds or "phones", which last anything from 10 to 100 milliseconds. The principal differences between the phonetic realizations of individual phonemes are segmental in character: formant frequencies, for example, are segmental properties. The suprasegmental properties of an utterance, on the other hand, are of three main sorts, having to do with voice quality, rhythm, and intonation. I shall have nothing to say about voice quality, and rather little about speech rhythm—the temporal structure of speech—though it is a fascinating subject in a rapid state of development. I shall concentrate almost entirely on intonation —on the way in which the pitch of the speaker's voice rises and falls as the utterance proceeds. I think it is true to say that intonation is one of the most challenging and at the same time elusive subjects in the whole of linguistics, and will probably be one of the last phenomena to be fully captured by man-made speech-processing systems.

I shall divide this chapter into three sections. First, I shall say something about the encoding of pitch-related information and the production of artificial pitch contours for specified utterances. Then I shall review some of the least controversial facts, few as they are, about the tones of voice that English people employ when they talk, and the factors which lead a person to adopt one tone rather than another. Finally, we will consider what use the speech-understanding systems of the future might make of the pitch contour of an utterance in deciding how to interpret it.

The Measurement and Manipulation of Pitch

There are many ways of encoding speech for transmission, but most of them rely on the fact that speech is a modulated sequence of hisses and buzzes, the modulation being effected by the cavities and constrictions of the vocal tract. Linear predictive coding, for example, separates the information about the speech into two streams: one specifies the transfer function of the vocal tract at intervals of, say, 10 milliseconds, and the other specifies whether, during each interval, the larynx was vibrating or not, and if so at what frequency. It is quite difficult to design a reliable voicing decision procedure, or to formulate a reliable algorithm for computing the larynx frequency, which of course determines the subjectively perceived pitch of the voice; but for the moment we will disregard these difficulties and adopt the convenient fiction that each syllable contains a voiced section (usually a vowel, though not always) of well-defined if varying pitch. One can in fact produce quite a realistic pitch contour for a natural utterance by assigning musical notes to the syllables and putting the resulting step function of time through a low-pass filter, with a cut-off at about 5 hertz; the pitch contour that results from this process must be advanced in time so as to allow for the finite delay introduced by the filter. Here is an original utterance of the sentence

I was thinking about buying another coat before the winter

and the utterance transformed by setting it, syllable by syllable, to the tune notated in figure 1. The original utterance was in fact uttered by my colleague Dr. C. J. Darwin, for quite other purposes.

One can play some quite amusing tricks with the intonation contours of recorded utterances, but pitch modification can also serve a serious research

Figure 1

objective—that of identifying the acoustic variables which convey particular kinds of linguistic information. The following example is adapted from
the admirable textbook by O'Connor and Arnold (1961), *Intonation of
Colloquial English*. The sentence

I thought she was married

can be said in at least two quite different ways: with the word "thought" at
a low pitch and the first syllable of "married" at a high pitch, or vice versa.
I think you will agree that the effect is totally different in the two cases; the
question arises whether this difference is entirely due to the difference in
pitch or to differences of other kinds such as timing or intensity. I therefore
simply interchanged the intonation contours of the two utterances without
changing the timing or intensity relationships, and you can judge the
results for yourselves. My own conclusion is that it is indeed the intonation
contour of each utterance which gives it its particular flavour.

Perhaps these examples will serve to illustrate the possibilities of pitch
modification and the utility of this technique in linguistic research. But to
say this is only to scratch the surface of the subject of intonation; what we
would really like to know is: what are the main intonational choices that are
open to the speaker; what factors lead him to choose one tone rather than
another; and what information does his eventual choice convey to the
hearer?

The Rise and Fall of English Speech

The taxonomy of English intonation is the work of many hands, and a task
that is still far from complete. But such authors as Bolinger (1972), Halliday
(1967), O'Connor and Arnold (1961), Crystal (1975), and Ladd (1980) all
recognise and distinguish between a small number of intonational gestures
which lend a special salience to the words on which they occur. These
"tones", as they are called, include three in particular, namely the "fall",
the "rise", and the "fall-rise", which I will now illustrate by three utterances
of the word "potatoes".

```
                    ta
fall:          po                                                        (a)
                         toes

                         toes?
rise:          po                                                        (b)
               ta

               ta      es
fall-rise:     po                                                        (c)
                  to
```

In the fall-rise the rise is spread over the last syllable, which is spun out a little bit to give time for the rise to make itself clearly heard.

The most obvious fact about these tones (and the much rarer "rise-fall", which I will leave on one side) is that they involve sudden large changes of pitch, which can, indeed, be completed in the course of a single short syllable. The three tones I have mentioned are the most widely used in England, and there is virtually no risk of the hearer mistaking any one of them for any other. Most of those present will, I think, have no difficulty in hearing utterance b as a question and utterance a as the answer to a question; but it would be a mistake to generalize and to suppose that every statement ends in a fall and every question in a rise. A generalization that is slightly nearer the truth is based on the distinction between two types of question: those, such as "Is it raining?", which expect a yes-or-no answer, and those, such as "Where's John?", which require a different sort of answer. Yes-no questions, or polar questions as they are usually called, are frequently spoken with a terminal rise, whereas the other sort of question, known to linguists as "Wh" questions, usually end with a fall. But the distinction between statements and questions in turn requires close examination. It is not too difficult to decide, in most cases, whether an utterance has the syntactic form of a statement or a question; the matter can be decided by simply inspecting the order of the words in the utterance. But an utterance which is interrogative in *syntactic* form may be no more than a dummy question to which the speaker does not really expect an answer, and in such a case it may well terminate with a fall rather than a rise even though it has the form of a polar question. An example would be the utterance

This is a lovely day, isn't it?

in which the last two words would normally be spoken with a fall, indicating that the speaker is not really asking for the independent opinion of the hearer. It is quite otherwise with the question

This is the right train, isn't it?

where the words "isn't it?" would almost certainly be said with a rise, for the very good pragmatic reason that someone asking this particular question will be very likely to want to know the answer. If this analysis is correct, it would seem that among those utterances which have the syntactic form of polar questions we must distinguish between those which, pragmatically speaking, are genuine requests for information, and those which are not; only the former will be spoken with a terminal rise. This hypothesis seems to be supported by the following pair of utterances:

Tell me: do you love her?

The question is: do you love her?

the first of which seems to call for a terminal rise and the latter (presumably intended only to provoke thought) for a terminal fall.

Similar complications arise with "Wh" questions, not all of which, by any means, demand a falling intonation at the end. In certain circumstances a speaker may be well advised to end a "Wh" question with a rise rather than a fall. Take, for example, someone talking to a little girl apparently lost in the street. They would be much more likely to say

```
        your
What's              dear?
          name
```

(with a terminal rise) than

```
          name
What's your
          dear?
```

(with a terminal fall); the latter might sound a bit bossy in the circumstances. And quite apart from such obvious but untidy facts about the ways in which circumstances affect a person's tone of voice, there is a broad class of utterances called "echo questions" which are best defined pragmatically rather than syntactically; their syntactic form is very widely variable, but they share the characteristic of throwing back at the hearer something he has just said. My favourite example of such an utterance is Lady Bracknell's exclamation, in "The Importance of Being Earnest", when she is told by her prospective son-in-law that he was found at Victoria Station in a handbag:

hand-

A

      bag!!!

It was not until I last heard these words uttered by Dame Edith Evans that I realized that this famous utterance can be appropriately realized with either a terminal rise or a terminal fall. A high fall on "handbag" has the affect of expressing horror rather than incredulity, for reasons that are not at all obvious. Indeed, the whole subject of intonation is riddled with facts of this kind, which are well known to actors and theatre directors but still defy the most strenuous attempts by academic linguists to bring them to some semblance of theoretical order.

This discussion of the tones of English speech and the pragmatic factors which influence a speaker in choosing a particular tone is very far from systematic, if only because we are still very far from an understanding of all those factors, including the emotions of the speaker and the cultural conventions which shape his or her linguistic behaviour. There are, however, some fairly hum-drum generalizations at a rather low level which now seem fairly secure and may be of practical use when it comes to making speech-understanding systems dimly sensitive to the rise and fall of a speaker's voice. They concern the role of intonation in revealing the stress patterns of words and word sequences, and its slightly different role in the marking of novelty and contrast.

Intonation and Stress

Stress is, in the first instance, a property of the syllable (the syllables of a word being, crudely speaking, those pieces into which it can be divided by hyphens). In every polysyllabic word the syllables are unequally stressed and one syllable bears a greater stress than any of the others. Thus the word "syllable" has a greater stress on its first syllable than on either of the other two, but in the word "divide" it is the second syllable that bears the heavier stress. In most utterances, most monosyllabic words are stressed; the principal exceptions are "closed class" words such as "of" and "the". The stressed syllables of an utterance partition it into "feet", each foot beginning with a stressed syllable; the feet correspond, roughly speaking, to the bars of a piece of metrical music. This fact connects the concept of stress with the concept of rhythm; one may think of the rhythm as a specification of the manner in which the syllables are grouped into metrical units, these in turn being grouped into high-level units. Liberman and Prince (1977) have developed this idea in detail, and have proposed that the rhythms of English utterances should be represented as binary trees, in which a unit at any level except the lowest branches into a "strong" and a "weak" sub-unit. The lowest-level units are the syllables; the next units up will be words or groups of syllables; and at higher levels still one will find sequences of words, including such units as noun phrases and whole clauses.

The relevance of stress to intonation can be nicely illustrated by considering a particular kind of syntactic entity: the composite noun, composed of two nouns strung together as in "lawn mower". As Chomsky and Halle pointed out in *The Sound Pattern of English*, it is usually the first noun in such a pair that carries the greater stress; but what is the acoustic evidence for this assertion? It is to be found in the intonation contours of the utterances in the following type of conversational fragment:

A: What's that?

             lawn

B: That's a

                      mower.

In the utterance attributed to B, which in its context may be safely assumed to terminate with a fall, the word "lawn" will receive a higher pitch than the word "mower"; the higher stress on "lawn" is realized by its higher pitch. But heavy stress is not always marked by high pitch; if the conversation had continued with A saying incredulously

             mower?

A

  lawn

then the word "lawn" would have occurred, not at the top of a fall, but at the bottom of a rise, and would therefore have received a lower pitch than the word "mower". This shows that stress is a more abstract concept than pitch, so that the relative stresses of two or more words or syllables cannot be inferred from their relative pitches without a considerable amount of contextual information.

To show that this phenomenon is not restricted to noun-noun pairs, one may consider the simple adjective-noun pair "black board", in which "board" is more heavily stressed than "black" (whereas in the compound "blackboard" the reverse would be the case). When this adjective-noun pair occurs at the end of an utterance with a terminal fall, the fall is located on the word "board", because this is the more heavily stressed word. But if the utterance ends with a rise, then it will be the same word that carries the rise and therefore starts at the bottom of the pitch contour. Broadly speaking, it is the most heavily stressed syllable in a particular environment that manifests the greatest pitch change, but even this generalization is not sufficiently reliable for the fully automatic assignment of relative stress values.

Intonation, Novelty, and Contrast

One important function of intonation is to draw attention to words which introduce new ideas into the conversation, or ideas which stand in contrast to those already current. An example of the use of intonation for signalling new information is provided by the utterance

No, Edinburgh is the capital of Scotland.

Spoken with a fall-rise on "Edinburgh" and a (high) fall on "Scotland", this utterance conveys the very strong impression that the speaker is correcting somebody's misapprehension that Edinburgh is the capital of some other country. The novel information in the utterance is carried by the word "Scotland", which must therefore receive the most salient intonational gesture available, namely the high fall; but almost equally important is the current information carried by "Edinburgh", so that this word merits a gesture of some sort, and the fall-rise seems to fill this role quite aptly. Had the utterance been spoken with a high fall on "Edinburgh" and a fall-rise on "Scotland", a quite different impression would have been created: the speaker would then have seemed to be correcting the mistaken idea that some other city than Edinburgh was the Scottish capital. The novel information in the utterance would then have been carried by the word "Edinburgh"; "Scotland", being already under discussion, would merit only the fall-rise.

A final example of the interaction of novelty and contrast in shaping the tone of an utterance I owe to Stephen Isard. Printed without italics or other such markings, the sentence

Fred called Harry a liar, and then he insulted him.

seems to have a clear meaning, part of which is that Fred insulted Harry. But spoken with a fall-rise on "he" and a high fall on "him", the utterance acquires a quite different meaning, namely that Harry insulted Fred. Presumably the very fact that the two pronouns are both the loci of intonational gestures warns the hearer not to adopt the "unmarked" interpretation, according to which Fred is the subject and Harry the object in both clauses. Phenomena of this kind have been elegantly and authoritatively discussed by Cutler and Isard (1980) and Ladd (1980).

The Role of Intonation in Automatic Speech Understanding

One can, I suppose, classify the potential uses of pitch information to a speech-understanding system under two main headings: its use for identifying the actual words of an utterance and establishing the syntactic relations between them (Vaissière 1981; Lea 1980), and its use in decoding that part of the speaker's message which is only implicit, not explicit, in what he actually says.

The identification of individual words in connected speech is now a practical possibility; but some parts of an utterance are much easier to decode than others, and one might expect the words which carry the most conspicuous pitch changes to be not only the most important but also the most clearly articulated words in the utterance; these words could well be used as "nuclei" for an "inside-out" recognition system.

A second use of pitch information for word identification would be in distinguishing between pairs like "green house" and "greenhouse" or between the noun "import" and the verb "import"; when such words occur in tonic position, the stressed syllable is identifiable as the one which shows the greatest pitch variation.

We have already discussed the use of intonation for signalling novelty or contrast; in both cases the hearer is well advised to pay special attention to the intonationally salient words or phrases, and the same could apply to a speech-processing system which took account of the relative importance that a speaker attached to the different words of his utterance. (I will leave on one side the question whether a human speaker would ever be content with a system which was designed to attend only to the most important words of his utterance, and to ignore the rest.)

But the really challenging problems of intonation, as far as speech-understanding systems are concerned, have to do with the role that it plays in the interpersonal relationships between the human participants in an ordinary conversation. Implicit messages such as "I have now finished speaking" or "Did you really mean that?" or "I don't expect you to answer this question" could, one imagines, be extracted from the intonation contours of utterances and put to good use by the systems of the future. But at the present time I doubt whether we could, even if we wished, design systems capable of detecting bonhomie, boredom, irony, or irritation in a person's tone of voice and responding in a manner becoming to a mere artefact. Not that this is any reason for not thinking about the problems of computer etiquette; the attempt to extend our technology to the construction of well-mannered computers could only have the effect of sharpening both our wits and our self-awareness.

It is perhaps fortunate that present-day computing systems are so exceedingly literal-minded. Most of us would, I suspect, feel very ill at ease with a speech-understanding system which responded differently according to whether one addressed it in a pleasant or a not-so-pleasant tone of voice. But in the *Times* of 28 June 1983 there appeared an article by Richard Stevens, an information-processing scientist, suggesting that the day is not far off when computers will be running programs with feelings and emotions of their own. "Programs that understand human feelings and emotions will replace others without that understanding, because they will better satisfy the user". I quote this article not because I agree or disagree with its author's prognostications, but simply because I believe that the attempt to make computational models of the production and comprehension of speech is the most promising road to a real understanding of what we are pleased to call our "emotions". The value of such an enterprise can be assessed quite independently of ethical questions about machines which, invented for the purpose of relieving human drudgery, end up by usurping human roles.

References

Bolinger, D. (ed.) 1972. *Intonation.* Harmondsworth: Penguin.

Crystal, D. 1975. *The English Tone of Voice.* London: Arnold.

Cutler, A., and S. D. Isard. 1980. The production of prosody. In *Language and Production*, volume 1: *Speech and Talk*, ed. B. L. Butterworth (London: Academic).

Halliday, M. S. 1967. *Intonation and Grammar in British English.* The Hague: Mouton.

Ladd, D. R. 1980. *The Structure of Intonational Meaning.* Bloomington: Indiana University Press.

Lea, W. A. 1980. Prosodic aids to speech recognition. In *Trends in Speech Recognition*, ed. W. A. Lea (Englewood Cliffs, N.J.: Prentice-Hall).

Liberman, M., and A. Prince. 1977. On stress and linguistic rhythm. *Linguistic Inquiry* 8, no. 2: 249–336.

O'Connor, J. D., and G. F. Arnold. 1961. *Intonation of Colloquial English.* London: Longman.

Vaissière, J. 1981. Speech recognition programs as models of speech perception. In *The Cognitive Representation of Speech*, ed. T. Myers et al. (Amsterdam: North-Holland).

IV

Vision

The chapters in this section are all to do with the problem of inferring the structure of a scene from two views, which may be either simultaneous, as in binocular vision, or successive, as in monocular motion perception. In order to solve this problem it is necessary to establish some sort of correspondence between the elements of the two images—or so it is usually supposed. However, in those chapters concerned with stereoscopic vision the "correspondence problem" is presumed to have been solved, and in the chapters on visual motion perception there is no discussion of the acute difficulty of translating a time-varying image into an optic flow field.

Chapter 20 was strongly influenced by Shimon Ullman's book *The Interpretation of Visual Motion*, which in turn was inspired by David Marr's idea that visual tasks are essentially computational problems. Our most significant result, I now believe, was the demonstration that the optic flow field in the image plane of a moving camera is the vector sum of a translational and a rotational component, all the depth information about the scene being contained in the translational component of the flow. The succeeding chapter, which is probably more relevant to human vision, appears here for the first time.

There is no disguising the mathematical nature of these chapters; their motivation was the discovery that some of the juiciest problems in visual kinematics had been overlooked by applied mathematicians, and that it was still possible in the 1980s to unearth such problems and solve them exactly. Though most of the solutions described are rather implausible as accounts of our own visual processes, if only because of their acute sensitivity to error, they provide a point of departure for heuristic approximations. John Mayhew's elegant explanation of Ogle's Induced Effect in terms of a computational theory of binocular vision (see chapter 26) was, he told me, sparked by my work on the possible role of the vertical dimension in stereoscopic vision—which is why he was kind enough to invite me to be a coauthor of the *Nature* paper that appears here as chapter 26.

The computational theory of vision and the design of computer vision systems are moving ahead very rapidly at the present time, partly (I regret to say) in response to military demands. At the time of writing (summer 1986), most published work on the determination of structure from motion has taken for granted the reality of the optic flow field; but acute difficulties are encountered when one attempts to compute the image velocity at more than a very few special points. What the visual system ultimately has to do is to infer from a $(2 + 1)$-dimensional image—or two such images—the spatio-temporal structure of a (3 + 1)-dimensional scene. Logically there is no need to solve this problem for a succession of well-defined instants of time; the visual system might well deal with it piecemeal, by determining independently the trajectories of a number of identifiable features.

20

The Interpretation of a Moving Retinal Image

H. C. Longuet-Higgins
and K. Prazdny

When the eye is in motion relative to the visible environment, a moving pattern of light falls upon the retina, and the resulting "optical flow field" supplies useful information not only about the motion but also about the three-dimensional structure of the scene (Helmholtz 1925; Gibson 1950, 1966, 1979; Gibson et al. 1955, 1957, 1959; Braunstein 1976). This information is inadequate, in general, for establishing the relative distances and velocities of all of the visible elements in the scene, if only because the line-of-sight velocity of a point source makes no difference to the retinal velocity of its image. But in practice the scene will usually consist of rigid objects of finite extent, and, if this condition is satisfied, the assumption of local rigidity can lead to a unique, and correct, three-dimensional interpretation of the moving retinal image (Ullman 1979).

There have been two somewhat different approaches to the interpretation of visual motion. One is based on an analogy with stereopsis, and the other appeals to the existence of receptors that respond to visual stimuli moving across the retina with specific velocities (Hubel and Wiesel 1968; Bridgeman 1972; Grusser and Grusser 1973; Sekuler and Levinson 1974, 1977). In the quasi-stereoscopic theory the visual problem is seen as that of collating the information from two or more discrete views of the scene. The first stage is to solve the "correspondence problem" (Marr and Poggio 1976; Ullman 1979) of establishing which elements in each image correspond to the same element in the scene; the second stage is to compute the structure from the finite disparity between the retinal positions of corresponding elements (Ullman 1979). The other approach (Gibson et al. 1955; Gordon 1965; Lee 1974; Koenderink and van Doorn 1976) takes as given the optical flow field itself, and attempts to infer the relative motion and the three-dimensional structure on the assumption that the scene is indeed locally rigid.

Whichever approach one decides to adopt, there is no great problem in calculating how the retinal image changes when the eye moves in a given manner relative to a scene of specified geometry. The real difficulties begin when one addresses the converse problem, that of proceeding from the optical flow field to conclusions about the motion and the structure. The difficulties are not severe if one assumes that the motion has no rotational component (Gibson et al. 1955; Lee 1974) or that its translational component is known (Koenderink and van Doorn 1976); but it is by no means obvious whether the visual system could, in principle, compute both the translational and the rotational motion of the eye relative to the scene from the optical flow field alone. This is the problem that we consider in the present chapter.

The plan of the chapter is as follows. In the following section we examine the form of the optic flow field due to arbitrary motion relative to a rigid scene. In the most general case the field is found to be the vector sum of a translational component and a rotational component. The translational velocity at any point is directed towards or away from a unique "vanishing point" determined by the relative translational motion. The rotational velocity field is fully determined by the angular velocity of the eye relative to the environment; it is entirely independent of the structure of the scene. Motion parallax cues (Helmholtz 1925), when they are available, are shown to provide a means of calculating both the translational and the rotational component of the relative motion; once this has been achieved, the structure of the scene can be fully determined from the translational component of the flow field.

Next we consider the case of a scene consisting of arbitrarily moving rigid objects with smooth, densely textured surfaces. The problem is to determine the translational and rotational motion of a given object, and the gradient of its surface at any point (Marr 1976), from the optic flow field due to the nearby texture elements. It is shown that all these unknowns may be computed from the field and its first and second spatial derivatives at the corresponding point on the retina. The first derivatives may be expressed in terms of the invariants discussed by Koenderink and van Doorn (1976), but the second derivatives are also needed for a full determination of the relative motion. They supply, incidentally, a check on the assumption of local rigidity. Plane surfaces are found to present special problems of visual interpretation.

Finally, we raise the possibility that the visual system may possess receptors that respond specifically to local deformations of the optic flow field, due to *relative* motion of neighbouring elements of the retinal image.

Motion through a Static Environment

To gain a qualitative insight into the form of the optic flow field it is helpful to think of the eye as a hemispherical pinhole camera, in arbitrary motion through a static environment. The motion at any instant may be resolved into two components: the translational velocity of the pinhole relative to the scene, and the angular velocity of the hemisphere about the pinhole, also measured relative to the scene. In purely translational motion (for which the angular velocity vanishes) the optic flow takes on a specially simple form: if the line of motion of the pinhole O intersects the hemisphere at the point Q, then every other image point on the hemisphere will move along the great circle that joins it to the point Q (Nakayama and Loomis 1974). So if Q is regarded as a "pole" on the hemisphere, a purely translational field is one for which the image velocity is everywhere directed along "lines of longitude", having a magnitude that depends on the detailed geometry of the scene (figure 1a).

If the hemisphere is rotating as well as translating, then every image point will acquire an additional velocity component corresponding to a rigid rotation of the hemisphere about some radius OR. The most general flow field due to motion through a static environment is thus the vector sum of a "polar" field due to the translation and an "axial" field due to the rotation; but there is no relation, in general, between the directions OQ and OR. The problem of "interpreting" the flow field amounts, then, to

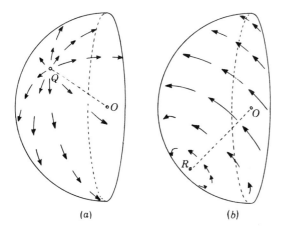

(a)   (b)

Figure 1
Typical translational ("polar") and rotational ("axial") components of the flow field on a hemispherical retina.

resolving it into an axial field (completely determined by the three components of the angular velocity) and a polar field attributable to the translation. If such a resolution can be effected, the presumption of a rigid scene is confirmed, and the three-dimensional structure follows straightforwardly from the translational field component (Gibson et al. 1955; Lee 1974).

The analysis that follows is largely concerned with the task of resolving the optic flow field into its rotational and translational components. In describing the flow field due to motion through a rigid scene, we have been idealizing the retina as a hemisphere. Spherical polar coordinates might be thought appropriate; but the choice of retinal coordinates is entirely a matter of convenience, and we prefer to work with plane projective coordinates (x, y) having the property that a great circle on the hemisphere corresponds to a straight line in the (x, y) plane. The reader who feels uncertain on this point may care to note that although the retina is not planar, neither is it a hemisphere with the lens at its centre; any retinal coordinate system is equally legitimate provided that it does not misrepresent the topology of the retinal image.

Consider a monocular observer moving through a static environment. Let O be the instantaneous position of the nodal point of the eye, and let $OXYZ$ be an "external" Cartesian coordinate system that is fixed with respect to the eye, OZ being the line of sight. Let (U, V, W) be the translational velocity of $OXYZ$ relative to the scene, and let (A, B, C) be its angular velocity. Then if (X, Y, Z) are the instantaneous coordinates of a texture element P in the scene, the velocity components of P in the moving frame will be (see figure 2)

$$\dot{X} = -U - BZ + CY,$$
$$\dot{Y} = -V - CX + AZ, \tag{1}$$
$$\dot{Z} = -W - AY + BX.$$

The retinal position of p, the image of P, may conveniently be represented by the "internal" coordinates

$$(x, y) = (X/Z, Y/Z); \tag{2}$$

it will move across the retina with velocity

$$(u, v) = (\dot{x}, \dot{y}). \tag{3}$$

Substituting from equations 1 and 2 into equation 3, we obtain

$$u = \dot{X}/Z - X\dot{Z}/Z^2$$
$$= (-U/Z - B + Cy) - x(-W/Z - Ay + Bx), \tag{4}$$

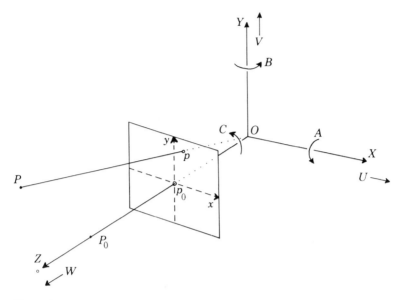

Figure 2
An external coordinate system $OXYZ$ moving with the eye, and the corresponding retinal coordinates (x, y). The distance OP_0 equals R.

$$v = \dot{Y}/Z - Y\dot{Z}/Z^2$$
$$= (-V/Z - Cx + A) - y(-W/Z - Ay + Bx), \tag{5}$$

and these equations may be written in the form

$$u = u^T + u^R, \quad v = v^T + v^R, \tag{6}$$

with

$$u^T = (-U + xW)/Z, \quad v^T = (-V + yW)/Z \tag{7}$$

and

$$u^R = -B + Cy + Axy - Bx^2, \quad v^R = -Cx + A + Ay^2 - Bxy. \tag{8}$$

The retinal velocity field is therefore the vector sum of a translational component (u^T, v^T) that is independent of (A, B, C) and a rotational component (u^R, v^R) that is independent of the three-dimensional structure of the scene. Introducing the coordinates

$$x_0 = U/W, \quad y_0 = V/W, \tag{9}$$

we may write the translational component in the form

$$u^T = (x - x_0)W/Z, \quad v^T = (y - y_0)W/Z. \tag{10}$$

It follows that

$$v^T/u^T = (y - y_0)/(x - x_0), \tag{11}$$

and that the translational flow component is everywhere along straight lines that meet at the "vanishing point" (x_0, y_0).

So, if the observer is able to resolve the retinal flow field into a rotational component of the form of equation 8 and a translational component that is everywhere directed away from (or towards) some retinal point (x_0, y_0), not only will this confirm his presumption that the scene is rigid, but also he will be able to compute his direction of motion,

$$U : V : W = x_0 : y_0 : 1, \tag{12}$$

and even to determine the relative depths of all the texture elements in the scene:

$$Z/W = (x - x_0)/u^T = (y - y_0)/v^T. \tag{13}$$

But to effect this resolution he must find values of $(A, B, C,)$ such that, when the corresponding rotational field (given by equation 8) is substracted from (u, v), the difference (u^T, v^T) is indeed identifiable as a pure translational field from which the structure of the scene can be found. The question thus arises: How can the observer discover what value to assign to his relative angular velocity (A, B, C)?

One very useful source of information, when it is available, is motion parallax (Helmholtz 1925). If, for example, the observer is walking past a dusty window, then two distinct flow fields will be generated on his retina, one due to the dust particles and the other due to the texture elements behind the window. (This situation illustrates the fact that the optic flow field is not necessarily a single-valued function of retinal position; it is possible, and indeed common, for distinct texture elements to cast their images, momentarily, on the same retinal point.)

Suppose, then, that at the time of observation there are two texture elements, P_1 and P_2, lying in the same direction (x, y) but at different depths, Z_1 and Z_2. Then their images p_1 and p_2 will have the same rotational velocities (u^R, v^R) but will differ in their translational velocities (u^T, v^T). Hence the difference in the retinal velocities of p_1 and p_2 will be

$$u_1 - u_2 = (-U + xW)(1/Z_1 - 1/Z_2) \tag{14}$$

and

$$v_1 - v_2 = (-V + yW)(1/Z_1 - 1/Z_2), \tag{15}$$

from which it follows that

$$\frac{v_1 - v_2}{u_1 - u_2} = \frac{-V + yW}{-U + xW} = \frac{y - y_0}{x - x_0}. \tag{16}$$

The relative velocity $(u_1 - u_2, v_1 - v_2)$ at (x, y) therefore points directly towards or away from the vanishing point (x_0, y_0), and this point can be located by using the motion parallax at a number of separate retinal positions. The concurrence of the relative velocity vectors at these positions supports the presumption that the scene is rigid.

Motion parallax thus enables the observer to locate the vanishing point (x_0, y_0) and hence to calculate his direction of motion from equation 12. But to calculate the relative Z coordinates of any two elements he also needs to know the angular velocity (A, B, C), and this he can compute as follows.

For any point on the line $(x = x_0)$, the value of u is given by

$$u(x_0, y) = -B + Cy + Ax_0y - Bx_0^2. \tag{17}$$

It follows that a plot of $u(x_0, y)$ against y is a straight line of slope $(C + Ax_0)$ and intercept $-B(1 + x_0^2)$. Likewise, a plot of $v(x, y_0)$ against x is a straight line of slope $-(C + By_0)$ and intercept $A(1 + y_0^2)$:

$$v(x, y_0) = Cx + A + Ay_0^2 - Bxy_0. \tag{18}$$

Knowing x_0 and y_0, the observer can thus compute (A, B, C) without difficulty; having done so, he can then obtain the relative depths of the texture elements from

$$\frac{Z}{W} = \frac{x - x_0}{u - u^R} = \frac{y - y_0}{v - v^R}, \tag{19}$$

where u^R and v^R have been calculated from equation 8. To speak of the observer solving such equations is not, of course, to imply that the visual system performs such calculations exactly as a mathematician would; its modes of operation may well be more "geometrical" than "algebraic", and the same applies to the other computations envisaged in this chapter. Our main point is that the equations demonstrate the feasibility of calculating both the motion and the structure from the optic flow field alone.

But if motion-parallax cues are not readily available, or if parts of the scene are in relative motion, then these methods fail. We therefore turn to the problem of determining the motion and the structure of an object with a smooth, densely textured surface.

Motion Relative to a Visually Textured Surface

If the scene consists of a number of rigid objects in relative motion, then, to determine his motion relative to any one of them, the observer will have to rely on information from a limited part of the visual field. We therefore envisage a situation in which the object of interest has a smooth, densely textured surface S; the observer's task is then to determine his motion relative to S, and the gradient of the surface at any given point P_0 lying on it.

Since P_0 is not necessarily in the observer's line of sight, we now adopt a coordinate system, $OXYZ$, that is orientated in such a way that P_0 has the coordinates $(0, 0, R)$ at the time of observation. As before, $OXYZ$ is assumed to move with the observer's eye. The surface S may than be described by the equation

$$Z(X, Y) = R + \alpha X + \beta Y + O_2(X, Y), \tag{20}$$

where $O_2(X, Y)$ means "terms of the second order in X and Y" and where (α, β) is the gradient of S at P_0. If $(x, y) = (X/Z, Y/Z)$ are local retinal coordinates, the equations 4 and 5 hold in the new interpretation, so that

$$u = (-U + xW)/Z - B + Cy + Axy - Bx^2, \tag{21}$$

$$v = (-V + yW)/Z - Cx + A + Ay^2 - Bxy. \tag{22}$$

Introducing the dimensionless depth coordinate

$$z = (Z - R)/Z = \alpha x + \beta y + O_2(x, y) \tag{23}$$

and the depth-scaled velocities

$$u_0 = U/R, \quad v_0 = V/R, \quad w_0 = W/R, \tag{24}$$

we may write equations 21 and 22 in the forms

$$u = (-u_0 + xw_0)(1 - z) - B + Cy + Axy - Bx^2, \tag{25}$$

$$v = (-v_0 + yw_0)(1 - z) - Cx + A + Ay^2 - Bxy. \tag{26}$$

(The local coordinates of p_0, the image of P_0, are, of course, $(x, y) = (0, 0)$.) The question now arises: can the observer derive all the unknown parameters u_0, v_0, w_0, A, B, C, α, and β from the velocity field (u, v) in the immediate neighbourhood of p_0?

Since S is smooth, by hypothesis, the derivatives of u and v with respect to x and y are well defined. At the point p_0, where $x = y = z = 0$, u and v take the values

$$u = -u_0 - B, \quad v = -v_0 + A; \tag{27}$$

their first derivatives are found to be

$$u_x = u_0\alpha + w_0, \quad u_y = u_0\beta + C,$$
$$v_x = v_0\alpha - C, \quad v_y = v_0\beta + w_0, \tag{28}$$

since

$$z_x = \alpha, \quad z_y = \beta. \tag{29}$$

If u_0 and v_0 could only be found, equation 27 would immediately give the values of A and B and equation 28 would supply the values of w_0, C, α, and β; but, as the equations stand, the values of α and β are inseparable from those of u_0 and v_0, and, in particular, there is no way of finding the relative magnitudes of these two pairs of quantities. This is the familiar problem of the "indeterminate depth scale" in a new guise.

There is, however, a way round the difficulty. The translational components of u and v correspond, as shown in the previous section, to flow along lines through the vanishing point:

$$(x_0, y_0) = (u_0/w_0, v_0/w_0). \tag{30}$$

Writing equation 25 in the form

$$u = (x - x_0)w_0(1 - z) - B + Cy + Axy - Bx^2, \tag{31}$$

we see that, if the (x, y) axes are reorientated in such a way that the y axis passes through (x_0, y_0), equation 31 reduces to

$$u = xw_0(1 - z) - B + Cy + Axy - Bx^2, \tag{32}$$

where all quantities now refer to the new coordinate system (figure 3).

On the y axis, where $x = 0$, u now assumes a particularly simple form, namely

$$u(0, y) = -B + Cy. \tag{33}$$

This equation asserts, in effect, that all those image points that lie on the (new) y axis at time t will still lie on a straight line at $t + \delta t$, namely the line

$$x = (-B + Cy)\delta t + O_2(\delta t). \tag{34}$$

In general, furthermore, there will be only one straight line of image points, through the origin, that at the time of observation is not bending in the (x, y) plane. Equations for finding this line, when it is unique, are given in the appendix, where it is also shown that, if S is planar, every line through the origin has this property, so that the present analysis fails.

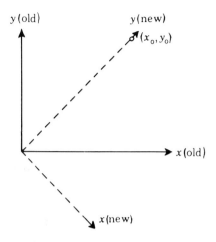

Figure 3

If the unbending line is indeed unique, then once it has been located and adopted as the y axis the problem is largely solved. For, by equation 30,

$$u_0 = x_0 w_0 = 0, \tag{35}$$

so that at the origin

$$u = -B, \quad v = -v_0 + A, \tag{36}$$

$$u_x = w_0, \quad u_y = C,$$
$$v_x = v_0 \alpha - C, \quad v_y = v_0 \beta + w_0, \tag{37}$$

and, by equation 32,

$$u_{xx} = -2w_0 \alpha - 2B, \quad u_{xy} = -w_0 \beta + A. \tag{38}$$

Expressions 36–38 constitute eight equations for the seven unknown quantities, A, B, C, v_0, w_0, α, and β; their consistency is a necessary condition for S to be rigid. The solution is immediate. By equations 36 and 37,

$$B = -u, \quad w_0 = u_x, \quad C = u_y, \tag{39}$$

and substitution in the first of equations 38 gives

$$\alpha = (u - \tfrac{1}{2} u_{xx})/u_x. \tag{40}$$

Introducing the observable quantities (see figure 4)

$$\rho = u_x - v_y, \quad \sigma = u_y + v_x, \tag{41}$$

we infer from equation 37 that

$$v_0\alpha = \sigma, \quad v_0\beta = -\rho, \tag{42}$$

whence

$$v_0 = \sigma/\alpha, \quad \beta = -\rho/v_0. \tag{43}$$

Finally, then, by equation 36,

$$A = v + v_0, \tag{44}$$

and it only remains to check that u_{xy} satisfies the second of equations 38.

Equations 39–44 show that if and when a unique "unbending line" of image points can be identified, then, if it is selected as the y axis, the seven parameters of relative motion (excluding u_0, which now vanishes) can be simply expressed in terms of the first derivatives of u and v with respect to x and y, and the second derivatives of u with respect to these variables.

There is, however, one perceptual situation that merits special discussion, namely that in which the observer's eye is turning steadily so as to maintain the point P_0 at the origin in the (x, y) plane. In this case the velocity (u, v) vanishes there, and, according to equation 36,

$$B = 0, \quad A = v_0. \tag{45}$$

It may then be preferable to calculate α from v_0 rather than from equation 40, since if w_0 is small this equation is ill conditioned. Combining equations 38 and 45, we now obtain

$$u_{xx} = -2w_0\alpha, \quad v_0 = u_{xy} + w_0\beta, \tag{46}$$

and from equation 42 we deduce that

$$v_0 = u_{xy} + \rho u_{xx}/2\sigma. \tag{47}$$

The gradient (α, β) is then calculated from equation 42, and the final check of consistency is supplied by the first of equations 46, with w_0 set equal to u_x.

It appears, then, that the observer gains certain computational advantages from tracking with his eye any surface whose gradient and relative motion are of special interest to him; this is an intuitively reassuring result.

Discussion

What we have shown, in effect, is that an observer can *in principle* determine the structure of a rigid scene and his direction of motion relative to it from the *instantaneous* retinal velocity field. If the scene consists of separate objects in relative motion, then a separate computation must be carried out

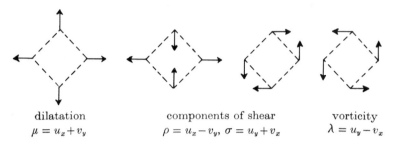

dilatation   components of shear   vorticity

$\mu = u_x + v_y$ $\rho = u_x - v_y, \; \sigma = u_y + v_x$ $\lambda = u_y - v_x$

Figure 4

on each one, requiring access to the flow at some retinal point and its first and second spatial derivatives at that point. Each computation checks the rigidity assumption on which it is based.

Whether the visual system actually operates in this way is, of course, another matter. Ullman (1979) has argued cogently for a "polar-parallel" scheme, which requires a time long enough for the observer to obtain at least three sufficiently distinct views of each object to determine its structure. The present scheme requires, instead, that the neighbourhoods involved in local computations subtend an angle large enough for the second derivatives of u and v to be estimated with accuracy.

Leaving aside the relative merits and domains of application of the two schemes, there is one feature of equations 42 et seq. to which we would like to draw attention, namely the quantities ρ and σ defined in equation 41. As pointed out by Koenderink and van Doorn (1976), there are four independent combinations of the flow-field derivatives that have specially simple transformation properties under rotation of the retinal axes. These combinations are illustrated in figure 4. The dilatation, μ, and the vorticity, λ, are separately invariant under rotation; the two components of shear, encountered in equation 41, are mixed together (but not with λ or μ) when the axes are rotated through an angle θ:

$$\rho \rightarrow \rho \cos 2\theta + \sigma \sin 2\theta,$$
$$\sigma \rightarrow -\rho \sin 2\theta + \sigma \cos 2\theta.$$

It would therefore not be surprising if the human visual system possessed channels tuned to these four basic types of "relative" motion, as well as the "absolute"-motion channels implicated in the waterfall illusion. Evidence has been obtained (Regan et al. 1978a,b, 1979) for channels sensitive to dilatation; if there also exist shear- and vorticity-sensitive channels, it might be possible to demonstrate their existence psychophysically.

Appendix

The computation described above hinges on the possibility of finding the line that joins the retinal origin to the vanishing point (x_0, y_0). This line has the peculiar property that image points lying on it at time t will still be in a straight line at time $t + \delta t$. If it is adopted as the y axis of a new coordinate frame, then the required kinematic parameters are simple functions of the retinal image velocity and its first and second derivatives in that frame.

In the original (x, y) system, by equation 30,

$$y_0/x_0 = v_0/u_0, \tag{A1}$$

and so the problem reduces to determining this ratio. Now, according to equations 25 and 26,

$$
\begin{aligned}
u_{xx} &= u_0 z_{xx} - 2w_0 \alpha - 2B, & v_{xx} &= v_0 z_{xx}, \\
u_{xy} &= u_0 z_{xy}, - w_0 \beta + A, & v_{xy} &= v_0 z_{xy} - w_0 \alpha - B, \\
u_{yy} &= u_0 z_{yy}, & v_{yy} &= v_0 z_{yy} - 2w_0 \beta + 2A.
\end{aligned}
\tag{A2}
$$

If the surface is highly curved at P_0, with radii of curvature much less than R (the distance of P_0 from the eye), then the terms in z_{xx}, z_{xy}, z_{yy} will outweigh the others, so that, to a first approximation,

$$v_0/u_0 = v_{xx}/u_{xx} = v_{xy}/u_{xy} = v_{yy}/u_{yy}. \tag{A3}$$

But if these ratios are markedly unequal, a more accurate calculation is needed. By equations A2,

$$
\begin{aligned}
u_{xx} - 2v_{xy} &= u_0 z_{xx} - 2v_0 z_{xy}, & v_0 z_{xx} &= v_{xx}, \\
v_{yy} - 2u_{xy} &= v_0 z_{yy} - 2u_0 z_{xy}, & u_0 z_{yy} &= u_{yy},
\end{aligned}
\tag{A4}
$$

Elimination of z_{xx}, z_{xy}, z_{yy} between these equations leads to

$$u_0{}^3 v_{xx} + u_0{}^2 v_0 (2v_{xy} - u_{xx}) + u_0 v_0{}^2 (v_{yy} - 2u_{xy}) - v_0{}^3 u_{yy} = 0, \tag{A5}$$

and this may be written in the alternative form

$$t = (v_{xx} + 2tv_{xy} + t^2 v_{yy})/(u_{xx} + 2tu_{xy} + t^2 u_{yy}), \tag{A6}$$

where

$$t = v_0/u_0. \tag{A7}$$

Equation A6 is a cubic equation in the required ratio t, but the relevant root can be quickly found by iteration if a first approximation is available from equation A3.

Difficulties arise, however, if S is planar, because then z_{xx}, z_{xy}, and z_{yy} all vanish, and so do all the coefficients in equation A5:

$$u_{xx} - 2v_{xy} = 0, \quad v_{xx} = 0,$$
$$v_{yy} - 2u_{xy} = 0, \quad u_{yy} = 0. \tag{A8}$$

Planarity is thus easily detected, but to determine the kinematic parameters is surprisingly difficult. One finds, in fact, that, when the second derivatives of z are set equal to zero in equations A2 the solution of these equations involves extracting the roots of a cubic equation; but there is no obvious way of calculating the appropriate root. Ullman's polar-parallel scheme (Ullman 1979, p. 173) also encounters difficulties with planar objects.

References

Braunstein, M. L. 1976. *Depth Perception through Motion*. London: Academic.

Bridgeman, B. 1972. Visual receptive fields to absolute and relative motion during tracking. *Science* 187: 1106–1108.

Gibson, E. J., J. J. Gibson, O. W. Smith, and H. Flock. 1959. Motion parallax as determinant of perceptual depth. *J. Exp. Psychol.* 58: 40–51.

Gibson, J. J. 1950. *The Perception of the Visual World*. Boston: Houghton Mifflin.

Gibson, J. J. 1966. *The Senses Considered as Perceptual Systems*. Boston: Houghton Mifflin.

Gibson, J. J. 1979. *The Ecological Approach to Visual Perception*. Boston: Houghton Mifflin.

Gibson, J. J., and E. J. Gibson. 1957. Continuous perspective transformations and the perception of rigid motion. *J. Exp. Psychol.* 54: 129–138.

Gibson, J. J., P. Olum, and F. Rosenblatt. 1955. Parallax and perspective during aircraft landings. *Am. J. Psychol.* 68: 372–385.

Gordon, D. A. 1965. Static and dynamic visual fields in human space perception. *J. Opt. Soc. Am.* 55: 1296–1303.

Grusser, O. J., and U. Grusser. 1973. Neuronal mechanisms of visual movement perception. In *Handbook of Sensory Physiology*, volume 7, part 3, ed. R. Jung (New York: Springer).

Helmholtz, H. von. 1925. *Treatise on Physiological Optics*. New York: Dover.

Hubel, D. H., and T. N. Wiesel. 1968. Receptive fields and functional architecture of monkey striate cortex. *J. Physiol. (Lond.)* 195: 215–243.

Koenderink, J. J., and A. J. van Doorn. 1976. Local structure of movement parallax of the plane. *J. Opt. Soc. Am.* 66: 717–723.

Lee, D. N. 1974. Visual information during locomotion. In *Perception: Essays in Honor of James J. Gibson*, ed. R. B. MacLeod and H. L. Pick (Ithaca, N.Y.: Cornell University Press).

Marr, D. 1976. Early processing of visual information. *Phil. Trans. R. Soc. Lond.* B 275: 483–534.

Marr, D., and T. Poggio. 1976. Cooperative computation of stereo disparity. *Science* 194: 283–287.

Nakayama, K., and J. M. Loomis. 1974. Optical velocity patterns, velocity sensitive neurons and space perception. *Perception* 3: 63–80.

Regan, D., and K. I. Beverley. 1978a. Illusory motion in depth. *Vision Res.* 18: 209–212.

Regan, D., and K. I. Beverley. 1978b. Looming detectors in the human visual pathway. *Vision Res.* 18: 415–421.

Regan, D., K. I. Beverley, and M. Cynader. 1979. The visual perception of depth. *Sci. Am.* 241: 122–133.

Sekuler, R., and E. Levinson. 1974. Mechanisms of motion perception. *Psychologia* 17: 38–49.

Sekuler, R., and E. Levinson. 1977. The perception of moving targets. *Sci. Am.* 236: 60–73.

Ullman, S. 1979. *The Interpretation of Visual Motion*. Cambridge, Mass.: MIT Press.

21 Further Thoughts on Visual Motion

H. C. Longuet-Higgins

In the preceding chapter Prazdny and I showed that if a scene consists of rigid textured surfaces, then the gradient of such a surface and the motion of the eye relative to it can in principle be determined from the velocity field of the moving retinal image together with its first and second spatial derivatives. A complementary problem is posed by the case in which the scene consists of a number of localised features such as corners or point sources of light. Ullman showed that if the image is an orthogonal projection of the scene, then three sufficiently different views are required for the solution of the structure-from-motion problem; this result implies that it is impossible in principle (even on the rigidity assumption) to compute the structure of a scene from an orthogonally projected image and the instantaneous velocities of the image points. One may therefore ask whether the same is true for perspective images. It transpires that in perspective projection the retinal positions and velocities of eight image points supply enough information for a simple computation of both the three-dimensional structure of the scene and the motion of the eye relative to the scene; the computation supplies, incidentally, three precise checks on the rigidity assumption. In this chapter I discuss the limitations of the algorithm and consider what information can be obtained from a less rigorous but more robust procedure.

An Eight-Point Velocity Algorithm

We start from equations 21 and 22 of chapter 20, written here as

$$u = (xW - U)/Z - B + Cy + Axy - Bx^2, \tag{1}$$

$$v = (yW - V)/Z + A - Cx - Bxy + Ay^2, \tag{2}$$

and begin by eliminating the unknown coordinate Z:

$$(u + B - Cy - Axy + Bx^2)(yW - V)$$
$$= (v - A + Cx + Bxy - Ay^2)(xW - U). \tag{3}$$

After a little rearrangement this reduces to

$$0 = (AU + BV) - x(AW + CU) - y(BW + CV) + uV - vU$$
$$+ (xv - yu)W - \tfrac{1}{2}(x^2 - y^2)(AU - BV) - xy(AV + BU)$$
$$+ \tfrac{1}{2}(x^2 + y^2)(AU + BV + 2CW). \tag{4}$$

In equation 4—and there is one such equation for each image point—the quantities x, y, u, and v are directly accessible to observation and the unknowns are the nine combinations of A, B, C, U, V, and W. In general the ratios of these nine unknowns can be found by solving eight simultaneous linear equations of the form of equation 4, one for each of eight image points; the solution will take the form

$$U : V : W : (AW + CU) : (BW + CV) : (AU + BV) : (AU - BV) : (AU + BV + 2CW) : (AV + BU)$$
$$t_1 : t_2 : t_3 : \quad t_4 \quad : \quad t_5 \quad : \quad t_6 \quad : \quad t_7 \quad : \quad t_8 \quad : \quad t_9$$
$$\tag{5}$$

If t_3 does not vanish, we may set $W = 1$ and infer that

$$U = t_1/t_3, \tag{6}$$

$$V = t_2/t_3, \tag{7}$$

$$C = (t_8 - t_6)/2t_3, \tag{8}$$

$$A = t_4/t_3 - CU, \tag{9}$$

$$B = t_5/t_3 - CV. \tag{10}$$

Having found A, B, C, U, and V, we can then use the remaining relations,

$$t_6/t_3 = AU + BV, \tag{11}$$

$$t_7/t_3 = AU - BV, \tag{12}$$

$$t_9/t_3 = AV + BU, \tag{13}$$

as checks on the rigidity assumption.

If t_3 does vanish, implying that $W = 0$, a different normalization condition must be used. A convenient one is to set

$$U = \cos\theta, \quad V = \sin\theta, \tag{14}$$

so that $U^2 + V^2 = 1$. Then

$$\theta = \arctan(t_2/t_1) \tag{15}$$

and the values of A, B, and C may be easily found from the relations

$$A + iB = (t_7 + it_9)/(t_1 + it_2), \tag{16}$$

$$C = (t_4 + it_5)/(t_1 + it_2). \tag{17}$$

Checks on the rigidity assumption are then supplied by verifying that the ratio on the right-hand side of equation 17 is real and that

$$t_6 = t_8 = At_1 + Bt_2 \tag{18}$$

If t_1, t_2, and t_3 all vanish, we must infer that the observer's translational velocity is zero, so that the optic flow field is entirely rotational and provides no information whatever about the structure of the scene.

Limitations of the Eight-Point Algorithm

The eight-point algorithm described above is, unfortunately, very sensitive to errors in the measured image velocities $u(x, y)$ and $v(x, y)$, essentially because the solution of the eight equations of the type represented by equation 4 does not respect the three relations that must hold between the nine combinations of the six velocity components A, B, C, U, V, and W. Quite apart from this, the equations become non-independent if the observer's line-of-sight velocity is tangent to the quadric surface (or, if this is not unique, to any quadric surface) passing through the eight visible points and the point O (the nodal point of the image-forming lens; see chapter 23). This degeneracy condition is fulfilled if as many as seven of the visible points lie in a plane; the case of a visually textured plane surface is, accordingly, given special treatment in chapter 26. In the next section I describe a rather different approach that can sometimes have practical applications and that probably has a good deal more relevance to the workings of the human visual system.

The Small-Object Approximation

Imagine the observer to be moving through a stationary scene, keeping his eye on a small object, or rather on a spot P_0 on its surface. Referring to equations 23–26 of chapter 20, and setting $R = 1$ for simplicity, we obtain the image velocity of any other point in the form

$$u = (-U + xW)(1 - z) - B + Cy + Axy - Bx^2, \tag{19}$$

$$v = (-V + yW)(1 - z) + A - Cx - Bxy + Ay^2. \tag{20}$$

In these equations it is illuminating to think of x, y, and z as the (scaled) *three*-dimensional coordinates of a point on the object relative to the fixation point P_0; if all three dimensions of the object are small compared with its distance, then x, y, and z will all be much less than unity.

We simplify equations 19 and 20 by dropping all the second-order terms in the local coordinates x, y, and z, and obtain

$$u = xW + U(z - 1) - B + Cy, \tag{21}$$

$$v = yW + V(z - 1) + A - Cx. \tag{22}$$

The assumption that the observer's eye is following the point P_0 asserts, in effect, that u and v both vanish when x, y, and z all vanish, so that

$$-U - B = 0 = -V + A \tag{23}$$

and u and v take the even simpler forms

$$u = Wx + Cy + Uz, \tag{24}$$

$$v = -Cx + Wy + Vz. \tag{25}$$

Equations 24 and 25 lead to a psychologically realistic hypothesis about the use of image velocities in assigning 3D structure to small irregular objects.

Let P_1, P_2, and P_3 be three other points on the object, and let p_1, p_2, and p_3 be their images. We may suppose that p_0, the image of P_0, lies inside the triangle $p_1 p_2 p_3$ (see figure 1), but nothing hinges on this. If P_0 lies out of the plane of P_1, P_2, and P_3, then as O moves p_0 will "move across" the triangle $p_1 p_2 p_3$ with a velocity which can be obtained by linear interpolation, as follows. If (x_i, y_i) are the image coordinates of p_i (relative to p_0, which lies at the origin in the image plane), then there will be a unique set of weights (a_1, a_2, a_3) such that

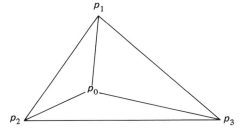

Figure 1

$$a_1 x_1 + a_2 x_2 + a_3 x_3 = 0, \tag{26}$$

$$a_1 y_1 + a_2 y_2 + a_3 y_3 = 0, \tag{27}$$

$$a_1 + a_2 + a_3 = 1. \tag{28}$$

(The three weights are, in fact, proportional to the areas of the three smaller triangles in figure 1.)

The relative velocity of the point p_0 and the triangle $p_1 p_2 p_3$ is then naturally defined as (u_4, v_4), where

$$u_4 = a_1 u_1 + a_2 u_2 + a_3 u_3, \tag{29}$$

$$v_4 = a_1 v_1 + a_2 v_2 + a_3 v_3, \tag{30}$$

and it follows immediately from equations 24 and 25 that

$$u_4 = U(a_1 z_1 + a_2 z_2 + a_3 z_3), \tag{31}$$

$$v_4 = V(a_1 z_1 + a_2 z_2 + a_3 z_3). \tag{32}$$

We can therefore determine the *direction* of (U, V) from the relative image velocity (u_4, v_4) of the point p_0 and the triangle $p_1 p_2 p_3$. The *magnitude* of (U, V) is, however, bound up in equations 24 and 25 with the magnitudes of the depth coordinates, so neither can be determined without a knowledge of the other. For want of further evidence, we therefore assume (U, V) to be a unit vector, setting

$$\begin{aligned} U &= \cos\phi, \\ V &= \sin\phi, \\ \phi &= \arctan(v_4/u_4). \end{aligned} \tag{33}$$

To find W and C, we eliminate z between equations 24 and 25:

$$(u \sin\phi - v \cos\phi) = W(x \sin\phi - y \cos\phi) + C(x \cos\phi + y \sin\phi). \tag{34}$$

If the (x, y) axes are reoriented so that (u_4, v_4) points along the x' axis, equation 34 becomes

$$v = Wy' - Cx', \tag{35}$$

an equation which asserts that the image velocity component perpendicular to the direction of (U, V) is attributable partly to the forward velocity W (which causes the image to expand) and partly to a rotation round the line of sight (which makes the image rotate in the opposite direction). The vector (u_4, v_4) lies, in fact, along the line joining the origin to the focus of expansion (a better term for what Prazdny and I referred to as the vanishing point).

The analysis of this section may be interpreted as demonstrating that something closely akin to motion parallax—the computation of the relative velocity (u_4, v_4)—can provide much useful information about the local structure of small non-planar objects. For a planar object, (u_4, v_4) will vanish, and therefore it supplies no useful information about the direction of (U, V).

To sum up: One can find the direction but not the magnitude of (U, V) in the small-object approximation, and the values of both W and C, by applying equation 35 to four or more image points. The uncertainty in the magnitude of (U, V) is equivalent to an uncertainty in the degree of "flatness" of the object. But if there are two or more objects in a stationary scene, one may be able to locate the focus of expansion in essentially the way that Prazdny and I described in chapter 20, with the relative velocity vector (u_4, v_4) playing a precisely similar role to the relative image velocity of two points at different depths that happen to lie in exactly the same direction.

22

The Reconstruction
of a Scene from
Two Projections

H. C. Longuet-Higgins

A simple algorithm for computing the three-dimensional structure of a scene from a correlated pair of perspective projections when the spatial relationship between the two projections is unknown is described here. This problem is relevant not only to photographic surveying (Thompson 1959) but also to binocular vision (Ogle 1964), in which the non-visual information available to the observer about the orientation and the focal length of each eye is much less accurate than the optical information supplied by the retinal images. The problem also arises in monocular perception of motion (Ullman 1979), in which the two projections represent views which are separated in time as well as in space. As Marr and Poggio (1976) have noted, the fusing of two images to produce a three-dimensional percept involves two distinct processes: the establishment of a $1:1$ correspondence between image points in the two views—the "correspondence problem"—and the use of the associated disparities for determining the distances of visible elements in the scene. I shall assume that the correspondence problem has been solved; the problem of reconstructing the scene then reduces to that of finding the relative orientation of the two viewpoints.

Photogrammetrists know that if a scene is photographed from two viewpoints, then the relationship between the camera positions is uniquely determined, in general, by the photographic coordinates of just five distinguishable points; but actually calculating the structure of the scene from five sets of image coordinates involves the iterative solution of five simultaneous third-order equations (Thompson 1959). I show here that if the scene contains as many as eight points whose images can be located in each projection, then the relative orientation of the two projections, and the structure of the scene, can be computed, in general, from the eight sets of image coordinates by a direct method which calls for nothing more difficult than the solution of a set of simultaneous linear equations.

Let P be a visible point in the scene, and let (X_1, X_2, X_3) and (X_1', X_2', X_3') be its three-dimensional cartesian coordinates with respect to the two viewpoints. The "forward" coordinates X_3 and X_3' are necessarily positive. The image coordinates of P in the two views may then be defined as

$$
\begin{aligned}
(x_1, x_2) &= (X_1/X_3, X_2/X_3), \\
(x_1', x_2') &= (X_1'/X_3', X_2'/X_3'),
\end{aligned}
\tag{1}
$$

and it is convenient to supplement them with the dummy coordinates

$$
x_3 = 1, \quad x_3' = 1
\tag{2}
$$

so that one can then write

$$
x_\mu = X_\mu/X_3, \quad x_\nu' = X_\nu'/X_3' \quad (\mu, \nu = 1, 2, 3).
\tag{3}
$$

As the two sets of three-dimensional coordinates are connected by an arbitrary displacement, we may write

$$
X_\mu' = R_{\mu\nu}(X_\nu - T_\nu),
\tag{4}
$$

where $\mathbf{T}$ is an unknown translational vector and $\mathbf{R}$ is an unknown rigid rotation matrix. (In this and subsequent equations I sum over repeated Greek subscripts.) The rotation $\mathbf{R}$ satisfies the relationships

$$
\mathbf{R\tilde{R}} = 1 = \mathbf{\tilde{R}R}, \quad \det \mathbf{R} = 1,
\tag{5}
$$

and it is convenient to adopt the length of the vector $\mathbf{T}$ as the unit of distance:

$$
\mathbf{T}_\nu^2 (= \mathbf{T}_1^2 + \mathbf{T}_2^2 + \mathbf{T}_3^2) = 1.
\tag{6}
$$

I begin by establishing a general relationship between the two sets of image coordinates—a relationship which expresses the condition that corresponding rays through the two centres of projection must intersect in space. We define a new matrix $\mathbf{Q}$ by

$$
\mathbf{Q} = \mathbf{RS},
\tag{7}
$$

where $\mathbf{S}$ is the skew-symmetric matrix

$$
\mathbf{S} = \begin{bmatrix} 0 & \mathbf{T}_3 & -\mathbf{T}_2 \\ -\mathbf{T}_3 & 0 & \mathbf{T}_1 \\ \mathbf{T}_2 & -\mathbf{T}_1 & 0 \end{bmatrix}.
\tag{8}
$$

Equation 8 may be written as

$$\mathbf{S}_{\lambda\nu} = \varepsilon_{\lambda\nu\sigma}\mathbf{T}_{\sigma'} \tag{9}$$

where $\varepsilon_{\lambda\nu\sigma} = 0$ unless (λ, ν, σ) is a permutation of $(1, 2, 3)$, in which case $\varepsilon_{\lambda\nu\sigma} = \pm 1$ depending on whether this permutation is even or odd. It follows from equations 4–9 that

$$\begin{aligned}
X'_\mu \mathbf{Q}_{\mu\nu} X_\nu &= \mathbf{R}_{\mu\kappa}(X_\kappa - \mathbf{T}_\kappa)\mathbf{R}_{\mu\lambda}\varepsilon_{\lambda\nu\sigma}\mathbf{T}_\sigma X_\nu \\
&= (X_\lambda - \mathbf{T}_\lambda)\varepsilon_{\lambda\nu\sigma}\mathbf{T}_\sigma X_{\nu'}
\end{aligned} \tag{10}$$

but because the quantity $\varepsilon_{\lambda\nu\sigma}$ is antisymmetric in every pair of its subscripts, the right-hand side vanishes identically:

$$X'_\mu \mathbf{Q}_{\mu\nu} X_\nu = 0. \tag{11}$$

Dividing equation 11 by $X'_3 X_3$, we arrive at the desired relationship between the image coordinates:

$$x'_\mu \mathbf{Q}_{\mu\nu} x_\nu = 0. \tag{12}$$

The next step is to determine the nine elements $\mathbf{Q}_{\mu\nu}$. There will be one equation of type 12 for every point P_i, namely

$$(x'_\mu x_\nu)_i \mathbf{Q}_{\mu\nu} = 0, \tag{13}$$

and in this equation the nine quantities $(x'_\mu x_\nu)_i$ are presumed to be known. The ratios of the nine unknowns $\mathbf{Q}_{\mu\nu}$ can therefore be obtained, in general, by solving eight simultaneous linear equations of type 13, one for each of eight visible points $P_1, \ldots, P_8$. I shall not yet discuss the special circumstances under which the solution fails; for the present, merely note that if the eight equations 13 are independent, their solution is entirely straightforward from a computational point of view.

The translational vector $\mathbf{T}$ must be calculated next. Multiplying $\mathbf{Q}$ on the left of equation 7 by its transpose, we obtain

$$\tilde{\mathbf{Q}}\mathbf{Q} = \tilde{\mathbf{S}}\tilde{\mathbf{R}}\mathbf{R}\mathbf{S} = \tilde{\mathbf{S}}\mathbf{S}, \tag{14}$$

so that, by the definition of $\mathbf{S}$,

$$\mathbf{Q}_{\mu\nu}\mathbf{Q}_{\mu\sigma} = \mathbf{T}_\mu^2\delta_{\nu\sigma} - \mathbf{T}_\nu\mathbf{T}_\sigma. \tag{15}$$

But $\mathbf{T}_\mu^2 = 1$ by equation 6, and so the trace of $\tilde{\mathbf{Q}}\mathbf{Q}$ must be

$$\mathbf{Q}_{\mu\nu}\mathbf{Q}_{\mu\nu} = \delta_{\nu\nu} - \mathbf{T}_\nu^2 = 2. \tag{16}$$

The nine elements of $\mathbf{Q}$ can therefore be normalized by dividing them by $\sqrt{\frac{1}{2}\,\text{trace}\,\tilde{\mathbf{Q}}\mathbf{Q}}$; the elements of the normalized matrix $\tilde{\mathbf{Q}}\mathbf{Q}$ can then be used for computing the ratios of the components of $\mathbf{T}$:

$$\tilde{Q}Q = \begin{bmatrix} 1 - T_1{}^2 & -T_1 T_2 & -T_1 T_3 \\ -T_2 T_1 & 1 - T_2{}^2 & -T_2 T_3 \\ -T_3 T_1 & -T_3 T_2 & 1 - T_3{}^2 \end{bmatrix}. \tag{17}$$

There are evidently three independent relationships between the diagonal and the off-diagonal elements of $\tilde{Q}Q$; these supply three independent checks on the results obtained so far. The absolute signs of the T_μ and the $Q_{\mu\nu}$ are still undetermined, but, as we shall see, these ambiguities are easily resolved later.

We are now in a position to compute the elements of the rotation matrix R. First note that equation 7 has a simple interpretation in terms of vector products. If we regard each row of Q and each row of R as a vector, then

$$Q_\alpha = T \times R_\alpha \quad (\alpha = 1, 2, 3) \tag{18}$$

and the condition for R to represent a proper rotation can be expressed in a similar form:

$$R_\alpha = R_\beta \times R_\gamma \tag{19}$$

for α, β, γ such that $\varepsilon_{\alpha\beta\gamma} = 1$. The problem is then to express the R_α in terms of T and the Q_α.

By equation 18, R_α is orthogonal to Q_α and may therefore be expressed as a linear combination of T and $Q_\alpha \times T$. We therefore introduce new vectors

$$W_\alpha = Q_\alpha \times T \quad (\alpha = 1, 2, 3) \tag{20}$$

and write

$$R_\alpha = a_\alpha T + b_\alpha W_\alpha. \tag{21}$$

Substitution into equation 18 gives

$$Q_\alpha = T \times (a_\alpha T + b_\alpha W_\alpha) = b_\alpha (T \times W_\alpha). \tag{22}$$

But as T is a unit vector,

$$T \times W_\alpha = T \times (Q_\alpha \times T) = Q_\alpha, \tag{23}$$

and so

$$b_\alpha = 1. \tag{24}$$

Turning to equation 19, we deduce that when $\varepsilon_{\alpha\beta\gamma} = 1$,

$$a_\alpha T + W_\alpha = (a_\beta T + W_\beta) \times (a_\gamma T + W_\gamma)$$
$$= a_\beta Q_\gamma - a_\gamma Q_\beta + W_\beta \times W_\gamma. \tag{25}$$

But in equation 25 the vectors $\mathbf{W}_\alpha$, $\mathbf{Q}_\beta$, and $\mathbf{Q}_\gamma$ are all orthogonal to $\mathbf{T}$, whereas $\mathbf{W}_\beta \times \mathbf{W}_\gamma$ is, by equation 20, a multiple of $\mathbf{T}$. It follows that in equation 25 the first term on the left equals the last term on the right,

$$a_\alpha \mathbf{T} = \mathbf{W}_\beta \times \mathbf{W}_\gamma, \tag{26}$$

and equation 21 finally becomes

$$\mathbf{R}_\alpha = \mathbf{W}_\alpha + \mathbf{W}_\beta \times \mathbf{W}_\gamma. \tag{27}$$

Having obtained in this way the vector $\mathbf{T}$ and the three rows of the matrix $\mathbf{R}$, we can at last find the three-dimensional coordinates X_μ, as follows.
 By equation 4,

$$X'_\mu = \mathbf{R}_{\mu\nu}(X_\nu - T_\nu),$$

from which it follows that

$$x'_1 = \frac{X'_1}{X'_3} = \frac{\mathbf{R}_{1\nu}(X_\nu - T_\nu)}{\mathbf{R}_{3\nu}(X_\nu - T_\nu)}. \tag{28}$$

Introducing the vectors

$$\mathbf{X} = (X_1, X_2, X_3), \quad \mathbf{x} = (x_1, x_2, 1), \tag{29}$$

we may write equation 28 in terms of the rows $\mathbf{R}_\alpha$ of the matrix $\mathbf{R}$:

$$x'_1 = \frac{\mathbf{R}_1 \cdot (\mathbf{X} - \mathbf{T})}{\mathbf{R}_3 \cdot (\mathbf{X} - \mathbf{T})} = \frac{\mathbf{R}_1 \cdot (\mathbf{x} - \mathbf{T}/X_3)}{\mathbf{R}_3 \cdot (\mathbf{x} - \mathbf{T}/X_3)}, \tag{30}$$

from which it follows that

$$X_3 = \frac{(\mathbf{R}_1 - x'_1 \mathbf{R}_3) \cdot \mathbf{T}}{(\mathbf{R}_1 - x'_1 \mathbf{R}_3) \cdot \mathbf{x}}. \tag{31}$$

The other unprimed coordinates are then given by equation 3 as

$$X_1 = x_1 X_3, \quad X_2 = x_2 X_3, \tag{32}$$

and the primed coordinates are finally obtained from equation 4.
 There are, in fact, four distinct solutions to the problem, associated with the alternative choices of sign for the components of $\mathbf{T}$ and the elements of $\mathbf{Q}$. But any doubt as to which choices to adopt is easily resolved: the condition that the forward coordinates of any point must both be positive will be satisfied if, and only if, both sets of signs are correctly chosen.
 There are certain "degenerate" eight-point configurations for which the algorithm fails because the associated equations 13 become non-independent.

A configuration will be degenerate if as many as four of the points lie in a straight line, or if as many as seven of them lie in a plane. Quite unexpectedly, degeneracy also arises if the configuration includes six points at the vertices of a regular hexagon, or consists of eight points at the vertices of a cube. The "invisibility" of such configurations to the eight-point algorithm may be demonstrated by arguments too long to be presented here; but the reasons for it are unconnected with any ambiguity in the interpretation of the resulting projections. A degenerate configuration immediately becomes "visible", however, if one of the offending points P_i is moved slightly away from its original position.

In general, then, the three-dimensional coordinates of a set of eight or more visible points may be obtained by the following algorithm:

(1) Set up eight equations of the form 13, and solve them for the ratios of the nine unknowns $\mathbf{Q}_{\mu\nu}$.

(2) Compute the matrix $\tilde{\mathbf{Q}}\mathbf{Q}$ and normalise the elements of $\mathbf{Q}$ by dividing them by $\sqrt{\frac{1}{2} \operatorname{trace} \tilde{\mathbf{Q}}\mathbf{Q}}$.

(3) Obtain the magnitudes and the relative signs of the $\mathbf{T}_\nu$ from equation 17; their absolute signs, and those of the $\mathbf{Q}_{\mu\nu}$, may have to be chosen arbitrarily at this stage.

(4) Define three new vectors by equation 20 and use equation 27 to calculate the rows of the matrix $\mathbf{R}$.

(5) Use equations 31 and 32 for computing the unprimed three-dimensional coordinates of all the visible points, and equation 4 for calculating the primed coordinates.

(6) Check that the forward coordinates X_3 and X_3' of any point are both positive. If both signs are negative, alter the signs of the $\mathbf{T}_\nu$ and return to step 5; if X_3 and X_3' are of opposite sign, reverse the signs of the $\mathbf{Q}_{\mu\nu}$ and return to step 4.

The algorithm yields the most accurate results when applied to situations in which the distance D between the centres of projection is not too small compared with their distances from the points P_i. If the projective coordinates are accurate to a few seconds of arc, the forward coordinates of the P_i can be estimated out to about $10D$ with great accuracy, and even as far as $100D$ if the P_i are adequately spaced in depth. This performance is comparable with that of the human visual system; but that does not, of course, imply that the eight-point algorithm is actually used in stereoscopic vision, as in binocular vision we have at least some information about the relative orientation of the two eyes. The most useful applications of the eight-point algorithm will probably be found in computer vision systems, where there is still a need for fast and accurate methods of converting two-dimensional images into three-dimensional interpretations.

I thank Drs A. L. Allan and K. B. Atkinson for the reference to Thompson, and the RS and SRC for support.

References

Marr, D., and T. Poggio. 1976. *Science* 194: 283–287.

Ogle, K. N. 1964. *Researches in Binocular Vision.* New York: Hafner.

Thompson, E. H. 1959. *Photogrammetric Record* 3, no. 14: 152–159.

Ullman, S. 1964. *The Interpretation of Visual Motion.* Cambridge, Mass.: MIT Press.

23

Configurations that Defeat the Eight-Point Algorithm

H. C. Longuet-Higgins

A few years ago I described an algorithm for locating eight or more points in three dimensions, given the 2D coordinates of their images in two separate projections (Longuet-Higgins 1981). The algorithm depends on the solution of eight simultaneous linear equations, but with certain "degenerate" eight-point configurations these equations become non-independent, so that the algorithm fails. Some configurations, such as the vertices of a cube, are found to be degenerate no matter how they are placed relative to the two centres of projection; such configurations may be described as "intrinsically" degenerate. But not all configurations remain degenerate if either of the viewpoints is moved; those that do not are "extrinsically" degenerate. The necessary and sufficient conditions for intrinsic degeneracy are now known (Longuet-Higgins 1984). In this chapter I derive a necessary and sufficient condition for degeneracy of either type: that the eight points lie on a quadric surface that passes through the two viewpoints.

We denote by X_μ and X'_ν ($\mu, \nu = 1, 2, 3$) the 3D coordinates of any visible point P with respect to cartesian frames centred at the two viewpoints O and O'; the plane projective coordinates of the two images of P are then

$$x_\mu = X_\mu/X_3, \quad x'_\nu = X'_\nu/X'_3, \tag{1}$$

where X_3 and X'_3 are the "forward" coordinates of a point so that $x_3 = 1 = x'_3$ by definition. The eight-point algorithm exploits an identity involving the coordinates x_μ and x'_ν, namely

$$\sum_{\mu\nu} x'_\mu Q_{\mu\nu} x_\nu = 0, \tag{2}$$

where the matrix $Q_{\mu\nu}$ is closely related to the displacement which transforms the X_μ into the X'_ν,

$$X'_\mu = \sum_v U_{\mu v}(X_v - T_v), \tag{3}$$

in which T_v is a translation vector and $U_{\mu v}$ a rigid rotation matrix. The relation is, in fact,

$$Q_{\mu v} = \sum_\kappa U_{\mu \kappa} S_{\kappa v}, \tag{4}$$

where S is the skew-symmetric matrix

$$S = \begin{bmatrix} 0 & T_3 & -T_2 \\ -T_3 & 0 & T_1 \\ T_2 & -T_1 & 0 \end{bmatrix}. \tag{5}$$

The fact that equation 2 is satisfied by every point which appears in both projections allows us, in general, to compute the ratios of the nine unknowns $Q_{\mu v}$ (and hence the T_v and the $U_{\mu v}$; see Longuet-Higgins 1981) by solving eight simultaneous linear equations of the form

$$\sum_{\mu v} (x'_{\mu i} x_{v i}) Q_{\mu v} = 0; \quad i = 1, \ldots, 8. \tag{6}$$

Trouble arises, however, if there exists a set of numbers c_i, not all zero, such that for all pairs of values of μ and v

$$\sum_1^8 c_i x'_{\mu i} x_{v i} = 0$$

—a condition which may conveniently be expressed in symbolic form:

$$\exists \{c_i\} \forall_{\mu v} : \sum_1^8 c_i x'_{\mu i} x_{v i} = 0. \tag{7}$$

Then (and only then) equations 6 become non-independent and fail to yield the relative values of the Q_μ. We therefore ask: What relative dispositions of the visible points $P_1, \ldots, P_8$ and the viewpoints O and O' will satisfy the degeneracy condition 7?

Now if any point P_i is to be visible in both projections, its "forward" coordinates X_{3i} and X'_{3i} must both be positive. Equation 7 will therefore possess a non-trivial solution $(c_1, \ldots, c_8)$ if and only if

$$\exists \{e_i\} \forall_{\mu v} : \sum_1^8 e_i X'_{\mu i} X_{v i} = 0, \tag{8}$$

the relation between e_i and c_i being

$$e_i = c_i / (X'_{3i} X_{3i}). \tag{9}$$

Substituting from equation 3 into equation 8, we obtain

$$\exists\{e_i\} \forall_{\mu\nu} : \sum_1^8 e_i \sum_\kappa U_{\mu\kappa}(X_{\kappa i} - T_\kappa)X_{vi} = 0. \tag{10}$$

Multiplying by $U_{\mu\lambda}$ and summing over λ, we succeed in eliminating the matrix U from the degeneracy condition, obtaining

$$\exists\{e_i\} \forall_{\lambda\nu} : \sum_1^8 e_i(X_{\lambda i} - T_\lambda)X_{vi} = 0, \tag{11}$$

which may be rewritten as

$$\exists\{e_i\} \forall_{\mu\nu} : \sum_1^8 e_i X_{\mu i} X_{vi} = X_{\mu 9} \sum_1^8 e_i X_{vi}, \tag{12}$$

where $X_{\mu 9}$ equals T_μ, by definition. We now show that equation 11 is satisfied if $P_1, \ldots, P_8$ and O' all lie on a quadric through the first viewpoint O, which is the origin of measurement of the coordinates X_μ. It is convenient to make a temporary change of notation, and denote these coordinates by X, Y, and Z; the equation of a quadric then takes the form

$$0 = [X\ Y\ Z\ 1]M \begin{bmatrix} X \\ Y \\ Z \\ 1 \end{bmatrix}, \tag{13}$$

where M is a real symmetric matrix. In the expansion of equation 13 there are ten separate terms; ten given points will lie on the same quadric if and only if the corresponding 10×10 determinant vanishes, namely

$$D_{10} = \begin{bmatrix} X_1{}^2 & Y_1{}^2 & Z_1{}^2 & X_1 Y_1 & X_1 Z_1 & Y_1 Z_1 & X_1 & Y_1 & Z_1 & 1 \\ \vdots & & & & & & & & & \vdots \\ X_{10}{}^2 & Y_{10}{}^2 & & & & & & & \cdots & 1 \end{bmatrix}, \tag{14}$$

where the terms in row i refer to the point P_i. If one of these points, say P_{10}, is the origin, then D_{10} vanishes if and only if its leading minor D_9 does so; this will happen if (in our earlier notation)

$$\exists\{e_i\}(\forall_{\mu\nu} : \sum_1^9 e_i X_{\mu i} X_{vi} = 0 \quad \text{(6 conditions)}$$

and $\tag{15}$

$$\forall_v : \sum_1^9 e_i X_{vi} = 0) \quad \text{(3 conditions)}.$$

The conditions 15 assert the existence of a linear relation between the rows of D_9; this is the necessary and sufficient condition that the points $P_1, \ldots, P_9$ lie on a quadric through the origin. So if the two viewpoints are at the origin and P_9 respectively, our immediate goal is to prove that equation 15 implies equation 12—that coquadricity implies degeneracy. The proof is simple: If e_9 in equation 15 is zero, then the two sums in equation 15 become sums from 1 to 8, and both sides of equation 12 vanish; if e_9 is not zero, the e_i may be normalized to make $e_9 = -1$, and equation 15 may be written in the form

$$\exists \{e_i\} \, (\forall_{\mu\nu} : \sum_1^8 e_i X_{\mu i} X_{\nu i} = X_{\mu 9} X_{\nu 9}$$

and   (16)

$$\forall_\nu : \sum_1^8 e_i X_{\nu i} = X_{\nu 9}),$$

from which equation 12 follows immediately.

To prove the converse—that degeneracy implies coquadricity—we note that the left-hand side of equation 12 is symmetric in μ and ν, and can therefore be diagonalized by a rotation of the coordinate axes about 0. We will, accordingly, reinterpret the $X_{\nu i}$ as coordinates in the rotated frame. In this frame both sides of equation 12 vanish when μ and ν are unequal:

$$\sum_1^8 e_i X_{\mu i} X_{\nu i} = X_{\mu 9} \sum_1^8 e_i X_{\nu i} = 0 \quad \text{for } \mu \neq \nu,$$ (17)

and the following are the only possibilities consistent with equation 17:

- The $X_{\mu 9}$ all vanish. This case is that in which P_9 and O coincide, so that a quadric can certainly be found that passes through $P_1, \ldots, P_8, P_9$, and O.
- The three quantities $\sum_1^8 e_i X_{\nu i}$ all vanish. In this case the sums in equation 17 will vanish for all pairs of values of μ and ν and by introducing $e_9 = 0$ we can ensure that the nine sums in equation 15 also vanish.
- Just one of the coordinates $X_{\mu 9}$ is non-zero, and the corresponding sum $\sum_1^8 e_i X_{\nu i}$:

$$\sum_1^8 e_i X_{\nu i} = 0 = X_{\nu 9} \quad \text{for } \nu \neq 3 \text{ (say)}$$ (18)

but

$$\sum_1^8 e_i X_{3i} \neq 0 \neq X_{39}.$$

Defining e_9 so that

$$\sum_1^9 e_i X_{3i} = 0,$$ (19)

we infer that

$$\forall_v : \sum_1^9 e_i X_{vi} = 0;$$ (20)

adding $e_9 X_{\mu 9} X_{v9}$ to each side of equation 17, we arrive at the condition

$$\exists\{e_i\} \forall_{\mu v} \sum_1^9 e_i X_{\mu i} X_{vi} = X_{\mu 9} \sum_1^9 e_i X_{vi} = 0.$$ (21)

Together, equations 20 and 21 ensure that the points $P_1, \ldots, P_8$ lie on a quadric through the two viewpoints O and O' ($= P_9$).

We see, then, that the necessary and sufficient condition for degeneracy—that $P_1, \ldots, P_8$ should lie on a quadric through O and O'—involves the eight visible points and two viewpoints on a completely equal footing. The question therefore arises: What becomes of the distinction between intrinsically and extrinsically degenerate configurations? Is it worth preserving, and if so what special cases is it useful to distinguish?

Before addressing these questions in detail it is helpful to put the degeneracy condition into an even more symmetrical form by passing to a coordinate system in which the first viewpoint is not at the origin but at the point P_0, with coordinates $X_{\mu 0}$ (the other viewpoint P_9 having coordinates $X_{\mu 9}$ as before). Then the coquadricity condition takes the new form: There exists a set of numbers $(e_0, e_1, \ldots, e_8, e_9)$, not all zero, such that

$$\forall_{\mu v} : \sum_0^9 e_i X_{\mu i} X_{vi} = 0 \quad \text{(6 conditions)}$$

$$\forall_v : \sum_0^9 e_i X_i = 0 \quad \text{(3 conditions)}$$ (22)

$$\sum_0^9 e_i = 0 \quad \text{(1 condition)}.$$

The distinction between intrinsic and extrinsic degeneracy is now to be found in the values of the e_i: If e_0 and e_9 both vanish, then the degeneracy is intrinsic; otherwise it is extrinsic.

Generally speaking, the various cases can be classified according to the number of non-zero coefficients that are involved in the linear relation expressed by equation 22. The most general case is that in which none of the e_i vanishes; in this case the degeneracy can be lifted by slightly displacing any one of the eight visible points or either of the two viewpoints. Correspondingly, any non-degenerate eight-point configuration can be made (extrinsically) degenerate by moving any one of the ten points on to the (usually unique) quadric passing through the other nine.

A linear relation between certain rows of the determinant D_{10} may be interpreted geometrically as implying that any one of the associated points lies on every quadric passing through the others. This will be the case for four or more points in a straight line, six or more points on a conic, seven or more points in a plane, or eight points forming a 'quadric octet'. The concept of a quadric octet rests on a theorem to the effect that for any set of seven points $P_1, \ldots, P_7$ in general positions there exists an eighth point P_8 such that any quadric through $P_1, \ldots, P_7$ also passes through P_8. The theorem depends on the fact that the quadrics passing through seven points constitute an only two-parameter family, so that if any three members of this family intersect in just one other point, then all the members of the family must do so.

To sum up: I have proved that the eight linear equations 6, on whose solution the eight-point algorithm depends, have no unique solution if and only if the eight visible points lie on a quadric through the two viewpoints. The ten points in question will satisfy this condition if (but not only if) any four of them are collinear, any six lie on a conic, any seven are coplanar, or any eight constitute a quadric octet.

These results have obvious implications for a variant of the eight-point algorithm that computes the observer's angular velocity and direction of motion from the retinal velocities of eight points. This kinetic eight-point algorithm may be regarded as a limiting case of the one discussed here, in which the viewpoints O and O' are very close together. We infer that the kinematic eight-point algorithm will fail if and only if the direction of the observer's translational velocity is tangent to some quadric through the eight visible points and the centre of projection. The intrinsically degenerate configurations of the eight points are, naturally, the same for both algorithms.

References

Longuet-Higgins, H. C. 1981. A computer algorithm for reconstructing a scene from two projections. *Nature* 293: 133–135. [Chapter 22 in present volume.]

Longuet-Higgins, H. C. 1984. Configurations that defeat the 8-point algorithm. In *Image Understanding 1984*, ed. S. Ullman and W. Richards (Ablex).

24

The Role of the
Vertical Dimension in
Stereoscopic Vision

H. C. Longuet-Higgins

Theoretical discussions of stereoscopic depth perception (see, for example, Foley 1980) have tended to ignore the vertical dimension; partly because the horizontal disparities between the retinal images are usually larger than the vertical disparities, but partly perhaps because it is easier to think—and certainly easier to draw—in two dimensions than in three. In this chapter I show that if the vertical dimension is reinstated, the full three-dimensional structure of a scene may in principle be computed from the two retinal images when all that is known about the orientation of the eyes is that the planes of their horizontal meridians accurately coincide.

If the world were two-dimensional, casting one-dimensional images on our retinas, then it would be impossible even in principle to determine the structure of a scene from the retinal images alone. Figure 1 shows why: if the filled circles represent one possible interpretation of a pair of images, then another equally consistent interpretation is obtained by rotating each pencil of rays through an arbitrary angle and relocating the visible points at the new intersections. There are, clearly, infinitely many such interpretations (a twofold infinity, in fact), between which it is impossible to choose without recourse to nonvisual information about the angle of convergence and the direction of gaze. But if photogrammetrists find it possible to reconstruct a scene from a pair of photographs when the relation between the camera positions is quite unknown (Longuet-Higgins 1981), why should the visual system not do likewise? Is it not possible that the apparent need for nonvisual information in the binocular estimation of depth is merely a consequence of adopting an oversimplified theory, rather than an inescapable limitation of binocular vision? The only way to settle the matter is, of course, to construct a fully three-dimensional theory and to see whether it suggests a way of overcoming this limitation.

The essential difference between two and three dimensions is that whereas in two dimensions all pairs of lines intersect (possibly at infinity),

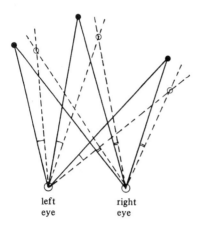

left
eye

right
eye

Figure 1
The impossibility of seeing where things are in a two-dimensional world.

in three dimensions it is quite exceptional for them to do so. If we think of the retinal images of a visible point as defining "rays" that travel outwards from the eyes in straight lines, then the condition that the two rays shall meet in space places a precise constraint on the relative orientation of the two eyes; a sufficient number of such constraints will uniquely determine their relative orientation.

Another way of seeing the importance of the vertical dimension is to notice that it enables the observer to estimate the relative distances of a point P from the two eyes, provided that P does not lie in the horizontal meridian. The ratio of the distances is simply $\tan\phi''/\tan\phi'$, where ϕ' and ϕ'' are the angular elevations of P as seen by the two eyes. It is this extra information, as we shall see, that gives a three-dimensional theory the deductive power that is denied to a two-dimensional one. The associated effects may be small, but they enable a system which takes account of vertical disparities to outperform, to an astonishing degree, one which merely treats them as tiresome discrepancies to be explained away or ignored altogether.

The Coordinates of a Visible Point

The various three-dimensional coordinates that we shall need are illustrated in figure 2. O' and O'' are the nodal points of the two eyes. The plane of the diagram is taken to be the common plane of their horizontal meridians, so that the axes $O'X'$, $O'Z'$, $O''X''$, and $O''Z''$ all lie in this plane. (The

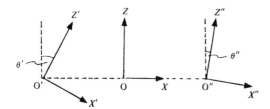

Figure 2
The plane of the horizontal meridians of the two eyes. O' and O'' are the nodal points of the left and right eyes, and O is the midpoint of $O'O''$.

vertical axes $O'Y'$ and $O''Y''$ cannot be seen, as they are perpendicular to the plane of the figure.) In addition to the local coordinate systems $O'X'Y'Z'$ and $O''X''Y''Z''$, we introduce a "cyclopean" coordinate system $OXYZ$ (Julesz 1971). The origin O lies at the midpoint of the interocular axis $O'O''$, and OX lies along this axis. OZ also lies in the horizontal plane, and θ' and θ'' (both measured clockwise) are the angles that the lines of regard $O'Z'$ and $O''Z''$ make with the cyclopean Z axis. Finally, the X coordinates of O' and O'' are assigned the values -1 and $+1$ respectively; this convention establishes the unit of length as one-half of the interocular distance. The retinal coordinates of the images of a visible point are defined by the equations

$$(x', y') = (X'/Z', Y'/Z'), \quad (x'', y'') = (X''/Z'', Y''/Z''); \tag{1}$$

the goal of the theory is to derive the cyclopean coordinates of a set of visible points, and the vergence angles θ' and θ'', from the retinal coordinates of their images.

We begin by expressing the local coordinates (X', Y', Z') and (X'', Y'', Z'') in terms of the cyclopean coordinates:

$$\begin{aligned}
X' &= (X + 1)\cos\theta' - Z\sin\theta', & X'' &= (X - 1)\cos\theta'' - Z\sin\theta'', \\
Y' &= Y, & Y'' &= Y, \\
Z' &= (X + 1)\sin\theta' + Z\cos\theta', & Z'' &= (X - 1)\sin\theta'' + Z\cos\theta'',
\end{aligned} \tag{2}$$

and vice versa:

$$\begin{aligned}
X + 1 &= X'\cos\theta' + Z'\sin\theta', & X - 1 &= X''\cos\theta'' + Z''\sin\theta'', \\
Y &= Y', & Y &= Y'', \\
Z &= -X'\sin\theta' + Z'\cos\theta'. & Z &= -X''\sin\theta'' + Z''\cos\theta''.
\end{aligned} \tag{3}$$

Equations 3 supply two alternative expressions for Z/Y, and if $Y \neq 0$ these must be equal (otherwise they are undefined):

$$-\frac{X'}{Y'}\sin\theta' + \frac{Z'}{Y'}\cos\theta' = -\frac{X''}{Y''}\sin\theta'' + \frac{Z''}{Y''}\cos\theta''. \tag{4}$$

The two pairs of retinal coordinates must therefore be connected by the useful relation

$$-\frac{x'}{y'}\sin\theta' + \frac{1}{y'}\cos\theta' = -\frac{x''}{y''}\sin\theta'' + \frac{1}{y''}\cos\theta''. \tag{5}$$

The occurrence of y' and y'' as denominators in equation 5 reminds us that the equation cannot be applied to points in the XZ plane, for which $y' = 0 = y''$. But for even a single point P with a finite elevation ($Y \neq 0$) the equation can tell us something about its position in space. To see this, suppose that the observer is looking straight ahead ($\theta' + \theta'' = 0$) and knows that he is, although he cannot estimate his angle of convergence $\theta' - \theta''$. Then, setting $\theta' = \theta$ and $\theta'' = -\theta$, we obtain

$$\left(\frac{x''}{y''} + \frac{x'}{y'}\right)\sin\theta = \left(\frac{1}{y''} - \frac{1}{y'}\right)\cos\theta$$

or

$$\tan\theta = \frac{y' - y''}{x''y' + x'y''}.$$

If P lies on the midplane $X = 0$, symmetry dictates that

$$x' + x'' = 0, \quad y' = y'',$$

so the expression for $\tan\theta$ is undefined ($=0/0$). But if P lies well away from both the planes $X = 0$ and $Y = 0$, then the observer can determine $\tan\theta$ from the vertical disparity $y' - y''$, and thus locate P in three dimensions. For once θ is known, equations 3 may be used to calculate

$$\frac{X+1}{Y} = \frac{x'}{y'}\cos\theta + \frac{1}{y'}\sin\theta = A, \text{ say,}$$

$$\frac{X-1}{Y} = \frac{x''}{y''}\cos\theta - \frac{1}{y''}\sin\theta = B, \text{ say,}$$

$$\frac{Z}{Y} = -\frac{x'}{y'}\sin\theta + \frac{1}{y'}\cos\theta = C, \text{ say;}$$

thereafter

$$X = \frac{A+B}{A-B}, \quad Y = \frac{2}{A-B}, \quad Z = \frac{2C}{A-B}.$$

(Moral: If you want to locate a point source in the dark, don't look straight at it!)

The Case of Three Visible Points

If as many as three points are visible, and none of the points lies on the horizontal meridian, then their cyclopean coordinates can be computed, in general, without any assumption about the vergence angles. Each of the visible points will yield an equation of type 5; so we can find the ratios of the four unknowns $\sin\theta'$, $\cos\theta'$, $\sin\theta''$, and $\cos\theta''$ by solving three simultaneous equations, one for each visible point (unless the equations turn out to be nonindependent—a case which we shall consider in a moment). If (x_i', y_i') and (x_i'', y_i'') are the retinal coordinates of the images of P_i $(i = 1, 2, 3)$, then the solution of the three simultaneous equations is

$$\frac{\sin\theta'}{D_1} = -\frac{\cos\theta'}{D_2} = \frac{\sin\theta''}{D_3} = -\frac{\cos\theta''}{D_4}, \tag{6}$$

where D_1, D_2, D_3, and D_4 are the determinants of the 3×3 matrices obtained by omitting, in turn, column 1, 2, 3, or 4 from the 3×4 matrix

$$\begin{vmatrix} -\dfrac{x_1'}{y_1'} & \dfrac{1}{y_1'} & \dfrac{x_1''}{y_1''} & -\dfrac{1}{y_1''} \\[2mm] -\dfrac{x_2'}{y_2'} & \dfrac{1}{y_2'} & \dfrac{x_2''}{y_2''} & -\dfrac{1}{y_2''} \\[2mm] -\dfrac{x_3'}{y_3'} & \dfrac{1}{y_3'} & \dfrac{x_3''}{y_3''} & -\dfrac{1}{y_3''} \end{vmatrix} = \mathbf{M}, \text{ say.} \tag{7}$$

Once D_1, D_2, D_3, and D_4 have been computed, the vergence angles are given by

$$\theta' = -\arctan\left(\frac{D_1}{D_2}\right), \quad \theta'' = -\arctan\left(\frac{D_3}{D_4}\right), \tag{8}$$

and the cyclopean coordinates can then be found by using equations 3:

$$\frac{X + 1}{Y} = \frac{x'}{y'}\cos\theta' + \frac{1}{y'}\sin\theta', \quad \frac{X - 1}{Y} = \frac{x''}{y''}\cos\theta'' + \frac{1}{y''}\sin\theta'',$$

$$\frac{Z}{Y} = -\frac{x'}{y'}\sin\theta' + \frac{1}{y'}\cos\theta', \text{ or } \frac{Z}{Y} = -\frac{x''}{y''}\sin\theta'' + \frac{1}{y''}\cos\theta''. \tag{9}$$

(A separate calculation is needed, of course, for each point.)

If the problem is being solved on a computer, the consistency of the solution can be checked by testing the relation

$$D_1{}^2 + D_2{}^2 = D_3{}^2 + D_4{}^2,\tag{10}$$

which follows from equation 6. The existence of this relation indicates that the two sets of retinal coordinates are not fully independent; they must be related if they are to admit a consistent three-dimensional interpretation.

As already remarked, the computation will fail if the three simultaneous equations of type 5 are not independent; for then the determinants D_1, D_2, D_3, and D_4 will all vanish. This will happen if each of the four quantities x'/y', $1/y'$, x''/y'', and $1/y''$ can be expressed as a linear combination of just two variables; because then each column of $\mathbf{M}$ can be expressed as a linear combination of any two of the other columns. But by equations 2, x'/y', x''/y'', $1/y'$, and $1/y''$ are linear combinations of the three ratios X/Y, $1/Y$, and Z/Y; so a necessary and sufficient condition for D_1, D_2, D_3, and D_4 to vanish is that these three ratios are connected by a linear relation of the form

$$\frac{1}{Y} = \lambda \frac{X}{Y} + \mu \frac{Z}{Y},$$

or

$$\lambda X + \mu Z = 1.\tag{11}$$

This is the equation of a vertical plane—that is, one which is parallel to the cyclopean Y axis. We infer that the three-point computation based on equation 5 fails, not only when one or more of the points P_i lies in the horizontal meridian, but also when all three points lie in a vertical plane.

In general, however, the observer can easily escape from this dilemma; all he has to do is to raise or lower his eyes and look again. This is because the concepts "horizontal" and "vertical" are not defined in relation to the observer's body, or even his head; the horizontal plane is just the common plane of the lines of regard $O'Z'$ and $O''Z''$. Without moving his head the observer can therefore rotate the cyclopean frame $OXYZ$ about its X axis in such a way as to move any visible point out of the XZ plane; and if the plane $P_1 P_2 P_3$ was initially parallel to the Y axis, it will no longer be after the rotation has been carried out (unless it was initially parallel to the YZ plane, i.e. perpendicular to the interocular axis). We infer that in attempting to locate three visible points in space a binocular observer will do well to explore the effect of moving his eyes, rather than gazing fixedly at one of the points and thereby annihilating the informative y' and y'' coordinates of its retinal images.

The Case of Two Visible Points

It might be supposed that three was the smallest number of visible points that could be accurately located in space solely on the basis of the retinal positions of their images. But a tally of the number of unknowns and the number of retinal coordinates indicates that just two points might be enough. With two points there are six cyclopean coordinates and two vergence angles to be determined, but each point supplies four retinal coordinates (x', y') and (x'', y''), making up the required total of eight. We now show that the optimism generated by this balance between the numbers of known and unknown parameters is not misplaced.

(The reader who is unfamiliar with complex numbers should skip to the last paragraph of this section.)

Our starting point is equations 9, which may be condensed into two equations by writing them in complex form:

$$\frac{(X + iZ) + 1}{Y} = \left(\frac{x'}{y'} + \frac{i}{y'}\right)\exp(-i\theta'),$$
$$\frac{(X + iZ) - 1}{Y} = \left(\frac{x''}{y''} + \frac{i}{y''}\right)\exp(-i\theta''). \tag{12}$$

Introducing the complex cyclopean coordinate $U = X + iZ$ and the complex retinal coordinates $\eta' = (x' + i)/y'$ and $\eta'' = (x'' + i)/y''$, and remembering that there are two visible points to be considered, we arrive at the set of equations

$$\frac{U_1 + 1}{Y_1} = \eta_1' \exp(-i\theta'), \quad \frac{U_1 - 1}{Y_1} = \eta_1'' \exp(-i\theta''),$$
$$\frac{U_2 + 1}{Y_2} = \eta_2' \exp(-i\theta'), \quad \frac{U_2 - 1}{Y_2} = \eta_2'' \exp(-i\theta''), \tag{13}$$

The ηs are known; the problem is to find the Us, the Ys, and the θs.

Eliminating U_1 from the first pair of equations, and U_2 from the second, we obtain

$$\frac{2}{Y_1} = \eta_1' \exp(-i\theta') - \eta_1'' \exp(-i\theta''),$$
$$\frac{2}{Y_2} = \eta_2' \exp(-i\theta') - \eta_2'' \exp(-i\theta''), \tag{14}$$

which enables us to obtain a simple relation between the altitude ratio Y_2/Y_1 and the angle of convergence $\theta' - \theta''$. Defining

$$t = Y_2/Y_1, \quad \xi = \exp[i(\theta' - \theta'')], \tag{15}$$

we infer from equations 14 that

$$t = \frac{\eta_1' - \eta_1''\xi}{\eta_2' - \eta_2''\xi}; \tag{16}$$

inverting this relation between t and ξ, we get

$$\xi = \frac{\eta_1' - \eta_2' t}{\eta_1'' - \eta_2'' t}. \tag{17}$$

But t is real and ξ is a complex number of modulus unity; it follows immediately that

$$(\eta_1' - \eta_2' t)(\bar{\eta}_1' - \bar{\eta}_2' t) = (\eta_1'' - \eta_2'' t)(\bar{\eta}_1'' - \bar{\eta}_2'' t). \tag{18}$$

Equation 18 is a quadratic equation in t with real coefficients. Since one of its roots—the one which equals Y_2/Y_1—is real, the other root must be real too; but at this stage there is no way of telling which root is the right one. We therefore take one of the roots at random and use it for calculating the various unknowns.

By equations 13,

$$\frac{U_1 - 1}{U_1 + 1} = \frac{\eta_1''\xi}{\eta_1'}, \quad \frac{U_2 - 1}{U_2 + 1} = \frac{\eta_2''\xi}{\eta_2'}, \tag{19}$$

from which the values of U_1 and U_2 follow immediately:

$$U_1 = \frac{\eta_1' + \eta_1''\xi}{\eta_1' - \eta_1''\xi}, \quad U_2 = \frac{\eta_2' + \eta_2''\xi}{\eta_2' - \eta_2''\xi}, \tag{20}$$

with ξ given by equation 17. But U_1 and U_2 encapsulate the values of X_1, Z_1, X_2, and Z_2, so these four cyclopean coordinates are now determined. Evidently the "forward" coordinates Z_1 and Z_2 must both be positive; if either is negative, the chosen root of equation 18 corresponds to an unrealistic interpretation of the retinal images. But if t passes this test, the values of Y_1 and Y_2 are still of interest. Their magnitudes follow from equation 14:

$$|Y_1| = \frac{2}{|\eta_1' - \eta_1''\xi|}, \quad |Y_2| = \frac{2}{|\eta_2' - \eta_2''\xi|}, \tag{21}$$

and their signs must be the same as those of the retinal coordinates y_1' (or y_1'') and y_2' (or y_2'') respectively. The vergence angles, finally, are given by equations 13 as

$$\theta' = \arg\left(\frac{\eta_1' Y_1}{U_1 + 1}\right), \quad \theta'' = \arg\left(\frac{\eta_1'' Y_1}{U_1 - 1}\right). \tag{22}$$

The retinal images of two points not lying in the horizontal meridian are therefore consistent with at most two complete specifications of the geometry of the system. We now examine the relation between these alternative interpretations.

The Visual Ambiguity of a Vertical Plane

As we have just seen, there are sometimes two distinct three-dimensional interpretations of the retinal images of just two visible points; and, as we saw above, a difficulty arises in locating three points in space on the basis of their retinal images if the points lie in a vertical plane. These phenomena turn out to be related: in both cases there are two alternative dispositions of the points, which will lead to identical retinal images if the vergence angles θ' and θ'' are assigned appropriate values. To show that this is so, I first give a geometrical description of the relation between the two interpretations, and then supply an informal proof based on the circle of Apollonius.

The plane of figure 3, like that of figure 2, is the plane $Y = 0$. The two visible points P_1 and P_2 are supposed to lie on vertical lines through the points N_1 and N_2, which lie in the XZ plane. C is the point at which $N_1 N_2$ meets the Z axis, so that $O'C = O''C, = R$ say. L_1 and L_2 are points on $N_1 N_2$ such that $CN_1 \cdot CL_1 = R^2$ and $CN_2 \cdot CL_2 = R^2$; M_1 and M_2 are the mirror images of L_1 and L_2 in the XY plane. Then the spurious interpretation of the retinal images is one which locates the visible points at Q_1 and Q_2, lying on vertical lines through M_1 and M_2 respectively.

The following conditions are necessary and sufficient for the pair of points (Q_1, Q_2) to present the same aspect as the pair (P_1, P_2) when viewed from either O' or O'':

(i) Q_1 and Q_2 must have the same angular elevations, as seen from O', as P_1 and P_2. This condition can be satisfied by construction:

$Q_1 M_1 : O'M_1 = P_1 N_1 : O'N_1; \quad Q_2 M_2 : O'M_2 = P_2 N_2 : O'N_2.$

(ii) The same must apply to the elevations as seen from O'':

$Q_1 M_1 : O''M_1 = P_1 N_1 : O''N_1; \quad Q_2 M_2 : O''M_2 = P_2 N_2 : O''N_2.$

Since condition i holds by construction, this condition can be restated in the form

$O'M_1 : O'N_1 = O''M_1 : O''N_1; \quad O'M_2 : O'N_2 = O''M_2 : O''N_2.$

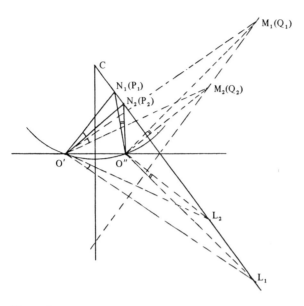

Figure 3
The alternative interpretations of the retinal images of a set of points lying in a vertical plane. P_1 and P_2 are the true positions of the visible points, and lie on vertical lines through N_1 and N_2; Q_1 and Q_2 are their spurious positions, lying on vertical lines through M_1 and M_2.

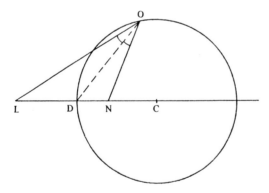

Figure 4
The circle of Apollonius.

(iii) The horizontal angles subtended by $N_1 N_2$ and $M_1 M_2$ must be the same, both at O' and at O'':

$$\angle M_1 O'M_2 = \angle N_1 O'N_2; \quad \angle M_1 O''M_2 = \angle N_1 O''N_2.$$

I now explain why these conditions are satisfied if Q_1 and Q_2 are constructed from P_1 and P_2 in the manner described. Figure 4 is the circle of Apollonius, in an unconventional guise. O is any point on the circumference of the circle; L and N are collinear with the centre C, and $CN \cdot CL = OC^2$. Two useful equalities hold, namely $OL : ON = DL : DN$ and $\angle LOD = \angle DON$. The first of these equalities ensures that in figure 3

$$O'L_1 : O'N_1 = O''L_1 : O''N_1; \quad O'L_2 : O'N_2 = O''L_2 : O''N_2,$$

and hence that condition ii holds as restated. The second equality ensures that

$$\angle L_1 O'L_2 = \angle N_1 O'N_2, \quad \angle L_1 O''L_2 = \angle N_1 O''N_2,$$

and hence that condition iii is also satisfied. So the construction described does indeed give two new points, Q_1 and Q_2, whose joint aspect is identical with that of P_1 and P_2 as viewed (with appropriate vergence changes) from either O' or O''.

A number of further results emerge from the theory; some of them are obvious:

• The geometrical transform which takes (P_1, P_2) into (Q_1, Q_2) also takes (Q_1, Q_2) into (P_1, P_2). (If it did not, we could generate further, distinct, interpretations.)

• The same transform may be applied to any number of points lying in the same vertical plane as P_1 and P_2, and the new set of points will present the same two aspects as the old set. It is therefore not surprising, in retrospect, that the deterministic computation described above broke down when applied to three points in a vertical plane.

• The spurious interpretation $(Q_1, Q_2, \ldots)$ will coincide with the correct one $(P_1, P_2, \ldots)$ if and only if the vertical plane containing the P_i intersects the interocular axis $O'O''$ at right angles. In this case it is unnecessary, as well as ineffective, for the observer to raise or lower his eyes in the hope of making the plane no longer vertical; the two roots of the quadratic equation 18 will coincide, and no question therefore arises as to which one corresponds to the correct interpretation.

• But if the (vertical) plane of the P_i is *nearly* perpendicular to $O'O''$, both interpretations will be physically acceptable, and it may be quite difficult to decide, even by raising the eyes, which is the correct one.

• The spatial positions of the spurious points Q_i depend only on the positions of the P_i and not on the vergence angles θ' and θ''. If this were not so, the Q_i would be revealed as spurious by seeming to move when the vergence angles were changed.

• But the two interpretations lead to different predictions as to how the retinal images are affected by rotating the eyes about the interocular axis. The correct interpretation must survive, but the spurious one will lead to an apparent distortion in the case of two visible points. With three or more visible points, however, the above analysis shows that there is no consistent alternative to the correct interpretation if the plane of the P_i is no longer vertical. A determined attempt to cling to the spurious interpretation when the eyes are raised or lowered could well lead, therefore, to a paradoxical percept.

• The situation illustrated in figure 3 was one in which both the correct and the spurious interpretation were physically realistic. But figure 5 shows that the spurious interpretation may well locate one or more of the Q_i behind the XY plane. In such a case, the correct interpretation is the only one that could possibly suggest itself.

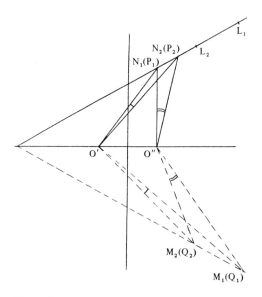

Figure 5
A case in which the alternative interpretation (Q_1, Q_2) is absurd.

Conclusions

The theory developed in this chapter demonstrates that the spatial positions of three visible points are uniquely determined, in general, by the locations of their images on the two retinas; and that even if only two points are visible, there are at most two solutions for their three-dimensional coordinates. The vertical dimension plays an essential role in the analysis; this fact strongly suggests that the vertical disparities of corresponding image elements may supply the optical cues to absolute distance and direction that are totally lacking in a two-dimensional theory of binocular vision. Vertical disparities are, however, much smaller than horizontal ones, and for this reason the predictions of the theory depend critically on its central assumption—that the planes of the two horizontal meridians accurately coincide.

Apart from showing how the structure of a scene may in principle be computed from a pair of retinal images, the theory predicts an unforeseen twofold ambiguity of interpretation in the case in which the visible points all lie in a vertical plane. (The author actually discovered the relation between the two interpretations of a vertical plane in the course of developing a suite of programs designed to implement the theory; this incident illustrates the value of computer implementations, not only for checking one's mathematics, but also in bringing to light exceptional cases.) It would be interesting to know whether, with impoverished visual stimuli, this ambiguity poses a serious perceptual problem, as it well might when all the visible points of a scene lie in a vertical plane that is nearly perpendicular to the interocular axis.

In short, the theory shows that vertical disparities could play an essential role in the binocular perception of absolute depth. Mayhew (1982) found this hypothesis to provide a quantitative explanation for Ogle's (1964) "induced effect".

Acknowledgements

My thanks are due to N. S. Sutherland and S. Isard for much useful advice and criticism, and to the Royal Society and the Science Research Council for research support.

References

Foley, J. M. 1980. Binocular distance perception. *Psychological Reviews* 87: 411–434.

Julesz, B. 1971. *Foundations of Cyclopean Perception.* University of Chicago Press.

Longuet-Higgins, H. C. 1981. A computer algorithm for reconstructing a scene from two projections. *Nature* 293: 133—135. [Chapter 22 in present volume.]

Mayhew, J. 1982. The interpretation of stereo-disparity information: The computation of surface orientation and depth. *Perception* 11: 387—403.

Ogle, K. N. 1964. *Research in Binocular Vision.* New York: Hafner.

25

A Computational Model of Binocular Depth Perception

J. E. W. Mayhew and
H. C. Longuet-Higgins

The binocular perception of depth may be regarded as proceeding in two stages: the establishment of a point-by-point correspondence between the left and right retinal images to extract disparity information, and the interpretation of the disparities to yield a three-dimensional percept. The position of an image point on the left retina can be represented by its plane projective coordinates (x, y); if (x', y') are the coordinates of the corresponding image point on the right retina, then the difference $x' - x$ is described as the horizontal disparity between the two image points, and $y' - y$ as the vertical disparity. The "correspondence problem"—that of computing the disparities—has been fully discussed in the literature (Ogle 1950; Julesz 1971; Nelson 1975; Marr and Poggio 1979; Mayhew and Frisby 1981), and we shall not consider it further. Our present concern is the "interpretation problem"—that of using the disparities for computing the three-dimensional structure of the scene.

As vertical disparities produced by local depth variations (in contrast to those produced by asymmetrical convergence) are commonly much smaller than horizontal ones (Ogle 1950; Mayhew 1982)—and necessarily vanish on the horizontal meridian—it is often supposed that only the horizontal disparities are relevant to the binocular perception of depth. There are two difficulties with this hypothesis. First, the horizontal disparities supply insufficient information, even in principle, for computing the absolute distances and directions of a set of visible points; they must be supplemented by independent information about the distance and direction of the fixation point, but non-visual estimates of these "viewing parameters" are notoriously unreliable. There is, however, a more serious difficulty: The binocular perception of a three-dimensional scene is profoundly altered by distorting one of the retinal images in the *vertical* dimension. If a cylindrical lens which induces a small vertical magnification is placed in front of one eye, then a visually textured surface in the fronto-parallel plane will acquire a pronounced tilt, as if it had been rotated about a vertical axis, although the horizontal disparities and the non-visual cues to fixation distance and direction are quite unaffected by the introduction of the lens. The question therefore arises: Could the vertical disparities supply the information about the viewing parameters that is required for deriving the structure of the scene from the horizontal disparities? The answer, as we shall see, is in the affirmative; and the hypothesis that the viewing parameters are derived from the vertical disparities rather than from non-visual information sources accounts quantitatively for the above phenomenon, which Ogle (1950) has described as the "induced effect".

It has recently been pointed out that a binocular system which takes account of the vertical as well as the horizontal image coordinates can in principle solve the interpretation problem without recourse to extra-retinal sources of information (Longuet-Higgins 1981, 1982); and also that there exists a remarkably simple approximate method of deriving the position and orientation of a visually textured plane from the horizontal and vertical disparities of a small number of texture elements lying in the plane (Mayhew 1982). Figure 1 illustrates the geometry of this situation. O and

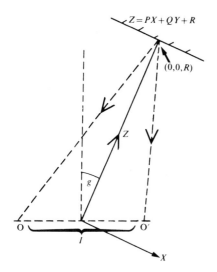

Figure 1
The coordinate system has origin at the midpoint of the line joining the optical centres of the eyes (O and O'). The line joining this point to the point of fixation $(0, 0, R)$ defines the Z axis; the X axis lies in the plane containing the line OO' and fixation point; and the line normal to this plane is the Y axis. The angle of gaze, g, is the angle OO' makes with the X axis. The analysis assumes that the eyes are free to rotate around their X and Y axes but not their Z axes.

O' are the nodal points of the two eyes, and the observer is looking—not quite straight ahead—at the plane $Z = PX + QY + R$, where the Z axis joins the midpoint of OO' to the fixation point $(0, 0, R)$ and makes an angle g with the forward direction. The capital letters refer to a coordinate system with the origin at the midpoint of the line joining the optical centres of the eyes. If the fixation distance R is large enough compared with the interocular distance I, then one can neglect, in the disparities, terms of the second order in I/R. It then becomes possible to use the algebra that Longuet-Higgins and Prazdny (1980) used in their analysis of the visual perception of motion; the problem is isomorphous with that presented by the stereoscopic viewing of an object at a moderate distance. If $\sin(g) = s$ and $\cos(g) = c$, one obtains, in this way,

$$H(x, y) = x' - x$$
$$= [(Pc + s)x + Qcy + (c - Ps)x^2 - Qsxy]I/R, \tag{1}$$

$$V(x, y) = y' - y$$
$$= [sy + (c - Ps)xy - Qsy^2]I/R. \tag{2}$$

These equations simplify if g is small enough for s and c to be replaced by g and 1 respectively, and for Pg and Qg to be neglected; in these conditions,

$$H(x, y) = x' - x = [(P + g)x + Qy + x^2]I/R, \tag{3}$$

$$V(x, y) = y' - y = (gy + xy)I/R. \tag{4}$$

These equations immediately suggest a way of computing the unknown parameters P, Q, R, and g. The equation for V implies that a plot of V/y against x gives a line of slope I/R and intercept gI/R, so that the values of R and g can be obtained from the vertical disparities of just two non-meridional points with different x coordinates (that is, points with $y \neq 0$ and $x_1 \neq x_2$). Explicitly,

$$R = I/V_{xy}, \quad g = V_y/V_{xy}, \tag{5}$$

where V_y and V_{xy} denote the coefficients of y and xy in the expression for V. Likewise, if H_x and H_y denote the coefficients of x and y in H, it follows from equation 3 that

$$P + g = H_x R/I, \quad Q = H_y R/I. \tag{6}$$

Substituting from equation 5 into equation 6, we infer that

$$P = (H_x - V_y)/V_{xy}, \quad Q = H_y/V_{xy}. \tag{7}$$

In short, the viewing parameters R and g can be directly computed from the vertical disparities alone; once they are known, the geometrical parameters P and Q may be computed from either equation 6 or equation 7, in which the viewing parameters do not appear explicitly. A computer simulation implementing equations 5 and 7 has shown that the small-angle approximations underlying these equations are indeed adequate for a wide range of reasonable surface orientations, viewing distances, and angles of gaze.

When a vertically magnifying lens is placed in front of one eye, the two retinal images become mutually incompatible, in the sense of ceasing to admit of a consistent three-dimensional interpretation. It is therefore quite surprising that the observer should obtain a clear three-dimensional percept, albeit a distorted one. The induced effect therefore offers a challenge to theories of stereopsis. Would a "seeing machine" which was based on a particular theory be subject to the induced effect, or would it arrive at a different interpretation of the two images, or fail to reach any interpretation at all? For example, machines based on the theories described in Longuet-Higgins 1981 and Mayhew and Frisby 1982 would not be subject to the induced effect and therefore may be excluded as models of the human visual process. Similarly, a full implementation of equations 1 and 2 would not in general show the induced effect, whereas a machine implementing the approximate solutions (equations 3 and 4) apparently interprets the two images in a way similar to that reported by human subjects. We shall now show that a system which computes P and Q directly from equation 7 will be subject to an induced effect of exactly the same nature and magnitude as that investigated by Ogle.

Suppose that a lens of horizontal magnification λ and vertical magnification μ is placed over the right eye. Then the new retinal coordinates for that eye will be

$$\hat{x} = \lambda x', \quad \hat{y} = \mu y',$$
(8)

so that the horizontal and vertical disparities will be

$$\hat{H} = \hat{x} - x$$
$$= \lambda[(P + g)x + Qy + x^2]l/R + (\lambda - 1)x,$$
(9)

$$V = \hat{y} - y$$
$$= \mu(gy + xy)l/R + (\mu - 1)y.$$
(10)

The new values of V_y and V_{xy} will therefore be

$$\hat{V}_y = \mu gl/R + (\mu - 1) = \mu(V_y + 1) - 1,$$
(11)

$$\hat{V}_{xy} = \mu I/R = \mu V_{xy}, \tag{12}$$

and the new values of H_x and H_y will be

$$\hat{H}_x = \lambda(P + g)I/R + (\lambda - 1) = \lambda(H_x + 1) - 1, \tag{13}$$

$$\hat{H}_y = \lambda QI/R = \lambda H_y. \tag{14}$$

The apparent values of P, Q, and R will therefore be

$$\hat{P} = (\hat{H}_x - \hat{V}_y)/\hat{V}_{xy} = [\lambda(H_x + 1) - \mu(V_y + 1)]/\mu V_{xy}, \tag{15}$$

$$\hat{Q} = \hat{H}_y/\hat{V}_{xy} = \lambda H_y/\mu V_{xy} = \lambda Q/\mu, \tag{16}$$

$$\hat{R} = I/\hat{V}_{xy} = I/\mu V_{xy} = R/\mu. \tag{17}$$

If λ and μ are both $\simeq 1$, the values of Q and R are not much affected, but with P it is an entirely different matter. To see this, suppose that P is actually zero, as it will be for a fronto-parallel plane. Then, according to equation 7, H_x and V_y must be equal, and so the apparent value of P, given by equation 15, will be

$$\hat{P} = (\lambda - \mu)(1 - V_y)/\mu V_{xy}. \tag{18}$$

As V_y is of order I/R, and λ and μ are close to 1, we may neglect V_y in the numerator and infer that

$$\hat{P} \simeq (\lambda - \mu)/V_{xy} = (\lambda - \mu)R/I. \tag{19}$$

Equation 19, with μ set equal to 1, becomes Ogle's own expression for the apparent tilt produced by a horizontally magnifying lens—an effect which can be understood in purely geometrical terms and which he therefore named the "geometric effect". Various predictions follow, and all are confirmed by Ogle's observations:

• The apparent tilt is proportional to the difference between the horizontal and vertical magnification, so that for a given value of R a vertical magnification induces an apparent tilt equal and opposite to that produced by an equivalent horizontal magnification. (The induced effect actually falls off at high magnification; this is not predicted by equation 19, but is presumably connected with the fact that $\hat{V}_y/\hat{V}_{xy}$ then implies an implausibly large value for the angle of gaze.)

• An ordinary spherical lens, with $\lambda = \mu$, induces no tilt.

• When $\mu = 1$ and $\lambda \simeq 1$, the induced tilt is proportional both to $\lambda - 1$ and to R. At a viewing distance $R = 40$ cm, Ogle found that the angle of tilt increased by 3–3.5° for every 1% increase in magnification. With an interocular distance $I = 6.5$ cm, equation 19 predicts a value for this ratio of

$$(180/\pi) \times (40/6.5) \times (1/100) = 3.53° \text{ per } \% \text{ magnification.}$$

In his experiments, Ogle actually used a null method of estimating the induced tilt of a vertical plane: the subject had to tilt the plane himself (in the opposite direction) until the apparent slope P became zero, that is, until $\hat{H}_x = \hat{V}_y$. This relationship entails that

$$\lambda(H_x + 1) = \mu(V_y + 1) \tag{20}$$

or

$$(\lambda - \mu) = \lambda H_x - \mu V_y = [\lambda(P + g) - \mu g]I/R. \tag{21}$$

Remembering that $\lambda \sim 1$ and $\mu \sim 1$, we get

$$\mu - \lambda \simeq PI/R, \tag{22}$$

showing that the actual value of P required to make $P = 0$ is

$$P = (\mu - \lambda)R/I. \tag{23}$$

This is, indeed, equal and opposite to the apparent tilt of a fronto-parallel plane under identical viewing conditions.

It has commonly been believed (see Foley 1980 for a review) that only the horizontal disparities convey useful information about the distances of objects, and only qualitative information at that. Vertical disparities, which arise when an object is nearer one eye than the other, have been regarded merely as something that the visual system must be capable of allowing for in fusing the two images into a unitary percept. Our approach to the problem, from an artificial-intelligence standpoint, has led to a computational solution of the interpretation problem which accounts quantitatively for the induced effect. Various explanations of this effect have been proposed (Ogle 1950; Julesz 1971; Foley 1980; Nelson 1977; Mayhew and Frisby 1981; Arditi et al. 1981), but none, we feel, follows so naturally from a theory of normal stereoscopic depth perception as the explanation proposed above. (The limitations of a recent theory which attempts to explain the induced effect without using vertical disparities [Arditi et al. 1981] have been criticized elsewhere [Mayhew and Frisby 1982].) Ogle's explanation, like ours, agrees quantitatively with the psychophysical magnitude of the induced effect, but requires the use of the vertical disparities on the vertical meridian to compute the compensatory rotation of the

Veith-Muller circle necessary to maintain the correct egocentric localization (this corresponds to the direction of gaze in our expressions). However, Ogle's theory fails to exploit the vertical-disparity information at other retinal locations and thus does not solve for the other viewing parameter, distance, which remains as an unknown scaling variable in his expression. Note that the retinal eccentricity of the location at which the disparity information is measured is of fundamental importance in our expressions relating horizontal and vertical disparity to the viewing and scene parameters (equations 1–4). Without the terms derived solely from the retinal eccentricity, the system of equations would be homogeneous and without a unique solution. The emphasis on a coordinate system derived from concern with corresponding points—the horopter and the Veith-Muller circle—may have masked the importance of these terms from Ogle's consideration, and may explain why, when he was so close to a complete solution, he failed to find it.

As our theory is formally complete, it predicts that the induced effect will result from any stimulus which supplies misleading cues about the viewing parameters—the distance and direction of the fixation point. Although the vertical disparities from any two retinal locations could be used to solve for the viewing parameters, and thus the computation could be essentially local to a particular region of retina, the results of the computation have global implications which can provide powerful constraints and checks on its consistency. In contrast to the interpretation of horizontal disparities where the results in one region of the retina exert little constraint on the interpretation at another region, the interpretation of the vertical disparities should give the same result everywhere. There are obvious advantages in making viewing-system parameters globally available, and so one might expect that the induced effect would act on the whole visual field even though vertical-disparity information could be derived from only a particular region of it. Ogle (1950) reports an experiment confirming this expectation. Vertical disparities from one part of the visual field changed the apparent depths of vertical rods (which of course cannot provide vertical-disparity information) in accord with the predictions of the induced effect. If the stimulus situation presents incompatible vertical-disparity information at different parts of the visual field or, alternatively, vertical-disparity information whose interpretation results in grossly implausible viewing-system parameters, one might expect some difficulty in perceiving the induced effect. This may explain why there may be some difficulty in producing the induced effect without the aid of a cylindrical lens (Arditi et al. 1981; Westheimer 1978).

Finally, it is of interest that Ogle reports excellent agreement in estimates of stereo acuity derived from experiments investigating the induced effect and other psychophysical procedures, which correspond to a sensitivity of about 0.2% magnification between the two eyes' images. The constraints that this degree of resolution imposes on the implementation of the processes described above are currently the subject of computational and psychophysical experimentation.

References

Arditi, A., L. Kaufman, and J. A. Movshon. 1981. *Vision Res.* 21: 755–764.

Foley, J. M. 1980. *Psychol. Rev.* 87: 411–434.

Julesz, B. 1971. *Foundations of Cyclopean Perception.* University of Chicago Press.

Longuet-Higgins, H. C. 1981. *Nature* 293: 133–134.

Longuet-Higgins, H. C. 1982. *Perception* 11: 405–407. [Chapter 24 in present volume.]

Longuet-Higgins, H. C., and K. Prazdny. 1980. *Proc. R. Soc.* B 208: 385–397.

Marr, D., and T. Poggio. 1979. *Proc. R. Soc.* B 204: 301–328.

Mayhew, J. E. W. 1982. *Perception* 11: 387–403.

Mayhew, J. E. W., and J. P. Frisby. 1981. *Artificial Intelligence* 17: 349–387.

Mayhew, J. E. W., and J. P. Frisby. 1982. *Vision Res.* 22: 1225–1228.

Nelson, J. 1975. *J. Theor. Biol.* 49: 1–88.

Nelson, J. 1977. *J. Theor. Biol.* 66: 203–266.

Ogle, K. N. 1950. *Binocular Vision.* Philadelphia: Saunders.

Westheimer, G. 1978. *Invest. Ophthalmol. Visual Sci.* 17: 545–551.

26   The Visual Ambiguity of a Moving Plane

H. C. Longuet-Higgins

In two previous papers (Longuet-Higgins and Prazdny 1980; Longuet-Higgins 1981) solutions were proposed to the problem of recovering the structure of a scene, and the motion of a monocular observer relative to the scene, from the motion of the optical image across the observer's retina. The problem, which has received the attention of many authors (Helmholtz 1866; Gibson 1950, 1966, 1979; Gibson and Gibson 1957; Gibson et al. 1955; Lee 1974; Nakayama and Loomis 1974; Braunstein 1976; Koenderink and van Doorn 1976; Ullman 1979), was found to present special difficulties if all the visible texture elements lay in the same plane. The rigidity assumption, which underlies the recovery of structure from visual motion, enabled one to decide whether or not the visible elements were coplanar, but not to locate the plane in which they lay. In a more recent investigation of the planar case, Tsai and Huang (1981) have shown that the parameters specifying the optic flow due to a textured plane give rise, in the general case, to two separate solutions for the orientation of the plane and the observer's motion relative to it. In this chapter the problem is examined afresh and it is shown that the spurious interpretation can be ruled out on geometrical grounds if the visible elements include some that lie in the forward direction (relative to the observer's linear velocity) and others that lie in the backward direction. At the end of the chapter examples are given to illustrate the ambiguity which remains if this condition is not satisfied.

The Eight Kinematic Parameters

Following Longuet-Higgins and Prazdny (1980), we envisage the observer as being in motion relative to the scene. The three-dimensional coordinates (X, Y, Z) of any texture element P in the scene are measured with respect to axes moving with the observer's eye, which has angular velocity (A, B, C) about these axes and linear velocity (U, V, W) along them. The time derivatives of the coordinates X, Y, and Z are then given by

$$\dot{X} = -U - BZ + CY,$$
$$\dot{Y} = -V - CX + AZ,$$
$$\dot{Z} = -W - AY + BX.$$
(1)

The element P will cast an image on the retina only if Z is positive; in this event the plane projective coordinates of the image will be

$$x = X/Z,$$
$$y = Y/Z,$$
(2)

and its velocity $(\dot{x}, \dot{y})$ across the retina will be

$$\dot{x} = (Wx - U)/Z - B + Cy - Bx^2 + Axy,$$
$$\dot{y} = (Wy - V)/Z + A - Cx - Bxy + Ay^2.$$
(3)

The case of interest is that in which the texture elements P all lie in the same plane, which may be represented by the equation

$$LX + MY + NZ = 1.$$
(4)

(In equation 4 the coordinate vector (L, M, N) is normal to the plane and has the dimensions of an inverse length; it points directly towards the plane and its length is the reciprocal of the distance of the plane from the origin. In what follows, the plane will sometimes be referred to as "the plane (L, M, N)".) Substituting

$$1/Z = Lx + My + N$$
(5)

into equation 3, we obtain, after collecting terms,

$$\dot{x} = -(UN + B) - x(UL - WN) - y(UM - C)$$
$$+ x^2(WL - B) + xy(WM + A),$$
(6)

$$\dot{y} = -(VN - A) - x(VL + C) - y(VM - WN)$$
$$+ xy(WL - B) + y^2(WM + A).$$
(7)

These equations show that each component of the image velocity is a second-order polynomial in the image coordinates, with coefficients that are simple combinations of the nine unknowns (A, B, C), (L, M, N), and (U, V, W). Evidently the five coefficients in equation 6 may be obtained from the values of $\dot{x}(x, y)$ for five image points by solving five simultaneous linear equations; the same applies to the five coefficients in equation 7. The values of $(WM + A)$ and of $(WL - B)$ given by the two calculations should, of course, agree. (Less obviously, the eight parameters in the two equations could be obtained from the velocities of just four image elements, by solving eight simultaneous linear equations, provided that no three of the elements are collinear.) In what follows we shall assume that the eight parameters have been successfully evaluated by such means and found to have the following values:

$$WM + A = a, \quad UN + B = b, \quad VL + C = c, \quad UL - WN = h,$$
$$VN - A = a', \quad WL - B = b', \quad UM - C = c', \quad VM - WN = k. \tag{8}$$

The problem is then to discover as much as possible about the nine unknowns (A, B, C), (L, M, N), and (U, V, W) from the eight quantities a, b, c, a', b', c', h, and k.

Solving the Equations

Setting

$$a + a' = 2p, \quad b + b' = 2q, \quad c + c' = 2r \tag{9}$$

and eliminating (A, B, C) from equations 8, we are left with five equations for six unknowns:

$$WM + VN = 2p, \quad UN + WL = 2q, \quad VL + UM = 2r,$$
$$UL - WN = h, \quad VM - WN = k. \tag{10}$$

The shortfall in the number of equations reflects the fact that the flow field cannot supply independent estimates of the observer's speed and distance from the plane; but equations 10 enable one, in fact, to compute the directions in which the vectors (U, V, W) and (L, M, N) must lie, and the product of their magnitudes. To demonstrate this, we begin by translating equations 10 into matrix notation. Defining

$$\mathbf{V} = (U, V, W), \quad \mathbf{N} = (L, M, N), \quad f = WN, \tag{11}$$

we can rewrite equations 10 in the form

$$\tfrac{1}{2}(\mathbf{V}\tilde{\mathbf{N}} + \mathbf{N}\tilde{\mathbf{V}}) = \begin{bmatrix} h + f & r & q \\ r & k + f & p \\ q & p & f \end{bmatrix} = \mathbf{S}, \text{ say,} \tag{12}$$

in which all the quantities in the matrix except f are presumed known. ($\mathbf{V}$ and $\tilde{\mathbf{V}}$ denote column and row vectors, respectively.)

Since $\mathbf{S}$ is symmetric, it can be transformed into a diagonal matrix $\mathbf{R}$ by an orthogonal matrix $\mathbf{T}$ (one whose inverse equals its transpose $\tilde{\mathbf{T}}$). Finding $\mathbf{T}$ involves determining the roots of the cubic equation in f obtained by equating the determinant of S to zero. If these roots are f_1, f_2, and f_3, then the relation between R, S, and T is

$$T S \tilde{T} = R = \begin{bmatrix} f - f_1 & & \\ & f - f_2 & \\ & & f - f_3 \end{bmatrix}. \tag{13}$$

One can view the diagonalization of S as a rotation applied to its constituent vectors V and N. Introducing the rotated vectors

$$v = TV, \quad n = TN, \tag{14}$$

we infer from equation 13 that

$$R = \tfrac{1}{2} T(V\tilde{N} + N\tilde{V})\tilde{T} = \tfrac{1}{2}(v\tilde{n} + n\tilde{v}). \tag{15}$$

In short, the orthogonal matrix T that transforms S into R rotates the vectors V and N into new vectors v and n such that

$$R = \begin{bmatrix} f - f_1 & 0 & 0 \\ 0 & f - f_2 & 0 \\ 0 & 0 & f - f_3 \end{bmatrix}$$
$$= \begin{bmatrix} v_1 n_1 & \tfrac{1}{2}(v_1 n_2 + n_1 v_2) & \tfrac{1}{2}(v_1 n_3 + n_1 v_3) \\ \tfrac{1}{2}(v_1 n_2 + n_1 v_2) & v_2 n_2 & \tfrac{1}{2}(v_2 n_3 + n_2 v_3) \\ \tfrac{1}{2}(v_1 n_3 + n_1 v_3) & \tfrac{1}{2}(v_2 n_3 + n_2 v_3) & v_3 n_3 \end{bmatrix}. \tag{16}$$

Much can be inferred from this equation about the vectors v and n.

First we show that at least one of the diagonal elements of R must vanish. For if none of them were zero, then the vanishing of the off-diagonal elements would imply that

$$v_1/n_1 = -v_2/n_2 = v_3/n_3 = -v_1/n_1, \tag{17}$$

leading to a contradiction. Without loss of generality we therefore assume that $f - f_2$ vanishes, that is, that

$$f = f_2. \tag{18}$$

Next we show that if neither $f - f_1$ nor $f - f_3$ vanishes, then f_2 must lie between f_1 and f_3. For in this case

$$v_1 n_1 \neq 0, \quad v_3 n_3 \neq 0, \quad v_1 n_3 + n_1 v_3 = 0, \tag{19}$$

from which it follows straightforwardly that $v_1 n_1$ and $v_3 n_3$ are of opposite sign, and the same applies to $f - f_1$ and $f - f_3$. Assuming, without loss of generality, that $f_1 < f_3$, we deduce that

$$f_1 < f < f_3 \tag{20}$$

and infer from equation 18 that f is the middle root of the cubic. Another immediate inference is that both v_2 and n_2 vanish; this follows from the vanishing of $v_2 n_2$ and $v_1 n_2 + n_1 v_2$ and the fact that $v_1 n_1$ does not vanish. The vectors $\mathbf{v}$ and $\mathbf{n}$ therefore take the forms

$$\mathbf{v} = (v_1, 0, v_3), \quad \mathbf{n} = (n_1, 0, n_3), \tag{21}$$

in which, by equations 19,

$$v_3/v_1 = -n_3/n_1, \quad v_1 n_1 > 0 > v_3 n_3. \tag{22}$$

Denoting the magnitudes of $\mathbf{v}$ and $\mathbf{n}$ by v and n respectively, we may write

$$\mathbf{v} = v(c, 0, s), \quad \mathbf{n} = n(c, 0, -s), \tag{23}$$

where s and c are the sine and cosine of some angle θ, yet to be determined. From equations 17, 18, and 23 we deduce that

$$f_2 - f_1 = v_1 n_1 = c^2 vn, \quad f_2 - f_3 = v_3 n_3 = -s^2 vn, \tag{24}$$

from which it follows at once that

$$vn = f_3 - f_1, \tag{25}$$

$$\mathbf{v} \cdot \mathbf{n} = v_1 n_1 + v_3 n_3 = 2f_2 - f_1 - f_3, \tag{26}$$

and

$$\cos 2\theta = c^2 - s^2 = (2f_2 - f_1 - f_3)/(f_3 - f_1). \tag{27}$$

So when they are all unequal the roots f_1, f_2, and f_3 give the product of the magnitudes of $\mathbf{v}$ and $\mathbf{n}$ and the scalar product $\mathbf{v} \cdot \mathbf{n}$, which has a direct physical interpretation as the reciprocal of the "time to collision"—the time that the observer would take to reach the plane $\mathbf{n}$ if he continued on course with uniform velocity $\mathbf{v}$. (A negative value for $\mathbf{v} \cdot \mathbf{n}$ means that the observer is now receding from the plane.)

The next most general case after $f_1 < f_2 < f_3$ is that in which two of these roots are equal, so that $f_1 = f_2 < f_3$ or $f_1 < f_2 = f_3$. If $f_1 < f_2 = f_3$, then, by equation 24, $s^2 = 0$ and $c^2 = 1$, so that 2θ, the angle between $\mathbf{v}$ and $\mathbf{n}$, equals 0. We infer that the observer is moving directly towards the plane. If, on the other hand, $f_1 = f_2 < f_3$, then $s^2 = 1$, $c^2 = 0$, $\cos 2\theta = -1$, and $2\theta = \pi$; the observer must be moving directly away from the plane.

Finally, it may happen that $f_1 = f_2 = f_3$, a case that deserves particular consideration. It can arise only if $v_1 n_1 = v_2 n_2 = v_3 n_3$, and since at least one of these products vanishes, they must all do so. If any of the components of $\mathbf{v}$, say v_1, does not vanish, then all the components of $\mathbf{n}$ must be zero (and vice versa). For if $v_1 \neq 0$, then $n_1 = 0$; but $v_1 n_2 + n_1 v_2 = 0$, and so $n_2 = 0$; for a similar reason, $n_3 = 0$. We infer that if $f_1 = f_2 = f_3$ then either $\mathbf{v} = 0$, and the observer's linear velocity is zero, or $\mathbf{n} = 0$, and the visible plane is at infinity. In neither event does the optic flow supply any depth information about the scene; it must be entirely attributed to the observer's rotation.

Alternative Interpretations

Having found values for the vectors $\mathbf{v}$ and $\mathbf{n}$, we can now retrace our steps and evaluate the vectors $\mathbf{V}$ and $\mathbf{N}$ from which they were derived, using the inverse transformation

$$\mathbf{V} = \tilde{\mathbf{T}}\mathbf{v}, \quad \mathbf{N} = \tilde{\mathbf{T}}\mathbf{n}. \tag{28}$$

But the values we obtain for $\mathbf{V}$ and $\mathbf{N}$ will clearly depend on the values assigned to $\mathbf{v}$ and $\mathbf{n}$, both of which depend on the value chosen for the angle θ. This angle is constrained but not determined by the value of $\cos 2\theta$ given by equation 27; reversing the sign of θ or adding π will make no difference to $\cos 2\theta$. Recalling that

$$\mathbf{v} = v(\cos\theta, 0, \sin\theta), \quad \mathbf{n} = n(\cos\theta, 0, -\sin\theta), \tag{29}$$

we see that the former operation interchanges the directions of $\mathbf{v}$ and $\mathbf{n}$ and the latter reverses their signs. So there are four distinct interpretations $(\mathbf{v}, \mathbf{n})$ consistent with the given values of the eight parameters, and this ambiguity naturally extends to the original vectors $\mathbf{V}$ and $\mathbf{N}$. If $(\mathbf{V}, \mathbf{N})$ is the veridical solution (the one which corresponds to reality), the other putative solutions are $(\mathbf{N}, \mathbf{V})$, $(-\mathbf{N}, -\mathbf{V})$, and $(-\mathbf{V}, -\mathbf{N})$. The question arises: Under what conditions might one of the spurious solutions represent a credible alternative to the veridical one?

The key to this dilemma is the obvious fact that the point (X, Y, Z) will be visible to the observer only if $Z > 0$. In the present context this criterion implies that a visible element in the direction (x, y) can be supposed to lie on the plane (L, M, N) only if

$$Lx + My + N > 0, \tag{30}$$

since the left-hand side of this inequality is the value of $1/Z$ for such an element. This condition immediately eliminates the spurious interpretation $(-\mathbf{V}, -\mathbf{N})$; the texture elements giving rise to the flow field must satisfy the inequality 30 or they would be invisible, but if they lay on the plane $(-L, -M, -N)$ the inequality would have to be violated.

The other spurious interpretations are those in which (i) the observer's velocity is N and the texture elements lie on the plane V or (ii) his velocity is $-N$ and the plane has coordinate vector $-V$. Now a ray from the direction (x, y) can come from a point on the plane V only if

$$Ux + Vy + W > 0, \tag{31}$$

whereas it can originate on the plane $-V$ only if

$$Ux + Vy + W < 0. \tag{32}$$

It follows that if the moving image elements are confined to that part of the visual field that satisfies 31, interpretation i is a possible interpretation on the flow field; and that if they all satisfy 32, interpretation ii is a possible interpretation. But if some lie in one part of the field and some in the other, neither interpretation can accommodate them all; the veridical interpretation is the only one that survives.

Another way of stating these conditions is in terms of the positions of the visible texture elements in space. The plane

$$UX + VY + WZ = 0 \tag{33}$$

divides space into two regions: a "forward" region, for which the left-hand side is positive, and a "backward" region, for which it is negative. (The distinction refers to the direction in which the observer is moving, rather than the direction in which he is looking.) The visible part of the forward region satisfies 31; the visible part of the backward region satisfies 32. We may therefore say that interpretation i is a possible alternative to the veridical interpretation if all the texture elements visible to the observer lie in the forward region of space, and ii is a possible interpretation if they all lie in the backward region; but if they are distributed over the two regions, then the only possible interpretation is the veridical one.

These conditions need qualification when the roots f_1, f_2, and f_3 are not all distinct. In the case $f_1 < f_2 = f_3$, as we saw earlier, the vectors v and n are parallel, and so the spurious interpretation i, obtained by interchanging V and N, is no different from the veridical one. Likewise, in the case $f_1 = f_2 < f_3$, in which v and n point in opposite directions, simultaneous interchange and reversal makes no difference, so interpretation ii coincides with the veridical interpretation. In both cases, since interpretations i and ii are mutually exclusive, the only possible interpretation is the veridical one.

An Algorithm

We are now in a position to propose an algorithm for computing the observer's motion and the structure of the scene from the eight parameters of the optic flow field, assuming that the two components of the field do indeed satisfy equations 14 and 15. Starting with values for $a, a', b, b', c, c',$ $h,$ and $k,$ one calculates $p, q,$ and r from equation 9 and proceeds to solve the cubic equation

$$\det \mathbf{S} = \begin{vmatrix} h + f & r & q \\ r & k + f & p \\ q & p & f \end{vmatrix}$$
$$= 0$$
$$= f^3 + f^2(h + k) + f(hk - p^2 - q^2 - r^2) + (2pqr - hp^2 - kq^2). \tag{34}$$

Four cases may be distinguished.

(i) The roots will all be equal (to zero) only if $p, q, r, h,$ and k all vanish; in this event no information can be obtained about the directions of $\mathbf{V}$ or $\mathbf{N}$, but the observer's angular velocity can be evaluated without further ado:

$$(A, B, C) = \tfrac{1}{2}(a - a', b - b', c - c'). \tag{35}$$

(ii) If $f_1 < f_2 = f_3$, then we need only compute the first row of the matrix $\mathbf{T}$, by solving the equation

$$\begin{bmatrix} h + f_1 & r & q \\ r & k + f_1 & p \\ q & p & f_1 \end{bmatrix} \begin{bmatrix} T_{11} \\ T_{12} \\ T_{13} \end{bmatrix} = 0. \tag{36}$$

The vectors $\mathbf{v}$ and $\mathbf{n}$ will satisfy

$$\mathbf{v} = v(1, 0, 0), \quad \mathbf{n} = n(1, 0, 0),$$

and the original vectors $\mathbf{V}$ and $\mathbf{N}$ will be given by

$$\mathbf{V} = v(T_{11}, T_{12}, T_{13}), \quad \mathbf{N} = n(T_{11}, T_{12}, T_{13}), \tag{37}$$

where their magnitudes v and n are subject to

$$vn = f_3 - f_1.$$

(iii) If $f_1 = f_2 < f_3$, then only the third row of $\mathbf{T}$ need be computed, by solving

$$\begin{bmatrix} h + f_3 & r & q \\ r & k + f_3 & p \\ q & p & f_3 \end{bmatrix} \begin{bmatrix} T_{31} \\ T_{32} \\ T_{33} \end{bmatrix} = 0. \tag{38}$$

The vectors $\mathbf{V}$ and $\mathbf{N}$ are now

$$\mathbf{V} = v(T_{31}, T_{32}, T_{33}), \quad \mathbf{N} = -n(T_{31}, T_{32}, T_{33}). \tag{39}$$

In cases ii and iii the quantity $Lx + My + N$ will be found to have the same sign for all the image elements (x, y); if this sign is negative, the signs of $\mathbf{N}$ and $\mathbf{V}$ must be reversed. Equations 36 and 38 do not, of course, determine the absolute signs of the elements of $\mathbf{T}$ to be substituted into equations 37 and 39.

(iv) In the most general case, $f_1 < f_2 < f_3$, it is necessary to find both the first row and the third row of $\mathbf{T}$, because $\mathbf{v}$ and $\mathbf{n}$ now take the forms

$$\mathbf{v} = v(c, 0, s), \quad \mathbf{n} = n(c, 0, -s), \tag{40}$$

in which

$$c = \cos\theta, \quad s = \sin\theta, \quad \cos 2\theta = (2f_2 - f_1 - f_3)/(f_3 - f_1). \tag{41}$$

Choosing freely one of the four values of θ consistent with equations 41, we obtain $\mathbf{V}$ and $\mathbf{N}$ from the equations

$$\mathbf{V} = v(c\mathbf{T}_1 + s\mathbf{T}_3), \quad \mathbf{N} = n(c\mathbf{T}_1 - s\mathbf{T}_3), \tag{42}$$

where $\mathbf{T}_1$ and $\mathbf{T}_3$ are the first and third rows of the matrix $\mathbf{T}$, derived from equations 36 and 38 respectively.

At this point there is a fourfold ambiguity in the pair of vectors $\mathbf{N}$ and $\mathbf{V}$. To resolve it we use the fact that if $\mathbf{N}$ as obtained from equation 42 really is the coordinate vector of the visible plane, then the scalar product $\mathbf{N} \cdot \mathbf{r}$, where $\mathbf{r} = (x, y, 1)$, must be positive for every image element (x, y). If $\mathbf{N} \cdot \mathbf{r}$ varies in sign over the elements, then $\mathbf{N}$ and $\mathbf{V}$ must be interchanged (by reversing the sign of θ or, equivalently, of $\mathbf{T}_3$). If $\mathbf{N} \cdot \mathbf{r}$ is negative for all the image elements, then adding π to θ (or multiplying $\mathbf{T}_1$ and $\mathbf{T}_3$ by -1) will have the desired effect of reversing $\mathbf{N}$ (and will reverse $\mathbf{V}$ as well). If now $\mathbf{V} \cdot \mathbf{r}$ is of variable sign over the elements, $\mathbf{V}$ can be uniquely identified as the velocity (U, V, W) and $\mathbf{N}$ as the coordinate vector (L, M, N); but otherwise there remains a twofold ambiguity: Should the two vectors really be interchanged, and, if necessary, reversed in sign to meet the condition that $\mathbf{N} \cdot \mathbf{r}$ be positive for every image element? There is no way of telling on the basis of the flow field alone.

Having computed the possible values of **N** and **V**, one can immediately obtain the corresponding values of the angular velocity (A, B, C). By equation 8,

$$A = \tfrac{1}{2}(a - a' + VN - WM),$$
$$B = \tfrac{1}{2}(b - b' + WL - UN), \qquad\qquad (43)$$
$$C = \tfrac{1}{2}(c - c' + UM - VL),$$

or, if the symbol $\times$ denotes a vector product,

$$(A, B, C) = \tfrac{1}{2}(a - a', b - b', c - c') + \tfrac{1}{2}(U, V, W) \times (L, M, N). \qquad (44)$$

The first term on the right hand side of equation 44 is directly determined by the optic flow field, but the value of the vector product is subject to any ambiguity as to the values of **V** and **N**. Interchange of these two vectors, with or without a reversal of both, reverses their vector product; so if **V** and **N** are the true values of (U, V, W) and (L, M, N), then a spurious interpretation of the flow field that interchanges their roles will under-estimate the observer's angular velocity by an amount **V** $\times$ **N**. S. J. Maybank (private communication) has recently shown that the angular velocity difference between the alternative interpretations is parallel to the vector product of the observer's angular velocity and the normal to the plane.

An Ambiguous Flow Field

A convenient example of an ambiguous flow field is provided by an aircraft approaching a horizontal landing strip at night, when nothing is visible except a few light sources on the ground. Figure 1a represents a side view of the approach; the vector **N** is directed vertically downwards, and **V**

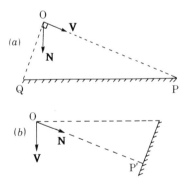

Figure 1

points slightly below the horizontal; the observer's angular velocity is not shown, but we might suppose the pilot to be fixing on the point P. We also suppose his field of view to be restricted to the forward part of the strip (to the right of Q). The spurious interpretation is as shown in figure 1b. In this interpretation the light sources lie on a nearly vertical plane, and the aircraft is descending vertically, having a finite angular velocity about the fixation point P'. A moment later this interpretation, if adopted, would become untenable; but if in the meantime the controls were adjusted accordingly, disaster might well result.

Figure 2 may help the reader's intuition about the nature of the ambiguity. The instantaneous flow field a, where all the visible elements lie below the upper edge of the rectangle, could arise either from the situation b— horizontal motion over a horizontal surface—or from the quite different situation c, in which the observer is in a descending lift, looking at the lower half of the wall of the shaft, and has an additional angular velocity $V \times N$. Figure 2d illustrates a situation equivalent to c as far as relative motion is concerned, namely one in which the absolute motion is attributed to the visible surface; in this case the textured plane is hinged about its upper edge H and is swinging towards the observer, generating the same flow field a as before.

Finally, although the *instantaneous* flow field sometimes permits two alternative interpretations in terms of motion relative to a textured plane, the spurious interpretation will become untenable after a finite time; other evidence, such as texture clues to distance, may well lead to its immediate rejection. In figure 2, for example, the interpretations b and c imply very different dependences of distance upon elevation in the field of view.

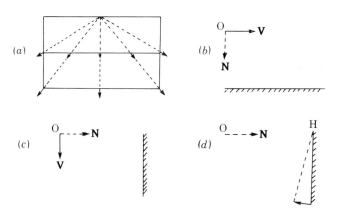

Figure 2

Conclusions and Discussion

The main conclusion established in this paper is that the optic flow field due to motion relative to a visually textured plane is sometimes ambiguous, that is, consistent with two quite distinct sets of values for the observer's linear and angular velocity and the coordinate vector of the plane. This conclusion was anticipated by Tsai and Huang (1981), but they failed to identify quite exactly the conditions for ambiguity to arise. It is true, as they found, that the flow field is unambiguous if two of the roots f_1, f_2, and f_3 are equal; but the converse is not true: In the case in which f_1, f_2, and f_3 are all unequal, the flow field will be unambiguous if it arises partly from the "forward" half of the plane and partly from the "backward" half, relative to the observer's linear velocity.

One unambiguous case ($f_1 < f_2 = f_3$) arises when the observer is moving straight towards the plane, another ($f_1 = f_2 < f_3$) when he is moving directly away from it. In all cases the difference ($f_3 - f_1$) gives the ratio of the observer's speed and distance from the plane; his time to impact is $1/(2f_2 - f_1 - f_3)$, and the angle between his linear velocity and the normal to the plane is

$$\arccos((2f_2 - f_1 - f_3)/(f_3 - f_1)).$$

The algorithm has been implemented and confirms the mathematical analysis in detail; but it would plainly be naive to imagine that it accurately describes how the human visual system estimates the positions and velocities of moving plane surfaces. Perhaps the result of the analysis will be of most interest to the designers of computer vision systems, as indicating that reliance on optic flow as a sole source of structural information could lead to trouble unless account is taken of its occasional ambiguity.

My thanks are due to S. Ullman, T. S. Huang, B. Buxton, and D. Hogg for helpful discussions, and to the Royal Society and the Science and Engineering Research Council for research support.

References

Braunstein, M. L. 1976. *Depth Perception through Motion.* London: Academic.

Gibson, J. J. 1950. *The Perception of the Visual World.* Boston: Houghton Mifflin.

Gibson, J. J. 1966. *The Senses Considered as Perceptual Systems.* Boston: Houghton Mifflin.

Gibson, J. J. 1979. *The Ecological Approach to Visual Perception.* Boston: Houghton Mifflin.

Gibson, J. J., and E. J. Gibson. 1957. Continuous perspective transformations and the perception of rigid motion. *J. Exp. Psychol.* 54: 129–138.

Gibson, J. J., P. Olum, and F. Rosenblatt. 1955. Parallax and perspective during aircraft landings. *Am. J. Psychol.* 68: 372–385.

Helmholtz, H. von. 1866. *Handbuch der physiologischen Optik.* Leipzig: Voss. English translation: *Physiological Optics,* ed. J. P. C. Southall. New York: Dover.

Koenderink, J. J., and A. J. van Doorn. 1976. Local structure of movement parallax of the plane. *J. Opt. Soc. Am.* 66: 717–723.

Lee, D. N. 1974. Visual information during locomotion. In *Perception,* ed. R. B. McLeod and H. L. Pick (Ithaca, N.Y.: Cornell University Press).

Longuet-Higgins, H. C. 1981. A computer algorithm for reconstructing a scene from two projections. *Nature* 293: 133–135. [Chapter 22 in present volume.]

Longuet-Higgins, H. C., and K. Prazdny. 1980. The interpretation of a moving retinal image. *Proc. R. Soc.* B 208: 385–397. [Chapter 20 in present volume.]

Nakayama, K., and J. M. Loomis. 1974. Optical velocity patterns, velocity sensitive neurons and space perception. *Perception* 3: 63–80.

Tsai, R. Y., and T. S. Huang. 1981. Estimating Three-Dimensional Motion Parameters of a Rigid Planar Patch. Research Report R-922, Coordinated Science Laboratory, University of Illinois.

Ullman, S. 1979. *The Interpretation of Visual Motion.* Cambridge, Mass.: MIT Press.

.

V

Memory

"A Holographic Model of Temporal Recall" (chapter 27) attracted altogether too much attention when it first appeared in print. I should have known better than to speculate so shamelessly about the neural mechanism of temporal memory; the idea of a neuron's "learning" a particular frequency has scarcely a leg to stand on. But the discussion the paper provoked—in both physical and physiological circles—testified to the fact that ideas, however far-fetched, are the life-blood of scientific research, and that a demonstration of how something could possibly happen (in this case, cued temporal recall) may be almost as welcome as the discovery of how it actually does happen.

The 1969 paper that appears here as chapter 29 should perhaps have been entitled "A *Quasi*-Holographic Associative Memory", in that it uses the idea of forming correlations without entering the frequency domain. Associative nets have since achieved considerable popularity in discussions of brain function; their patrons have included such luminaries as Dennis Gabor, Teuvo Kohonen, Leon Cooper, John Hopfield, Francis Crick, Gerald Edelman, and Geoffrey Hinton. My present feeling on the matter is that they probably fulfil just one humble but vital role in human memory: that of establishing the link between a neural address (a subset of the input fibres) and the information stored there (the associated set of output fibres).

27

A Holographic Model of Temporal Recall

H. C. Longuet-Higgins

How do we manage to recognize immediately, and to recall without effort, familiar words, sentences, and other behavioural sequences? I suggest that we employ a system which is the temporal analogue of optical holography (Gabor 1948, 1949; Julesz and Pennington 1965). The analogy between holography and visual memory has already attracted attention in the literature, but this is not quite the thought that I shall pursue here; rather I shall consider the time dimension, because any perceptual event must certainly be associated with cerebral happenings which are extended not only in space but in time. If a system of this kind were indeed used by the brain, not only would some familiar phenomena of perception be naturally explained, but the cells or cell clusters responsible for laying down sensory information should have a certain property which might be accessible to experimental test.

The system which I have in mind is most easily described with the aid of a concrete example. Imagine a bank of resonators, rather like the strings of a piano. Their resonant frequencies v_k are supposed to be evenly distributed over a certain frequency band, with a spacing equal to μ, and the bandwidth of each resonator will be assumed equal to the same constant μ. Each resonator is supposed to be coupled to the input signal $f(t)$ according to the equation

$$\ddot{x}_k + (4\pi\mu)\dot{x}_k + 4\pi^2(\mu^2 + v_k^2)x_k = A_k f(t),$$

where x_k denotes the displacement of the kth resonator and A_k is a coupling constant. Then it can be shown that the total response of the bank, conveniently defined as

$$g(t) = \sum_k (\dot{x}_k + 2\pi\mu x_k),$$

will be proportional to $f(t)$ provided (a) that the coupling coefficients A_k are all equal, (b) that $f(t)$ contains no frequencies lying outside the range of the bank, and (c) that μ is sufficiently small—that the resonators are sufficiently densely distributed over the frequency range.

I now imagine that after the passage of a signal $f(t)$, the coupling constant of each resonator is capable of being altered by an amount proportional to the work recently done on it by the signal, that is,

$$\Delta A_k = \lambda \int_{-\infty}^{0} f(t)\dot{x}_k(t)e^{4\pi\mu t}dt,$$

where the quantity λ is supposed to be the same for each resonator. If the signal consisted of a pulse $f_1(t)$ followed immediately by another signal $f_2(t)$, then it can be shown that, if the coupling constants are subsequently adjusted as shown, a later input of the same pulse will immediately evoke a response $g_2(t)$ proportional to $f_2(t)$. This phenomenon is the mathematical analogue of the following holographic observation: A collimated laser beam is split into two parts; one is directly incident on a photographic plate, and the other falls on an object, the light from which is also incident on the plate. The plate is developed and replaced by its positive print, the hologram; the object is removed, and the hologram is illuminated with the first part of the same laser beam. An observer looking through the hologram then beholds the absent object in its original position. The mathematical analogy is not, however, quite complete; whereas the hologram records the square of the Fourier transform of the wavefront leaving the object, the bank of resonators records the square of the Laplace transform of $f(t)$, because to record the Fourier transform would require a violation of causality.

This result can be generalized in two stages. First, it can be shown that if a signal $f(t)$ is arbitrarily partitioned into an earlier part f_1 and a later part f_2, then after the bank has "memorized" the whole signal, the input of f_1 will evoke a more or less distinct "echo" of g_2 immediately afterwards. The distinctness of the echo will be greater the more closely the temporal autocorrelation function of $f_1(t)$ approximates to a delta function at the origin. Second, the bank may be used for memorizing, at widely different times, a number of different signals $f^{(n)}$, $n = 1, 2, 3, \ldots$. If these signals are so different that their mutual correlations can be neglected, then the later input of $f_1^{(m)}$ will evoke a more or less distinct echo of $g_2^{(m)}$ uncontaminated by any of the other signals that have also been recorded in the bank.

If the bank is used, in this way, for recording a number of different signals, there will obviously be a limit to the length of any one signal that can be recorded. This limit is, in fact, the reciprocal of the frequency spacing μ. But the bank can be made to regenerate signals of much greater length by connecting it to a regenerative feedback mechanism such that when the response g_n appears the signal f_n is fed back into the bank. Then, if the signals (f_1 then f_2), (f_2 then f_3), and so on, have all been recorded, the input of f_2 will cause the bank to re-create the long sequence (g_2 then g_3 then g_4 then g_5 and so on).

The resemblance of such behaviour to that of memory is sufficiently striking for one to wonder whether the brain may not employ systems of this general kind for recording temporal sequences such as those which are involved in speech and kinaesthetically controlled movement. If so, perhaps groups of cells could be detected which have the property of becoming more responsive to particular frequencies the more they are stimulated at those frequencies. Cells are already known which display an accurately sinusoidal metabolism, and have been tentatively identified as "biological clocks" (Chance et al. 1967). Could such cells by vitally involved in the processes of temporal recall?

I thank Dr. A. Moscowitz, Dr. L. Harmon, and Dr. B. Julesz for helpful criticism, and the Bell Telephone Laboratories for their hospitality in the course of this work.

References

Chance, B., K. Pye, and J. J. Higgins. 1967. *IEEE Spectrum* 4, no. 8: 79.

Gabor, D. 1948. *Nature* 161: 777.

Gabor, D. 1949. *Proc. R. Soc.* A 197: 454.

Julesz, B., and K. Pennington. 1965. *J. Opt. Soc. Am.* 55: 604.

28

The Non-Local Storage of
Temporal Information

H. C. Longuet-Higgins

The central problem confronting students of the brain is to interpret the findings of experimental psychology in physical and physiological terms. One of the main difficulties in this enterprise is to set up theoretical models which are both realistic in relation to what we know about the central nervous system and tractable in the sense of yielding definite and interesting psychological predictions. As Weiskrantz (1968) has pointed out, it is easy to fall victim to conceptual fashions, and one must be on guard against taking, for example, computer analogies too literally. But this does not mean that a student of the real nervous system (r.n.s.) can get along without any concepts at all; and concepts, as Young (1964) has shown in his studies of "addressing" in the octopus brain, are nothing less than the raw material of theories.

The concept that I particularly want to talk about in this chapter is that of non-local information storage, with particular reference to the time dimension. There are both experimental and theoretical difficulties in supposing that our long-term memories operate according to purely local storage principles, not the least of which is that they must be "content-addressable", not merely "location-addressable" (Miller 1968). I shall begin by reviewing some of these difficulties, and then present a blueprint of a primitive content-addressable temporal memory (Longuet-Higgins 1968). Although this simple model is most unlikely to apply in detail to our brains, it may be of some interest to neurophysiologists as showing that the storage and instant retrieval of temporal information can be achieved in a physical system of relative simplicity.

Local and Non-Local Information Storage

The distinction between local and non-local information storage is well illustrated by the difference between photography and holography. In photography we have a typical example of local information storage: there is a one-to-one correspondence between points on the object and grains on the plate, and every scene has to be recorded on a separate print. There are, however, three objections against supposing that our memories are stored like the pictures in a photograph album. First, if every item of my recorded experience were stored in a separate piece of neural tissue, I should either run out of store abruptly at an early age or much of my cortex would remain unused for most of my life. Secondly, there is the addressing problem. If I want to look up a particular photograph—say the one in which my niece was making a face at the camera—I must either hunt through the whole album to find it or consult an enormous ready-made index, in which case I am not relying solely on the album itself. The third difficulty with the idea that our memories are stored locally is their sturdiness against anatomical damage. If each item were recorded in a separate small region, then removal of cortical tissue should result in irretrievable loss of specific memories. In fact this does not seem to happen, though it is very difficult to be sure.

With holography the situation is different (Gabor 1948, 1949; Stroke 1966). A hologram is an optical record in which every grain has been influenced by light from every point on the object and therefore records something about the object as a whole. This many-to-many relation between the grains on the plate and the points on the object has two interesting consequences. First, although in ordinary light the hologram is a meaningless jumble of grey markings, a scene recorded on it will spring to life when the plate is illuminated by part of the wavefront which was originally incident upon it. (This is essentially why holography demands laser illumination and highly stable optics; only coherent light sources can yield accurately reproducible wavefronts.) Secondly, if the hologram is so illuminated, a passable image of the object can be conjured up even when part of the hologram has been ablated.

In most current applications of holography the wavefront used for reconstructing the recorded scene is a collimated beam, such a beam also having been incident on the plate during the recording. But Stroke et al. (1965) have shown that it is possible to use for the reconstruction a wavefront from part of the scene itself; if the hologram is illuminated with light from one part of the scene, the rest will appear also, though some-what blurred. A further possibility, of considerable interest in the present connexion, is that of recording several scenes on the same hologram. Then if light from part of one scene is allowed to fall on the hologram, what appears is the whole of that particular scene. The degree of blurring will depend on the amount of regularity in each recorded scene, and on the degrees of resemblance between the recorded scenes, but within these important limitations a multiply exposed hologram will behave as an associative or content-addressable memory.

As an analogue of the long-term memory, then, holography is free from the three objections which apply to photography—a fact which has not escaped attention in the literature (Julesz and Pennington 1965). There is no sharp limit on the number of scenes which can be recorded on one hologram, though an attempt to record too many will result in a severe deterioration in clarity of recall. The addressing problem is solved automatically: a scene can be recalled in outline by supplying any part of it, and—which is a positive advantage—in no other way. And, as already remarked, an ablated hologram can be used to reconstruct images which, although fuzzier than those obtainable from the original hologram, are complete in their main features.

The mathematical theory of holography has been well worked out (Stroke 1966), so there is no need to go into it here; but one or two general remarks may be helpful. First, if one tried to find on a hologram an "engram" sufficient for reconstructing a recorded scene, one would look in vain. This is because the pattern on a hologram is basically ambiguous, like the Patterson function of a crystal. What is recorded is essentially the power spectrum of the object wave, regarded as a superposition of spatial Fourier components. Each grain carries a record of the intensity of a particular component—which is a feature of the wave as a whole—but the phase relations between the components are not recorded. They can be reconstructed, but only by supplying information from outside—by putting in enough of the object wave to determine them. The recorded features are themselves non-local, each referring to some internal relationship between the parts of the object. Only when some "absolute" information is made available can the "relative" information embodied in the hologram be used to recreate the original object.

A Temporal Analogue of Holography

In trying to make theories of the memory one cannot afford to ignore the time dimension. Any incoming stimulus must give rise to a pattern of cerebral events which are extended not only in space but in time, and to define an input signal precisely we must specify not only its neural path or paths but also the temporal relations between the events which compose it. It is therefore natural to ask whether the principle of non-local information storage, realized in space by the holograph, could also be realized in time.

A temporal holograph, or "holophone", would be a physical system which could record several functions of time in such a way that input of an extract from one recorded signal would immediately evoke the continuation of that signal. Let us now see how such a system might be constructed.

In holography one records the power spectrum of a pattern, regarded as a superposition of Fourier components. So the holophone should have elements which can record the power spectrum of a time-varying signal. In holography the incident wavefront is mediated by a set of developed grains in a photographic emulsion. By analogy, in the holophone the incoming signal should be mediated by a set of narrow-pass filters whose transmittances can be increased in accordance with how they have responded to past signals. In viewing a hologram our eyes resynthesize the signals transmitted by the individual grains on the plate. The holophone must therefore possess an output channel which can combine the signals emerging from the individual filters.

Let us imagine, then, a bank of narrow-pass filters, each of which can be regarded as an oscillator with a certain resonant frequency and damping constant. Taken together they will behave rather like the strings of a piano, which can be set into oscillation by singing into the piano with the sustaining pedal held down. In this case the air acts as both input and output channel, and one hears afterwards the combined effect of the individual oscillations. The holophone is a similar system, but with the additional property that one can increase the transmittance of each filter, after the passage of a signal, in proportion to the amount of power dissipated by that filter. The memory of the holophone then resides in the transmittances of the individual filters, just as the memory of a holograph resides in the transparencies of the individual grains on the hologram. I shall now show that the holophone will behave, within limits, as an associative temporal memory.

Mathematical Theory of the Holophone

For simplicity we adopt a linear model, and assume that each filter in the bank behaves as a damped harmonic oscillator. In unforced motion an oscillator with displacement x, circular frequency ω, and damping constant μ would satisfy the differential equation

$$\ddot{x} + 2\mu\dot{x} + (\mu^2 + \omega^2)x = 0.$$

We suppose that an incoming signal $f(t)$ imparts to the oscillator an additional acceleration

$A f(t) = \ddot{x} + 2\mu\dot{x} + (\mu^2 + \omega^2)x,$

where A is an *adjustable* coupling constant. Defining the complex parameter $p = \mu + iw$, with complex conjugate $p^* = \mu - iw$, we may write the full equation of motion in the form

$(p + d/dt)(p^* + d/dt)x = Af.$

Introducing the time-varying coordinates

$y = p^*x + \dot{x}, \quad y^* = px + \dot{x},$

we deduce that

$(p + d/dt)y = Af = (p^* + d/dt)y^*.$

The sum

$y + y^* = 2(\mu x + \dot{x})$

is a convenient measure of the "response" of the oscillator, and is, evidently, accessible to instantaneous measurement.

Our first task is to calculate the response function $K(\tau)$ of the filter, defined by the equation

$$y(t) + y^*(t) = \int_0^\infty K(\tau)f(t - \tau)d\tau.$$

We note that

$$\int_{-\infty}^0 A f(t)e^{pt}dt = \int_{-\infty}^0 \left(py + \frac{dy}{dt}\right)e^{pt}dt = [ye^{pt}]^0_{-\infty} = y(0),$$

and likewise that

$$\int_{-\infty}^0 A f(t)e^{p^*t}dt = y^*(0).$$

Hence

$$y(0) + y^*(0) = \int_0^\infty A(e^{-p\tau} + e^{-p^*\tau})f(-\tau)d\tau,$$

from which it follows that

$K(\tau) = A(e^{-p\tau} + e^{-p^*\tau}) = 2Ae^{-\mu\tau}\cos\omega\tau.$

In general, then, a filter will continue to respond long after the end of the signal that excites it—an important point to bear in mind if one wishes to look for corresponding entities in the brain.

Next we must say something about the manner in which the responses of the individual filters are to be combined to produce the output signal, which we may call $g(t)$. The simplest way is just to add them together:

$$g(t) = \sum_k [y_k(t) + y_k^*(t)].$$

Then for the whole filter bank the response function $M(\tau)$, defined by

$$g(t) = \int_0^\infty M(\tau)f(t - \tau)d\tau,$$

will be

$$M(\tau) = \sum_k A_k(e^{-p_k\tau} + e^{-p_k^*\tau}).$$

Provided that the resonant frequencies ω_k, $k = 1, 2, \ldots$, are sufficiently densely distributed over the given range, this sum may be approximated as an integral. Let us assume that μ has the same value for each filter, and that the circular frequency of the kth filter is $k\mu$, so that $p_{k+1} - p_k = i\mu$. Then for small μ and non-negative τ,

$$M(\tau) = \frac{1}{i\mu} \int_\mu^{\mu+i\infty} A(p)(e^{-p\tau} + e^{-p^*\tau})dp$$
$$= \frac{1}{i\mu} \int_{\mu-i\infty}^{\mu+i\infty} A(p)e^{-p\tau}dp,$$

where the set of coupling constants A_k has been replaced by the analytic function $A(p)$. (This function is defined by the condition that it takes the real value A_k both at $p = \mu + i\omega_k$ and at $p = \mu - i\omega_k$.) The above relation only holds, of course, for non-negative τ, because $K(\tau)$ vanishes when $\tau < 0$.

An interesting special case is when all the A_k are equal to the same real constant A. Then $A(p)$ also equals A, and we obtain

$$H(\tau) = \frac{A}{i\mu} \int_{\mu-i\infty}^{\mu+i\infty} e^{-p\tau}dp = \frac{2\pi A}{\mu}\delta(\tau).$$

We infer that when all the coupling constants are equal, $g(t)$ is identical with $f(t)$, apart from a constant factor, so that the output stops as soon as the input stops, although the individual filters keep on oscillating.

Now we come to the actual recording process. A signal $f(t)$, which is over by the time $t = 0$, is to be recorded. To achieve this we must have measured the integral

$$\int_{-\infty}^{0} (y_k + y_k^*)fe^{2\mu t}dt = 2\int_{-\infty}^{0} (\dot{x}_k + \mu x_k)fe^{2\mu t}dt$$

for each of the filters. Having done this, we record $f(t)$ by adjusting A_k by an amount

$$\Delta A_k = 2\lambda \int_{-\infty}^{0} (\dot{x}_k + \mu x_k)fe^{2\mu t}dt,$$

where λ is the same for all the filters. For small μ the integral may be interpreted as the work "recently" done on the kth filter by the signal $f(t)$. An alternative and more convenient expression for ΔA_k is

$$\Delta A_k = \lambda A_k \phi(p_k)\phi(p_k^*) = \lambda A_k \phi(p_k)\phi(2\mu - p_k),$$

where

$$\phi(p) = \int_{-\infty}^{0} f(t)e^{pt}dt.$$

The equivalence of the two expressions is established as follows:

$$\int_{-\infty}^{0} yfe^{2\mu t}dt = \int_{-\infty}^{0} dt \int_{-\infty}^{t} dt' A f(t')e^{p(t'-t)}f(t)e^{2\mu t}$$

$$= A \int_{-\infty}^{0} dt \int_{-\infty}^{t} dt' f(t')e^{pt'}f(t)e^{p*t},$$

and likewise

$$\int_{-\infty}^{0} y^* fe^{2\mu t'}dt' = A \int_{-\infty}^{0} dt' \int_{-\infty}^{t'} dt f(t)e^{p*t}f(t')e^{pt'}.$$

Addition of these two equations gives

$$\int (y + y^*)fe^{2\mu t}dt = A \int_{-\infty}^{0} dt \int_{-\infty}^{0} dt' f(t')e^{pt'}f(t)e^{p*t} = A\phi(p)\phi(p^*),$$

establishing the required result.

Having recorded $f(t)$ in this way, we now feed in another input signal, $f'(t)$. What will emerge? To answer this question we must find $\Delta M(\tau)$, the change in the response function of the holophone due to the recording of $f(t)$. For simplicity let us suppose that all the A_k were originally equal to $\mu/2\pi$. Then after the recording they will have the values

$$A_k = (\mu/2\pi)[1 + \lambda\phi(p_k)\phi(2\mu - p_k)].$$

The leading term, as we have seen, will contribute an amount $\delta(\tau)$ to the response function $M(\tau)$. The term in λ will make an extra contribution equal to

$$\Delta M(\tau) = \lambda(\mu/2\pi)\sum_k (p_k)\phi(2\mu - p_k)(e^{-p_k\tau} + e^{-p_k^*\tau}).$$

Converting this sum into an integral, we obtain

$$\Delta M(\tau) = \frac{\lambda}{2\pi i}\int_{\mu-i\infty}^{\mu+i\infty} \phi(p)\phi(2\mu - p)e^{-p\tau}dp.$$

(The coefficient of $e^{-p\tau}$ in the integrand is, as required, an analytic function of p taking the same real value at $\mu - i\omega$ as at $\mu + i\omega$.) Substituting for $\phi(p)$ and $\phi(2\mu - p)$ from their definitions, we obtain the more explicit expression

$$\Delta M(\tau) = \lambda \int_{-\infty}^{0} dt_1 \int_{-\infty}^{0} dt_2 f(t_1)f(t_2)e^{2\mu t_2}\delta(t_1 - t_2 - \tau)$$

$$= \lambda \int_{-\infty}^{0} f(t_1)e^{2\mu(t_1-\tau)}f(t_1 - \tau)dt_1.$$

The total output signal is therefore

$$g'(t) = f'(t) + \Delta g'(t),$$

where

$$\Delta g'(t) = \lambda \int_{0}^{\infty} d\tau \int_{-\infty}^{0} dt_1 f(t_1)e^{2\mu(t_1-\tau)}f(t_1 - \tau)f'(t - \tau).$$

That is to say,

$$\Delta g'(t) = \lambda \int_{0}^{\infty} C(\tau)f'(t - \tau)d\tau,$$

where

$$C(\tau) = \int_{-\infty}^{0} f(t_1)e^{2\mu(t_1-\tau)}f(t_1 - \tau)dt_1.$$

What has happened, then, is that the recording of $f(t)$ has altered the response function of the holophone by an amount equal to $\lambda C(\tau)$, where C is a time-weighted autocorrelation function of the recorded signal $f(t)$. (See Gabor 1968.) We might suppose that if $f(t)$ was a randomly varying function of time $C(\tau)$ would be small except near $\tau = 0$, and we would conclude that

$$\Delta g'(t) \propto \int_0^\infty \delta(\tau)f'(t-\tau)d\tau = f'(t).$$

If this were so, then g' would stop as soon as f' stopped, apart from a very indistinct "echo". In general this conclusion is valid, but it demands re-examination if f' is strongly correlated with f. To see why, let us suppose that f' is identical with a certain section of f, so that while f' is not zero it satisfies the relation

$$f'(t) = f(t-\theta),$$

where θ is some fairly long interval. Going back to our expression for $\Delta g'$, we may rewrite it thus:

$$\Delta g'(t) = \lambda \int_{-\infty}^0 C'(t-t_1)f(t_1)dt_1,$$

where

$$C'(t-t_1) = \int_0^\infty f(t_1-\tau)e^{2\mu(t_1-\tau)}f_1(t-\tau)d\tau.$$

(In writing C' as a function of $t-t_1$ we are supposing that t is a time after the end of f'; if it were not, C' would depend on both t and $t-t_1$.) In this form $\Delta g'$ appears as the convolution of f with the mutual correlation of f and f', and in view of our assumed relation between f and f' we may expect $C'(t-t_1)$ to be small unless t_1 is close to $t-\theta$. In these circumstances,

$$\Delta g'(t) \propto \int_{-\infty}^0 \delta(t_1-t+\theta)f(t_1)dt_1 = f(t-\theta).$$

This is our central result. It shows that if f' is an extract from a randomly varying recorded signal f, then the output signal which emerges after the end of the input f' is no ordinary echo of f' but a very special sort of echo which is in fact the rest of the recorded signal f, in the correct temporal relation to the part which was fed in. In making this statement we must bear in mind that even when f is random C' will not be exactly a delta function of $t_1 - t + \theta$, so that there is inevitably quite a lot of noise accompanying the "playback". A preliminary investigation of this matter, which I plan to discuss in a later publication, seems to show that the signal-to-noise ratio for random recorded signals equals the length of f' divided by the length of f. The quality of reproduction is therefore rather poor.

To complete our investigation let us see how the holophone will perform if we record on it a number of different signals. For definiteness let us suppose that we have recorded two signals f_1 and f_2, and then feed in a signal which is uncorrelated with f_1 but is identical with a section of f_2. If the intensities λ_1 and λ_2 with which the two signals have been recorded are sufficiently small, they will make additive contributions to the response function, and we may write

$$\Delta M(\tau) = \Delta_1 M(\tau) + \Delta_2 M(\tau).$$

The output produced by f' will also be additive:

$$\Delta g'(t) = \Delta_1 g'(t) + \Delta_2 g'(t).$$

Since f' is uncorrelated with f_1, $\Delta_1 g'$ will merely be an indistinct echo of f'; but as we have just seen, $\Delta_2 g'$ will bear a strong resemblance to the part of f_2 which followed the section corresponding to f'. The generalization to several signals is immediate. If an input signal is highly correlated with just one recorded signal, then the output which it evokes will be the continuation of that signal, rather noisy but in real time. We have therefore done what we set out to do, namely to design a content-addressable temporal memory.

Possible Relevance to the Brain

Whether holophonic principles have any relevance to the phenomena of associative recall remains, of course, to be seen. But the fact that an adaptive filter bank could behave as a content-addressable memory raises some questions of neurophysiological interest. For example: are there cells in the cerebral cortex which respond specifically to particular rhythms, just as there are known to be cells which fire only in the presence of specific visible features? Is it possible to detect arrays of cells which, when briefly stimulated, discharge rhythmically for some time afterwards? If so, can their thresholds for rhythmic firing to altered by rhythmic stimulation? Perhaps the most useful task the theoretician can perform is to raise such questions rather than to speculate upon their answers.

Acknowledgements

I am much indebted to the Bell Telephone Laboratories for their hospitality during the early part of this work, and to many colleagues there for helpful criticism. My special thanks are due to H. L. Frisch, D. Gabor, A. Moscowitz, and E. Wasserman for invaluable encouragement.

References

Gabor, D. 1948. *Nature* 161: 777.

Gabor, D. 1949. *Proc. R. Soc.* A 197: 454.

Gabor, D. 1968. *Nature* 217: 584.

Julesz, B., and K. Pennington. 1965. *J. Opt. Soc. Am.* 55: 604.

Longuet-Higgins, H. C. 1968. *Nature* 217: 104.

Miller, G. A. 1968. *Proc. R. Soc.* B 171: 276–386, at 361.

Stroke, G. W. 1966. *An Introduction to Coherent Optics and Holography.* New York: Academic.

Stroke, G. W., R. Restrick, A. Funkhouser, and D. Brumm. 1965a. *Phys. Lett.* 18: 274.

Stroke, G. W., R. Restrick, A. Funkhouser, and D. Brumm. 1965b. *Appl. Phys. Lett.* 6: 178.

Weiskrantz, L. 1968. *Proc. R. Soc.* B 171: 276–386, at 335.

Young, J. Z. 1964. *A Model of the Brain.* Oxford: Clarendon.

29

A Non-Holographic Model of Associative Memory

D. J. Willshaw,
O. P. Buneman, and
H. C. Longuet-Higgins

The remarkable properties of the hologram as an information store have led some people (Van Heerden 1963; Pribram 1969) to wonder whether the memory may not work on holographic principles. There are, however, certain difficulties with this hypothesis if the holographic analogy is pressed too far; how could the brain Fourier-analyze the incoming signals with sufficient accuracy, and how could it improve on the rather feeble signal-to-noise ratio (Willshaw and Longuet-Higgins 1969) of the reconstructed signals? Our purpose here is to show that the most desirable features of holography are manifested by another type of associative memory, which might well have been evolved by the brain. A mathematical investigation of this non-holographic memory shows that in optimal conditions it has a capacity which is not far from the maximum permitted by information theory.

Our point of departure is Gabor's (1968a, b) observation that any physical system which can correlate (or for that matter convolve) pairs of patterns can mimic the performance of a Fourier holograph. Such a system, which could be set up in any school physics laboratory, is shown in figure 1. The apparatus is designed for making "correlograms" between pairs of pinhole patterns, and then using the correlogram and one of the patterns for reconstructing its partner. One of the pinhole patterns is mounted at A, and the other at B. The distance between them equals f, the focal length of the lens L. A viewing screen is placed at C, at a distance f from the lens, and a diffuse light source is mounted behind A. The pattern of bright dots appearing at C is the correlogram between the pattern at A and the pattern at B. Formally, $C = \bar{A} * B$, where the asterisk stands for convolution and $\bar{A}$ is the result of rotating the pattern A through half a turn round the optical axis. If A and B were interchanged, the pattern at C would be $\bar{B} * A = A * \bar{B} = \bar{C}$, so that the correlogram would be inverted. This is clear enough if B is a pinhole, and shows that the order of the patterns is important.

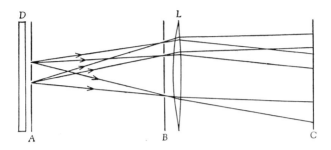

Figure 1
Constructing a correlogram. *D* is a diffuse light source; *L* is a lens; *C* is the plane of the correlogram of *A* with *B*.

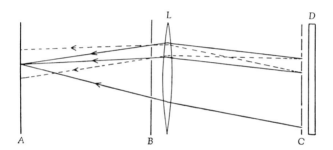

Figure 2
Reconstructing a pattern. Solid lines: paths traversed in figure 1. Broken lines: paths not traversed in figure 1.

To recover pattern *A* from pattern *B* we convert the correlogram into a pattern of pinholes in a black card and place the light source behind it, so that the light shines through *C* and *B* on to a viewing screen at *A* (figure 2). A pattern of spots now appears on the viewing screen. All the spots of the original pattern *A* are present, but a number of spurious spots as well. If the pinholes were infinitesimal and there were no diffraction effects the reconstructed pattern would be $\bar{C} * B = A * \bar{B} * B$, just as in Fourier holography. If *B* were a random pattern, one could argue, $\bar{B} * B$ would approximate to a delta function at the origin, so that the reconstructed pattern would look like a slightly bespattered version of the original pattern *A*. How can we pick out the genuine spots from the others?

To solve this problem let us simplify the set-up by removing the lens (figure 3). Suppose, for example, that *A* has two holes and *B* has three. Then the pattern *C* will consist of six bright spots (barring coincidences). When these spots are converted into pinholes and illuminated from the right, a

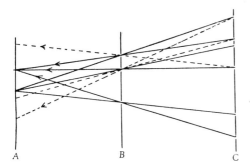

A   B   C

Figure 3

total of 18 ($=6 \times 3$) rays will emerge from B and impinge on the screen
at A. But we shall not see eighteen spots on this screen, because six of the
rays will converge, in sets of three, on to the two points of the original
pattern. The other twelve rays will give rise to spurious spots, but (again
barring coincidences) these spots will be fainter than the genuine ones. We
can therefore expect to be able to pick out the wheat from the chaff with a
detector with a threshold slightly less than three units of brightness.

This reasoning applies equally to the "correlograph", with lens, illustrated
in figures 1 and 2. So, having found how to get rid of the unwanted
background in reconstructing A from B and C, we can now envisage the
possibility of constructing multiple correlograms, comprising all the spots
present in $C_1 = \bar{A}_1 * B_1$ or in $C_2 = \bar{A}_2 * B_2$, and so on. Presentation of B_1
should evoke A_1, presentation of B_2 should evoke A_2, and so on, up to the
limit set by the information capacity of the system. But what is this limit?

To answer this question let us evade the complicated (and basically
irrelevant) issues raised by the finite wavelength of light, edge effects, and
so on, and pose the question in terms of a discrete, and slightly more
abstract, model. We suppose A, B, and C to be discrete spaces, each
containing N points, a_1 to a_N, b_1 to b_N, and c_1 to c_N. The point-pair (a_i, b_j)
is mapped on to the point c_k if $i - j = k$ or $k - N$. Conversely, the
point-pair (c_k, b_j) is mapped on to a_i if the same condition is met. Imagine
now that we have R pairs of patterns which we wish to associate together,
each pair consisting of M points selected from A and another M selected
from B. The total number of point-pairs determined by all the pairs of
patterns will be RM^2, and we may think of this number of "rays" striking
C. If they impinge at random, the probability of any point c_k not being
struck will be

$$\exp(-RM^2/N) = 1 - p, \text{ say.}$$

The correlogram for the whole set of R pairs will then consist of the remaining pN points of C.

Now consider the reconstruction process. One of the B-patterns, comprising M of the points b_1 to b_N, is selected and combined with the correlogram to produce pNM "rays" impinging on A. Each point of the original A-pattern will receive exactly M rays, so that we should set the threshold of our detector at M if we want to pick up all the original points. Now consider any one of the $N - M$ other points in A. It may receive a ray through any one of the M "holes" in B; the probability that it receives a ray through a given hole is just p, for this is the chance that the point on C "behind" the hole belongs to the correlogram. The chance of an unwanted point reaching the threshold is thus p^M, and the probable number of spurious points of brightness M is consequently $(N - M)p^M$. If M is a fairly large number, this will be a sensitive function of p, and for given N and M the critical value of p above which spurious points begin to appear may be found from the relation

$$(N - M)p^M = 1.$$

Alternatively, this may be viewed as a relation which sets a lower limit to the value of M for given values of N and p. A slightly safer estimate is given by

$$Np^M = 1, \text{ or } M = -\log N/\log p.$$

If M falls below this value, the reconstruction will be marred by spurious points.

Next we enquire about the amount of information stored in the memory when R pairs have been memorized and M satisfies the aforementioned condition for accurate retrieval. We can evoke any one of R A-patterns by presenting the appropriate B-pattern. There are $\binom{N}{M}$ possible A-patterns altogether, so the amount of information needed to store any one of them is $\log\binom{N}{M}$, which is roughly $M\log N$ natural units of information. The total amount of information stored is, therefore, approximately $I = RM\log N$ natural units. But according to our original calculation of p

$$RM^2 = -N\log(1 - p),$$

and if we are working at the limit of accurate retrieval

$$M = -\log N/\log p \simeq \log_2 N$$

(see below). It follows immediately that

$$I = N\log p\log(1 - p).$$

As one might have anticipated, this expression has its maximum value when p is 0.5—when the correlogram occupies about half of C.

What is remarkable is the size of I_{max}:

$$I_{max} = N(\log 2)^2 \text{ natural units} = N \log 2 \text{ bits.}$$

The maximum amount of information that could possibly be stored in C is N bits. So the correlograph, in this discrete realization, stores its information nearly ($\log_e 2 = 69$ per cent) as densely as a random-access store with no associative capability.

As described, the discrete correlograph, like the holograph, will "recognize" displaced patterns. If an A-pattern $\{a_i\}$ and a B-pattern $\{b_j\}$ have been associated, then presentation of the displaced B-pattern $\{b_{j+d}\}$ will evoke the displaced A-pattern $\{a_{i+d}\}$.

But the resemblance does not cease there. Just as in holography, the information to be stored is laid down in parallel, non-locally, and in such a way that it can survive local damage. In parallel, because each mapping $(a_i, b_j) \to c_k$ can be effected without reference to any other; the same applies to the reconstructive mappings $(c_k, b_j) \to a_i$. Non-locally, because the presence of a_i in an A-pattern is registered at M separate points on the correlogram, one for each point of the B-pattern. And robustly, because if the system is not stretched to its theoretical limit it can (as we shall show elsewhere) be used for the accurate reconstruction of A-patterns even when some of the correlogram is "ablated" and/or the B-patterns are inaccurately presented. But it can be made secure against such contingencies only by sacrificing storage capacity—as one would expect.

In our discussion of the process of reconstruction we had occasion to note that a point c_k might owe its presence on the correlogram to the joint occurrence of (a_i, b_j); but that if a pattern were presented containing the point b_{j+d}, the "ray" (c_k, b_{j+d}) would light up the point a_{i+d}, which might never have occurred in any A-pattern. It was this feature which underlay the ability of the system to recognize displaced patterns; but the same feature is a slight embarrassment when one comes to consider how a discrete correlograph, with the reconstructive facility, could be realized in neural tissue. We will not dwell on this point, except to acknowledge that it was drawn to our attention by Dr F. H. C. Crick, to whom H. C. L.-H. is indebted for provocative comments. But it led us on to a further refinement of our model, in which a given point c_k is admitted to the correlogram only if the particular pair (a_i, b_j) occurs in one of the pairs of patterns, and not otherwise. On this assumption there might be as many as N^2 separate point-pairs to take into account, and a correspondingly large number of points in the space C.

In this form our associative memory model ceases to be a correlograph, having lost the ability to recognize displaced patterns, but its information capacity is now potentially far greater than before. To show this, we will adopt a rather different type of representation, in which the points of A become N_A parallel lines and those of B become N_B parallel lines. The points of C are the $N_A N_B$ intersections between the lines a_i and the lines b_j.

In this network model, as before, a particular point of C is included in the active set if the pair of lines (a_i, b_j) which pass through it have been called into play in at least one association of an A-pattern with a B-pattern. Let us suppose that R pairs of patterns have been associated in this way, each pair comprising a selection of M_A lines from A and M_B lines from B. Then the chance that a given point of C has not been activated by the recording is

$$\exp(-RM_A M_B/N_C) = 1 - p, \text{ say,}$$

where we have written N_C for $N_A N_B$. If B-patterns are being used to recall A-patterns, then there will be a minimum value of M_B such that if the threshold on the A-lines is set at M_B (so as to detect all the genuine lines) spurious lines will begin to be detected as well. (The argument is just the same as that applied to the correlograph earlier on.) This minimum value of M_B is given by

$$N_A p^{M_B} = 1$$

or

$$M_B = -\log N_A / \log p \simeq \log_2 N_A.$$

Now the amount of information stored in the memory when R pairs of A-patterns have been memorized is roughly

$$I_A = RM_A \log N_A.$$

But from our equation for $1 - p$

$$RM_A M_B = -N_C \log(1 - p).$$

Therefore

$$I_A = N_C \log p \log(1 - p),$$

showing that, as in the correlograph, the density with which the associative net stores information is 69 per cent of the theoretical maximum value. We note, in passing, that I_B, defined as $RM_B \log N_B$, is also equal to $N_C \log p \log(1 - p)$.

An associative network of this kind also operates (i) in parallel, (ii)

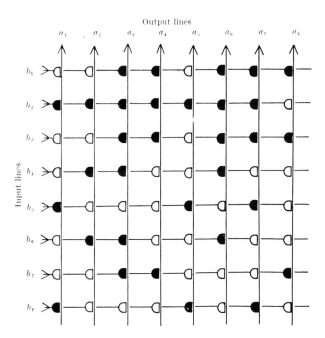

Figure 4
An associative net.

non-locally, and (iii) in such a way that local damage or inaccuracy is not necessarily disastrous. We intend to go into the details of iii elsewhere. We now succumb to the temptation of indicating how such an associative memory might be realized in neural tissue, though, as Brindley (1967) has pointed out, function need not determine structure uniquely.

The system we have in mind is represented diagrammatically in figure 4. The horizontal lines are axons of the N_B input neurones b_1, b_2, ..., while the vertical lines are dendrites of the N_A output neurones a_1, a_2, ... At the intersection of b_j with a_i is a modifiable synapse c_{ij}. This synapse is initially inactive, but becomes active after a coincidence in which a_i and b_j are made to fire at the same time by some external stimulus. Such a coincidence is supposed to occur if an A-pattern containing a_i is presented in association with a B-pattern containing b_j. After the activation of c_{ij} (which we regard as a permanent effect) the firing of b_j will locally depolarize the membrane of a_i. The output neurone a_i is then supposed to fire if M_B or more input cells depolarize it simultaneously.

In figure 4 we indicate what the state of the network would be after it had learned to associate the following pairs of patterns:

B-pattern	A-pattern
1, 2, 3	4, 6, 7
2, 5, 8	1, 5, 7
2, 4, 6	2, 3, 6
1, 3, 7	3, 4, 8

The synapses indicated by solid semicircles would be active, those indicated by open semicircles being still inactive. In this particular example, N_A and N_B are both 8, and M_A ($\simeq \log_2 N_B$) and M_B ($\simeq \log_2 N_A$) are both 3. R, the number of pairs of patterns associated, has been chosen so as to make p, the proportion of synapses active, close to 0.5; in fact p equals 0.5 exactly. These various numbers illustrate the system working near its maximum capacity. The reader may verify that every B-pattern except the first evokes the correct A-pattern at a threshold of 3; the only mistake the system makes is that when supplied with the B-pattern 1, 2, 3 it responds with an A-pattern 3, 4, 6, 7 containing four elements.

To summarize: We have attempted to distil from holography the features which commend it as a model of associative memory, and have found that the performance of a holograph can be mimicked and actually improved on by discrete non-linear models, namely the correlograph and the associative net just described. Quite possibly there is no system in the brain which corresponds exactly to our hypothetical neural network; but we do attach importance to the principle on which it works and the quantitative relations which we have shown must hold if such a system is to perform, as it can, with high efficiency.

References

Brindley, G. S. 1967. *Proc. R. Soc.* B 168: 361.

Gabor, D. 1968a. *Nature* 217: 1288.

Gabor, D. 1968b. *Nature* 217: 584.

Pribram, K. H. 1969. *Sci. Am.* 220: 73.

Van Heerden, P. J. 1963. *Appl. Optics* 2: 393.

Willshaw, D., and H. C. Longuet-Higgins. 1969. In *Machine Intelligence 4*, ed. D. Michie (Edinburgh University Press).

30

Reply to P. J. van Heerden's "Models for the Brain"

D. J. Willshaw, H. C. Longuet-Higgins, and O. P. Buneman

Editor's note: The reply follows the article by van Heerden, which is reprinted here in its entirety.

Models for the Brain (van Heerden)

Willshaw, Buneman, and Longuet-Higgins (1969) have proposed a non-holographic associative memory model for the brain. They also criticize the proposal made by myself (van Heerden 1963a) and by Pribram (1966, 1969) that the brain would be organized on the holographic principle. They say: "How could the brain Fourier-analyse the incoming signals with sufficient accuracy, and how could it improve on the rather feeble signal to noise ratio of the reconstructed signals?"

In an earlier paper (van Heerden 1963b), in which the potential of the hologram for retrieving information was first pointed out, I calculated the signal to noise ratio. As an example I showed that, theoretically, in a hologram of a library of 300 books in coded form of 200 pages each, one single line could instantaneously be recognized and located. The hologram contains half the information held in the ideal matched filter. One can show, for example, that two holograms, in the two arms of a Michelson interferometer, perform the same function as one matched filter. Further, the hologram of a symmetric image, which has half the information of a general image, is identical with the matched filter (van Heerden 1963b). It therefore seems correct to say that the signal to noise ratio of the hologram is 50 per cent of ideal. No method of information retrieval can have a signal to noise ratio better than the hologram by more than a factor of two.

In a book on the subject (van Heerden 1968) I discussed further how the brain could work physically very well as a three-dimensional hologram. If we have a three-dimensional network of neurones, in which each neurone is connected to a few adjacent ones, and if a neurone in a certain layer, in receiving a signal, will send this on to a few neurones in the next layer, then signals will propagate in this network as a wave propagates in an elastic medium. If, moreover, the ability of the neurones to propagate received signals can be permanently enhanced by frequent use, then the network must act as a three-dimensional hologram, with a storage capacity of the order of the number of neurones present in the network.

For recognizing, we need a two-dimensional hologram for fast search, combined with a three-dimensional hologram which has a large capacity for storing information that is readily accessible (van Heerden 1968). This is still not sufficient, however, to explain the wonderful human capacity for recognizing. We can recognize a person, even one we have not met for a long time, at any distance and from many different angles. A fixed hologram memory would not be able to perform this operation. The flexibility needed can be provided by optical means: for example, a zoom lens can carry out a search to match the size of the image received to the image stored. It seems not too far-fetched to imagine that a neurone network has this flexibility. It could be realized by extended variable fields, analogous to those used in electron optics, to produce different gradients in the speed of propagation of the network by electrical or chemical means. This could effect a change in focal distance, or a rotation of the image, or small distortions, to achieve a clear, sharp recognition signal in the image plane.

Although the hologram principle is natural for a neurone network, it does not exclude the possibility that another model such as the correlogram of Willshaw, Buneman, and Longuet-Higgins is actually realized in the brain. One has first, however, to show that such a model is reasonable. Their model, in the optical form they propose, seems to have a low storage capacity because of the diffraction of any kind of wave field (this is not irrelevant!). In the network model they propose, on the other hand, they do obtain the same storage capacity as the holographic model, but it seems to lack the flexibility for recognizing images which are displaced, of different size, or slightly distorted. One more aspect to be considered is the fact that three-dimensional holograms are capable of storing time dependent signals (van Heerden 1963a). The recognition of speech, and our ability to speak or run or drive a car, is one more aspect of information processing in the brain which must be explained by any model.

References

Pribram, K. H. 1966. In *Macromolecules and Behavior*, ed. J. Gaito. (New York: Appleton-Century-Crofts).

Pribram, K. H. 1969. *Sci. Am.* 220: 73.

van Heerden, P. J. 1963a. *Applied Optics* 2: 393.

van Heerden, P. J. 1963b. *Applied Optics* 2: 387.

van Heerden, P. J. 1968. *The Foundation of Empirical Knowledge, with a Theory of Artificial Intelligence*. Wassenaar, The Netherlands: Wistik.

Willshaw, D. J., O. P. Buneman, and H. C. Longuet-Higgins. 1969. *Nature* 222: 960. [Chapter 29 in present volume.]

Reply (Willshaw, Longuet-Higgins, and Buneman)

Van Heerden has discussed some of the differences between his holographic model of memory (van Heerden 1963a) and a pair of non-holographic models that we put forward last year (Willshaw et al. 1969). We alluded to the poor signal-to-noise ratio of the holograph when it is used to reconstruct a stored pattern from a fragment of that pattern; van Heerden's comment refers to the signal-to-noise ratio with which one can locate a given fragment in a large text, and this is quite a different matter. Van Heerden himself showed that the signal-to-noise ratio in the reconstruction of random patterns was equal to the size of the fragment divided by the size of the whole pattern, and the same applies to the reconstruction of a temporal signal from a short cue (Willshaw and Longuet-Higgins 1969).

Our first model, the correlograph, was designed to re-create accurately one binary pattern from another, having recorded a cross-correlation between the two. To do this with accuracy it was necessary to put a threshold on the output of the device, so that the relatively weak unwanted signals would not appear in the reconstruction. Regarding the output pattern or patterns (several input-output pairs can be stored simultaneously) as constituting the stored information, we found that the information storage density could be as high as 69 per cent of the theoretical maximum without loss of accuracy in recall.

These remarks apply equally to our other model, the associative net. Although more information can be stored in the associative net, we lose the ability to produce a displaced output from a correspondingly displaced input. In this and in some other respects the net behaves like a discrete version of van Heerden's (1963b) three-dimensional hologram, but, again, threshold elements are used to clean up the output patterns, a result which cannot be achieved in a purely linear device.

In its optical form the correlograph is, indeed, severely limited by diffraction and cannot be taken literally as a physical model for memory; nor did we intend that it should. But we felt that its logic, which is easy to appreciate, might possibly be realized in the nervous system. For instance, an associative net might be made to function as a correlograph by "tying together" certain of its switches. But there was no evidence that any such tying takes place and we therefore put forward the associative net as the more likely model. It could be simply realized, as we pointed out, by a system of neurones with thresholds and modifiable synapses; both these properties are known to occur peripherally in the nervous system (Eccles 1957, 1964), and probably occur centrally as well (Burns et al. 1968).

Although there is no conclusive neurophysiological evidence to support our theory against van Heerden's, the ability of parts of the nervous system to propagate waves according to Huygens's principle would be difficult to reconcile with the observed non-linearity of some neural responses, and the existence of a stable periodic source of excitation has yet to be demonstrated. We also feel that in any model of the brain it is of advantage to be able to modify synapses as well as nerve cells. The ratio of synapses to nerve cells in the cerebral cortex seems to be of the order $10^4 - 10^5$, so that the information that could be stored synaptically would be correspondingly higher (Cragg 1967). As to the remarkable flexibility of the human perceptual apparatus, we feel that neither his model nor ours can be held to account for this in their present forms.

References

Burns, B. D., T. V. P. Bliss, and A. M. Uttley. 1968. *J. Physiol.* 195: 339.

Cragg, B. G. 1967. *J. Anat.* 101: 639.

Eccles, J. C. 1957. *The Physiology of Nerve Cells.* Baltimore: Johns Hopkins University Press.

Eccles, J. C. 1964. *The Physiology of Synapses.* Berlin: Springer-Verlag.

van Heerden, P. J. 1963a. *Applied Optics* 2: 387.

van Heerden, P. J. 1963b. *Applied Optics* 2: 393.

Willshaw, D. J., and H. C. Longuet-Higgins. 1969. In *Machine Intelligence* 4, ed. D. Michie (Edinburgh University Press).

Willshaw, D. J., O. P. Buneman, and H. C. Longuet-Higgins. 1969. *Nature* 222: 960. [Chapter 29 in present volume.]

31   Theories of Associative Recall

H. C. Longuet-Higgins,
D. J. Willshaw, and
O. P. Buneman

The problem of how the brain stores and retrieves information is ultimately an experimental one, and its solution will doubtless call for the combined resources of psychology, physiology, and molecular biology. But it is also a problem of great theoretical sophistication; and one of the major tasks confronting the brain scientist is the construction of theoretical models which are worthy of, and open to, experimental test. In this review we shall be concerned with the latter aspect of the problem of memory, which has attracted quite a lot of attention in the last few years. It is early yet to judge the relative merits of the various models in any detail; but as we shall see, most of those which have been developed beyond their initial hypotheses have a certain family resemblance, and it seems as if we may now be in possession of the basic ideas which will be needed for the understanding of one of the central problems of memory, namely the mechanism of associative recall.

The most convenient definition of associative recall, for our purposes, is in terms of stimuli and responses. Consider a physical system occupying a certain region of space—a "black box", in fact. The box has an input channel and an output channel, each capable of transmitting very complex signals. The input signals are of two kinds, which we may designate as conditioned stimuli (CS) and unconditioned stimuli (UCS). Before the system has memorized anything, any UCS will evoke a certain response which will emerge along the output channel. During the learning phase the system is subjected to a succession of UCS, each of which is accompanied by a certain CS, simultaneously or nearly so. After learning is completed the input of a CS will evoke the same response as the UCS which accompanied it during learning; the system will respond to the conditioned stimuli in the absence of the unconditioned stimuli.

A very simple system of just this kind was postulated by Hebb (1949), who advanced a famous hypothesis about the modification of synaptic connections between neurons. The axons of two neurons A and B are connected to the body or the dendrites of a third cell C. The synapse BC is unmodifiable, and an impulse from B will invariably excite C. The synapse AC is initially ineffective; but if C is fired by B at the moment when an impulse arrives from A, then the synapse AC is facilitated, so that thereafter an impulse from A may suffice to excite C without the assistance of an impulse from B. The cell C thus learns to respond to the CS from A in the same manner as it originally responded only to the UCS from B.

There are certain difficulties, however, in generalizing this simple system into an acceptable theory of associative recall. First, an associative memory must be able to associate signals which are highly unexpected, in the sense of having a low prior probability, and it would be extravagant to reserve a separate cell for every conceivable input signal. And even if this were not so, the memory would be unable to establish arbitrary associations unless there existed at least one cell C connected from (i.e. postsynaptically connected with) every possible pair of cells A and B. These remarks underline the desirability of constructing theoretical models in which, after the establishment of many arbitrary associations, the relevant information will have been stored sufficiently densely not to waste too many modifiable elements. Another generally desirable feature is that the modifications which result from a particular association should be fairly widely distributed over the system, so that the recall of a particular response is not too sensitive to local damage, or to inaccuracy in the CS which should evoke it. And finally, though this is still a largely unsolved problem, the system must be able to associate together signals which are temporally as well as spatially complex, and this calls for components with characteristic frequencies or time constants.

In the following paragraphs we shall not attempt a complete survey of all the published literature on learning in the nervous system, but will concentrate on the rather few papers which have dealt specifically with the neurological problem just posed. The ideas and models which we shall discuss are scattered fairly widely in the literature, in such diverse fields as neuroanatomy, the technology of pattern recognition, and applied optics. We will begin with the optical and quasi-optical models.

Optical Models

The forerunner of most of the current optical models was a paper by Beurle (1956), though Beurle's ideas were couched not in optical but in neurological terms. Like Cragg and Temperley (1954) and Griffith (1963, 1965),

Beurle explored the hypothesis that the seat of the memory is macroscopically homogenous, such structure as it possesses being adequately describable in terms of local neural connections. This assumption implies that its behaviour can be adequately specified by a set of differential equations, expressing the manner in which it transmits waves of excitation and the manner in which the local parameters of the equations are altered after the passage of such waves. The mathematical details of Beurle's paper need not detain us, as the underlying assumptions are difficult to reconcile with the known structural complexity of the cortex; but one particularly attractive idea emerged from Beurle's analysis, namely that two different waves spreading across the cortex might together generate an interference pattern from which either wave alone could subsequently regenerate the other. Broadly enough interpreted, this suggestion could hardly be doubted, and it was explicitly referred to by van Heerden in a pair of papers (1963a,b) which first took seriously the analogy between associative memory and the optical technique of holography.

Holography was invented by Gabor in 1948 (see also Gabor 1949, 1951) for recording photographically an interference pattern between two light waves in such a way that either light wave, when falling on the interference pattern, regenerates the other. For this purpose spatially coherent light is required, and it was not until the advent of the laser and the technical developments made by Leith and Upatnieks (1962), Stroke (1966), and others that holography became a practically useful technique for the storage and retrieval of information. The best-known holographic experiment is that in which the beam from a laser is split into two by a half-silvered mirror. One part, the reference beam B, is shone directly on to a photographic plate; the other is used to illuminate an object in such a way that the light wave A scattered by the object also falls on the plate. The plate records an interference pattern, and is developed and printed as a positive transparency. When this transparency—the "hologram"—is now illuminated by the reference beam B, the light wave A is regenerated, and an observer looking through the hologram sees a clear image of the original object, as through a window. Remarkably enough, this image is three-dimensional, and can be seen through any part of the hologram, indicating that every point on the object affects every point on the plate, and conversely that every point on the plate records something about the object as a whole. In both these senses the information storage is non-local, or distributed in the sense of the previous section, and it is probably this fact which has most strongly commended holography to some neurologists as a memory model (Westlake 1967; Pribram 1966, 1969).

But there is another feature of holographic recording which is possibly of greater theoretical interest, and it is rather less well known. This is the possibility of storing many different associations on the same hologram. To do this one replaces the direct reference beam of the previous experiment by the light scattered by a second object, so that the plate records the interference pattern between two scattered waves (Stroke 1966). Either scattered wave will then regenerate the other, though with some loss of definition. But before developing the plate one can expose it to many different pairs of scattered waves: A_1 and B_1, A_2 and B_2, and so on. Then, provided that each pair of scattered waves is effectively random, one can recover the image of any recorded object by illuminating the hologram with the laser light scattered by its partner (which must be placed accurately in its original position). The more pairs of objects that are associated in this way, the worse the definition in the reconstructed image; but this fact merely exhibits the finite information-storage capacity of any physical system—a limitation from which the brain can hardly be exempt.

The theory of the two-dimensional hologram was worked out in detail by van Heerden (1963a). He calculated the signal-to-noise ratio of the reconstructed image, and showed how the phenomenon of ghost images could be used for recognizing and locating a small fragment in a larger pattern, using an apparatus of the type described in the next paragraph. In a later paper (van Heerden 1963b) he showed theoretically that optical information could also be stored in light-sensitive three-dimensional systems such as discoloured crystals. The information is stored, as in the two-dimensional hologram, as a series of interference patterns between pairs of plane parallel waves. Many different pictures could be stored in the same crystal, if each was illuminated by a different plane wave, and the number of bits of retrievable information was comparable to the number of colour centres in the crystal, so that the system could be regarded as rather efficient. Relating these results to the suggestions of Beurle (1956), van Heerden stressed the need for exact phase relations between the waves to be maintained over large distances. He postulated a calibrating system of pulses to compensate for any variation in the speed of propagation, and suggested that the memory may comprise two subsystems, one for search and recognition and the other for actual storage. But though his model is mathematically attractive, its physical assumptions are rather speculative in relation to the brain, so we will pass on to consider the underlying theory, which does seem to have more relevance to our neurological problem.

Perhaps the easiest holographic experiment to analyse theoretically is Fourier holography, illustrated in figure 1. T is a transparency, illuminated

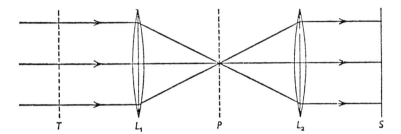

Figure 1
A Fourier holograph. T is a transparency, illuminated from the left by a collimated laser
beam. L_1 and L_2 are convex lenses of focal length d, separated by a distance $2d$. P is a plate
holder for the hologram. S is a viewing screen.

from the left by a collimated laser beam. P is a plate holder and S a
ground-glass viewing screen. L_1 and L_2 are convex lenses of focal length d,
and each of the distances TL_1, L_1P, PL_2, and L_2S is equal to d. When P is
empty an inverted image of T is thrown on to S. A photographic plate at
P records the intensity of the light at each point in its plane, and is
developed and printed as a hologram whose transparency at every point is
proportional to this intensity. With the hologram in position the inverted
image at S is slightly but not seriously blurred; the interesting point is that
part of the transparency can now be screened from the laser and the whole
of its image is still visible at S. Why?

The basic physical fact we need is that when coherent light is passing
through both focal planes of a lens the electric fields in the two planes are
Fourier transforms of one another. So if $F(x, y)$ is the field at the transparency
and $f(u, v)$ the field at P, then

$$f(u, v) = \int\int F(x, y) \exp 2\pi i(ux + vy)dxdy.$$

The light intensity at P is the square modulus of f, namely f^*f, where
the asterisk denotes the complex conjugate; so the transparency of the
hologram is proportional to f^*f, which is just the two-dimensional power
spectrum of the pattern $F(x, y)$. Now suppose that F is in two parts, F_1 and
F_2, and that we illuminate F_1 but cover up F_2. The wave reaching the
hologram will be f_1, the Fourier transform of F_1, and the wave emerging
from the other side will be $f_1(f_1^* + f_2^*)(f_1 + f_2)$. Of particular concern to
us is the component $f_1f_1^*f_2$. When Fourier transformed by the second lens
(see appendix) this gives F_2 (upside down) slightly blurred by convolution
with the Fourier transform of $f_1^*f_1$, which is the autocorrelation function of

F_1. The reason why the blurring is generally slight is that if F_1 is an effectively random pattern its autocorrelation function will be small and random except in the immediate neighbourhood of the origin; that is, the pattern F_1 will not be a good match with a displaced version of itself. Hence the appearance of F_2 on the viewing screen even when that part of the transparency is screened from illumination by the laser.

Instead of raising the embarrassing question whether the skull can contain anything corresponding to a laser, perhaps we should say something about a mathematically similar model designed to do in the dimension of time what the holograph does in space. At present perhaps the model is of more logical than neurological significance, but it is too early as yet to be certain.

Temporal Holography

In Fourier holography we record the power spectrum of a spatial pattern and use it to modulate the Fourier transform of part of the pattern, recovering the other part by what may be described as Fourier synthesis. Longuet-Higgins (1968a,b) showed that precisely similar operations could be applied to time-dependent signals, using a device which he has named the "holophone". This is essentially a bank of narrow-pass filters connected in parallel to the input channel and similarly connected to the output channel through amplifiers of variable gain. The battery of amplifiers corresponds mathematically to the light-sensitive grains of the holographic plate. When a signal is put into the device, each filter transmits a certain amount of energy, and the gain of its amplifier is turned up by a proportional amount. The gains of the amplifiers thus represent the power spectrum of the recorded signal. Several signals can recorded in this way, and the amplifier gains will then represent the sum of their power spectra. Now suppose that a recorded signal is in two parts, an earlier part $F_1(t)$ and a later part $F_2(t)$. Then arguments very similar to those of the preceding section show that if $F_1(t)$ alone is sent along the input channel, the output channel will emit both $F_1(t)$ and $F_2(t)$, in the correct temporal relation. The later part, F_2 (and for that matter the cue F_1), will be accompanied by a certain amount of noise in the form of an "echo" unless F_1 happens to be a single sharp pulse, and this echo will be more noisy the shorter the cue and the greater the combined length of the recorded signals (Willshaw and Longuet-Higgins 1969).

As an information storage and retrieval device the holophone has advantages and disadvantages which correspond exactly with those of the holograph. It can be used for storing several complex signals, though the signal-to-noise ratio falls in proportion to the number stored. The storage is non-local: damage or ablation affects all the stored signals a little, rather than any one of them in particular, or any part of one. And both the holograph and the holophone are content-addressable, in the sense that mere presentation of a "CS" is enough to evoke the appropriate response, without any need to locate its address in the system. But both systems suffer from a certain rigidity: a recorded pattern or signal will evoke its partner or proper successor only if it is presented at exactly the right scale (for the holograph) or exactly the right tempo (for the holophone). If one is thinking of the former device in connexion with visual learning, or the latter in connexion with the learning of sequential routines, this is obviously a serious limitation. Also, a holophone has to meet rather stringent specifications in order to function properly: it can record a signal of duration D only if the inverse bandwidth of each filter exceeds D, the inverse frequency separation between neighbouring filters also exceeds D, and the resonant frequencies of the filters are not subject to drift. Nevertheless, the possibility of storing temporal signals in frequency space does raise the question whether some parts of the cortex may not code temporal signals in this sort of way, and whether there may not be systems of cells or neural circuits which respond selectively to particular frequencies—most likely in the range from 100 to 10 cycles.

Correlation Models

As already remarked, the output of a holograph, when it is used to store pairs of patterns and to recall a particular one from its partner, is mathematically expressible in terms of convolutions and correlations involving the patterns concerned—and, indeed, those not concerned (see appendix). It does this by storing the superimposed power spectra of the various pairs, rather than their internal correlations. But there is a well-known theorem to the effect that the power spectrum and the autocorrelation function of a pattern are Fourier transforms of each other, so that to record the one is equivalent, in terms of information, to storing the other. Could one therefore not imagine storing directly the correlations between or within the various input signals, without the need for Fourier-analysing the signals and all the apparatus which that entails? Various authors have pointed out that the performance of the holograph can be crudely mimicked by simple optical devices working with ordinary incoherent light. But the first person to put forward a detailed model of associative memory based on the correlation principle seems to have been Roy (1960, 1962). Roy's papers are concerned with associative recall in time, and describe a device incorporating a large number of delay lines, each of which is involved in recording the autocorrelation for a particular time interval—though Roy does not say so explicitly. The time scale is quantized, and the information is stored in a number of units rather like potentiometers, but the input-output characteristics of the system are virtually identical with those of the holophone (a later proposal). The same problem of tempo arises—if it really is a problem—and Roy has considered how it might be overcome by cunning neural circuitry (private communication). But although the general idea is attractive, we are still without any quantitative estimate of the storage efficiency of the device, and it is not easy to see how its relevance to the brain could be established by physiological experiments—a dilemma which should not, of course, be regarded as nullifying a good idea.

So, many of the features of holographic recording might be retained, and some of the technical difficulties avoided (Gabor 1968, 1969), if one could store correlations directly rather than in the form of power spectra. This theoretical suggestion was explored in Willshaw et al. 1969, and as that analysis led to some useful conclusions about information storage efficiency we shall summarize it.

We began by considering an optical device, the correlograph (figure 2), which could form on a viewing screen S the cross-correlation between two pinhole patterns B and A. In the case illustrated B consists of two pinholes and A of three, so that the "correlogram" comprises six bright spots. The correlogram is copied as a third pinhole pattern C, and is substituted for S, which in turn is mounted where B was before. Light from a diffuse source is now allowed to shine through C and A, and a pattern of bright spots appears on S. But the 18 rays now passing through do not produce as

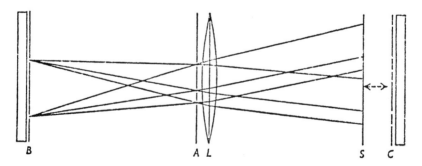

Figure 2
The distances AB and LS are both equal to the focal length of L. In the reconstruction of B from A, S is replaced by C, which is illuminated from the right.

many bright spots on S; six of them converge in sets of three on to the sites of the original pinholes in B, and the other 12 rays strike S at random points. Using a detector with a threshold of three brightness units we can therefore reconstruct the original B pattern with full accuracy.

We went on to consider the logic of the device. Because of the focusing action of the lens, any ray through A and B parallel to a given line will illuminate the same point on S, so that there is a many-to-one mapping from point pairs in A and B on to points in S. This makes it possible to recover a displaced B-pattern from a correspondingly displaced A-pattern, but seriously limits the number of pattern pairs that can be associated in one correlogram. We therefore turned our attention to a logically related but very different-looking model, in which every pair of "points" in A and B is mapped on to just one point of a third set S. A natural realization of this model is the "associative net", in which (figure 3) the "points" of A are

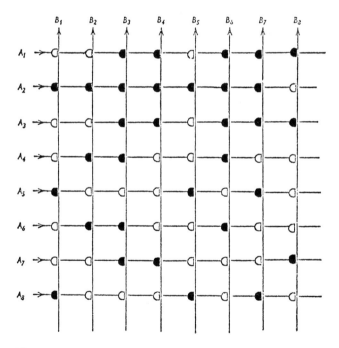

Figure 3

An associative net. The input lines $(A_1 \ldots A_8)$ run horizontally; the output lines $(B_1 \ldots B_8)$ run vertically. The filled or open semicircles represent switches which have or have not been turned on. Four associations have been recorded:

A-pattern	B-pattern	A-pattern	B-pattern
1, 2, 3	4, 6, 7	2, 4, 6	2, 3, 6
2, 5, 8	1, 5, 7	1, 3, 7	3, 4, 8

input fibres running from left to right, the "points" of B are output fibres running upwards, and those of S are on-off switches at the intersection. The theory is as follows. Let there be N_A A-lines, N_B B-lines, and $N_A N_B$ switches. Let a typical A-pattern consist of impulses coming along M_A of the A-lines chosen at random, and let a typical B-pattern likewise involve M_B B-lines. Then an A-impulse will cross a B-impulse at each of $M_A M_B$ intersections, and at each of these the switch is turned on if it is not already on. After a number of pairs of patterns, say R pairs, have been associated in this way, a certain fraction p of the switches will have been turned on; if the patterns are random, p will approximately be given by

$$p = 1 - \exp(-RM_A M_B/N_A N_B).$$

After the storage, the recall. An A-pattern is put in, and each B-line of the associated B-pattern receives impulses through M_A switches (which, by hypothesis, have all been turned on). But a B-line not belonging to the B-pattern will also receive a certain number of impulses. The chance that it receives an impulse through every one of its M_A intersections with the active A-lines is in fact p^{M_A}. So if each B-line has a firing threshold equal to M_A, not only will all those lines fire which belong to the B-pattern, but a further $N_B p^{M_A}$ will probably fire as well. The critical value of p will therefore be that for which this number is approximately unity; that is,

$$\log_e N_B = -M_A \log_e p.$$

With this value of p, how much information will have been stored? A single B-pattern requires

$$\log_2 \binom{N_B}{M_B}$$

bits to specify it, so if R B-patterns can be accurately retrieved the available information stored is

$$R \log_2 \binom{N_B}{M_B} = RM_B \log_2 N_B \text{ bits approximately.}$$

Combining these three equations, we deduce that the number of bits stored is

$$N_A N_B \log_2 p \log_e(1 - p),$$

which has its maximum when $p = \frac{1}{2}$, and is then $0.693 N_A N_B$ bits. This maximum will in fact never be attained, because the derivation assumes that N_B is virtually infinite; but it does show that under ideal conditions the associative net is more than 50% efficient in the use it makes of its $N_A N_B$

binary switches. Another conclusion of almost equal importance emerges at once from the second equation above. When $p = \frac{1}{2}$, M_A should be about $\log_2 N_B$ (though this is a lower limit, of course), and therefore much smaller than N_B itself. The input signals should therefore comprise rather small numbers of pulses if the system is to be an efficient information store.

In a subsequent paper (Willshaw and Longuet-Higgins 1970) it has been shown that the associative net can be made to function accurately even if the A-patterns—the "conditioned stimuli"—are defective in a certain fraction of their M_A impulses, and even if the system is partially ablated, in the sense that some of the switches which should be turned on are taken away or turned off at random. To guard against such handicaps the mean number of impulses in an A-pattern must be raised above the minimal value quoted above, and substantially fewer associations than before can be stored if the output is not to be contaminated with spurious pulses. As a result, the information storage density drops sharply—a phenomenon which one might have anticipated from the Winograd-Cowan theorem (1963), which states that if a logical function is to be implemented with unreliable components, then there is a lower limit to the redundancy which must be built into the system if the output is to be accurate.

To sum up this section, we must say that it is indeed possible to mimic many of the most attractive features of holographic memories with devices which store correlations directly rather than as power spectra. In particular, the associative net resembles the holograph in operating with fully parallel logic, in storing its information non-locally, and in allowing the storage of many different associations in the same system. It differs from the holograph in not requiring any transformation of the input and output signals or any coherent source of excitation for this purpose, in employing threshold elements to get rid of unwanted noise in the recall, and in using on-off switches rather than grains of variable transparency for storing the individual bits of information which go to make up the recorded associations. In the last three respects it harmonizes distinctly better with our neurophysiological knowledge, particularly if the Hebb synapse is the basic modifiable element in the animal cortex. We shall have more to say on this last point in later sections.

Adalines and Perceptrons

A single output line of an associative net, connected to many input lines through as many modifiable switches, bears a strong superficial resemblance to the "Adaline" (adaptive linear classifier) invented by Widrow in 1960 (see Widrow 1964). The Adaline is a pattern-classifying device to which patterns are presented as ordered sets of N numbers $(x_1, x_2, \ldots, x_N)$. There are N input lines, and each x_i in every pattern is either 0 or 1. The pattern $(x_1, x_2, \ldots, x_N)$ may be regarded as a point in N-dimensional space; the two classes to which the patterns are to be assigned may be designated as C and C'. There *may* exist a plane P such that all the points of class C and the point $(0, 0, \ldots, 0)$ lie on the same side of P, and all the points of C' lie on the other side of P; if so, the patterns are said to be linearly separable. In this case the Adaline can be taught to separate them—to emit a pulse when presented with a pattern of class C', and not to emit a pulse for a pattern of class C. What it does is to form the sum

$$w_1 x_1 + w_2 x_2 + \cdots + w_N x_N,$$

where the w_i are the current values of N adjustable weights. If this sum exceeds the current value of an adjustable threshold t, a pulse is output; otherwise not. If when a pattern of class C is presented a pulse is (incorrectly) output, the operator lowers w_i by a predetermined amount δw if x_i was 1, raises t by a predetermined amount δt, and presents the incorrectly classified pattern again. If, on the other hand, a pattern of class C' fails to provoke a pulse, the threshold is lowered and the weights raised, by the same amounts. If a pattern is correctly classified, the threshold and the weights are left as they were. Ultimately, it can be proved, the Adaline responds correctly to every pattern.

An output line of an associative net resembles an Adaline in forming a weighted sum, at any stage, of the ones and zeroes coming along its input lines and in outputting a pulse, or not, according as the resulting sum exceeds or falls short of a certain threshold. And if a pulse ought to be output, those weights which are not already 1 are altered from 0 to 1. But there are important differences, which must not be overlooked. First, the threshold of an associative net is, by hypothesis, fixed in magnitude—a hypothesis which may of course be invalid for real neural networks. Secondly, each weight in the associative net is assumed to be 0 or 1; if a switch is off $w_i = 0$, and if it is on $w_i = 1$. And thirdly, the switches in the associative net can only be switched on, not off. These handicaps might occasion some surprise that the net can work so efficiently under good conditions. The explanation seems to be that when about half the switches have been turned on, most of them will either be off or be on because just one association demands it. For this statement to hold, the number of stored associations multiplied by the number of ones in an input signal must not exceed the number of input lines—a conclusion to which Marr (1969) and Brindley (1969) have been led in recent neurological studies.

It is not possible, however, to teach an Adaline or an output line of an associative net to classify a given set of patterns in an entirely arbitrary fashion. For large N most arbitrary divisions of a large set of patterns into patterns of class C and patterns of class C' are such that no plane can be drawn between the C points and the C' points. The corresponding limitation for the associative net is that if two input patterns both fire a given output line, then any third pattern whose ones are entirely included among those of the first two patterns must also fire that line. So to achieve more general classifications some further apparatus is needed. In their book on perceptrons, Minsky and Papert (1969) deal elegantly with this general problem; but we must be content to refer to the fundamental theorem on which their work is based. (The perceptron was invented by Rosenblatt [1958, 1962], but since that time the word has widened considerably in application.) To state the theorem we need the idea of a "mask". A mask is a device which can be applied to a pattern and outputs a 1 if all the x_i belonging to a given subset are equal to 1; otherwise it outputs a 0. Then the theorem states that, given any classification of a set of input patterns into patterns of class C and patterns of class C', there exists a set of masks such that if each mask is connected to one input line of an Adaline, whose weights and thresholds are suitably adjusted, the system will output a pulse if and only if the input pattern is of class C'. Such a two-layer system, incorporating a set of masks and a linear threshold device, is called a two-layer perceptron. Informally speaking, the first layer is the "coder", and the second layer, the Adaline, is the "memory", since it is there that the learning, if any, takes place. The problem of choosing a suitable set of masks for a particular classification task is a problem of great interest, and is Minsky and Papert's main concern in their book. For us the essential point is that a two-layer perceptron can learn any classification task if it is equipped with an appropriate set of masks; and we shall see that the concept of a mask in a two-layer perceptron is virtually identical with Marr's concept of a "codon" in his theory of the cerebellum (1969), to which we now turn.

The Cerebellar Cortex

The cerebellar cortex is one of the most tantalizing organs of the brain, because of its extremely orderly structure, which has been the subject of intensive study ever since Ramón y Cajal (1911) first mapped its main features. In bald and inadequate outline, the cerebellum has (Eccles et al. 1967) one set of outputs—the inhibitory outputs of the Purkinje cells—

and two sets of inputs. The simpler set of inputs is along the climbing fibres, each of which is polysynaptically connected to just one Purkinje cell and is capable of exciting the Purkinje cell without apparent assistance. The more complex set of inputs is along a much greater number of mossy fibres, which are connected in a few-to-few fashion to the dendrites of the extremely numerous granule cells. The axons of the granule cells are monosynaptically connected to the dendrites or the bodies of the Purkinje cells. These axons are the parallel fibres; and whereas each parallel fibre may form a synapse with perhaps 500 Purkinje cells, each Purkinje cell receives synaptic connexions from hundreds of thousands of parallel fibres. (Also ministering in some way to the needs of the Purkinje cells are the stellate cells and the basket cells, which are also controlled by the parallel fibres; and the activity in the parallel fibres is regulated by Golgi cells, which sample the mossy-fibre activity and also that of the granule cells. We may ignore these complications for the moment.)

The crux of Marr's theory (1969) is that the Purkinje cells are the output lines of an associative net (though his paper slightly predates Willshaw et al. 1969). A given Purkinje cell can be made to fire by the appropriate UCS, provided by its climbing fibre; but if this firing is accompanied by a CS in the form of a parallel-fibre input, then the CS alone will later suffice to fire the Purkinje cell. This process of conditioning is achieved, in Marr's view, by facilitation of the synapses between the relevant parallel fibres and the Purkinje cell; if the Purkinje-cell threshold is low enough, a set of impulses along these fibres will fire it without any input from the climbing fibre. Marr therefore postulates that the parallel fibre–Purkinje cell synapses are potentially excitatory and can be activated in the manner of Hebb synapses—a nice firm experimental prediction.

Marr's second hypothesis concerns the translation from mossy-fibre input into parallel-fibre activity. This process he regards as fulfilling the same function as the masks in the two-layer perceptron (see above), though he uses the phrase "codon representation" to designate the transformation to which a particular mossy-fibre input is subjected before being referred to the Purkinje cells. He gives quantitative reasons why a granule cell should receive rather few synapses from mossy fibres—why, in other words, patterns can be rather well separated with quite few masks.

According to this view, which harmonizes most attractively with the known anatomy, the cerebellar cortex behaves as a battery of two-layer perceptrons, if the word "perceptron" is allowed to encompass a learning machine in which a particular weight, once altered, cannot be altered back again. The system is supposed to learn two kinds of task, under cerebral instruction: the performance of complex movements and the maintenance of posture and balance. The primary instructions (UCS) are received along the climbing fibres, which originate in the cells of the inferior olivary nucleus; whenever an olivary cell fires, it sends an impulse to its Purkinje cell. The Purkinje cell is also provided, via its mossy-fibre input, with information (CS) about the context in which its olivary cell fired. Later, when the action has been learnt, occurrence of the context alone is enough to fire the Purkinje cell, which then initiates the next elementary movement; the action thus progresses as it did during rehearsal.

The suggestion that the cerebellum learns motor skills in this way is due to Brindley (1964); but Marr develops the idea in considerable detail, both mathematical and anatomical. In particular, he works out the possible range of codon sizes, and finds that they should be very small (4 or 5) in relation to the number of active mossy fibres (500–1500). He also points out that the stellate and basket cells, which inhibit the Purkinje cells, may very well serve the purpose of adjusting the Purkinje-cell threshold (downwards if the mossy-fibre or granule-cell activity is unusually high), and that the Golgi cells may perhaps act similarly in controlling the codon size. (These hypotheses, though appealing, are not crucial to the theory.) Marr does not, however, consider the Purkinje cells collectively, and therefore he draws no conclusion about the density, in bits per modifiable synapse, with which the available information is stored. The amount of available information, in the absence of redundancy, is

$$R \log_2 \binom{N}{M},$$

where N is the number of output lines, M the number which were active in any response, and R the number of learned responses. But the analysis above showed that for an associative net with constant output thresholds this amount of information was indeed comparable with the total number of adjustable switches; so there can be little doubt that Marr's model of the cerebellar cortex is capable of storing its output information efficiently— without wasting too many modifiable synapses.

Sequential Models

Similar ideas to those underlying Marr's theory have been used by Brindley (1969) in the construction of nerve-net models which will learn large numbers of elementary "word" sequences and are economical in storage space and realistic in their neurological components. The task is to memorize say 10^5 three-word sequences composed from a vocabulary of say 10^4

words, so that when the first two words of a sequence are supplied the third will be reliably recalled. The proposed models store their information in modifiable synapses; their connexions need to be specified only in a general way, and they can tolerate the destruction of many cells. The model which Brindley favours most is built with Hebb synapses and demands an observationally plausible number of inputs to each cell. Brindley shows that this model stores its information economically—that it does not waste a large fraction of its modifiable synapses—and suggests that such economy can be achieved only if there is an abundance of cells with many independent inputs and rather low thresholds. This conclusion harmonizes very satisfactorily with the theory of the associative net. Brindley deals with the problem of timing by postulating delay lines and repeater cells which keep the first "word" in hand till the second word arrives. Doubtless there are such components in our temporal memories, but there is obviously room for much more theoretical work on timing devices, particularly in relation to the question of variability of tempo (see above). A final point in favour of Brindley's scheme is its embryological plausibility, for which he presents detailed arguments; but these, regrettably, would take us outside the scope of this review.

Discussion

In this chapter we have not attempted to review, or even to refer to, all the good work which has been devoted to the study of the memory. In particular we have not felt competent to undertake any discussion of the abundant psychological evidence relating to associative memory, or to place the various theoretical models in any precise relation to the anatomy of the brain, except in so far as this has already been done by Marr for the cerebellar cortex. We have concentrated on one particular problem: How is it possible to construct, with mainly parallel logic, an associative information store which can learn to associate very many pairs of conditioned and unconditioned stimuli, when the individual stimuli are so complex that they cannot be anticipated in any detail before they arrive? And how can this task be performed with the maximum economy in the use of modifiable elements? In reviewing the published work on this problem we have been struck by the way in which people in quite diverse fields have converged upon the same general ideas: namely that this end is well served by storing the correlations between the separate components of each CS and the corresponding UCS, that it is entirely satisfactory to store these correlations indiscriminately in a large number of binary stores, that some kind of threshold logic is essential if one is to obtain accurate responses after learning, and that systems of this general design can be made to store the relevant information at a high density in bits per register. Furthermore, such systems can be made tolerant to extensive damage, or to inaccuracy in the conditioned stimuli, by a corresponding sacrifice in information-storage density—a possibility which arises from the distributed manner in which each individual association is stored. And last but not least, it appears that the cerebellum may very well be an information-processing system of just this kind.

Finally, a word about the particular problem of temporal recall. Just as the holograph can be mimicked by the correlograph and the associative net, so the holophone, which stores temporal variations in frequency space, can be mimicked by a system incorporating a large number of delay lines. We really have insufficient evidence at present on which to base a theoretical decision; frequency analysis is certainly a neurological possibility, as something of the kind is obviously done by the ear, but the finite speeds of neural impulses would provide an obvious basis for neural models based on the delay principle. Perhaps both types of coding are used in the brain; experiment alone can decide.

Mathematical Appendix: Fourier Holography

As remarked above, the electric-field amplitude $f(u, v)$ reaching the plane P is the Fourier transform of that leaving T. That is,

$$f(u, v) = \int \int F(x, y) \exp[2\pi i(ux + vy)] dx dy,$$

where u and v are holographic coordinates which have been normalized by dividing by the laser wavelength and by the focal length of L_1. A second Fourier transformation, effected by L_2,

$$F'(x, y) = \int \int f(u, v) \exp[2\pi i(xu + yv)] du dv$$
$$= F(-x, -y),$$

gives the inverted image F' on the screen S in the absence of the hologram. With the hologram in position, illuminated by light passing through the first part of the transparency, the light reaching S is the Fourier transform of $f_1 f^* f$, where $f = f_1 + f_2$. To determine the contribution of the particular term $f_1 f_1^* f_2$ we use the theorem which states that the transform of a product is the convolution of the transforms of the individual factors. It follows that the transform of $f_1 f_1^*$ is

$$\int\int F_1'(x - x', y - y')F_1(x', y')dx'dy'$$

$$= \int\int F_1(x' - x, y' - y)F_1(x', y')dx'dy',$$

which is the autocorrelation function of F_1, and may be written as $C(x, y)$. Convolving this with F_2', the Fourier transform of f_2, we obtain

$$\int\int C(x - x', y - y')F_2'(x', y')dx'dy',$$

a blurred, inverted image of F_2. If F_1 is irregular, $C(x, y)$ will be small and random except at the origin, and in these circumstances F_2 will be discernible in spite of the blurring, especially if it is made up of a number of small bright spots.

An important question about the holograph, used as an associative memory, concerns the signal-to-noise ratio of the output signal evoked by a given input. The same problem arises in any device which stores correlations between pairs of patterns; the more pairs that are stored, the noisier the recall. Suppose (to change our notation slightly) that a holograph or linear correlograph has been loaded with R pairs of patterns: F_1 and G_1, F_2 and G_2, etc. Then the input of F_1 will evoke the composite output

$$F_1\%(H_1'\%H_1 + H_2'\%H_2 + \cdots),$$

where the % sign has been used for convolution, a dash denotes inversion of a pattern, and

$$H_1 = F_1 + G_1, H_2 = F_2 + G_2, \text{ etc.}$$

When this expression is expanded, just one of the 4^R terms is that which enables F_1 to recall G_1, namely $F_1\%F_1'\%G_1$; all the others count as noise. More detailed analysis shows that the signal-to-noise ratio in the recall of G_1, if all the patterns are chosen completely at random and are of comparable intensity, is the area covered by F_1 divided by the combined area of all the recorded patterns. This fact underlines the necessity of filtering the output through a battery of threshold elements, such elements being not only practically but logically necessary if the system is to be used for *recognizing* patterns rather than just recalling them.

References

Beurle, R. L. 1956. Properties of a mass of cells capable of regenerating pulses. *Phil. Trans. R. Soc.* B 240: 55.

Brindley, G. S. 1964. The use made by the cerebellum of the information that it receives from sense organs. *Int. Brain Res. Org. Bull.* 3: 80.

Brindley, G. S. 1969. Nerve net models of plausible size that perform many simple learning tasks. *Proc. R. Soc.* B 174: 173.

Cragg, E. C., and H. N. V. Temperley. 1954. The organisation of neurones: A co-operative analogy. *Electroenceph. Clin. Neurophysiol.* 6: 85.

Eccles, J. C., M. Ito, and J. Szentagothai. 1967. *The Cerebellum as a Neuronal Machine.* Berlin: Springer-Verlag.

Gabor, D. 1948. A new microscopic principle. *Nature* 161: 777.

Gabor, D. 1949. Microscopy by reconstructed wavefronts. *Proc. R. Soc.* A 197: 187.

Gabor, D. 1951. Microscopy by reconstructed wavefronts. II. *Proc. Phys. Soc.* 64: 449.

Gabor, D. 1968. Improved holographic model of temporal recall. *Nature* 217: 1288.

Gabor, D. 1969. Associative holographic memories. *IBM J. Res. Div.* 13: 156.

Griffith, J. S. 1963. A field theory of neural nets. I. Derivation of field equations. *Bull. Math. Biophys.* 25: 111.

Griffith, J. S. 1965. A field theory of neural nets. II. Properties of the field equations. *Bull. Math. Biophys.* 27: 187.

Hebb, D. O. 1949. *The Organization of Behavior.* New York: Wiley.

Leith, E. N., and J. Upatnieks. 1962. Reconstructed wavefronts and communication theory. *J. Opt. Soc. Am.* 2: 387.

Longuet-Higgins, H. C. 1968a. Holographic model of temporal recall. *Nature* 217: 104.

Longuet-Higgins, H. C. 1968b. The non-local storage of temporal information. *Proc. R. Soc.* B 171: 327.

Marr, D. 1969. A theory of cerebellar cortex. *J. Physiol. (Lond.)* 202: 437.

Minsky, M., and S. Papert. 1969. *Perceptrons.* Cambridge, Mass.: MIT Press.

Pribram, K. H. 1966. Some dimensions of remembering: Steps towards a neuro-psychological model of memory. In *Macromolecules and Behavior*, ed. J. Gaito (New York: Appleton-Century-Crofts).

Pribram, K. H. 1969. The neurophysiology of remembering. *Sci. Am.* 220: 73.

Ramón y Cajal. 1911. *Histologie du Système Nerveux de l'Homme et des Vertébrés.* Paris: A. Maloine.

Rosenblatt, F. 1958. The perceptron. A probabilistic model for information storage and organisation in the brain. *Psychol. Rev.* 65: 386.

Rosenblatt, F. 1962. *Principles of Neurodynamics.* Washington, D.C.: Spartan.

Roy, A. E. 1960. On a method of storing information. *Bull. Math. Biophys.* 22: 139.

Roy, A. E. 1962. On a method of storing information. II. A further study of model properties. *Bull. Math. Biophys.* 24: 39.

Stroke, G. W. 1966. *An Introduction to Coherent Optics and Holography.* New York: Academic.

van Heerden, P. J. 1963a. A new optical method of storing and retrieving information. *Appl. Optics* 2: 387.

van Heerden, P. J. 1963b. Theory of optical information storage in solids. *Appl. Optics* 2: 393.

Westlake, P. R. 1967. Towards a theory of brain functioning: The possibilities of neural holographic processes. In Proceedings of the Twentieth Annual Conference on Engineering in Medicine and Biology, IEEE.

Widrow, B. 1964. Pattern recognition and adaptive control. *Trans. AIEEE Appl. Indust.* 83: 269.

Willshaw, D. J., and H. C. Longuet-Higgins. 1969. The holophone—Recent developments. In *Machine Intelligence 4*, ed. D. Michie (Edinburgh University Press).

Willshaw, D. J., and H. C. Longuet-Higgins. 1970. Associative memory models. In *Machine Intelligence 5* (Edinburgh University Press).

Willshaw, D. J., O. P. Buneman, and H. C. Longuet-Higgins. 1969. Non-holographic associative memory. *Nature* 222: 960. [Chapter 29 in present volume.]

Winograd, S., and J. D. Cowan. 1963. *Reliable Computation in the Presence of Noise.* Cambridge, Mass.: MIT Press.

Index

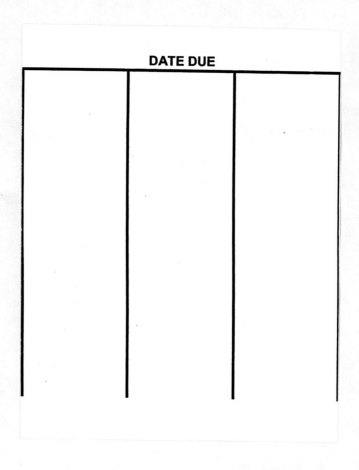

DATE DUE